P9-AGP-191

GLUTATHIONE (GSH)

YOUR BODY'S MOST POWERFUL PROTECTOR

JIMMY GUTMAN MD, FACEP

EDITED & ILLUSTRATED BY STEPHEN SCHETTINI

FOREWORD BY
DR. EARL MINDELL, R.Ph., Ph.D

KUDO.CA COMMUNICATIONS INC.
MONTREAL, CANADA

www.kudo.ca

This book discusses the manufacture and use of glutathione (GSH) by the human body and proposes strategies that, according to scientific research, may benefit us in times of sickness and of health. Knowledge of GSH is very much in its infancy but is evolving in leaps and bounds as new preventive and therapeutic possibilities become apparent. Readers with existing medical conditions, anyone on medication and those undergoing medical treatment of any sort are encouraged *to seek the advice of a qualified medical professional* before making use of the recommendations in this book.

The authors and publisher expressly disclaim responsibility from the use or application of information described in this book.

GLUTATHIONE—YOUR BODY'S MOST POWERFUL PROTECTOR
by Jimmy Gutman MD, FACEP.
Editor: Stephen Schettini; illustration & design: Stephen Schettini
© Copyright 2002 Jimmy Gutman & Stephen Schettini, Montreal, Canada

PUBLICATION HISTORY

1st edition, 1998: The Ultimate GSH Handbook
ISBN 0-9687078-0-7
Published in Canada by Gutman & Schettini, Montreal

2nd edition, 2000: Glutathione—Your Body's Most Powerful Healing Agent
ISBN 0-9687078-2-3
Published in Canada by Gutman & Schettini Inc., Montreal

3rd edition, 2002: Glutathione—Your Body's Most Powerful Protector
ISBN 0-9731409-0-9
Published in Canada by Communications Kudo.ca Inc., Montreal

This book may not be reproduced or transmitted in any form by any means including electronic, mechanical, photocopying recording or information storage system without written permission from the publisher, except for the use of brief quotations in a review.

KUDO.CA COMMUNICATIONS
Montreal, Canada
www.kudo.ca

WHAT HEALTH PROFESSIONALS
ARE SAYING ABOUT THIS BOOK

"Thorough and fascinating"
A thorough and fascinating synopsis of glutathione. Easy to read. Covers the topic completely and backs up all statements with reliable medical references. Stop searching libraries and the internet…it's all here.

JAMES WEISS MD, FCCP
PULMONARY AND INTERNAL MEDICINE
LOS ANGELES, CA

"Cutting edge"
This book provides access to the cutting edge of one of today's hottest research topics – glutathione in health and illness. Reading it will open up a new world of discovery. I highly recommend this book to everyone from fellow researchers to those interested in improving their health.

DR. JEAN MARCOUX MD, FRCP(C)
CHAIRMAN, ADVISORY BOARD OF THE AMERICAN LUNG ASSOCIATION, HOUSTON

"Highly recommended"
For the growing number of people interested in complementary medicine – a synthesis of alternative and conventional treatments for illness – it will be obvious that this book by Jimmy Gutman and Stephen Schettini is timely. Glutathione plays a pivotal role in the defense against both aging and disease, and this well executed and researched publication makes that very clear. I highly recommend GLUTATHIONE—YOUR BODY'S MOST POWERFUL PROTECTOR to anyone intent on living a healthier life naturally.

PHYLLIS BALCH CNC
Author, "PRESCRIPTION FOR NUTRITIONAL HEALING"
and, "PRESCRIPTION FOR DIETARY WELLNESS"

"Most complete, up-to-date and readable"
"GLUTATHIONE—YOUR BODY'S MOST POWERFUL PROTECTOR" is the most complete, up-to-date and readable reference I've yet seen on the essential issue of anti-oxidant supplementation with GSH. I recommend it.

RONALD KLATZ, MD, DO
PRESIDENT, AMERICAN ACADEMY OF ANTI-AGING MEDICINE (A⁴M)
[WWW.WORLDHEALTH.NET]

"Demystifies the subject"
Many facts and fantasies exist regarding glutathione – where it works, when it works, how to raise its levels. Given glutathione's impending widespread integration into clinical practice it is refreshing to pick up a source that demystifies the subject.

DR. ROGER D. ANDERSON
DIRECTOR, ANDERSON CLINICAL RESEARCH

"Read this book"

How can this one substance address so many health issues? It's because glutathione is the body's 'decision maker' of oxidant-antioxidant balance. Dr. Gutman has compiled the cream of the latest GSH research and put it between two covers. Read this book and you'll understand the critical importance of GSH to the health of every cell in your body.

Dr. Bikul Das
Researcher in molecular biology
Author, "The Science Behind Squalene"

"Invaluable"

Firstly, Dr. Gutman's book collects all the tremendously important scientific reports about glutathione into a single source. Secondly, it explains it in plain English. It is an invaluable addition to any health library and to the understanding of this crucial topic.

Allan Somersall PhD, MD
Physician, Nutritionist, Chemist
Author, "Breakthrough in Cell Defense"

"World-wide research"

Like the use of antioxidant vitamins and minerals two decades ago, GSH therapy is causing quite a stir among the medical community and patients alike. Researchers are already familiar with the healing power of GSH in chronic illnesses like cancer, viral hepatitis, autoimmune diseases, diabetes and atherosclerosis. Dr. Gutman's book compiles worldwide research findings and details the entire range of ailments caused or exacerbated by low GSH levels. In these pages you will find all the information you need to take advantage of increased glutathione levels.

Zoltan P. Rona MD, MSc
Author, "The Joy of Health"
Medical Editor, "Encyclopedia of Natural Healing"

"A wealth of information"

After decades of research into glutathione I can say without the slightest hesitation that glutathione is absolutely critical to our well-being. This molecule's protective functions and its effects on the human immune response give it a role in a huge number of potential clinical applications. My research has also convinced me that GSH levels can be effectively raised by the use of natural dietary proteins. The recent surge of interest in GSH has led to an abundance of new knowledge. But knowledge is one thing—applying it is another. How do we medical researchers get this information into the hands of everyday people in a language they can understand? Dr. Gutman has explained the intricacies of GSH research from the standpoint of his broad experience of medicine. He takes the reader on a fascinating journey through this newly charted territory, providing a wealth of information in plain English. If you think that GSH is just another antioxidant, this book will make you sit up and think again.

Gustavo Bounous MD, FRCSC
Glutathione Researcher & Career Investigator
of the Medical Research Council of Canada

To my wife Susan and our children Evan and Bianca. Through the hours, days and weeks that I was immersed in this important project their love and patience has never wavered.

ACKNOWLEDGMENTS

I have worked through hundreds of theoretical papers, laboratory experiments, and clinical studies by Dr. Gustavo Bounous, and speak with him frequently and at great length. With prodigious wit, charm and wisdom Dr. Bounous has conveyed to me and to many other health professionals the extraordinary powers of glutathione (GSH). My debt to him is immeasurable.

Thanks to Howdy Meghdady, and Roman Motyka for hanging tough. Thanks to Hinda Packard, Gary Groner, Denis Goyette and Chris Tselios for their work on the book. Thanks to John Molson, the best medical student I've ever had. Special thanks to Deb Moore who knows her Epstein from her Einstein and kept egg off our faces. And finally, thanks to two people I've never met, but who have made a profound contribution to our knowledge of glutathione: Alton Meister and Mary Anderson.

JIMMY GUTMAN MD

CONTENTS

FIGURES

FOREWORD
by Dr. Earl Mindell

Knowledge of the role of antioxidants has increased dramatically in recent years. Doctor Gutman's first edition of this book in 1998—The Ultimate GSH Handbook—contributed greatly to the understanding of our body's most essential naturally occurring antioxidant, glutathione. I am pleased to introduce this third edition of his veritable catalog of glutathione research.

Since the release of that book, the Four Aces (vitamins A, C, E and selenium) have continued to attract attention. The A vitamins (beta-carotene, alpha-carotene, lutein and lycopene) have been studied and shown to promote amazing results. Vitamin C and the bioflavonoids, vitamin E and the whole family of tocopherols show great promise against cancer treatment and prevention. Vitamin C is constantly in the news showing its effects against oral, esophageal and stomach cancers. Selenium is used by the body in close conjunction with glutathione and has been demonstrated around the world to lessen the incidence of certain cancers, including the most common among men—prostate cancer.

Recent research has introduced health professionals and the general public to such antioxidants as grape seed extract, grape skin, pine bark extract, as well as other proanthocyanidins. The Japanese also consider coenzyme Q10 and green tea to be potent antioxidants. Soy foods rich in antioxidants as well as garlic are in the news almost every day. In the USA, the FDA has at long last allowed soy food labels to bear the statement that just twenty-five grams of soy foods will lower cholesterol—one of the greatest risk factors for heart disease.

Radical oxygen molecules accelerate the aging process and lead to degenerative diseases that are slowly killing us. We are not really dying of old age—nine out of ten people in the Western world die from preventable heart disease, stroke or cancer. Until recently, the amino acid antioxidants—especially glutathione—have not received the important recognition they deserve in the battle against free radicals and oxidative stress. This book amply corrects that oversight.

I first encountered glutathione in the late 1970's while researching my Ph.D. dissertation, at which point it's crucial importance was only just becoming apparent. Since then, the volume of scientific publications on GSH has increased exponentially. Unfortunately, this information was until recently only accessible to the scientific community. Here, Dr. Jimmy Gutman interprets this highly technical research within the framework of a single, exhaustive compendium and makes it accessible to all readers.

For good reason I have referred to glutathione in my own books as the "Triple Threat Amino Acid." Although strictly speaking it is not a simple amino acid but a 'tripeptide' of three amino acids, the power of glutathione goes well beyond its unrivalled antioxidant abilities. It also binds to toxic substances enabling the body to carry them away harmlessly and is a key player in the immune system—our front line defense against infection and cancer.

This book succinctly describes the importance of GSH, how it detoxifies your body and its role in the immune system. It tells you how to raise your glutathione levels and outlines its potential role in cancer prevention and treatment and the slowing of the aging process. Dr. Gutman describes its potential clinical application in Parkinson's disease and Alzheimer's disease, heart disease, stroke, cholesterol maintenance, diabetes, AIDS, multiple sclerosis, lung and digestive diseases and many more ailments.

Glutathione is truly your body's most powerful healing agent.

EARL MINDELL R.PH., PH.D.

PREFACE

My medical specialty has been emergency medicine. I have spent many long shifts in the E.R. but have also been engaged in research, teaching and management. I am what is called an *academic clinician*. Today I practice family medicine but my focus is still principally on teaching, an experience that has prepared me well to write this book.

As an emergency doctor it is no easy task to make snap decisions with unflappable confidence. It is yet another task to impart this skill to a student. In the end, there is no greater sense of accomplishment than to see a novice initially sickened at the sight of blood turn into a team leader running major trauma codes. Such accomplishment continually reinforces my love of teaching. This book springs from the same love. I have tried to present this material in a proficient but concise manner, hoping to avoid overwhelming the reader with technicalities and jargon. Our intention is obviously to reach the broadest possible audience. However, medical science being what it is, a good amount of terminology has crept into the text. For your convenience you will find an extensive glossary at the end of the book.

My approach here is based on the teaching method I developed with medical interns and students—I provide the material, but learning it is your responsibility. A book of this size covering so many disease areas—each one bristling with its own medical specializations—can only skim the surface. To thoroughly understand the remarkable advantages of GSH you may choose to go beyond this introductory text. Apart from the contents of each chapter, I consider the critical part of this book to be the extensive reference lists at the end of each chapter. I hope you will delve into this material.

Having said that, I sincerely hope that this modest volume provides some insight and encourages you to explore the remarkable world of GSH and the human immune response system.

Our mandate is to provide up-to-date information by constantly revising and expanding this book. To do so effectively, we depend in part on your feedback. Please let us know what you think, and especially what you would like to see in future editions.

JIMMY GUTMAN MD, FACEP

Editor's note

In the spring of 1997 Dr. Jimmy Gutman spoke to me for the first time of GSH, also known as *glutathione*. This small protein had first been found in the body decades ago, but wasn't particularly well-studied. Nowadays, he told me, it is receiving much more attention. Indeed, today there are natural ways to actually raise GSH levels within the body, with a resulting boost to the immune system.

The facts he was giving me combined with the excitement in his voice made me sit down and listen. After several conversations I began to glimpse for the first time the comings and goings of the immune system and the unique story of GSH in sickness and in health.

It turned out to be a tale of lifeless molecules fitting into the biochemical jigsaw puzzle as if they knew precisely where to go and what to do. I was dazzled by the processes of life and profoundly impressed by the body's relentless drive to stay healthy. I realized more vividly than ever that an optimized immune response is preventive medicine *par excellence*.

Dr. Gutman has been studying and spreading the GSH word far and wide, with gratifying results. His examination of the many scientific studies described in this book has made him, I believe, one of the most widely-informed physicians in the world on the role of GSH. As a result, he has received endless requests to put his knowledge into print. He envisioned a book that summarized his considered opinions and, most importantly, pointed to their scientific origins.

Which is where I come into the picture. Dr. Gutman knew of my experience in writing and designing medical textbooks and asked me to work with him on this project. The result is one of the most fruitful and enjoyable relationships of my career. Dr. Gutman is responsible for the content of this book; I, for its delivery.

My objective has been to apply a guiding eye to the presentation of information and to become an advocate for the reader, with the ultimate objective of making the subject accessible to the widest possible audience. There were many changes and corrections in the development of this book, but there was little dissent. Thanks to his close scrutiny, Dr. Gutman's scientific rigor has survived the almost endless process of editing. For my part, I am satisfied that anybody who wants to do so can, with a little effort, read and follow any part of this book.

Some readers may be uncomfortable with the wide use of scientific terminology. Unfortunately, without the language of medicine it is impossible to pull back the skin and expose the remarkable role of GSH in the immune system. To help you understand and acquaint yourself with these words we have provided a detailed glossary near the end of the book.

It's been a pleasure and an eye-opener to work with Dr. Gutman. I'm not a doctor but I am sometimes a patient, and I've learned over the years that scientific training alone does not necessarily make a good doctor. In fact, it seems that only a few physicians possess the essential spirit of healing. But Dr. Gutman is one of them. He combines personal integrity and compassion with a rigorous sense of scientific enquiry. I hope that through studying this book you will come to value his knowledge as much as I do.

STEPHEN SCHETTINI

Stephen Schettini is a Montreal writer, illustrator and designer of scientific books for professionals and for the general public. He has developed extensive training guides and learning programs on the cardiovascular system, arthritis, hormone replacement therapy, allergies & antihistamines, dermatology and prostate cancer. He has also co-authored the preceding two editions of this book with Dr. Jimmy Gutman (formerly published by G&S Health Books), The Osteoporosis Remedy (published by Avery Penguin Putnam) and The Science Behind Squalene (with Dr. Bikul Das). Stephen is director of Kudo.ca Communications, and his portfolio can be viewed at www.kudo.ca.

INTRODUCTION

Pick up a medical journal or health magazine and the chances are you'll find yet another article describing the benefits of GSH (glutathione). A computer search of traditional medical literature over the past three years returns a list of more than five thousand articles on the subject. Medical science has known of this tiny protein for over three-quarters of a century, so why all this sudden attention? It concerns new discoveries about GSH and the part it plays in human immune response.

At the same time, North Americans in unprecedented numbers are taking an active part in maintaining their health. We increasingly accept greater responsibility for our own well-being and are learning more and more about preventive maintenance. This feeds a growing industry based on nutritional supplements, fitness and diet. Our interest is timely but not coincidental. Average age in the industrialized world is on the rise, and our already overburdened health care systems are facing the additional strain of a disproportionately large geriatric population. We also have environmental problems to contend with: the depletion of the ozone layer, general pollution, the spread of environmental toxins and poisons. These things are only imperfectly understood even by experts. The media broadcasts frightening news of infections that are increasingly resistant to present-day antibiotics. Diseases unknown twenty years ago are now household words: AIDS, chronic fatigue syndrome, Gulf War syndrome, fibromyalgia, and others. The inescapable stress of our life styles fosters the development of cancer, heart disease and gastrointestinal problems. Antibiotic medications are becoming less effective as microscopic organisms begin to outwit us. The old attitude of fixing people only when their bodies break is giving way to the realization that it's preferable to prevent a health problem than to deal with it once it arrives—if indeed it can then be dealt with.

Today we see a shift in two directions. On the one hand, there are continuous advances in the technology and expertise of medical science. On the other, interest in alternative (also known as "complementary") medicine is growing. Most exciting of all, practitioners of medical science are crossing the great divide. After decades of exclusion, complementary regimens and therapies are finally being placed in the scientific spotlight. This is great news for patients and practitioners everywhere.

The result is a shift towards more comprehensive therapies. For the first time in decades, doctors are emphasizing diet, life style, physical exercise and spiritual well-being as integral components of health maintenance and therapy. In addition to balanced eating habits and fresh foods, dietary regimes include vitamin supplements and other natural products. These products enhance our well-being in various ways, many of which are still being discovered. Their contributions to the prevention of the diseases of aging are encouraging.

This book is about GSH—a substance manufactured naturally by the body to battle disease and aging. It will tell you how to elevate your body's GSH levels, helping you defend it against the pollution and disease of the twenty-first century.

Doctors and patients alike should develop an open-minded but cautious approach to all possible diagnostic and therapeutic tools, both conventional and alternative. That is the approach we have taken in this book. We have looked at both ways of elevating GSH levels. All information is based on hard scientific research. To simplify presentation we have avoided the intrusion of superscripts and footnotes, but all sources are listed for each chapter. The volume, variety and reliability of research data on GSH is staggering, and leaves the importance of glutathione beyond doubt. We encourage you to study these papers but not to get bogged down in dry facts, so we've also included anecdotal stories to show that GSH is not an abstract idea but something that affects our health and well-being every day.

Our hope is that this book will help you help yourself and your loved ones. Good reading, and good health!

GLUTATHIONE IN THE BODY
[CHAPTERS I TO 4]

*Part One describes glutathione (GSH) in general terms.
Its four chapters describe GSH itself, its role in
detoxification, the part it plays in immune response,
and how to boost your GSH levels. Part Two describes
the role played by low GSH levels in the development of
specific diseases and how GSH supplementation can
help the body fight back. Part Three discusses the
preventative advantages of GSH supplementation for
those in good health.*

IMPORTANT NOTE

GLUTATHIONE AS A DIETARY SUPPLEMENT

Before continuing we must clarify one particular aspect of the
glutathione story. When people find out about GSH, they want to
go to their health store, buy some and 'take' it. Although it can be
found in this form, eating glutathione has negligible effects on your
health. It is quickly broken down in your digestive tract and eliminated. GSH must be manufactured within your cells, which is
exactly where it appears—in every cell of your body. The only effective way to do this is to give your body the building blocks it
needs to manufacture glutathione for itself. Some pharmaceutical
drugs have been developed to provide these precursors and there
are also natural ways to raise glutathione levels, notably the use of
undenatured (bioactive) whey proteins. These are referred to
thoughout this book and are described in chapter 4.

Figure 1 — Possible clinical applications for elevated glutathione levels

Neurology
- ❏ Parkinson's disease
- ❏ Alzheimer's disease
- ❏ Seizures
- ❏ Multiple sclerosis

Eye diseases
- ❏ Cataracts
- ❏ Macular degeneration
- ❏ Glaucoma

Cardiovascular
- ❏ Prevent heart disease
- ❏ Prevent stroke
- ❏ Prevent atherosclerosis
- ❏ Prevent reperfusion injury

Digestive system
- ❏ Inflammatory bowel disease
- ❏ Hepatitis
- ❏ Malnutrition
- ❏ Pancreatitis
- ❏ Peptic ulcer

Toxicology
- ❏ Certain drug overdoses
- ❏ Tobacco smoke, auto exhaust
- ❏ Pollutants including heavy metals, pesticides
- ❏ Prevents hearing loss from noise pollution
- ❏ Detoxifies many well-known carcinogens.

Infectious disease and immunology
- ❏ Anti-viral (AIDS, hepatitis, herpes, common cold, etc.)
- ❏ Bacterial infection
- ❏ Certain autoimmune dysfunction
- ❏ Chronic fatigue syndrome
- ❏ Immunosuppression

Cancer
- ❏ Cancer prevention
- ❏ Suppress tumor growth
- ❏ Eliminate carcinogens, mutagens
- ❏ Retard oxidative damage to DNA
- ❏ Prevent wasting disease
- ❏ Ease side effects of chemo- and radiotherapy

Pulmonary
- ❏ Break up mucus (esp. cystic fibrosis)
- ❏ Asthma
- ❏ Chronic bronchitis
- ❏ Emphysema
- ❏ Pulmonary fibrosis

Metabolic
- ❏ Enhances athletic performance
- ❏ Decreases recovery time from physical stress/injury
- ❏ Decreases cholesterol and oxidation of LDL
- ❏ Supports hemoglobin in kidney failure

CHAPTER I
GLUTATHIONE (GSH)

You may or may not have heard of 'glutathione.' However, researchers and scientists continue to discover the importance of this substance in health and disease and in the next few years its name will become as well known as terms like 'cholesterol' or 'vitamin.' Your life depends on glutathione. Without it, your liver would shrivel up and die from the overwhelming accumulation of toxins, your cells would disintegrate from unrestrained oxidative stress and, as if you needed more problems, your body would have little resistance to bacteria, viruses or cancers. So many protective systems of the body, including its use of vitamins C and E, depend heavily upon this remarkable molecule.

THE IMPORTANCE OF GLUTATHIONE

Glutathione's importance to your health cannot be overstated. Your immune system is constantly on the prowl for pathogens—agents of cellular damage, toxicity and disease. To neutralize them the body needs a ready supply of glutathione. If it doesn't have enough, some of the invaders will get through, infecting the body and/or contributing to aging, long-term accumulative damage—even eventual cancer. We can't avoid illness and aging altogether—though a few scientists are pursuing the age-old dream of immortality—but by keeping our intracellular glutathione levels up we also keep our immune system on the ball and fully armed. GSH is fundamental to the immune response.

RESEARCH ON GLUTATHIONE

In the last twenty years the volume of research into GSH has grown immensely. A huge variety of theoretical papers, bench-top laboratory experiments, epidemiological studies, animal projects and—most importantly—clinical trials on humans, has linked glutathione to an extraordinary variety of illnesses. The list is long and would be hard to believe were it not for the strength and credibility of the research. However, it is now clear that glutathione's role in the immune response, detoxification and antioxidation is pivotal. Without it, many bodily processes would fail.

All the information in this book is derived from the scientific reports listed at the end of each chapter. Hundreds of articles have described how elevated glutathione levels help combat the infirmities of aging, such as Parkinson's disease, Alzheimer's disease, cataract formation, macular degeneration, and cancers of aging (e.g. prostate cancer). You will find references to all these subjects listed in the index.

GSH is also known to play a crucial role in the cardiovascular system, helping prevent heart disease, stroke, atherosclerosis and reperfusion injury. In an ideal situation where the patient is exercising, eating properly, avoiding tobacco and maintaining a good general lifestyle, raising glutathione levels can actually help reverse atherosclerosis (see chapter 9).

In the digestive system glutathione helps the body fight inflammatory bowel disease, hepatitis, malnutrition, pancreatitis and peptic ulcer. Its antioxidant properties and its role in maintaining the immune response have led to interesting strategies against these all-too-common problems (see chapter 15).

Overdosing of certain drugs has been treated for some time with a variety of GSH-enhancing drugs that have become mainstays in critical care medicine. However only recently has it been recognized that GSH is a powerful detoxifier of many other nasty substances—including those released from cigarette smoke and auto exhaust, such pollutants as heavy metals and pesticides, and many well-known carcinogens. Believe it or not, the evidence shows that GSH even helps prevent hearing loss from noise pollution (see chapter 17).

In infectious disease and immunology, glutathione's anti-viral properties help the body fight AIDS, hepatitis, herpes and the common cold. Its role in combating bacterial infection has also been clearly described. Although raised GSH levels do not effect a "cure," they elevate and sustain our natural immune response, providing reinforcement to deal with the threats at hand and minimizing damage. GSH also has potential applications against some autoimmune dysfunctions, chronic fatigue syndrome and states of immunosuppression.

The immune system is on constant alert against the threat of cancer. Glutathione helps prevent carcinogenesis (the transformation of normal cells into cancer cells) by eliminating carcinogens and mutagens from the body and by slowing down oxidative damage to DNA and other sensitive structures within the cell. In cases of diagnosed cancer, glutathione has been shown to suppress tumor growth, prevent the wasting disease associated with advanced cancer and ease the side effects of chemotherapy and radiotherapy (see chapter 5).

In pulmonary or respiratory medicine, raised glutathione levels have been used for many years in Europe and now increasingly in North America. Glutathione can break up mucus (especially in cystic fibrosis), reduce the danger of asthmatic attacks, aid in both acute and chronic bronchitis and fight emphysema and pulmonary fibrosis. All these mechanisms are described in chapter 14.

We have also included chapters on glutathione's many metabolic functions, including its role in complications of diabetes, reduction of cholesterol and oxidation of bad cholesterol (LDL), and its support of red blood cell levels in patients suffering from kidney failure.

Finally, we present research emphasizing the importance of glutathione in the healthy individual. For the physically active, GSH enhances athletic performance, decreases recovery time from physical stress and aids in immune function. For the average person, its role in health maintenance just can't be overestimated. Glutathione modulation is an essential part of staying young, active and healthy (see chapters 23 and 24).

In his book on antioxidants (What You Should Know About the Super Antioxidant Miracle) Dr. Earl Mindell states "We literally cannot survive without this miraculous antioxidant." Dr. John T. Pinto of the Sloan Kettering Cancer Center in New York proclaims, "It is the master antioxidant." Jean Carper in her book Stop Aging Now! claims, "You must get your levels of glutathione up if you want to keep your youth and live longer. High levels of GSH predict good health and a long life. Low levels predict early disease and death."

Closer to the raw science of glutathione, Dr. Gustavo Bounous, a researcher and leading authority on GSH and nutrition at McGill University in Montreal says, "In view of existing scientific data, all we can expect from the environment is continued pollution, ozone depletion, and the increased virulence of infections. I think that enhancing glutathione levels will allow for a better quality of life."

You don't have to be a scientist to understand that as society 'progresses' we become increasingly dependent upon technology and have to live with its many unhealthy by-products. Not all of them are as tangible as toxic waste. There's the stress and hurry of modern life—few of us take the time to listen closely to our bodies' demands, to eat and exercise accordingly, nor even to rest as often as we might need. We are driven by forces that sometimes leave us numb to our spiritual and physical needs. Our whole being is affected, but a strong immune system can help take the physiological brunt of it. What it needs is regular maintenance and the all-important raw materials to make glutathione.

GSH—THE MOLECULE

Glutathione is the general term for glutathone sulfhydryl, abbreviated as GSH. The 'SH' represents the critically active sulfur sulfhydryl group. GSH is a peptide (very small protein) that occurs naturally within the body, where it is assembled by individual cells from its three components—the aminoacids glycine, glutamate (glutamic acid), and the all-important cysteine. Because it contains three amino acids it is referred to as a tripeptide. Glutathione's molecular structure is represented in figure 2.

Of these three amino acids, cysteine is the hardest to find. Cysteine is a sulfur-containing amino acid that contributes the sulfhydryl group to the molecule, making it also the most important of these raw ingredients. When cells have cysteine, they can efficiently manufacture GSH. However, this amino-acid is absent or deficient in many diets. Also, it must be in an accessible form. Cysteine has trouble surviving the trip from your mouth to your cells unless it's part of a larger protein.

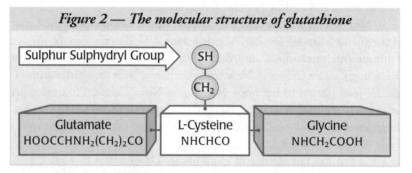

Figure 2 — The molecular structure of glutathione

Without adequate cysteine, cells can't produce enough GSH and the body suffers on three fronts: cellular oxidation contributes to general decline and aging, toxins accumulate in the body causing further damage, and the immune system is compromised, leaving us vulnerable to disease.

On the other hand, there are many benefits for the body with elevated glutathione levels. Its metabolic functions include:

❑ Enhanced immune function
❑ Elimination of toxins
❑ Elimination of carcinogens
❑ Antioxidant cell protection
❑ Protection against ionizing radiation
❑ DNA synthesis and repair
❑ Protein synthesis
❑ Prostaglandin synthesis
❑ Leukotriene synthesis
❑ Amino acid transport
❑ Enzyme activation and regulation

These functions can be summarized into three general categories:

1 ANTIOXIDANT—GSH is the most powerful antioxidant occurring naturally in your body. The effectiveness of other antioxidants like vitamins C and E depends on glutathione. This is described in the following pages.

2 DETOXIFIER—Dozens of toxins are eliminated by the GSH enzyme system, including drug metabolites, pollutants, carcinogens and radiation damage. It's no surprise that GSH concentrations are highest in the liver, the body's major detoxifying organ (see chapter 2).

3 IMMUNE SYSTEM ENHANCER—The immune system is dependent upon GSH for its proper functioning, in particular the creation and maintenance of T-cell lymphocytes, the body's frontline defense against infection. See chapter 3 for details.

These three functions are not separate. As far as the immune system is concerned, it is just using GSH to do its job. A GSH molecule may neutralize a free radical, be recycled by the GSH system and then eliminate a stray toxin. The remainder of part 1 describes these functions in detail and how we can maintain them. Before we look at its antioxidant role we must describe the processes of oxidation.

OXIDATION AND ANTIOXIDATION

Today there is enormous growth in the markets for preventative and anti-aging medicine, and much time and money has been spent looking into the wear and tear of living, breathing and eating. This non-stop activity places continuous stress on every cell of the body, and every cell must respond or suffer damage. Terms like oxidation, free radical, oxyradical and antioxidant are used to describe these processes. What do they mean?

Each and every cell in the body is a biological machine that is gradually worn down by the work of staying alive. It's an imperfect system. Like all machines, cells derive their energy from the consumption (oxidation) of fuel—nutrients and oxygen—but at a price. This process produces harmful waste products (free radicals or oxyradicals). One of our cells' most routine tasks is to neutralize and remove these wastes, and the key substance it uses is glutathione. Glutathione is the body's principal antioxidant. When it runs out, oxyradicals proliferate, slowly but surely wreaking havoc. In Part Two you will see that severe GSH deficiency is common to many diseases, especially in their advanced, chronic conditions.

How do oxyradicals form? If you were to look inside a cell you'd see thousands of tiny chemical reactions that use oxygen to metabolize nutrients and release energy. This is the necessary process of oxidation. But oxidation produces harmful byproducts—oxyradicals, or unstable atoms.

An atom is a nucleus orbited by electrons. By working in pairs like children on a seesaw electrons maintain a balanced and stable orbit. But sometimes during oxidation an electron is knocked off its orbit, leaving its partner unbalanced, as shown in figure 3. The remaining electron spontaneously corrects the imbalance by stealing a neighbor's electron, which then does the same again. Imagine a playground full of children jumping from seesaw to seesaw. The resulting chain reaction of disrupted molecules can cause untold damage to individual cells. Fortunately, our cells are equipped with natural antioxidants—agents that neutralize free radicals by giving them an electron, rather as a playground monitor ensures that each child has a partner.

This process of oxidation and antioxidation occurs continuously. Oxidation isn't a bad thing—after all, it provides energy and is also a frontline defense against bacteria and viruses. But if our diet lacks certain nutrients or vitamins, or if our body experiences excessive oxidative stress and increased oxyradical production, individual cells inevitably suffer. This isn't surprising. After all, oxidation causes metal to rust, apples to rot and butter to turn rancid. It also causes natural aging in humans. But its effects don't end there. Free radicals can damage or destroy cell walls, cause cell death (apoptosis) and disrupt DNA patterns, potentially leading to cancer.

Lipid peroxidation (a precipitous oxidative chain reaction) is responsible for the breakdown of fats, particularly 'bad' cholesterol (LDL-cholesterol) which damages arteries and leads to blocked blood vessels, heart disease and stroke (see chapter 9). The list of ailments caused by oxidation and free radical formation grows longer every day. In fact, a whole new field of medicine has developed, called 'Free Radical Biology.' It studies the diseases and potential damaging effects of oxidative stress. Today there is no doubt that antioxidants help diminish cell damage, lessen the threat of disease and slow the harmful effects of aging.

Many factors contribute to oxidative stress. Some of them are poor diet, pollution, drugs, radiation, stress, trauma, injury, burns, aging and infection by bacteria or viruses. Each time your immune system confronts a threat, free radicals are released. Free radicals are also created in large numbers during exercise, when more energy is used and the rate of oxidation increases, and every time your body encounters fatigue, illness, inflammation, pollution, toxins and radiation. As you will see in the following paragraphs, glutathione is the body's key natural antioxidant. You can minimize oxidative damage by raising intracellular GSH levels and keeping them there.

GLUTATHIONE—THE MASTER ANTIOXIDANT

How does GSH work with other antioxidants? They all have their advantages and disadvantages. You should never stop using established supple-

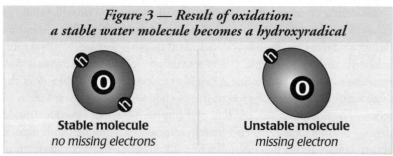

Figure 3 — Result of oxidation:
a stable water molecule becomes a hydroxyradical

Stable molecule
no missing electrons

Unstable molecule
missing electron

Figure 4 — Glutathione molecules neutralize free radicals by handing off an electron, then pair off to remain neutral themselves

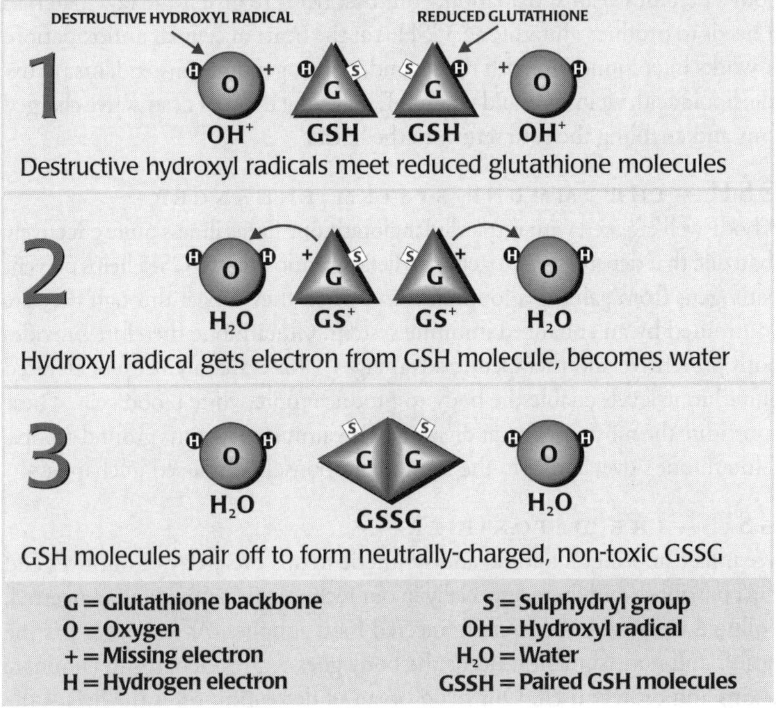

1 — DESTRUCTIVE HYDROXYL RADICAL / REDUCED GLUTATHIONE

OH⁺ GSH GSH OH⁺

Destructive hydroxyl radicals meet reduced glutathione molecules

2

H_2O GS⁺ GS⁺ H_2O

Hydroxyl radical gets electron from GSH molecule, becomes water

3

H_2O GSSG H_2O

GSH molecules pair off to form neutrally-charged, non-toxic GSSG

G = Glutathione backbone	S = Sulphydryl group
O = Oxygen	OH = Hydroxyl radical
+ = Missing electron	H_2O = Water
H = Hydrogen electron	GSSH = Paired GSH molecules

ments like vitamins C and E. These substances act synergistically with GSH—i.e., they enhance each other's effectiveness. We call GSH the master antioxidant because it replenishes the action of many other antioxidants. When vitamins C and E pick up an oxyradical they must hand it off to the GSH system so they are free to go back and get others. GSH similarly neutralizes peroxide and lipoic acid. In fact, all of these antioxidants help to neutralize each other, and glutathione is at the center of cellular antioxidation. It is GSH—not the vitamin—that ultimately neutralizes the radical. A GSH molecule encounters a destructive, positively-charged hydroxyl radical and gives it an electron, turning it into harmless water. The GSH molecule has not become a radical but pairs up with another radicalized GSH molecule to form neutral, non-toxic GSSG.

Another synergistic antioxidant is selenium. Studies show it to be clinically similar to glutathione and it is an integral component of the important enzyme GSH-peroxidase. For this reason selenium is considered a GSH-booster.

None of these important but lesser antioxidants occur naturally in the cell—only glutathione. All others are obtained from the food we eat. GSH is a vital, natural component of your cells—an endogenous antioxidant. It is manufactured within from amino-acid precursors. If you want to boost your body's defenses against oxidation, your best bet is to give it the raw materials it needs to produce glutathione. GSH is at the heart of cellular antioxidation. It works in conjunction with the secondary (exogenous) antioxidants peroxide, lipoic acid, vitamin C and vitamin E, relieving them of destructive charged ions and enabling them to return to the battle.

GSH—THE IMMUNE SYSTEM ENHANCER

A body well-stocked with intracellular glutathione fights illness more effectively than one that depends on exogenous (dietary) antioxidants. GSH helps prevent pathogens from gaining a foothold. And when they do get through they are confronted by an enhanced immune system. Glutathione therefore provides both preventive and therapeutic advantages. This is mainly because elevated glutathione levels enable the body to produce more white blood cells. These constitute the most important division of the immune system's ground-troops. Glutathione's overall role in the immune response is discussed in chapter 3.

GSH—THE DETOXIFIER

We inhale and ingest natural and synthetic toxins every day of our lives and can't possibly avoid them, especially in our technological times, our congested, polluted cities and with our engineered food supplies. As long as it has the health and nourishment it needs the body goes to great lengths to eliminate toxins and protect itself. Our main organ of detoxification is the liver—the largest organ in the body and also the depository of the body's highest con-

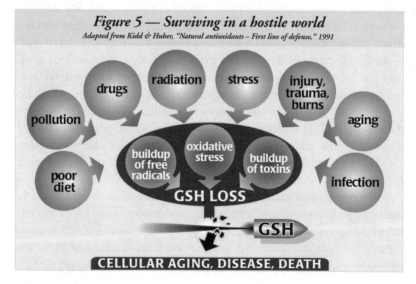

Figure 5 — Surviving in a hostile world
Adapted from Kidd & Huber, "Natural antioxidants – First line of defense," 1991

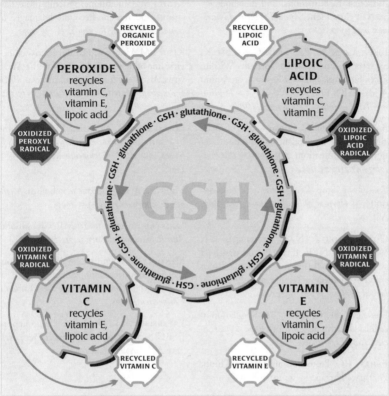

Figure 6 — Inside each cell of the body the gears of antioxidation are driven by glutathione (GSH) as it recycles peroxide, lipoic acid, vitamin C and vitamin E and gets them back to work

centrations of glutathione. Experimental studies have shown that low glutathione levels lead to poor liver function, and result in unnecessarily large quantities of toxins circulating through the body. There, they continuously damage individual cells and organs. Chapter 2 describes the role of glutathione in detoxification. The liver and its function is described in chapter 11.

CONCLUSION

Glutathione carries out many crucial functions in our body, of which three stand out. GSH is 1) the most important naturally-occurring antioxidant in our cells, 2) a key enzyme system for the detoxification of countless noxious substances and 3) a critical element that sustains the functioning and well-being of our immune systems. These vital roles are now beyond doubt and considerable research is underway to uncover the full range of clinical applications for the preventative and therapeutic roles of elevated GSH levels.

GLUTATHIONE (GSH)

BEUTLER E. Nutritional and metabolic aspects of glutathione. *Annual Review of Nutrition 9:287-302, 1989*

BRAVERMAN E, PFEIFFER C, BLUM K, SMAYDA R. The Healing Nutrients Within: Facts, Findings, and New Research on Amino Acids. [ISBN 0-87983-706-3] *Keats Publishing, New Canaan, Connecticut, 1987*

BRAY T, TAYLOR C. Enhancement of tissue glutathione for antioxidant and immune functions in malnutrition. *Biochemistry Pharmacology 47:2113-23, 1994*

CARPER J. Stop Aging Now! [ISBN 0-06-018355-1] *HarperCollins Publishers, New York, NY, 1995*

COMMANDEUR JNM, STIJNTJES GJ, VERMEULEN NPE. Enzymes and transport systems involved in the formation and disposition of glutathione s-conjugates. *Pharmacological Reviews 47: 271-330, 1995*

DENEKE SM, FANBURG BL. Regulation of cellular glutathione. *American Physiological Society L163-L173, 1989*

FAHEY, RC. Protection of DNA by Thiols. Pharmac. Therapeut. 39: 101-108, 1988

KIDD PM. Glutathione: Systemic protectant against oxidative and free radical damage. *Alternative Medicine Review 2:155-176, 1997*

KIDD PM, Huber W. Natural antioxidants – First line of defense in Living with the AIDS virus: A strategy for long term survival. *PMK Biomedical-Nutritional Consulting: 115-142, 1991*

LOMAESTRO B, MALONE M. Glutathione in health and disease: Pharmacotherapeutic Issues. *Annals of Pharmacotherapy 29:1263-73, 1995*

MEISTER A. Glutathione metabolism. *Methods in Enzymology 252:3-7, 1995*

MEISTER A, ANDERSON ME. Glutathione. *Ann Revue Biochemistry 52:711-60, 1983*

MINDELL E. What you should Know About the Super Antioxidant Miracle. [ISBN 0-87983-721-7] *Keats Publishing, New Canaan, Connecticut, 1996*

PRESSMAN AH. The GSH Phenomenon. [ISBN 0-312-15135-7] *St. Martin's Press, New York NY. First Edition, 1997*

CHAPTER 2
GSH AND DETOXIFICATION

TOXINS, GLUTATHIONE AND HEALTH

Medical science and public health measures have notably reduced death rates and prolonged the average life span, especially in developed countries. But development has its downside. Our environment contains tens of thousands of confirmed toxic substances, and the pace of life and consumer-oriented marketing promote bad lifestyle habits which we all adopt to some extent. We in the twentieth-century can expect a longer life span than our ancestors, but one potentially burdened by chronic ailments. The full promise of longevity is blunted.

What's remarkable is that we don't succumb even earlier to the daily onslaught of toxins in our food, air and water. We have our body's defense mechanisms to thank, notably the GSH detoxification process. But like all biological systems, even this can be overwhelmed by extensive or prolonged attack and may eventually begin to function poorly.

Although GSH was discovered in 1888 by De-Rey-Pailhade, it was not until the 1970's that its detoxifying role was recognized. Over the past thirty years scientific understanding of this process has unfolded slowly, but the huge resurgence of interest in preventive medicine and in GSH is giving rise to new discoveries. The liver and the kidney are the major organs of detoxification and elimination and have the highest levels of intracellular GSH in the body (see figure 7). GSH is the most important thiol (sulfur-containing amino-acid) in living systems. It plays a critical role not only in humans and mammals, but in all vertebrates and even in insects, plants and micro-organisms.

The team of biochemists D.P. Jones, L.A. Brown and P. Sternberg from Emory School of Medicine in Atlanta wrote, "GSH has multiple functions in detoxification and its depletion has been associated with an increased

ORGAN	GSH (μ-mol/g)
Liver	7.3
Kidney	4.0
Lung	2.9
Heart	2.4
Brain	1.5

Figure 7 — Organ GSH content in lab animals

risk of chemical toxicity…GSH can be depleted by different agents (and GSH) plasma levels vary with gender, age, race and dietary habits." They go on to suggest that by monitoring glutathione levels we can measure an individual's risk of falling prey to environmental toxins.

H. Lew and A. Quitanihila, physiologists at the University of California, verified the upside of this discovery. The increased liver GSH levels seen in actively trained, physically fit individuals leave them better equipped to handle toxic threats from such substances as acetaminophen. R.J. Flanagan and T.J. Meridith at the Poisons Unit of Guy's Hospital in London reviewed the use of N-acetyl-cysteine (NAC)—a GSH-enhancing drug—as a detoxifying treatment. They believe that besides its common use as a treatment for acetaminophen overdose, research will show its potential to detoxify the body of carbon monoxide, carbon tetrachloride, chloroform, and other harmful compounds.

CASE STUDIES

Whether accumulated over the years or ingested in one dose, many organic and inorganic toxins are cleared from the body by the action of GSH. Without sufficient glutathione supplies, these toxins can push the body into a slow or precipitous decline. Fortunately, drug-induced or dietary supplementation to raise GSH levels can sometimes help reverse this process. The following stories illustrate this.

Lara, a 28-year-old technical writer, did what she could to live a healthy life-style. She exercised regularly but found it increasing difficult over the years to get what she needed nutritionally. Many foods she had previously enjoyed—including dairy and meat products—left her feeling bloated, cranky and fatigued. She found herself taking various supplements to round off her dietary needs, but felt she was "left short." In addition, trips downtown were fraught with episodes of itchy, runny eyes and nose, headache and shortness of breath. Perfumes, auto exhaust and other odors made her feel 'sick' so she avoided crowds. Fortunately, the nature of her job allowed her to do most of her work at home. After a visit to a local clinic she was diagnosed as agoraphobic. This made no sense to her because she loved going out. A nutritionist suggested that she was in fact suffering from multiple chemical sensitivity and prescribed the GSH-enhancing drug NAC for detoxification. After a few weeks of cramps, diarrhea, sweating and considerable urination she began to improve. She started cautiously reintroducing previous favorites back into her diet. She remains on her low dose of NAC and her tolerance of external smells continues to improve.

Linda was a recently unemployed 24 year-old office manager whose common-law husband had abruptly moved out of their apartment. After drinking two bottles of wine, she swallowed 30-40 tablets of extra strength (500 mg) acetaminophen. The next morning, after the effects of the alcohol had worn off, she showed up at the emergency department of the local hospital. Her stomach was not pumped because it had been so long since she took the pills. Her acetaminophen blood level was at 150 micrograms per milliliter (μg/ml)—enough to damage the liver if left untreated—and her initial liver enzyme profile was already showing mild abnormalities. A dose of NAC (N-acetyl-cysteine) treatment was given immediately and continued every four hours for the next three days. Oral charcoal was also used on the first day. Her liver enzyme abnormalities worsened over the first forty-eight hours but were finally reversed and returned to normal. Although suffering from nausea and cramps during her hospital stay, she was glad to be alive. After being cleared by the psychiatric consultant, she was sent home.

PREVENTION

A serious shortcoming of traditional medicine is its focus on treatment rather than prevention. This isn't without cause. The need to see people who are sick or suffering is always more pressing than the good intention to meet those in good health. And there's no shortage of disease out there—if anything, there's a shortage of doctors. It has fallen to other branches of the healing arts to address the issue of maintaining well-being. Nutrition-sensitive approaches can teach us a great deal. But the real strength of such health maintenance is self-awareness. We must study for ourselves, and learn to take control of the conditions that affect our well-being. As much as possible, we should avoid whatever harmful influences we can, then identify the unavoidable ones and provide our body with whatever resources it needs to fight them.

SMOKING AND TOBACCO

Medically, statistically and economically, the greatest risk to health in North America is tobacco use. The huge body of scientific evidence accumulated over the past decades leaves no doubt that cigarette smoking profoundly increases the risk of contracting Chronic Obstructive Pulmonary Disease (COPD, including asthma, chronic bronchitis and emphysema), cancer and cardiovascular disease. Despite years of successful lobbying and denial, the tobacco industry has recently been forced to admit what the medical community has known for ages—cigarettes kill.

Figure 8 — Everyday toxins (you're better off outdoors!)

Source: OTT AND ROBERTS, "Everyday exposure to toxic Pollutants," Scientific American 278(2);86-91, 1998

EXPOSURE	Respirable particles (µg/cubic meter) 0 · 100 · 200 · 300	Toxic, volatile, organic compounds (µg/cubic meter) 1 · 10 · 10² · 10³ · 10⁴
Photocopier with dry toner (formaldehyde, styrene, etc.)	▬ (~50)	▬▬▬ (~10²)
Room with smokers (benzene, many others)	▬▬▬ (~100)	▬▬ (~50)
Carpeted home (pesticides, other etc.)	▬ (~25)	▬ (~30)
Steamy bathroom (chloroform)	▬ (~10)	▬▬▬ (~10³)
Dry-cleaning in closet (perchloro-, trichloro-ethane)	▬ (~10)	▬▬▬▬ (~10³)
Enclosed parking garage (benzene, many others)	▬ (~50)	▬▬▬ (~10²)
Fireplace (benzene, many others)	▬▬ (~100)	▬ (~20)
Kitchen fumes (many different compounds)	▬▬▬ (~200)	▬ (~20)
Household cleaners (paradichlorobenzene, etc.)	▬ (~30)	▬▬▬ (~10²)
Outdoors in the city (many different compounds)	▬ (~15)	▬ (~10)
Outdoors in the suburbs (many different compounds)	▬ (~10)	▬ (~10)

Cigarette smoke releases thousands of different chemicals and a single puff contains literally trillions of free radicals. The smoke actually burns away antioxidant vitamins like C and E and other nutrients, but even worse is the inflammation it causes in the lungs. This is the principal source of oxidative stress. The degree of lung inflammation and injury is directly related to the extent of oxidation caused by cigarette smoke. In addition, the tar from tobacco products contains potent carcinogens that cause not only lung cancer but all sorts of other tumors. GSH is well known to scavenge these free radicals and to neutralize many of the toxins by conjugation and elimination. If you're not ready to quit smoking, or if you can't avoid second-hand smoke, elevated GSH levels will help protect you.

Many studies have outlined the role of GSH in preventing or suppress-ing the damage caused by smoking. Clinicians have even gone as far as attempting to treat some of these consequences —not just prevent them— with glutathione-enhancing drugs like NAC. A more detailed analysis and review of clinical studies can be found in chapter 14.

RADIATION

Ionizing radiation is a known cause of cancer, and does other kinds of harm as well. It is one of the most extensively studied of all carcinogens and accounts for about three percent of all cancers. Some radiation comes from natural sources such as cosmic rays and natural radioactive minerals. The most com-mon source is sunlight, which carries the increased threat of ultraviolet radiation due to depletion of the protective ozone layer. Other sources include nuclear waste from energy plants, industrial waste, weapons test residue and certain building materials. X-rays from radiographs, mammograms, CT-scans and other medical test equipment are all weak, but have a cumulative effect over time.

Exposure to radiation results in the formation of hydroxyradicals—the most reactive of all free radicals. Many studies have shown that GSH plays a key role in its neutralization. Some physicians are raising GSH levels of patients in radiotherapy. This tends to reduce the side-effects they experience and can even enhance the effectiveness of the therapy itself.

L.A. Applegate at the Swiss Institute for Experimental Cancer Research conducted studies on human cells cultured in the laboratory. First, his team depleted their glutathione levels with the drug BSO, then they exposed the cells to radiation. They found a significantly higher proportion of DNA mutations, and therefore an increased risk of developing cancer. J. Navarro and a team of Spanish doctors showed that humans exposed to radiation suffered from significant GSH abnormalities.

V.N. Bhattathiri led a research team in India to study patients suffering from oral cancer. Each patient's GSH levels were measured before radiation therapy and correlated to the side-effects of the therapy. It was clear that the lower their initial GSH levels, the more injury they suffered. Following these tests the team felt able to identify any patient's susceptibility to radiation damage by measuring their GSH levels. They recommended that treat-ment dosages be adapted to the individual's ability to withstand the therapy.

A group of genetic researchers at the University of Nurnberg in Germany studied the potential use of NAC (a GSH-enhancing drug) to protect hu-man white blood cells from X-ray damage. Cells pretreated with NAC clearly had a protective advantage over untreated ones. Glutathione and its role in cancer, chemotherapy, and radiotherapy is discussed in chapter 5.

Enhanced GSH levels can also reduce the damaging effects of sunburn. It is believed that skin damaged by sunburn can develop various forms of skin cancer. Chapter 21 reviews some important studies relating to sun exposure, ultraviolet-radiation damage and glutathione.

HEAVY METAL TOXICITY

Heavy metals are metals from periodic table groups IIA through VIA. The semi-metallic elements boron, arsenic, selenium, and tellurium are often included. Many are essential in small quantities but can accumulate to toxic levels. Absorbed from the environment and food chain, they gradually build up in biological systems—from plants to the human body—and can grow into a significant health hazard. Such metals as arsenic are actually used as poisons. Nutritional supplements like iron or medications like bismuth are helpful or essential at appropriate doses, but quickly become toxic at higher levels. Here is a list of potential heavy metal toxins:

❑ Arsenic	❑ Copper	❑ Selenium
❑ Arsine	❑ Gold	❑ Silver
❑ Bismuth	❑ Iron	❑ Thallium
❑ Cadmium	❑ Lead	❑ Tin
❑ Chromium	❑ Mercury	❑ Vanadium
❑ Cobalt	❑ Nickel	❑ Zinc

Heavy metals exert their influence on all sorts of tissue and can affect many bodily systems. The nervous system, the renal (kidney) system, the cardio-vascular (heart and circulation) system, the hematological (blood) system, the gastrointestinal (digestive) system and many others are affected one after the other. Heavy metals exact their damage by generating free radicals or by interfering biochemically with normal metabolic functions.

Glutathione and its associated enzymes help regulate and eliminate many of these metals. Clinical studies have outlined the role of GSH in heavy metal toxicology and its role has been described in the way cells process arsenic, arsine, bismuth, cadmium, chromium, cobalt, copper, gold, iron, lead, mercury, nickel, selenium, silver, thallium, tin, vanadium and zinc. Of all these substances, mercury seems to be the most GSH-depleting.

MERCURY TOXICITY

The heavy metal mercury is an insidious but potent toxin that warrants special attention. It is all too common in our environment and is fraught with controversy, most notably when the topic of mercury amalgams (dental fillings) comes up. I have seen usually staid and sober medical and dental professionals coming close to blows over this issue at educational conventions. However, one of the tenets of the Hippocratic oath is, "Above all, do no harm." There certainly is sufficient clinical evidence to force a much closer look at the use of this important neurotoxin in clinical applications.

Mercuric substances can be either organic or inorganic. Inorganic forms include pure or elemental mercury (quicksilver), or the salts of mercury (mercuric chloride, mercuric oxide and others). These can be inhaled or ingested. High-risk occupations include dentistry, manufacture of batteries, explosives and jewelry, photographic development and taxidermy. Organic mercury comes in many forms, methyl-mercury being the most common— and also highly toxic. Poisoning by this form usually follows accidental ingestion. Farm workers, embalmers and producers of pesticides, fungicides, insecticides, bactericides, drugs and preservatives are all at risk.

Although primarily a neurotoxin (nerve poison), mercury can cause a broad range of problems, including kidney failure, severe nausea and vomiting, diarrhea, oral lesions (stomatitis), lung inflammation (pneumonitis) and rashes. It affects the nervous system with symptoms as subtle as emotional instability, anxiety, memory loss, and lethargy. The expression "Mad as a hatter" has an interesting basis in fact. Hat-makers in the nineteenth century used elemental mercury to form and weigh down their hats, and often paid a high neurological price for repeatedly handling this toxin. Serious mercury poisoning includes tingling or loss of sensation in the extremities, poor coordination, tremors, slurred speech and tunnel vision. These symptoms can progress to paralysis, coma and death.

Traditional treatment of mercury toxicity requires binding of the metal to larger organic molecules, a process called chelation. Chelating agents may be administered orally (e.g. D-penicillamine), intra-muscularly (e.g. Dimercaprol, BAL) or intravenously. Once chelated, the mercury complex is eliminated through normal excretion of urine or stool.

It has been long known that glutathione is a primary cellular defense against mercury toxicity. It starts out by effectively quenching the formation of free radicals. Even more critical is its ability to bind directly to mercuric compounds, enabling the cell to expel and the body to excrete them.

A recent article from the International Archives of Occupational and Environmental Health measured the impact of mercury exposure on glutathione levels. Forty-two workers from a chloralkali factory exposed to elemental mercury were compared to seventy-five non-exposed workers from a lime production plant. As expected, blood levels of mercury were higher in mercury workers, but so were levels of lipid peroxidation. Evidently, the detoxifying effects of glutathione peroxidase were significantly decreased.

In the laboratory, many studies have shown how glutathione protects cells from toxicity. By raising GSH levels, a team of toxicologists from the University of Arizona was able to decrease mercury-induced kidney damage. An Argentinean team had equal success using NAC to preserve renal (kidney) function. Similar positive results were found using glutathione monoester, selenium, and other agents to enhance GSH levels.

Experimentation on the liver, nerve and small intestine and other tissues, and even in fetal development verify that mercury drains the glutathione system, that decreased GSH levels lead to increased toxic damage by mercury, and that elevating or sustaining glutathione significantly protects cells against mercury poisoning.

DENTAL AMALGAMS

There's quite a controversy surrounding the alleged ill-effects of mercury from dental fillings (amalgams). The mercury in these so-called 'silver' fillings makes them malleable and strong. It has been a mainstay of dentistry for decades. Studies show that for average individuals not otherwise exposed to mercury, these filling represent the predominant source of exposure. The same studies also indicate that urinary mercury excretion is significantly higher in individuals with these fillings, and that these excretion levels correspond to the amount of filling in their mouths. A German study determined that the long-term excretion of mercury could be cut by five-fold after amalgam removal. A recent study from the Journal of Dental research by G. Sandborgh-England concluded that "…the process of removing amalgam fillings can have a considerable impact on Hg (mercury) levels in biological fluids."

The sixty-four thousand dollar question is whether or not this higher level of mercury exposure actually produces ill-effects. A recent study by the Australian W. Blumer, looked at 80 patients with dental amalgams who also showed symptoms of chronic mercury toxicity. Using the chelator EDTA to flush mercury from the body, it was found that the urine of patients with fillings had significantly higher levels of mercury. The fillings were removed and patients continued to take oral chelators along with selenium supplementation (to raise glutathione peroxidase). After three months patients were either symptom-free or greatly improved.

Proponents of the amalgam-toxicity school of thought are seeking ways to detoxify both patients and the dental professionals who are exposed daily to mercury vapors. Merely removing the exposure is not enough—like other heavy metals, mercury remains imbedded intracellularly in deeper tissues unless appropriately chelated or removed.

NAC (N-acetylcysteine) raises GSH levels and has been used to detoxify organic mercury. Researchers from the Department of Environmental Medicine at the University of Rochester, NY showed that oral NAC profoundly accelerates urinary methylmercury excretion to levels as much as ten times more than usual. NAC is able to detoxify mercury compounds.

One of the foremost scientists dealing with heavy metal and mercury toxicity is Dr. David Quig of Chicago, Illinois. He has elaborated the interplay of mercuric compounds, glutathione, cysteine and other metallothioneins (organic metal-sulfur compounds). He feels the long-term effects of consistent low-level mercury exposure have been underestimated. According to him, the most effective way to eliminate these toxins from deep tissue like the brain is by eating high-quality whey protein. Although the bioactivity of natural whey can easily be denatured, good quality whey protein can have significant GSH-enhancing properties. Studies using undenatured whey protein are currently underway by several research groups. The protein precursors of GSH act here as oral chelating agents.

High levels of mercury poisoning are often treated by emergency dialysis (blood filtration). American military doctors at their Health Sciences Department of Pharmacology at Bethesda, Maryland carried out an experiment to improve this treatment, with revealing results. Using dialysis they investigated the ability of ten different chelating agents to remove mercury from blood fluid. Most kidney specialists were surprised to find that NAC was very effective, even surpassing more traditional agents. Clinicians are now starting to apply this knowledge to their daily practice, using GSH therapy as a complement to their usual emergency treatments.

CASE STUDY

Sheryl was a 32-year-old mother of four who had fallen ill following the caesarian delivery of her last child two years earlier—the surgical incision was taking far too long to heal. Her gynecologist was puzzled and noted some muscular atrophy. She experienced periods of such profound weakness that she was bedridden for days. Over the next 18 months this weakness recurred and she was eventually admitted to hospital. Various diagnoses were considered, including multiple sclerosis and chronic fatigue syndrome, but supportive treatment for these conditions didn't help. Then her dentist suggested that mercury toxicity might be a contributing factor so she had her mercury amalgams removed.

Herbal supplementation was attempted to rid her of residual mercury. Her symptoms improved modestly. Some internet research led the dentist to Immunocal, which he suggested to Sheryl. Within five days she experienced a marked increase in strength. After ten days she was walking without pain. Two weeks later she rode her bike for the first time in 2½ years. Three weeks later, she felt "almost back to normal." She still feels well and continues to raise an active family.

LEAD POISONING

Plumbism—lead poisoning—is a public health problem that dates back to Roman times. The name comes from the use of lead (Latin: *plumbium*) in plumbing. Other forms of exposure have been common for centuries through cooking and eating utensils, pottery, and the use of lead in paints (fortunately discontinued in most house-paints). Moonshine liquor is sometimes prepared using automobile radiators, pipes and barrels soldered with lead. Mechanics, battery manufacturers, solderers and other tradespeople are subject to occupational exposure.

Lead poisoning is often difficult to diagnose. The symptoms can be subtle and very non-specific. Nevertheless, acute poisoning can be accompanied by severe nausea and vomiting, diarrhea, kidney failure, seizures, coma, paralysis, and death. Continuous, repeated exposure can result in anemia, weakness, aches and pains and irritability, not to mention a host of intellectual dysfunctions from learning disabilities to profound mental behavioral changes. The treatment is removal of the source of exposure and chelation therapy.

Like mercury, lead is detoxified at the cellular level by the glutathione enzyme system. The pro-oxidant effect of lead is counterbalanced by the antioxidant capabilities of GSH and the lead molecule itself can be conjugated or bound to glutathione, after which it is eliminated from the body.

Lead toxicity affects many tissues including the central and peripheral nervous system, the liver, the kidneys and red blood cells. Depleted GSH stores usually indicate increased severity of the disease. Restoration of glutathione levels is protective and helps eliminate lead. Raising GSH levels with agents like NAC, and the use of selenium have been shown to be a useful complement to traditional therapies, acting at the level of the liver, kidney, red blood cells and even the lens of the eye to counteract the deleterious effect of lead poisoning.

The anemia (loss of red blood cells) that is characteristic of lead toxicity is caused by several different factors, among them high levels of oxidative stress. This leads to lipid peroxidation of the red blood cell membrane, followed by cell disruption. A Japanese research group studied workers with a high occupational lead exposure by measuring their lipid peroxidation levels, lead concentration and glutathione peroxidase activity. The results show that lead levels and peroxidation levels seem to be directly related, and levels of the essential GSH-peroxidase fell as lead levels rose.

Environmental illness

Chronic exposure to xenobiotics (substance foreign to the body) may lead to subtle and hard-to-pinpoint changes in health, and may also lead to full-blown syndromes known as Environmental Illnesses (EI). These often reveal themselves in a combination of minor complaints—such as headaches, fatigue and lethargy—that tend to confuse diagnosis. They may be quite profound, as in the case of MCS (multiple chemical sensitivity) which has only recently become accepted as a legitimate diagnosis. For similar reasons, it was years before the medical community recognized Gulf War Syndrome as a specific illness.

There are many sources of xenobiotic exposure around the home. Carpets may hide pesticides carried in on footwear; steamy bathrooms contain chloroform; dry-cleaned clothes hanging in your closet give off fumes of perchloroethane and trichloro-ethane; fireplaces produce benzene and household cleaners contain paradichlorobenzene. In the office, photocopy toner releases formaldehyde and styrene, among other chemical pollutants. Enclosed parking garages are another source of benzene, among other chemicals. The air outdoors in the city or even the country contains many different compounds that we should ideally avoid. And of course, rooms in which people are smoking tobacco contain dozens of carcinogens and other toxic chemicals. We should be careful when using mildew removers, mothballs, scented detergents, fabric softeners, lawn fertilizers, pesticides, solvents and cleansers, paints, heating fuels, certain insulation materials and even products used to manufacture mattresses and furniture. A brief list of substances detoxified by GSH conjugation is shown in figure 9. Fortunately, a wealth of published information can help you keep track of these substances and where they are used. You'll find some excellent guides at your local bookstore.

Because the number of poisons in the general environment is large, exposure to environmental pollutants is unavoidable. In addition, concentrations of specific substances are high in certain workplaces. In an article on chemical toxicity in industrial workers, D.V. Parke and A. Sapota made a powerful statement about threats that can be counteracted by GSH. They claim that many industrial workers with symptoms of systemic inflammation are often misdiagnosed as suffering from rheumatoid arthritis, viral infections, connective tissue diseases and other such maladies. Physicians need to be informed more thoroughly about the ability of chemical pollutants to imitate inflammatory diseases.

Exposure to certain chemicals in the workplace has been connected to the development of cancer. R.K. Ross and his colleagues at the University of Southern California linked a deficiency of GSH enzymes to bladder cancer in workers exposed to arylamines—are also present in cigarette smoke.

CHRONIC FATIGUE SYNDROME, GULF WAR SYNDROME AND MULTIPLE CHEMICAL SENSITIVITY

These three health problems are dealt with together here for several reasons. They are mutually connected to a combination of environmental exposure to toxins, inappropriate immunological response and genetic predisposition. Because symptoms may be intermittent and vary from one person to another, many doctors are reluctant to offer firm clinical diagnoses, and these disease names and definitions have taken the medical community a long time to accept. Some small groups of physicians still feel these diseases are just various manifestations of a psychological disease.

Multiple chemical sensitivity is an environmental disease in which the buildup of various toxins reaches a dangerous threshold with few or minor symptoms. Any additional toxicological load may be the last straw that triggers a cascade of symptoms, often mimicking other diseases. Such circumstances make clear diagnosis very difficult. The onus is on the patient to avoid further exposure. The health practitioner must suggest detoxification strategies. The use of glutathione-enhancing treatments will undoubtedly become standard in the future.

A recent article in the American Journal of Medicine by I.R. Bell, C.M. Baldwin and G.E. Schwartz at the University of Arizona set out to summarize the relation of chronic fatigue syndrome to chemical sensitivity. They determined that severe chemical sensitivity is a factor in about one-fifth to one-half of chronic fatigue patients, and in about 5% of the American population. Between 15 and 30% of the general population report at least minor problems with chemical intolerances.

A paper entitled 'Gulf War Illnesses: complex medical, scientific and political paradox,' published by the Institute for Molecular Medicine in California, also makes a link with chronic fatigue syndrome. There is a higher incidence of CFS among Gulf War Veterans than in the general population. Since it may mimic other chronic multi-organ or immunological dysfunctions, there is danger of misdiagnosis and mistreatment.

Scientists at the Center for Environmental Hazards Research in New Jersey have determined that even when chronic fatigue syndrome and multiple chemical sensitivity syndrome are diagnosed among Gulf War Veterans, their symptoms differ substantially from the CFS and MCS diagnoses in the population at large. Discrepancies are found in immunological parameters, demographics and prognosis.

A discussion of chronic fatigue syndrome (CFS), also called chronic fatigue/immune dysfunction syndrome (CFIDS), would not be out of place in our chapter on immunology (chapter 3). From a causal point of view,

CFS is less of a toxicological problem and more typical of an immune disorder. It is best classified as a post-viral or post-infectious syndrome. The causal sequence often begins with an acute viral illness. This is usually followed by an overactive lymphatic response—swollen glands or lymph node enlargement (a symptom of "glandular fever"). For unknown reasons, some people develop an abnormal immunological and neuro-endocrinological response. This inability to fight health threats combines with an imbalance in the body's hormonal secretions, then begins to produce the symptoms of CFS.

Rheumatologists have now better defined the syndrome to enable more accurate diagnosis. It is characterized by persistent fatigue, musculo-skeletal pain, sleep disturbance and cognitive and psychological abnormalities. A clear test for CFS does not yet exist, but researchers are trying to elaborate the many subtle biochemical and physiological changes that take place. One such group is led by Dr. Paul Cheney, one of the first clinicians to describe the syndrome in the late 1980's and early 90's. Founder and director of the Cheney Clinic in North Carolina, his research is on the cutting edge of our understanding of chronic fatigue. He believes that although the initial event may be viral, it is subsequent abnormalities in protein synthesis and enzyme

---

Figure 9 — A short list of substances detoxified by GSH conjugation; there are countless others

❑ **Acetaminophen** (Tylenol, Atasol, others)

❑ **Other pharmaceuticals** (Adriamycin, etc.)

❑ **Acetone** (common solvent, cleaner, industrial agent)

❑ **Aflatoxin B1** (natural toxin, carcinogen from moldy nuts etc.)

❑ **Aliphatic hydrocarbons** (vinyl chloride, hexachlorohexane, plastics etc.)

❑ **Aromatic hydrocarbons** (solvents, fuels, bromobenzenes, chlorobezenes, etc.)

❑ **Nitrosamines** (smoked foods, salami, hot dogs, etc.)

❑ **Benzopyrenes** (barbecued foods, fuel exhaust, cigarettes, etc.)

❑ **Heavy metals** (lead, mercury, cadmium, cobalt, copper, etc.)

❑ **Organophosphate pesticides** (parathione, others)

❑ **Peroxides** (lipid peroxides, cholesterol peroxides, others)

❑ **Isothiocyanates**

❑ **Carbamates, thiocarbamates**

❑ **Arylamines, arylhalides** (industrial exposures, etc.)

❑ **Sulfates, nitrocompounds, naphthalene** (fuel, fuel by-products, etc.)

production that lead to liver and intracellular detoxification failure.

Dr. Cheney initially used oral glutathione or injectable glutathione and later the GSH precursor drug NAC (N-acetylcysteine), all with modest success. When bioactive, undenatured whey protein became available, many patients responded with dramatic results. This dietary source of GSH precursors is described in chapter 4.

The well-recognized German immunochemist Dr. Wulf Droge has coined the term "Low CG Syndrome" to describe a number of disease states associated with a depletion of cysteine and glutathione. These include chronic fatigue syndrome, AIDS, certain cancers, sepsis, Crohn's disease, ulcerative colitis, major trauma and others.

CASE STUDY

William, a lawyer from Alabama, noticed a change in his health at age 39. His initial visits to a number of physicians were neither conclusive nor accurate in their diagnoses, nor were any treatment options helpful. He was unable to carry on his usual demanding workload and was forced to end his law practice in 1994. His own research led him to a local CFS support group. They suggested that he consult a prestigious south-eastern clinic specializing in chronic fatigue. Initial treatment with vitamins, nutrients and dietary changes proved minimally successful. The head of this clinic was investigating the use of undenatured whey protein and after 12 weeks, William's improvement was noticeable. Three months later, he woke up one morning and "felt well again." That day he picked up his golf clubs for the first time in five years. Today he is shooting in the low 90's and will be restarting his practice in the fall.

CONCLUSION

The number of toxins our bodies must deal with every day is truly remarkable. To cope with this burden a fit, rested, well-fed person must maintain adequate immunological and biochemical defenses. The role played by GSH in these defense systems cannot be overstated. Glutathione detoxifies a large number of pollutants, carcinogens, heavy metals, herbicides, pesticides and radiation. We are exposed every day to toxins like cigarette smoke, automobile exhaust, food preservatives and dental amalgam and our body depends on GSH for their removal. Substances that raise GSH levels are being used with increasing frequency in the field of toxicology with considerable success.

GSH & DETOXIFICATION

ABT G, VAGHEF H, GEBHART E, ET AL. The role of N-acetylcysteine as a putative radioprotective agent on X-ray-induced DNA damage as evaluated by alkaline single-cell electrophoresis. *Mutation Research 384: 55-64, 1997*

APPLEGATE LA, LAUTIER D, FRENK E, TYRRELL RM. Endogenous glutathione levels modulate the frequency of both spontaneous and long wavelength ultraviolet induced mutations in human cells. *Carcinogenesis 13: 1557-1560, 1992*

AUST SD, CHIGNELL CF, BRAY TM, KALYANARAMAN B. MASON RP. Free radicals in toxicology. *Toxicology and Applied Pharmacology 120:168-178, 1993*

AWASTHI YC, DAO DD. Glutathione-mediated detoxification mechanisms of human placenta. *Placenta Suppl. 3: 289-301, 1981*

BAKER DH, CZARNECKI-MAULDON GL. Pharmacological role of cysteine in ameliorating or exacerbating mineral toxicities. *American Institute of Nutrition 117:1003-1010, 1987*

BAKER MA, DILLARD CJ, TAPPEL AL. Effect of gold on selenium and glutathione peroxidase activities in rat tissues. *Drug Nutr. Interact. 3: 141-152, 1985*

BALLATORI N. Glutathione mercaptides as transport forms of metals. *Adv. Pharmacol. 27: 271-298, 1994*

BALLATORI N, LIEBERMAN MW, WANG W. N-acetylcysteine as an antidote in methylmercury poisoning. *Environ. Health Perspect. 106: 267-271, 1998*

BALLATORI N, WANG W, LIEBERMAN MW. Accelerated methylmercury elimination in gamma-glutamyl transpeptidase-deficient mice. *American J. Pathol. 152: 1049-1055, 1998*

BARBARO G, DI LORENZO G, RIBERSANI M, ET AL. Serum ferritin and hepatic glutathione concentrations in chronic hepatitis C patients related to the hepatitis C genotype. *J. Hepatol. 30: 774-782, 1999*

BELL IR, BALDWIN CM, SCHWARTZ GE. Illness from low levels of environmental chemicals: relevance to chronic fatigue syndrome and fibromyalgia. *American J. Med. 105(3A): 74S-82S, 1998*

BERGEROW J, ZANDER D, FREIER I, DUNEMANN L. Long-term mercury excretion in urine after removal of amalgam fillings. *Int. Arch. Occup. Environ. Health 66: 209-212, 1994*

BHATTATHIRI VN, SREELEKHA TT, SEBASTIEN P, ET AL. Influence of plasma GSH level on acute radiation mucositis of the oral cavity. *Int. J. Radiat. Oncol. Biol. Phys. 29: 383-386, 1994*

BIAGLOW JE, VARNES ME, EPP ER, ET AL. Role of GSH and other thiols in cellular response to radiation and drugs. *Drug Metabolism Review 20:1-12, 1989*

BLAIR PC, THOMPSON MB, BECHTOLD M, ET AL. Evidence for oxidative damage to red blood cells in mice induced by arsine gas. *Toxicology 63: 25-34, 1990*

BLUMER W. Mercury toxicity in dental amalgam fillings. *J. Adv. In Med. 11: 219-221, 1998*

BOSE S, MUKHOPADHYAY B, CHAUDHURY S, BHATTACHARYA S. Correlation of metal distribution, reduced glutathione and metallothionine levels in liver and kidney of rat. *Indian J. Exp. Biol. 32:679-681, 1994*

BULAT P, DUJIC I, POTKONJAK B, VIDAKOVIC A. Activity of glutathione peroxidase and superoxide dismutase in workers occupationally exposed to mercury. *Int. Arch. Occup. Environm. Health 71 Suppl: S37-S39, 1998*

Bump EA, Brown JM. Role of GSH in the radiation response of mammalian cells in vitro and in vivo. *Pharmacology and Therapeutics 47:117-136,1990*

Burton CA, Hatelid K, Divine K, et al. Glutathione effects on toxicity and uptake of mercuric chloride and sodium arsenite in rabbit renal cortical slices. *Environ. Health Perspect. 103 Suppl 1: 81-84, 1995*

Chaudhari A, Dutta S. Alterations in tissue GSH and angiotensin converting enzyme due to inhalation of diesel engine exhaust. *Journal of Toxicology and Environmental Health 9:327-337, 1982*

Chen CY, Huang YL, Lin TH. Lipid peroxidation in liver of mice administered with nickel chloride: with special reference to trace elements and antioxidants. *Biol. Trace Elem. Res. 61: 193-205, 1998*

Chen TS, Richie JP Jr, Lang CA. Life span profiles of glutathione and acetaminophen detoxification. *Drug Metab. Dispos. 18: 882-887, 1990*

Chhabra SK, Hashim S, Rao AR. Modulation of hepatic glutathione system of enzymes in suckling mouse pups exposed translactationally to malathione. *J. Appl. Toxicol. 13: 411-416, 1993*

Cross CE, Halliwell B, Borish ET, et al. Oxygen radicals and human disease. *Annals of Internal Medicine 107:526-545, 1987*

Daggett DA, Nuwaysir EF, Nelson SA, et al. Effects of triethyl lead administration on the expression of glutathione S-transferase isoenzymes and quinone reductase in rat kidney and liver. *Toxicology 117: 61-71, 1997*

Daggett DA, Oberley TD, Nelson SA, et al. Effect of lead on rat kidney and liver: GST expression and oxidative stress. *Toxicology 128: 191-206, 1998*

DeLeve LD, Kaplowitz N. GSH metabolism and its role in hepatotoxicity. *Pharmacology and Therapeutics 52:287-305, 1991*

Droge W, Holme E. Role of cysteine and glutathione in HIV infection and other diseases associated with muscle wasting and immunological dysfunction. *FASEB. J. 11: 1077-1089, 1997*

Eke BC, Vural N, Iscan M. Combined effects of ethanol and cigarette smoke on hepatic and pulmonary xenobiotic metabolizing enzymes in rats. *Chem. Biol. Interact. 102: 155-167, 1996*

Ercal N, Treeratphan P, Hammond TC, et al. In vivo indices of oxidative stress in lead-exposed C57BL/6 mice are reduced by treatment with meso-2,3-dimercaptosuccinic acid or N-acetyl-cysteine. *Free Radic. Biol. Med. 21: 157-161, 1996*

Ercal N, Treeratphan P, Lutz P, et al. N-acetylcysteine protects Chinese hamster ovary (CHO) cells from lead-induced oxidative stress. *Toxicology 108: 57-64, 1996*

Ferguson CL, Cantilenia LR Jr. Mercury clearance from human plasma during in vitro dialysis: screening systems for chelating agents. *J. Toxicol. Clin. Toxicol. 30: 423-441, 1992*

Flanagan RJ, Meredith TJ. Use of N-acetylcysteine in clinical toxicology. *American J. Med. 91(3C): 131S-139S, 1991*

Garner M, Reglinski J, Smith WA, Stewart MJ. The interaction of colloidal metals with erythrocytes. *J. Inorg. Biochem. 56: 283-290, 1994*

Girardi G, Elias MM. Effectiveness of N-acetylcysteine in protecting against mercuric chloride-induced nephrotoxicity. *Toxicology 67: 155-164, 1991*

Girardi G, Elias MM. Effect of different renal glutathione levels on renal mercury disposition and excretion in the rat. *Toxicology 81: 57-67, 1993*

Goshorn RK. Chronic fatigue syndrome: a review for clinicians. *Semin. Neurol. 18: 237-242, 1998*

GRAF P, SIES H. Hepatic uptake of cadmium and its biliary release as affected by dithioerythritol and glutathione. *Biochem. Pharmacol. 33: 639-643, 1984*

GSTRAUNTHALER G, PFALLER W, KOTANKA P. Glutathione depletion and in vitro lipid peroxidation in mercury or maleate induced acute renal failure. *Biochem. Pharmacol. 32: 2969-2972, 1983*

GURER H, OZGUNES H, NEAL R, ET AL. Antioxidant effects of N-acetylcysteine and succimer in red blood cells from lead-exposed rats. *Toxicology 128: 181-189, 1998*

GYURASICS A, KOSZORUS L, VARGA F, GREGUS Z. Increased biliary excretion of glutathione is generated by the glutathione-dependant hepatobiliary transport of antimony and bismuth. *Biochem. Pharmacol. 44:1275-1281, 1992*

HANADA K, SAWAMURA D, TAMAI K, HASHIMOTO I, KOBAYASHI S. Photo-protective effect of esterified GSH against ultraviolet B induced sunburn cell formation in the hairless mice. *Journal of Investigative Dermatology 108:727-730, 1997*

HASAN M, HAIDER SS. Acetyl-homocysteine thiolactone protects against some neurotoxic effects of thallium. *Neurotoxicology 10: 257-261, 1989*

HIROTA Y. Effect of methylmercury on the activity of glutathione peroxidase in rat liver. *Am. Ind. Hyg. Assoc. J. 47: 556-558, 1986*

HOUSER MT, MILNER LS, KOLBECK PC, ET AL. Glutathione monoethyl ester moderates mercuric chloride-induced acute renal failure. *Nephron 61: 449-455, 1992*

HSU JM. Lead toxicity as related to GSH metabolism. *Journal of Nutrition 101:26-33, 1981*

HULTBERG B, ANDERSON A, ISSAKSON A. Alterations of thiol metabolism in human cell lines induced by low amounts of copper, mercury or cadmium ions. *Toxicology 126: 203-212, 1998*

JONES DP, BROWN LA, STERNBERG P. Variability in glutathione-dependant detoxification in vivo and its relevance to detoxification of chemical mixtures. *Toxicology 105: 267-274, 1995*

KATAWA M, SUZUKI KT. The effect of cadmium, zinc or copper loading on the metabolism of amino acids in mouse liver. *Toxicology Letters 20:149-154, 1984*

KELLY GS. Clinical applications of N-acetylcysteine. *Altern. Med. Rev. 3: 114-127, 1998*

KEOGH JP, STEFFEN B, SIEGERS CP. Cytotoxicity of heavy metals in the human small intestinal epithelial cell line I-407: the role of glutathione. *J. Toxicol. Environ. Health 43: 351-359, 1994*

KIDD PM. GSH: Systemic protectant against oxidative and free radical damage. *Alternative Medicine Review 2:155-176, 1997*

KIDD PM. The free radical oxidant toxins of polluted air. in: LEVINE SA, KID PM. *Antioxidant Adaptation – Its role in free radical pathology 69-103, 1985*

KRETZSCHMAR M, KLINGER W. The hepatic GSH system – influences of xenobiotics. *Experimental Pathology 38:145-164, 1990*

LASH LH, ZALUPS RK. Alterations in renal cellular glutathione metabolism after in vivo administration of a subtoxic dose of mercuric chloride. *J. Biochem. Toxicol. 11: 1-9, 1996*

LEE TC, WEI ML, CHANG WJ, ET AL. Elevation of glutathione levels and glutathione S-transferase activity in arsenic-resistant Chinese hamster ovary cells. *In Vitro Cell Dev. Biol. 25: 442-448, 1989*

LEW H, QUINTANILHA A. Effects of endurance training and exercise on tissue antioxidative capacity and acetaminophen detoxification. *Eur. J. Drug Metab. Pharmacokinet. 16: 59-68, 1991*

LIVARDJANI F, LEDIG M, KOPP P, ET AL. Lung and blood superoxide dismutase activity in mercury vapor exposed rats: effect of N-acetylcysteine treatment. *Toxicology 66: 289-295, 1991*

LUND ME, BANNER W JR, CLARKSON
TW, BERLIN M. Treatment of acute methylmercury ingestion by hemodialysis with N-
acetylcysteine (Mucomyst) infusion and 2, 3-
dimercaptopropane sulfonate. *J. Toxicol. Clin.
Toxicol. 22: 31-49, 1984*

MOLIN M, BERGMAN B, MARKLUND SL,
ET AL. Mercury, selenium, and glutathione
peroxidase before and after amalgam removal
in man. *Acta Odontol. Scand. 48: 189-202, 1990*

MOLIN M, MARKLUND SL, BERGMAN B,
NILSSON B. Mercury, selenium, and glu-
tathione peroxidase in dental personnel. *Acta
Odontol. Scand. 47: 383-390, 1989*

NAVARRO J, OBRADOR E, PELLICER JA,
ET AL. Blood glutathione as an index of ra-
diation-induced oxidative stress in mice and
humans. *Free Radic. Biol. Med. 22: 1203-1209,
1997*

NEAL R, COOPER K, GURER H, ERCAL N.
Effects of N-acetylcysteine and 2, 3-dimercapto-
succinic acid on lead induced oxidative stress
in rat lenses. *Toxicology 130: 167-174, 1998*

NICOLSON GL, NICOLSON NL. Gulf War
illnesses: complex medical, scientific and political paradox. *Med. Confl. Surviv. 14: 156-165,
1998*

ORNAGHI F, FERRINI S, PRATI M,
GIAVINI E. The protective effects of N-acetyl-
L-cysteine against methyl mercury
embryotoxicity in mice. *Fundam. Appl.
Toxicol. 20: 437-445, 1993*

OTHMAN AI, EL MISSIRY MA. Role of selenium against lead toxicity in male rats. *J.
Biochem. Mol. Toxicol. 12: 345-349, 1998*

OTT WR, ROBERTS JW. Everyday exposure to
toxic pollutants. *Scient. Ameri. 278(2):86-91, 1998*

PARKE DV, SAPOTA A. Chemical toxicity and
reactive oxygen species. *Internat. J. of Occupational
Med. and Environmental Health 9:331-340, 1996*

PLANAS-BOHNE F, ELIZALDE M. Activity
of glutathione-S-transferase in rat liver and
kidneys after administration of lead or cadmium. *Arch. Toxicol. 66: 365-367, 1992*

POLLET C, NATELSON BH, LANGE G, ET
AL. Medical evaluation of Persian Gulf veter-
ans with fatigue and / or chemical sensitivity.
J. Med. 29: 101-113, 1998

QUEIROZ ML, PENA SC, SALTES TS, ET
AL. Abnormal antioxidant system in erythro-
cytes of mercury-exposed workers. *Human
Exp. Toxicol. 17: 225-230, 1998*

QUIG D. Cysteine metabolism and metal toxicity. *Altern. Med. Rev. 3: 262-270, 1998*

REA WJ ET AL. Food and chemical sensitivity after environmental chemical overexposure.
Annals of Allergy 41:101-110, 1987

REICKS M, RADER JI. Effects of dietary tin
and copper on rat hepatocellular antioxidant
protection. *Proc. Soc. Exp. Biol. Med. 195:123-
128, 1990*

ROSS RK, JONES PA, YU MC. Bladder cancer epidemiology and pathogenesis. *Seminars
in Oncology 23:536-545, 1996*

SANDBORGH-ENGLAND G, ELINDER CG,
LANGWORTH S, ET AL. Mercury in biological fluids after amalgam removal. *J. Dental Res.
77: 615-624, 1998*

SANDHIR R, GILL KD. Effect of lead on
lipid peroxidation in liver of rats. *Biol. Trace
Elem. Res. 48: 91-97, 1995*

SARAFIAN TA, BREDESEN DE, VERITY
MA. Cellular resistance to methylmercury.
Neurotoxicity 17: 27-36, 1996

SARKAR D, DAS D, BHATTACHARYA S.
Role of exogenous reduced glutathione on time
dependant 203Hg distribution in liver and kidney of a freshwater teleost, Anabas testudineus.
Biomed. Environ. Sci. 10: 60-64, 1997

SASAKURA C, SUZUKI KT. Biological inter-
action between transition metals (Ag, Cd,
Hg), selenide/sulfide and *selenoprotein P. J.
Inorg. Biochem. 71: 159-162, 1998*

SELIG C, NOTHDURFT W, FLIEDNER TM.
Radioprotective effect of N-acetylcysteine on
granulocyte/macrophage colony-forming cells
of human bone marrow. *J. Cancer Res. Clin.
Oncol. 119: 346-349, 1993*

SHI X, FLYNN DC, LIU K, DALAL N. Vanadium (IV) formation in the reduction of vanadate by glutathione reductase/NADPH and the role of molecular oxygen. *Ann. Clin. Lab. Sci. 27: 422-427, 1997*

SINGHAL RK, ANDERSON ME, MEISTER A. Glutathione, a first line defense against cadmium toxicity. *FASEB J. 1: 220-223, 1987*

SMITH CV, JONES DP, GUENTHNER TM, LASH LH, LAUTERBERG BH. Compartmentalization of GSH: implications for the study of toxicity and disease. *Toxicology and Applied Pharmacology 140:1-12, 1996*

SMITH TK. Dietary modulation of the glutathione detoxification pathway and the potential for altered xenobiotic metabolism. *Adv. Exp. Med. Biol. 289: 165-169, 1991*

STOHS SJ, BAGCHI D. Oxidative mechanisms in the toxicity of metal ions. Free Radic. Biol. Med. 18: 321-336, 1995

SUGAWARA E, NAKAMURA K, MIYAKE T, ET AL. Lipid peroxidation and concentration of glutathione in erythrocytes from workers exposed to lead. *Br. J. Ind. Med. 48: 239-242, 1991*

THOMPSON AM. The oxidizing capacity of the Earth's atmosphere: Probable past and future changes. *Science 256: 1157-1165, 1992*

VALLIS KA. GSH deficiency and radiosensitivity in AIDS patients. *Lancet 337:918-919, 1991*

VIJAYALAKSHMI K, SOOD PP. Ameliorative capacities of vitamins and monothiols post therapy in the restoration of methylmercury altered glutathione metabolism. *Cell. Mol. Biol. 40: 211-224, 1994*

VOS O, ROOS-VERHEY WSD. Endogenous versus exogenous thiols in radioprotection. *Pharmacology and Therapeutics 39:169-177, 1988*

WALTHER UI, MUCKTER H, FICHTI B, FORTH W. Influence of glutathione on zinc-mediated cellular toxicity. *Biol. Trace Elem. Res. 67: 97-107, 1999*

WOODS JS, ELLIS ME. Up-regulation of glutathione synthesis in rat kidney by methyl mercury. Relationship to mercury-induced oxidative stress. *Biochem. Pharmacol. 50: 1719-1724, 1995*

WRIGHT LS, KORNGUTH SE, OBERLY TD, SIEGEL FL. Effects of lead on glutathione S-transferase expression in rat kidney: a dose-response study. *Toxicol. Sci. 46: 254-259, 1998*

XIE J, FUNAKOSHI T, SHIMADA H, KOJIMA S. Comparative effects of chelating agents on pulmonary toxicity of systemic nickel in mice. *J. Appl. Toxicol. 16: 317-324, 1996*

ZALUPS RK, BARFUSS DW. Participation of mercuric conjugates of cysteine, homocysteine, and N-acetylcysteine in mechanisms involved in the renal tubular uptake of inorganic mercury. *J. American Soc. Nephrol. 9: 551-561, 1998*

ZHANG Q, ZHOU XD, DENNY T, ET AL. Changes in immune parameters seen in Gulf War veterans but not in civilians with chronic fatigue syndrome. *Clin. Diagn. Lab. Immunol. 6: 6-13, 1999*

CHAPTER 3
GSH AND THE IMMUNE SYSTEM

THE IMMUNE SYSTEM

It's surprising how many people still believe that catching a cold is the result of sitting in a draft or going out with wet hair. It is a simple and well-established fact that the common cold is a contagious, transmittable disease. We don't catch colds from cold air, in spite of the disease's name. Both the expression and the misconception are deeply ingrained in our culture. But it is exposure to the actual virus that causes illness.

Others might blame their cold on being stressed out, overworked or having exercised too much. They are much closer to the truth. Although these factors in themselves do not *cause* a cold, they do make us more susceptible to the cold virus. By overdoing it, these patients have temporarily diminished their immune resources and suffer the consequences—the virus overpowers them. Most visits to the doctor follow the failure of the immune system to deal with a particular threat. The good news is, the immune system can be reinforced.

Few people are aware of this, even those who consciously work at their well-being. Many of us know well enough how to take care of the heart and muscles, but only a few pay attention to the immune system, even though this is our front line defense against all infectious and destructive attacks. To maintain a good immune response we should exercise regularly (45 to 60 minutes, 3 times weekly), eat regular and varied meals, maintain an ideal body weight, sleep regularly (8 hours for young adult, less for elderly), supplement our diet with vitamins, minerals & micronutrients, avoid undue stress and, funnily enough, laugh a lot. We should also avoid radiation and toxins, abuse of tobacco, alcohol and caffeine and the unnecessary use of antibiotics and steroids. See figure 10.

The immune defense is an extraordinarily sophisticated system. A microscopic examination of any part of the human body shows it teeming with microorganisms such as bacteria, parasites and fungi, and that's just inside us. The environment from which we get our air, water and food is also saturated with microorganisms. It is amazing that we survive at all.

Traditionally, we consult a physician only when a disease has actually taken hold. Often, the doctor launches an offensive or 'attack' strategy with antibiotics, antiviral compounds or chemotherapy in an attempt to exterminate the invader. Despite drug side-effects and other drawbacks this offensive strategy has proven widely effective. It's the best way we've found to fight the war.

But it's preferable to avoid the war altogether. After all, the battleground is your body. Even when medicine wins, the carnage remains. Drug side-effects and chemotherapy after-effects are like the random destruction of war in which innocent bystanders die. We can't overemphasize the value of a defensive strategy—a preventive medicine that stops invaders establishing a beachhead and avoids all-out conflict. An optimized immune system is without question the best prevention. We can do this by nurturing and feeding it just as we tend to the rest of our body.

THE IMMUNE RESPONSE
The immune response seeks out, identifies, and attacks threatening microorganisms, allergens, cancer cells and grafted tissue—collectively called antigens. The body's reaction is called an antigen response.

When a pathogen enters the blood stream, immune cells are activated. There are several types, including the polymorphonuclear cells that form pus. These large cells simply engulf pathogens and digest them. The smaller but much more sophisticated lymphocytes deal with pathogens by adapting a specific defense to them.

B-cell lymphocytes identify pathogens and mark them as targets for T-cell lymphocytes. Helper T-cells alert immune cells to join the battle, killer T-cells destroy the intruder, and suppressor T-cells switch off the immune response when the job is done.

The healthy immune response can become compromised, however. There may be too few immune cells, the cells themselves may be incompetent, or they may be overwhelmed by a particularly aggressive pathogen. In many cases, the adaptive side of the immune system identifies and subsequently remembers the chemical signature of a pathogen and is able to handle it more effectively the next time around. This leads to partial or complete immunity. For example, you only catch the measles once.

The immune system is impressive, but not infallible. It can sometimes respond to threats as if they were non-threats and to normal metabolic functions as if they were attacks on the body. We want our immune response to protect against infection, ignore harmless substances, accept transplanted organs, not attack its own organs and protect the body against carcinogenesis and tumor growth. We want to avoid recurrent infection, allergic response to harmless substances, rejection of transplanted organs, auto-immune disease in which the body attacks its own systems, and cancer. See figure II.

The two most common unwanted immune responses are autoimmune disease and allergies. In autoimmune disease the body mistakes normal tissue for a foreign antigen and attacks it, leading to the destruction of healthy tissue. In the case of allergies, the immune system mistakes a harmless substance for a potentially dangerous one and reacts with an aggressive, sometimes deadly response. Some autoimmune diseases are:

❏ Lupus
❏ Myasthenia gravis
❏ Chronic fatigue syndrome
❏ Rheumatoid arthritis
❏ Multiple sclerosis

❏ Polymyositis
❏ Scleroderma
❏ Lou Gehrig's disease (ALS)
❏ Grave's disease
❏ Crohn's Disease

THE IMMUNE SYSTEM AND GSH

Our account of polymorphonuclear cells and lymphocytes in the previous section describes only a part of the immune system. B-cell lymphocytes account for about 10% of all circulating lymphocytes and work by releasing immunoglobulins to attack and destroy invading pathogens. About 80% of lymphocytes are T-cells. When this system is disrupted the doors to infection open and health is compromised. For example, the human immunodeficiency virus (HIV) destroys helper T-cells and leaves killer T-cells cut off and powerless. As a result, invading micro-organisms that the body would normally shrug off are able to cause the severe infections that characterize AIDS.

GSH plays a central role in the functioning of our immune cells. Dr. Gustavo Bounous, a leading expert on GSH says, "The limiting factor in the proper activity of our lymphocytes is the availability of GSH." This is strikingly clear in the example of the human immunodeficiency virus, or HIV—the cause of AIDS (see chapter 12).

AIDS is essentially a T-cell dysfunction. Patients typically suffer from low GSH levels and especially from low T-cell GSH count. Several studies have shown that GSH levels can predict an AIDS patient's chances of survival and quality of life.

Healthy growth and activity of immune cells depends upon the availability of GSH. Experimental depletion of GSH severely diminishes the ability of these cells to fight pathogens and leaves the door wide open to disease. In numerous studies the level of intracellular GSH in the lymphocytes corresponds directly to the effectiveness of immune response. In the simplest terms, GSH is a sort of 'food' for the immune system.

In some autoimmune diseases such as rheumatoid arthritis (chapter 6), lupus (SLE) and in normal aging (chapter 6), T-cell lymphocytes show a weakened response to antigens. In addition these chronic inflammatory conditions have been associated with low serum and red blood cell GSH concentrations.

A lymphocyte attacks a pathogen by releasing powerful oxidizing chemicals such as peroxide and protects itself against these chemicals by neutralizing them with GSH. Also, lymphocytes must replicate themselves over and over again (monoclonal expansion) in order to attack the whole pathogen population. This requires the use of oxygen and releases further oxidants. In order to continue multiplying efficiently GSH is once again required to counteract the effects of oxidation. So fighting off infection consumes GSH in two ways— by using it to stabilize free radicals and also to grow immune cells. This is apparent in acute infections such as bacterial pneumonia. In chronic infections such as hepatitis C or AIDS, GSH depletion is even more pronounced. Recent research has demonstrated that elevated GSH levels enable the immune system to address these infections more effectively.

Doctor Bounous with his McGill University team measured the immune response of laboratory animals fed a whey protein isolate rich in GSH precursors (later trademarked Immunocal). These animals demonstrated both higher intracellular GSH levels and a heightened response to immune challenge. Interestingly, animals fed a similar diet of cysteine-enriched casein (see chapter 4) did not benefit from the same effects.

So the protective activity of GSH is two-fold—it enhances the activity of immune cells and also functions as an antioxidant within them.

A frightening number of antibiotic-resistant bacterial infections such as flesh-eating disease, vancomycin-resistant enterococcus and methicillin-resistant staphylococcus have made their way into our hospitals and communities. Some health professionals believe that viruses such as those causing AIDS and Hepatitis C are just the tip of the iceberg, and that a wave of newly emerging pathogens is on its way. Old foes like tuberculosis, previously thought to have

Figure 10 — The do's and don'ts of immune system maintenance

DO	DON'T
❏ Exercise regularly (45-60 min., 3 times weekly)	❏ *Abuse tobacco*
❏ Eat regular & varied meals	❏ *Abuse alcohol*
❏ Maintain ideal body weight	❏ *Abuse caffeine*
❏ Sleep regularly (8 hours for young adult, less for elderly)	❏ *Use antibiotics inappropriately*
❏ Supplement your diet with vitamins, minerals & micronutrients	❏ *Use steroids inappropriately*
❏ Avoid undue stress	❏ *Expose yourself to radiation*
❏ Laugh a lot	❏ *Expose yourself to toxins*

been eliminated, are back with a vengeance and are no longer susceptible to previously successful treatments. Enhancing our GSH levels is a practical precaution against this ominous trend.

Conclusion

The immune system uses various cells to fight off infection and other threats and the healthy growth and activity of these cells depends upon the availability of GSH. Glutathione is at the heart of all immune functions and low GSH levels are seen in many diseases, especially AIDS which is characterized by a severely compromised immune system.

Raising and maintaining GSH levels can minimize the risk of these diseases. Although only very ill people are severely deficient in GSH, those in good or fair health can benefit from GSH supplementation, especially in these days when we are exposed as never before to environmental toxins and drug-resistant bacteria. The use of GSH supplementation to fight specific diseases is discussed in part 2.

Without question, the best type of preventive medicine is an optimized immune system and a critical strategy to optimize it is by feeding it GSH.

Figure 11 — Desired and undesired immune responses

	Desired response	Undesired response
Infectious agent	Protective immunity	Recurrent infection
Harmless substance	No response	Allergy
Transplant organ	Acceptance	Rejection
Self organ	Self-tolerance	Auto-immune disease
Tumor	Tumor immunity	Cancer

GSH & THE IMMUNE SYSTEM

ANDERSON ME. GSH and GSH delivery systems. *Advances in Pharmacology 38:65-78, 1997*

BOUNOUS G, BATIST G, GOLD P. Immunoenhancing property of dietary whey proteins in mice: role of glutathione. *Clinical and Investigative Medicine 12:154-161, 1989*

BOUNOUS G, GOLD P. The biological activity of undenatured dietary whey protein in mice: role of glutathione. *Clinical and Investigative Medicine 14:296-309, 1991*

BOUNOUS G, KONGSHAVN P. Influence of dietary proteins on the immune system of mice. *Journal of Nutrition 112:1747-1755, 1982*

BOUNOUS G, KONGSHAVN P. Differential effect of dietary protein type on the B-cell and T-cell immune responses in mice. *Journal of Nutrition 115:1403-1408, 1985*

DROGE W, POTTMEYER-GERBER C, SCHMIDT H, NICK S. Glutathione augments the activation of cytotoxic T lymphocytes in vivo. *Immunobiology 172:151-156, 1986*

FIDELUS RK, GINOUVES P, LAWRENCE D, TSAN MF. Modulation of intracellular glutathione concentrations alters lymphocyte activation and proliferation. *Experimental Cell Research 170:269-275, 1987*

FIDELUS RK, TSAN MF. Glutathione and lymphocyte activation: a function of aging and autoimmune disease. *Immunology 61:503-508, 1987*

FURUKAWA T, MEYDANI SN, BLUMBERG JB. Reversal of age associated decline in immune responsiveness by dietary glutathione supplementation in mice. *Mechanisms of Aging and Development 38:107-117, 1987*

GMUNDER H, DROGE W. Differential effects of glutathione depletion of T-cell subsets. *Cellular Immunology 138:229-237, 1991*

HAMILOS DL, WEDNER HJ. The role of glutathione in lymphocyte activation. *Journal of Immunology 135:2740-2747, 1985*

KIDD PM. Glutathione: Systemic protectant against oxidative and free radical damage. *Alternative Medicine Review 2:155-176, 1997*

ROTILIO G, KNOEPFEL L, STEINKUHLER C, PALMARA AT, CIROLO MR, GARACI E. Effects of intracellular redox status on cellular regulation and viral infection. in: *Oxidative Stress, Cell Activation and Viral Infection, C. Pasquier et al (eds.), 1994*

CHAPTER 4

RAISING GSH LEVELS

If glutathione is manufactured within the body, what can we do to maintain or increase GSH levels? Some pharmaceutical drugs can do it, and so can some natural sources. Eating glutathione cannot. There are many ideas about how to raise GSH levels in the body but only a few actually work—and some of them have side effects. In order to take advantage of the great potential of GSH in health and disease we must dispel the myths and clarify the facts. This requires an understanding of the biochemical make-up of this important protein.

GSH is a tripeptide—a protein made up of three amino acids—in this case, glycine, glutamate (glutamic acid), and cysteine. The chemical structure of glutathione does not easily survive the digestive process, so eating it will not raise GSH levels. The body manufactures it within the cell from building blocks (precursors) of GSH in our food. Glycine and glutamate are readily available in North American diets, but cysteine-containing proteins are much harder to come by. Figure 12 shows sources of these three component amino-acids of glutathione.

Cysteine—a sulfur-containing, or "thiol" amino acid—is responsible for the biological activity (bioactivity) of the whole molecule. Cysteine as an isolated amino acid has trouble getting from your mouth to your cells. Much of it is broken down or altered in the digestive tract and bloodstream. So we must take cysteine in a form that resists breakdown. If the body doesn't get these sulfur-containing amino acids into the blood, we can't make GSH.

Other thiol amino acids include cystine (different from cysteine) and methionine. Cystine is known as a "disulfide" amino acid because it contains two cysteine molecules connected by their sulfur atoms—a so-called 'dilsulfide bridge.' Cystine is not generally found as a free amino acid. Methionine may serve as a glutathione building block, but it has the tendency to convert into homocysteine, which raises the risk of heart disease.

There are several ways to raise GSH levels. All the pharmaceutical and natural products listed in figure 13 are described in this chapter. We also explain how GSH works with other nutrients or co-factors.

GSH PRECURSORS & CELLULAR MANUFACTURE

The building blocks (precursors) glutamate, cysteine and glycine from any source must be in a form that can be transported from the mouth, through the digestive system, into the blood and finally through the cell wall. Once there, the cell combines them into GSH. Glutamate is derived from food

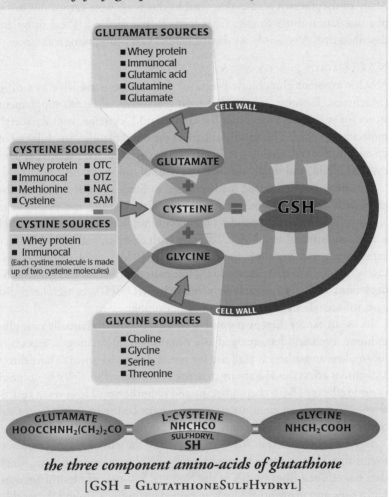

Figure 12 — GSH is manufactured in each cell of the body from three amino-acid precursors (building blocks)—glutamate, glycine, and most importantly cysteine, which contains the biologically active sulfhydryl group (SH). Some dietary sources are shown.

GLUTAMATE SOURCES
- Whey protein
- Immunocal
- Glutamic acid
- Glutamine
- Glutamate

CYSTEINE SOURCES
- Whey protein
- Immunocal
- Methionine
- Cysteine
- OTC
- OTZ
- NAC
- SAM

CYSTINE SOURCES
- Whey protein
- Immunocal

(Each cystine molecule is made up of two cysteine molecules)

GLYCINE SOURCES
- Choline
- Glycine
- Serine
- Threonine

CELL WALL

GLUTAMATE + CYSTEINE + GLYCINE = GSH

| GLUTAMATE $HOOCCHNH_2(CH_2)_2CO$ | L-CYSTEINE $NHCHCO$ SULFHDRYL SH | GLYCINE $NHCH_2COOH$ |

the three component amino-acids of glutathione

[GSH = GlutathioneSulfHydryl]

sources containing uncooked glutamic acid, glutamine and glutamate. It is found in undenatured why protein. Cysteine comes from such protein sources as eggs, raw milk, undenatured whey protein and in small amounts from other foods. The amino acid methionine can break down into cysteine. Various pharmaceutical drugs serve as cysteine delivery systems. Glycine is found in foods rich in the amino acids choline, glycine, serine and threonine. Only when these three precursors are absorbed by the body and have passed through the wall of individual cells can the body manufacture glutathione.

DRUGS

Many of the research studies described in this book were carried out using pharmaceutical drugs to raise GSH levels in test subjects. These drugs are described first. Afterwards, we discuss natural GSH-promoting substances.

NAC (N-ACETYL-CYSTEINE)

NAC is a potent glutathione precursor that has been available as a drug (Mucomist, Parvolex, etc.) and also on the shelves of health supplement stores for years. It is a variant of the amino acid L-cysteine, with an 'acetyl' molecule attached. This greatly enhances the bioavailability (usefulness) of cysteine to the cell, enabling it to survive the trip from the digestive system into the blood, and finally through the walls of individual cells.

For many years this drug has been used to break up mucus in lung diseases such as cystic fibrosis, chronic bronchitis, asthma and emphysema and is still the standard treatment for acetaminophen overdose. Most GSH studies on humans used NAC. Together with other animal and laboratory experiments they measured the effectiveness of NAC against a host of diseases characterized by oxidative stress, free radical formation and glutathione depletion. Such diseases include infection by AIDS/HIV, cancer, heart disease, tobacco damage and heavy metal poisoning.

Its use in cancer therapy is exciting because it can substantially raise glutathione levels and has emerged as a promising anticarcinogen, especially for smokers and others at high risk for cancer. It is also known to have direct anti-tumor effects and its ability to detoxify normal cells helps it counteract the side effects of both chemotherapy and radiotherapy. However, it's effectiveness depends on circumstances and it must be used wisely. Cancer patients wishing to take NAC must discuss it with their oncologist.

NAC has been used in AIDS research since the early 1990's when it was found that HIV patients become profoundly glutathione deficient. Much data has resulted from studies at the National Institute of Health, Stanford University, and many other highly respected institutions around the world.

NAC therapy has two common problems: firstly, it is a pharmaceutical drug and carries a certain toxicity itself; secondly, NAC-induced GSH levels reach a rapid peak and decline within hours. The drug is thus described as having a short half-life. Rapid peaks are often followed by a rapid drop, often to below normal levels. To maintain constantly elevated GSH levels, NAC must be swallowed or injected several times per day, and this is very hard on the body. Many people eating NAC report unwanted symptoms,

Figure 13 — GSH-promoting substances described in this chapter

Drugs	Natural products	GSH co-factors
NAC	Oral Glutathione	Selenium
SAM	Cysteine	Vitamin B1
OTC	Methionine	Vitamin B2
OTZ	Melatonin	Vitamin B6
Procysteine	Glutamine	Vitamin B12
GSH monoesters	Lipoic Acid	Folate, Folic acid
GSH diesters	Silymarin (milk thistle)	Vitamin C
	Whey Proteins	Vitamin E
	Bioactive whey proteins (Immunocal®)	Other nutrients

including rash, wheezing, nausea, vomiting, cramps and diarrhea. Others find the smell and taste unacceptable. Although rare, death has been reported in association with NAC. However, it is still the most commonly used way to raise glutathione levels in clinical settings.

Treating drug overdoses or acute pulmonary disease with NAC requires the monitoring of health professionals. Suggested non-prescription oral doses range from 200-2,400 mg/day depending on one's health.

SAM (S-ADENOSYL-METHIONINE)
SAM is a form of methionine already partially converted to cysteine. It can be useful in the treatment of cirrhosis and cholestasis and is becoming popular in Europe as a mood stabilizing medication. Its possible use in America as an antidepressant is under investigation. SAM is expensive to synthesize and may react poorly with other antidepressants. Its side effects at therapeutic doses can include dry mouth, agitation and gastrointestinal problems.

OTC AND OTZ
OTC (ornithine decarboxylase, procysteine) and OTZ (oxothiazolidine carboxylate) are synthetic delivery sources—a substrate for the enzyme 5-oxyprolinase which first converts them to s-carboxy-cysteine, and later hydrolyzes them to cysteine, which the liver uses to make GSH. However, the required enzyme 5-oxyprolinase is not present in all tissue and the value of OTC/OTZ is limited. Most studies have used either laboratory animals or human tissue cultures. Small studies have been conducted with AIDS and cancer patients, and further work is in progress. These drugs are not readily available to doctors or the general public.

GSH MONOESTERS, GSH DIESTERS
These synthetic compounds make quite effective GSH delivery systems but

they can be metabolized into alcohol, which potentially depletes GSH. Very few studies have been carried out on humans, but well-recognized GSH researchers such as the late Alton Meister and Mary Anderson have been optimistic about further elaboration of its clinical applications. However, the long-term safety of these products is open to question.

NATURAL PRODUCTS

ORAL GLUTATHIONE

Why not just eat GSH? After all, it is freely available in fresh fruits, vegetables and meats. It is also is commercially available in pill form or powder from a variety of chemical companies. Unfortunately, pre-manufactured GSH is not particularly helpful to the body. A small amount of reduced protein-bound GSH may make it into the blood stream, but most is lost to the digestive process and cannot effectively raise intracellular GSH levels. Researchers have demonstrated oral GSH's poor bioavailability, especially in the liver where it is most needed. E.W. Flagg and his team at Emory University, Atlanta even point to a possible *decrease* in blood GSH after oral ingestion of GSH-containing foods. In medical terms, oral GSH has negligible effect on immunologic parameters.

CYSTEINE (L-CYSTEINE)

The availability of cysteine determines how much GSH we can synthesize. Why not just eat this non-essential amino acid? It is available through pharmacological supply outlets and at health food stores and may in fact raise intracellular GSH to a small degree. However, cysteine as a dietary supplement can promote hypercysteinemia and potential toxicity. Because cysteine is easily oxidized in the digestive tract, its absorption into the bloodstream and cells is limited. Cysteine that manages to reach the bloodstream is further oxidized into potentially toxic by-products, some of which contain the hydroxyl radical—a highly reactive oxidant. This defeats its intended purpose as an antioxidant.

Clinical proof that dietary cysteine has a negligible effect upon immune response has been demonstrated by the Montreal researchers Drs. Gustavo Bounous and Gerry Batist. They compared specific protein precursors in the bioactive whey-protein Immunocal with a cysteine/casein combination. Animals fed oral cysteine showed no positive response.

METHIONINE (L-METHIONINE)

Methionine is an essential amino acid present in many foods and has been identified as a GSH precursor. It is also available from pharmacological supply outlets and health food stores. The metabolic transformation of methionine into GSH is a complex process, greatly affected by other factors. For example, methionine levels are very low when liver disease is present and non-existent in newborns. Above certain doses it can be toxic. Of great concern, methionine is also a precursor of homocysteine, recently identified as a high risk factor in the development of atherosclerosis (hardening of the arteries).

Melatonin

Melatonin is a naturally-occurring hormone manufactured by the pineal gland, which lies deep within the brain. Melatonin is a derivative of the amino acid tryptophan and the neurotransmitter serotonin. It has long been recognized for its role in the regulation of sleep and waking cycles and has gained popularity as a supplement for the treatment of jet lag, insomnia and other sleep disturbances.

Like most hormones, melatonin is rarely involved in just a single function. Recent research has led to a great number of papers describing the functions of melatonin, including potential anti-aging effects, application against Alzheimer's disease, cluster headaches, cancer prevention, cancer therapy, and as an immunostimulant. Melatonin is known to be a powerful antioxidant and plays a role in stimulating other antioxidants as well.

Apart from its ability to function independently as an antioxidant, melatonin has been shown to effectively raise glutathione levels in many tissues including the brain, liver, muscle and blood serum. Some of its positive benefits have been ascribed specifically to this ability.

An interesting scientific study measured melatonin levels against glutathione levels during sleep. A research team at the University of Texas showed that subjects given melatonin doubled their brain glutathione levels within 30 minutes. Like GSH anywhere in the body, it eliminates toxic hydroxyl radicals, but this brain GSH is more effective with sleep. It seems that melatonin may protect brain and nerve tissue because of its GSH-enhancing ability. Several European studies have supported these findings.

This same team in Texas led by R.J. Reiter has published many papers linking melatonin to GSH production. In a sports physiology experiment, muscle glutathione was measured before and after extended exercise. By using melatonin to pre-treat subjects before the stress of exercise, the usual, significant decreases in GSH levels due to oxidative stress were eliminated.

The long term safety of melatonin has not yet been established and response to it varies from person to person. This product should only be used in consultation with an appropriate health professional.

Glutamine

Glutamine (GAM) is the most abundant free amino acid found in the body.

It is common in both blood and muscle tissue, and is the second most common amino acid in the brain after glutamic acid (GA). The three semi-essential amino acids—glutamine, glutamic acid and gamma-amino butyric acid (GABA)—are closely related and are classified as glutamate amino acids. Glutamate is a salt of glutamic acid.

Described by Dr. Eric Braverman as "the brain's three musketeers," GAM, GA, and GABA are close in name and category but quite different in function. In the brain, GABA serves as a inhibiting (calming) neurotransmitter, GA as an excitatory neurotransmitter and GAM mainly as an energy source and mediator of both GA and GABA. Some proponents of glutamine have referred to it as "brain fuel."

These three amino acids usually fall into the same discussion because they have the ability to metabolize into one another. For example, if the brain senses a lack of glutamic acid it may draw glutamine from the muscles into the bloodstream, pass it through the blood-brain barrier and transform it into glutamic acid or glutamate.

Nitrogen is a critical component of all amino acids and is often released when they are broken down. Unfortunately this free nitrogen is easily converted to ammonia—especially toxic to nerve tissue and the brain. The liver must work hard to convert nitrogen into urea so it can be excreted in the urine. On the other hand, nitrogen may also attach itself to glutamic acid, forming glutamine. Because glutamine is unique among amino acids—the only one with two nitrogen molecules—glutamic acid serves as a "sink" to collect free nitrogen, protecting many tissues from harm.

Glutamine is crucial to the metabolism and maintenance of muscle. It is also the primary nutrient for cells lining the intestinal tract. In periods of stress or severe illness, glutamine levels may fall. That's why it is such a useful supplement for athletes, surgical patients, those suffering from the muscle wasting of AIDS or cancer and for various gastrointestinal disorders.

Glutamine can also boost the immune system, act as a cancer preventative and treatment, detoxify the body and support liver metabolism. Dr. Ronald Klatz of the American Academy of Anti-Aging Medicine (A⁴M) describes glutamine as a 'growth-hormone releaser' and an anti-aging agent. The overlap of the possible clinical applications of glutamine and glutathione is no coincidence. Glutamine supplies the body with glutamate (glutamic acid), the second most important component of GSH after cysteine.

Whether taken orally or intravenously, glutamine supplementation raises glutathione concentrations. T.R. Harward in Florida and M. Basoglu in Turkey conducted similar studies to measure the fortifying effect of glutamine on GSH levels in the gut. Levels of lipid peroxidation and oxidative stress both fell in these experiments. Y. Cao in Arkansas found a three-fold increase in intestinal GSH after glutamine supplementation.

R. Denno and J.D. Rounds of Harvard University conducted a study on parenteral nutrition—nutrients delivered by routes other than the stomach and gut. This is very important during long surgery and under other special circumstances. They showed that when glutamine was included, plasma glutathione levels rose significantly and supported liver functions. R.W. Hong from the same team showed that glutamine supplementation improved survival odds against such toxic threats as acetaminophen overdose by preserving glutathione stores in the liver.

Glutamine also plays a role in cancer therapy. Tumor cells often act as a trap, stealing glutamine from other parts of the body and leading to muscle wasting and atrophy. For this reason, many cancer therapists avoided glutamine in the past, fearing they would be feeding the cancer. It is now known that just the opposite is true. Glutamine promotes GSH production, heightening the immune system's defense against tumor cells and making it easier for normal tissue to tolerate chemotherapy and radiotherapy.

Another University of Arkansas study led by Dr. K. Rouse showed how oral glutamine supplementation could lower glutathione in tumors—making them more susceptible to chemotherapy—and raise glutathione in healthy cells—making them more resistant to chemotherapy. S. Yoshida and A. Kaibara conducted similar experiments in Japan and concluded that glutamine supplementation prevents deficiencies of glutamine and glutathione and improves protein metabolism in cancer victims.

Glutamine is found in many plant and animal food sources but is easily destroyed by cooking. Raw spinach and parsley are good sources. Chicken, fish, pork and beef are high in glutamine. However, eating raw meats carries certain health risks. Braver individuals may eat sushi, carpaccio, kibbi, or steak tartar—all uncooked animal products.

Glutamine is being widely researched as a nutritional supplement for certain hospitalized patients. More research is still needed and the appropriate dosage for various scenarios is still unclear. The amount demanded by the body during periods of physical stress is still unknown. Store-bought tablets contain as little as 0.5 grams (500 mg). It also comes in powder form—often taken in daily doses of 4 or 5 grams. In extreme situations—following a bone marrow transplant, for example—doses as high as 40 grams per day have been given. Supplemental glutamine must be kept absolutely dry or it will degrade into ammonia.

Completely healthy individuals don't need supplemental glutamine. It can provoke such side effects as gastrointestinal upset. Older people and patients with impaired kidney and liver failure should be cautious. Any serious use of this supplement should be monitored by a health professional.

Lipoic acid

Also called alpha-lipoic acid or thioctic acid, lipoic acid is a disulfide compound that acts as an effective antioxidant, a neutralizer of various toxins including some heavy metals, and an important co-enzyme for recycling other antioxidants including vitamin C, vitamin E and glutathione. Lipoic acid occurs naturally in your body but has also recently appeared on the shelves of health food stores. It is being actively investigated by the scientific community for its medical merits.

Research has revealed the benefits of lipoic acid for such conditions as diabetes, HIV infection and AIDS, liver disease, lead and cadmium toxicities, cataracts, poisoning by amanita mushrooms, reperfusion injury (following stroke and heart attack) and vitamin E deficiencies. It also extends the endurance of body builders and their recovery time from injury. You may notice that its advantages entirely overlap those of glutathione. Lipoic acid is vital for converting glutathione back and forth from its oxidized (GSSG) to its reduced (GSH) form (see figure 6, chapter 1). It regenerates vitamin C, vitamin E and coenzyme Q10. It can also provide reduction redox support to other sulfur groups and NADPH energy reactions.

Although lipoic acid has been described by many researchers as an antioxidant in its own right, scientists such as H. Bast and G.R. Haenen from the Department of Pharmacochemistry in the Netherlands believe that lipoic acid actually protects against lipid peroxidation by keeping GSH in its reduced (non-oxidized) state, and that GSH is the active antioxidant in this scenario. In fact, they showed that lipoic acid in the absence of glutathione actually promotes oxidation. One reason glutathione has been called the "master antioxidant" is because its critical enzyme glutathione-reductase maintains lipoic acid in its reduced (non-oxidative) state.

The ability of lipoic acid to enhance GSH function has been demonstrated by other scientists. E. Buses in Germany established that the protection offered by lipoic acid against radiation damage results from improved cell viability due to elevated glutathione levels.

Some leading American researchers in lipoic acid, headed by L. Packer, work at the University of California in Berkeley, . They describe lipoic acid as providing intact cystine, which makes cysteine available to the cells. It is clinically significant that lipoic acid helps restore glutathione when it is deficient. Recommended dosages range from 100 to 200 mg per day.

Silymarin (milk thistle)

The milk thistle plant, known scientifically as *Silybum marianum* has been used by herbalists for centuries to treat a variety of liver disorders, including hepatitis, alcoholic cirrhosis, jaundice and gallbladder disease, and to fight a number of toxins, including amanita poison mushrooms. The active ingredient of milk thistle is silymarin, a compound made up of the flavonoids silybin, silydianin, and silychristin, and is found in the seeds.

Many clinicians have studied this herbal extract and its use in toxicology and liver disease. It seems to stimulate the growth and regeneration of injured liver cells. However, its bioflavonoids seems to act primarily as free radical scavengers and to support detoxification enzyme pathways.

Further studies describing this action have demonstrated silymarin's impressive ability to promote glutathione production. It clearly prevents lipid peroxidation and maintains GSH levels. Silybin has a protective effect on acetaminophen overdoses—traditionally treated with the drug NAC. Silymarin can increase GSH by as much as 35% in certain glutathione-deficient states and accelerates detoxification of xenobiotics accordingly.

Recommended doses vary greatly, from 50 to 500 milligrams three times a day. Toxic reactions can include gas, cramps and diarrhea. Liver diseases should never be treated without the advice of a health professional.

WHEY PROTEINS
Whey, a large group of proteins, is a constituent of milk from all mammals, including human beings. The most commonly available whey comes from cow's milk. Raw milk contains 5 to 10% protein, of which 80% is casein and 20% whey. Casein is a mainstay of cheese production. For a long time whey was treated as an insignificant byproduct of the dairy industry but its advantages as a nutritional supplement are now creating a new surge of interest.

Many milk derivatives and whey products are marketed to health-conscious people. These products are extremely variable in their protein content, their concentration, the forms of proteins present, and other factors which determine the bio-effectiveness of the product, including the level of protein denaturation. Denaturation refers to a breakdown in the protein structure that may not affect its food value but that can affect its biological action (bioactivity) in the body. Many nutritionists point out that the fat or lactose content of milk products may still be high enough to cause concern. Others have reservations about the milk industry and its liberal use of antibiotics and steroids to boost production. And we cannot ignore the very real issue of fat-soluble and water-soluble environmental toxins passing into the milk.

Fresh milk whey contains potent GSH precursors such as lactoferrin, beta-lactalbumin, and serum albumin that are easily denatured. When consumed intact they are easily digestible and their constituent breakdown products pass readily into the bloodstream, serving as cysteine and cystine delivery systems. From there they are taken to individual cells, where these precursors are transported through the cell wall and metabolized into GSH.

These precursors are fragile and easily denatured. They contain thermo-labile components that are easily disturbed by heating and a mechanical shape that is quickly broken down by physical stresses such as shaking or churning. By the time most milk products reach your table their bioactivity is entirely lost, although their food value remains. Milk products are usually pasteurized several times to guard against bacterial contamination. This almost inevitably destroys their usefulness as glutathione precursors.

In order to maintain these precursors in a bioactive form, special means must be designed and used to extract whey proteins from milk and the process must be carefully monitored. Concentrations of protein in whey products range from as little as 20% to over 90%. They vary greatly in their make-up, as well as to the extent which GSH precursors are denatured or broken down. Some are bioactive. Most are not.

BIOACTIVE WHEY PROTEINS (IMMUNOCAL)

Bioactive whey proteins contain high levels of non-denatured protein and are also called undenatured whey proteins. In scientific terms, they preserve the original bioactivity of the thermolabile components and mechanical shape of the proteins, guaranteeing the highest level of GSH-promoting activity.

Our knowledge of the GSH-sustaining effect of dietary whey proteins is the result of research begun at McGill University in Montreal in the early 1980's. Dr. Gustavo Bounous was studying protein supplementation when by chance he discovered the bioactive potential of whey protein. He investigated this protein's effect on the immune system and published some exciting results. His findings encouraged many other scientific teams to study these GSH-enhancing qualities in tests on a wide variety of diseases. Dr. Bounous and his team went on to develop Immunocal—a whey protein made under conditions that maximize the protein's bioactivity.

Immunocal has been patented for its immuno-sustaining and GSH-enhancing effects. It is extracted exclusively from milk produced without an-

Figure 14 — Whey protein variables
Concentration of total protein
Types of proteins
Degree of denaturization (breakdown)
Fat content
Lactose content
Bioavailability
Biological Activity
Contaminants, toxins

tibiotics or steroids. The process produces 90%-pure whey protein and has received a patent for its method of use. It has also been recently granted a USA patent as a chemotherapeutic agent. It is the first natural supplement to receive such recognition.

Its history is backed up by phase I, II and III clinical trials including research into infectious disease (HIV/AIDS, hepatitis, Lyme disease, bacterial infections), cancer therapy, pulmonary disease, chronic fatigue syndrome and other disorders associated with high oxidative stress and low glutathione activity. It has been sold in Europe and the Orient by pharmaceutical distributors. In North America this all-natural product is available without prescription, although certain governmental agencies and insurance companies will reimburse patients with a physician's prescription.

Undenatured whey protein is a natural extract of milk and an ideal solution—a safe, dependable, effective way to raise and sustain GSH levels.

CO-FACTORS FOR GSH PRODUCTION

SELENIUM

The trace element selenium functions principally as an antioxidant but has other functions in protein synthesis and other metabolic processes, and acts synergistically (hand-in-hand) with other antioxidants—in particular vitamin E. Its clinical applications have received a great deal of attention and we are about to see an increase in the number of clinical trials using this mineral.

Plants absorb sodium selenite—an inorganic compound in the soil—and convert it into organic seleno-methionine. When we eat these plants the seleno-methionine is either used to make protein or converted once again, this time into seleno-cysteine. The cysteine portion of this molecule contributes to GSH production. The selenium portion is an essential component of the critically important enzyme glutathione peroxidase.

Browsing through a list of selenium research and clinical trials, one is reminded of GSH research and clinical trials. Both deal with the same types of disease, clinical symptoms and outcome. Selenium has been linked with heart disease and atherosclerosis, cancer treatment and prevention, liver and pancreatic function, detoxification of heavy metals, immune support, male infertility, AIDS, Crohn's disease, pancreatitis, cystic fibrosis and multiple sclerosis—a reflection of the contents of this book on GSH.

Most scientists agree that the principal way in which selenium fights these diseases is by elevating levels of glutathione peroxidase, the only known metabolically active form of selenium in the body.

A recent study sponsored by the National Cancer Institute (USA) caused quite a stir. Having examined favorable reports about selenium being cancer-preventive, it began a study on skin cancer. Patients were given either selenium or a placebo, and monitored for eight years for any recurrence of their skin lesions. Initial results were disappointing—there was no evidence that selenium protects against skin cancer recurrences. However, they were startled to find that their test group suffered significantly lower rates of other cancers, including lung, prostate and colon cancers (see chapters 5, 14 and 15). These unexpected findings rolled over into a host of new studies, some of which are still in progress.

Selenium is found abundantly in foods grown in selenium-rich soil and from the meat and dairy products of animals who have been raised on those plants. The suggested daily intake is 40 to 70 micrograms (mcg)—an amount found in normal diets and not requiring supplementation.

Be careful—too much selenium has a well-known toxicity and some individuals suffer ill effects at doses as low as 250 mcg/day. At 1,000 mcg/day, many symptoms become apparent. Selenium is usually sold in doses ranging from 25 to 200 mcg. It may be a natural food supplement but it must be approached with caution. People in good health with a reasonable diet should take no more than 25 to 50 mcg/day.

Vitamins B1, B2

The water-soluble vitamins B1 (thiamine) and B2 (riboflavin) were two of the first vitamins discovered back in the 1920's and 30's. They each perform several important functions in our body. Vitamin B1 is essential for carbohydrate metabolism and energy production. It also helps conversion of fatty acids into steroid hormones. Vitamin B2 is just as involved in energy production and hormone regulation and helps combine individual amino acids into larger proteins, glutathione being one of them.

Vitamins B1 and B2 maintain glutathione and its related enzymes in their active forms, enabling GSH to function at its optimum capacity. They are integral constituents of coenzymes that produce glutathione reductase and NADPH—essential for recycling oxidized glutathione (GSSG) back to reduced glutathione (GSH), the active form.

The currently recommended daily intake of these two vitamins is 1 to 2 milligrams. Most clinicians believe that these values are far too low and it's just a matter of time before they are raised. Doses of 50 to 150 mg are not uncommon and many feel that the optimum level lies between 25 and 300 mg/day. It is apparently not toxic—these higher doses have revealed no adverse effects. Nutritionists at times prescribe 500 mg/day for some conditions, but for most near-normal states 10 to 50 mg/day should suffice.

GLUTATHIONE

Vitamins B6, B12, & folic acid

Like their cousins B1 and B2, vitamins B6 (pyridoxine) and B12 (cobalamin) are also water soluble. Both play an indirect but important role in glutathione metabolism. Vitamin B6 is one of the most widely used vitamins in our body and contributes to over sixty enzyme systems. It is crucial for the metabolism and function of many amino acids and essential fatty acids, so the majority of our tissues depend on it. Vitamin B12 acts as a coenzyme in the production and regulation of red blood cells, myelin and other neurological tissues. It is prone to depletion in various diseases including malabsorption, alcoholism, pernicious anemia and the complications of strict vegetarianism.

Folic acid—also known as folate or folacin—takes part in a number of various processes including DNA synthesis and neurotransmission. It works together with vitamin B12 in amino acid metabolism and protein synthesis. Its role in cardiovascular disease has been recently highlighted—it lowers elevated homocysteine levels, a serious risk for cardiovascular disease. Folate tends to shunt cysteine preferentially towards glutathione production rather than homocysteine production.

North American recommended daily dietary allowances for vitamins B6, B12 and folate are 0.5 to 2 mg, 1 to 2 mcg, and 150 to 250 mcg respectively. Some nutritionists may recommend as much as 50 to 500 mg of vitamin B6, 100 to 500 mcg of vitamin B12, and 400 to 2,000 mcg of folic acid. Vitamin B12 has negligible toxicity but vitamin B6 can be neurotoxic at higher doses. Folic acid is relatively safe unless taken alone by someone deficient in certain B-vitamins, particularly B12. Under normal circumstances we recommend a maximum 10 to 50 mg of B6, 10 to 50 mcg of B12, and 400 mcg of folic acid per day.

Vitamin C

The water-soluble vitamin C has various names, including ascorbate and ascorbic acid. It has been a focus for antioxidant research longer than any other antioxidant. Linus Pauling, the foremost researcher in vitamin C is considered by many to be the grandfather of free radical biology. He blazed the trail along which this and many other books have evolved. Thousands of articles have been written about it and research is still going strong. Yet even after all this time the topic of vitamin C in health and disease is still fraught with controversy.

The classic disease of vitamin C deficiency is scurvy. More recently, the use of vitamin C has been studied in cancer, anti-aging medicine, cardiovascular disorders, emotional or physical stress, and of course in immunology and infectious disease. It is an antioxidant but performs many other functions in our body. It is involved in bone, cartilage and soft tissue repair, support of various biologic systems including the recycling of B-vitamins, folic acid and other antioxidants, iron storage and a list of other life-sustaining functions far too long and involved for us to discuss in this book.

It is mentioned here because of its important links with glutathione metabolism. It is intimately involved in the GSH-driven glutathione-transhydrogenase enzyme system which keeps GSH, vitamin C, vitamin E and other antioxidants in their reduced (non-oxidized) state.

Numerous studies have demonstrated the ability of vitamin C to support glutathione levels and activity. C.S. Johnston, C.G. Meyer and J.C. Srilakshmi from Arizona State University conducted a double blind study comparing the GSH levels of three groups—one ate a low-vitamin C diet, another ate vitamin C at 500 mg/day, and the third received 2,000 mg/day. Those taking the vitamin had significantly higher GSH red blood cell counts than the low-vitamin C group. There was little difference in glutathione level between the two groups taking vitamin C.

The converse is equally true. Vitamin C is far less effective and rapidly depleted without adequate glutathione. When a vitamin C molecule mops up a free radical, it effectively neutralizes it. However, the vitamin C complex is now tied up. It is either ejected from the cell and eliminated by the body, or it is recycled to go back and do more work. In the latter case, glutathione is the recycling agent. GSH and GSH enzymes accept the free radical from the vitamin C complex and free it up to get back to work. This cycle drives antioxidant function in our bodies (see figure 6, chapter 1).

S. Mendiratta, J.M. May, and Z.C. Qu of Vanderbilt University in Nashville carried out a persuasive study demonstrating this phenomenon in human plasma and red blood cells. When GSH content was intentionally depleted with the chemical diamide, vitamin C was either eventually lost from the plasma or severely functionally impaired in the red blood cells, remaining in its oxidized state (dehydro-ascorbate). Glutathione enabled its transformation back into the functional form, ascorbate.

There is still much disagreement over the appropriate dosage of vitamin C. Although both the American and Canadian recommended daily allowances of vitamin are in the range of 30 to 60 mg/day, many scientists and nutritionists feel that this figure is far too low. Advocates of megadosing with vitamin C are not adverse to taking 10, 20, or 30 thousand mg/day.

It is well documented that supplies of vitamin C beyond a certain threshold are eliminated from the body, often accompanied by cramps and diarrhea. Other researchers feel that vitamin C is potentially harmful at high doses. It may serve as a pro-oxidant, and also strongly competes with other antioxidants, occasionally impairing their function. E.W. Flagg and her team at

Emory University in Atlanta showed that high levels of vitamin C intake corresponded to lowered GSH levels.

If glutathione levels are adequate, no more than 200 to 1,000 mg/day of vitamin C is necessary.

Vitamin E

The fat soluble vitamin E is America's second most popular supplement after vitamin C. Given the wealth of information and positive clinical studies done on this vitamin, its popularity will probably continue to grow. Some have estimated that if all North Americans took adequate vitamin E supplements, health-care costs could be reduced by billions of dollars.

Studies have shown benefits in cancer prevention and therapy, cardiovascular disease, diseases of aging, wound healing, neurodegenerative disease and many other states of health. Besides its clearly defined role as an antioxidant, it plays a part in detoxification of many compounds and in the immune system.

Like vitamin C, vitamin E has an important role in the GSH-driven glutathione-transhydrogenase enzyme system which keeps GSH, vitamin C, vitamin E and other antioxidants in their reduced (non-oxidized) state (see figure 6, chapter 1). Studies with GSH and vitamin E resemble those with GSH and vitamin C because these antioxidants depend on each other for proper function and recycling. The synergistic effect of vitamin E and glutathione can be attributed to vitamin E's ability to help GSH with antioxidation, and to its direct modulation of glutathione-related enzymes.

Vitamin E comes in several forms, natural and synthetic. This vitamin actually represents different substances of which alpha-, beta-, delta-, and gamma-tocopherols are the most active. The natural form of tocopherol most often found is D-alpha-tocopherol, which is more potent and bioavailable than the synthetic DL-alpha-tocopherol.

The daily recommended allowances range from 25 to 50 IU (international units), however studies hint that most of us would experience more benefit at much higher doses. Popular regimens use doses from 100 to 1200 IU/day. With adequate GSH levels, it is unlikely that one needs more than 400 IU/day. At excessive levels, vitamin E is toxic and can provoke gastrointestinal, cardiovascular and neurological side-effects.

Other micronutrients

Magnesium deficiency can lead to impairment of the enzyme gamma glutamyl transpeptidase, important in the synthesis of glutathione.

Vanadium is a trace element that depends on glutathione to remain in a reduced (non-oxidized) state and to increase its bioavailability. Under certain conditions, vanadium may recycle GSH. However, vanadium in high ns is toxic and may deplete glutathione.

ency is also detrimental to glutathione metabolism, reducing
ration, especially in red blood cells. Zinc also carries a certain
...y, and may reduce GSH at high levels.

CONCLUSION

For our bodies to sustain healthy glutathione levels, the limiting factor in
our daily intake of food is usually the amino acid cysteine. It must be in a
form that can survive the trip from our mouths to our cells. Unfortunately,
merely eating either glutathione or the free amino acid cysteine does not give
the cell what it needs to manufacture glutathione.

Several drugs and natural products can do this efficiently. NAC (N-acetylcysteine) is a powerful drug that is commonly used in critical care medicine,
toxicology, and pulmonary medicine. It has been the most researched of all
the GSH-promoting modalities, and newer clinical applications are being
developed all the time.

Many natural products exert some of their positive effects by supporting
or directly raising glutathione levels. Undenatured whey protein isolates are
an exciting development and one, brand-named Immunocal®, has been
patented to augment glutathione levels and enhance immune function. Ongoing clinical trials are underway to test it with a number of different medical
conditions.

RAISING GSH LEVELS

ALMASIO P, BORTOLINI M, PAGLIARO L, ET AL. Role of s-adenosyl methionine in the treatment of intrahepatic cholestasis. *Drugs 40: (S3): 111-123, 1990*

ANDERSON ME. GSH and GSH delivery compounds. *Advances in Pharmacology 38:65-78, 1997*

ANDERSON ME, LEVY EJ, MEISTER A. Preparation and use of glutathione monoesters. *Methods Enzymol. 234: 492-499, 1994*

ANDERSON M, POWRIE F, PURI R, MEISTER A. Glutathione monoethyl ester: Preparation, uptake by tissues, and conversion to glutathione. *Archives Biochemistry and Biophysiology 239:538-48, 1985*

ANONYMOUS, record supplied by publisher. Monograph: Alpha-lipoic acid. Altern. *Med. Rev. 3: 308-311, 1998*

BALANSKY RB, D'AGOSTINI F, ZANACCHI P, DE FLORA S. Protection by N-acetylcysteine of the histopathological and cytogenical damage produced by exposure of rats to cigarette smoke. *Cancer Lett. 64: 123-131, 1992*

BARLOW-WALDEN LR, REITER RJ, ABE M, ET AL. Melatonin stimulates brain glutathione peroxidase activity. *Neurochem. Int. 26: 497-502, 1995*

BASOGLU M, YILIRGAN I, AKCAY F, ET AL. Glutathione and nitric oxide concentrations in glutamine-infused rabbits with intestinal ischemia/reperfusion. *Eur. J. Clin. Chem. Clin. Biochem. 35: 415-419, 1997*

BAST H, HAENEN GR. Interplay between lipoic acid and glutathione in the protection against microsomal lipid peroxidation. *Biochem. Biophys. Acta. 963: 558-561, 1988*

BAST H, HAENEN GR. Regulation of lipid peroxidation by glutathione and lipoic acid : involvement of liver microsomal vitamin E free radical reductase. *Adv. Exp. Med. Biol. 264: 111-116, 1990*

BAUR A, HARRER T, PEUKERT M, ET AL. Alpha-lipoic acid is an effective inhibitor of human immuno-deficiency virus (HIV-1) replication. *Klin. Wochenschr. 69: 722-724, 1991*

BIEWENGA GP, HAENEN GR, BAST. The pharmacology of the antioxidant lipoic acid. *Gen. Pharmacol. 29: 315-331, 1997*

BIRNBAUM S, WINITZ M, GREENSTEIN J. Quantitative nutritional studies with water soluble, chemically defined diets. III - Individual amino acids as sources of "non-essential" nitrogen. *Archives Biochemistry and Biophysics 72:428-36, 1957*

BISHAYEE A, CHATTERJEE M. Selective enhancement of glutathione S-transferase activity in liver and extrahepatic tissues of rat following oral administration of vanadate. *Acta. Physiol. Pharmacol. Bulg. 19: 83-89, 1993*

BISHAYEE A, CHATTERJEE M. Time course effects of vanadium supplement on cytosolic reduced glutathione level and glutathione S-transferase. *Biol. Trace Elem. Res. 48: 275-285, 1995*

BJORKMAN L, LANGWORTH S, LIND B, ET AL. Activity of antioxidative enzymes in erythrocytes and concentration of selenium in plasma related to mercury exposure. *J. Trace Elem. Electrolytes Health Dis. 7: 157-164, 1993*

BONGERS V, DE JONG J, STEEN I, ET AL. Antioxidant-related parameters in patients treated for cancer chemoprevention with \N-acetylcysteine. *Eur. J. Cancer 31A:921-923, 1995*

BOUNOUS G, GOLD P. The biological activity of undenatured whey proteins: The role of glutathione. *Clinical Investigative Medicine 14:296-309, 1991*

BOUNOUS G, KONGSHAVN P. Influence of dietary whey proteins on the immune system of mice. *Journal of Nutrition 112:1747-55, 1982*

BOUNOUS G, LETOURNEAU L, KONGSHAVN P. Influence of dietary protein type on the immune system of mice. *Journal of Nutrition 113:1415-21, 1983*

Bounous G, Batist G, Gold P. Immuno-enhancing property of dietary whey protein in mice: Role of glutathione. *Clinical Investigative Medicine 12:154-61, 1989*

Bounous, Dr. Gustavo Bounous G, Shenouda N, Kongshavn P, Osmond D. Mechanism of altered B-cell response induced by changes in dietary protein type in mice. *Journal of Nutrition 115:1409-17, 1985*

Bray T, Taylor C. Enhancement of tissue glutathione for antioxidant and immune functions in malnutrition. *Biochemistry Pharmacology 47:2113-23, 1994*

Busse E, Zimmer G, Schopohl B, Kornhuber B. Influence of alpha-lipoic acid on intracellular glutathione in vitro and in vivo. *Arzneimittelforschung 42: 829-831, 1992*

Campos R, Garrido A, Guerra R, Valenzuela A. Silybin dihemisuccinate protects against glutathione depletion and lipid peroxidation induced by acetaminophen on rat liver. *Planta Med. 55: 417-419, 1989*

Cao Y, Feng Z, Hoos A, Klimberg VS. Glutamine enhances gut glutathione production. *J. Parenter. Enteral Nutr. 22: 224-227, 1998*

Clark LC, Combs GF Jr, Turnbull BW, et al. Effects of selenium supplementation for cancer prevention in patients with carcinoma of the skin. A randomized controlled trial. Nutritional Prevention of Cancer Study Group. *JAMA 276: 1957-1963, 1996*

Clark LC, Dalkin B, Krongrad A, et al. Decreased incidence of prostate cancer with selenium supplementation : results of a double-blind cancer prevention trial. *Br. J. Urol. 81: 730-734, 1998*

Clark LC, Hixson LJ, Combs GF Jr, et al. Plasma selenium concentration predicts the prevalence of colorectal adenomatous polyps. *Cancer Epidemiol. Biomarkers Prev. 2: 41-46, 1993*

Combs GF Jr, Clark LC, Turnbull BW. Reduction of cancer risk with an oral supplement of selenium. *Biomed. Environ. Sci. 10: 227-234, 1997*

Conaway CC, Jiao D, Kelloff GJ, et al. Chemopreventive potential of fumaric acid, N-acetylcysteine, N-(4-hydroxyphenyl) retinamide and beta-carotene for tobacco-nitrosamine-induced lung tumors in A/J mice. *Cancer Lett. 124: 85-93, 1998*

Constantinescu A, Pick U, Handelman et al. Reduction and transport of lipoic acid by human erythrocytes. *Biochem. Pharmacol. 17: 253-261, 1995*

Costagliola C, Menzione M. Effect of vitamin E on the oxidative state of glutathione in plasma. *Clin. Physiol. Biochem. 8: 140-143, 1990*

D'Agostini F, Bagnasco M, Giunciuglio D, et al. Inhibition by N-acetylcysteine of doxorubicin-induced clastogenicity and alopecia, and prevention of primary tumors and micrometastasis in mice. *Int. J. Oncol. 13: 217-224, 1998*

Davreux CJ, Soric I, Natens AB, et al. N-acetylcysteine attenuates acute lung injury in the rat. *Shock 8: 432-438, 1997*

Denno R, Rounds JD, Faris R, et al. Glutamine-enriched total parenteral nutrition enhance plasma glutathione in the resting state. *J. Surg. Res. 15: 35-38, 1996*

Dickenson A. Benefits of nutritional supplements. *Council for Responsible Nutrition. 1-68, 1998*

Droge W. Cysteine and glutathione deficiency in AIDS patients: a rationale for the treatment with *N-acetyl-cysteine*. *Pharmacology 46: 61-65, 1993*

Dworkin BM. Selenium deficiency in HIV infection and the acquired immunodeficiency syndrome (AIDS). *Chem. Biol. Interact. 91: 181-186, 1994*

Flagg EW, Coates RJ, Eley JW, et al. Dietary glutathione intake in humans and the relationship between intake and plasma total glutathione level. *Nutrition and Cancer 21: 33-46, 1994*

Floreani M, Skaper SD, Facci L, et al. Melatonin maintains glutathione homeostasis in kainic acid-exposed rat brain tissues. *FASEB J 11: 1309-1315, 1997*

GREGUS Z, STEIN AF, VARGA F, KLASSEN CD. Effect of lipoic acid on biliary excretion of glutathione and metals. *Toxicol. Appl. Pharmacol. 114: 88-96, 1992*

HAN D, HANDELMAN G, MARCOCCI L, ET AL. Lipoic acid increases de novo synthesis of cellular glutathione by improving cysteine utilization. *Biofactors 6: 321-338, 1997*

HAN D, TRITSCHLER HJ, PACKER L. Alpha-lipoic acid increases intracellular glutathione in a human T-lymphocyte Jurkat cell line. *Biochem. Biophys. Res. Commun. 207: 258-264, 1995*

HARA M, ABE M, SUZUKI T, REITER RJ. Tissue changes in glutathione metabolism and lipid peroxidation induced by swimming are partially prevented by melatonin. *Pharmacol. Toxicol. 78: 308-312, 1996*

HARWARD TR, COE D, SOUBA WW, ET AL. Glutamine preserves gut glutathione levels during intestinal ischemia/reperfusion. *J. Surg. Res. 56: 351-355, 1994*

HEALTH CANADA. Nutrition recommendations: *The report of the Scientific Review Committee. Health Canada, 1990*

HIRAI R, NAKAI S, KIKUISHI H, KAWAI K. Evaluation of the immunological enhancement activities of Immunocal. *Otsuka Pharm Co. Dec. 13, 1990*

HOLDINESS MR. Clinical pharmacokinetics of N-acetylcysteine. *Clin. Pharmacokinet. 20: 123-134, 1991*

HONG RW, ROUNDS JD, HELTON WS, ET AL. Glutamine preserves liver glutathione after lethal hepatic injury. *Ann. Surg. 215: 114-119, 1992*

INSTITUTE OF MEDICINE, FOOD AND NUTRITION BOARD. Public policy news – Translating the science behind the dietary reference intakes. *J. American Diet. Assoc. 98: 756, 1998*

IP C. Comparative effects of antioxidants on enzymes involved in glutathione metabolism. *Life Sci. 34: 2501-2506, 1984*

JACOB C, MARET W, VALLEE BL. Selenium redox biochemistry of zinc-sulfur coordination sites in proteins and enzymes. *Proc. Natl. Acad. Sci. USA. 96: 1910-1914, 1999*

JAIN A, MADSEN DC, AULD P, ET AL. L-2-Oxothiazolidine-4-carboxylate, a cysteine precursor, stimulates growth and normalizes tissue glutathione concentrations in rats fed a sulfur amino acid-deficient diet. *J. Nutr. 125: 851-856, 1995*

JIANG LJ, MARET W, VALLEE BL. The glutathione redox couple modulates zinc transfer from metallothionein to zinc-depleted sorbitol dehydrogenase. *Proc. Natl. Acad. Sci. USA. 95: 3483-3488, 1998*

JOHNSTON CS, MEYER CG, SRILAKSHMI JC. Vitamin C elevates red blood cell glutathione in healthy adults. *American J. Clin. Nutr. 58: 103-105, 1993*

KALAYJIAN RC, SKOWRON G, EMGUSHOV RT, ET AL. A phase I/II trial of intravenous L-2-oxothiazolidine-4-carboxylic acid (procysteine) in asymptomatic HIV-infected subjects. *J. Acq. Immune Def. Syndr. 7: 369-374, 1994*

KALEBIC T, KINTER A, POLI G, ET AL. Suppression of human immunodeficiency virus expression in chronically infected monocyte cells by glutathione, glutathione ester, and N-acetylcysteine. *Proc. Natl. Acad. Sci. USA. 88: 986-990, 1991*

KAPLOWITZ N, AW T, OOKHTENS M. The regulation of hepatic glutathione. *Ann Revue Pharmacology and Toxicology 25:715-44, 1985*

KELLY GS. Clinical applications of N-acetylcysteine. *Altern. Med. Rev. 3: 114-127, 1998*

KLATZ R. Grow young with HGH [ISBN 0-06-098434-1]. *Harper Perennial. 1997*

KLIMBERG VS, McCLELLAN JL. Claude H. Organ Jr. Honorary Lectureship. Glutamine, cancer, and its therapy. *American J. Surg. 172: 418-424, 1996*

KOCH S, LEIS A, STOKIC D, KHAWLI F ET AL. Side effects of IV N-acetylcysteine. *American Journal Respirology and Critical Care Medicine 149:A321, 1994*

KOTLER M, RODRIGUEZ C, SAINZ RM, ET AL. Melatonin increases gene expression for antioxidant enzymes in rat brain cortex. *J. Pineal Research 24: 83-89, 1998*

LEDERMAN MM, GEORGER D, DANDO S, ET AL. L-2-Oxothiazolidine-4-carboxylic acid (procysteine) inhibits expression of the human immunodeficiency virus and expression of the interleukin-2 receptor alpha chain. *J. Acq. Immune Def. Syndr.* 8: 107-115, 1995

LEVY EJ, ANDERSON ME, MEISTER A. Transport of glutathione diethyl ester into human cells. *Proc. Natl. Acad. Sci. U.S.A.* 90: 9171-9175, 1993

LEVY EJ, ANDERSON ME, MEISTER A. Preparation and properties of glutathione diethyl ester and related derivatives. *Methods Enzymol.* 234: 499-505, 1994

LIEBERMAN S, BRUNING N. The Real Vitamin and Mineral Book. Second Ed., *Avery Pub., NY,* 1997

LOCKITCH G. Selenium: clinical significance and analytical concepts. *Crit. Rev. Clin. Lab. Sci.* 27: 483-541, 1989

LOMAESTRO B, MALONE M. Glutathione in health and disease: Pharmacotherapeutic Issues. *Annals of Pharmacotherapy* 29:1263-73, 1995

LOOK MP, ROCKSTROH JK, RAO GS, ET AL. Serum selenium, plasma glutathione (GSH) and erythrocyte glutathione peroxidase (GSH-Px)-levels in asymptomatic versus symptomatic human immunodeficiency virus-1 (HIV-1)-infection. *Eur. J. Clin. Nutr.* 51: 266-272, 1997

MANT T, TEMPOWSKI J, VOLANS G, TALBOT J. Adverse reactions to acetylcysteine and effects of overdose. *British Medical Journal 2* 89:217-19, 1984

MAY JM, MENDIRATTA S, HILL KE, BURK RF. Reduction of dehydroascorbate to ascorbate by the selenoenzyme thioreoxin reductase. *J. Biol. Chem.* 272: 22607-22610, 1997

MEISTER A, ANDERSON ME. Glutathione. *Ann Revue Biochemistry* 52:711-60, 1983

MEISTER A. New aspects of glutathione biochemistry and transport, selective alteration of glutathione metabolism. Nutrition Revue 42:397-410, 1984

MENDIRATTA S, QU ZC, MAY JM. Erythrocyte ascorbate recycling: antioxidant effects in blood. *Free Radic. Biol. Med.* 24: 789-797, 1998

MIGUEZ MP, ANUNDI I, SAINZ-PARDO LA, LINDROS KO. Hepatoprotective mechanism of silymarin: no evidence for involvement of cytochrome P450 2E1. *Chem. Biol. Interact.* 91: 51-63, 1994

MISSO NL, POWERS KA, GILLON RL, ET AL. Reduced platelet glutathione peroxidase activity and serum selenium concentration in atopic asthmatic patients. *Clin. Exp. Allergy* 26: 838-847, 1996

MUZES G, DEAK G, LANG I, ET AL. Effect of silymarin (Legalon) therapy on the antioxidant defense mechanism and lipid peroxidation in alcoholic liver disease. *Orv. Hetil.* 131: 863-866, 1990

NATH KA, SALAHUDEEN AK. Autoxidation of cysteine generates hydrogen peroxide: cytotoxicity and attenuation by pyruvate. *American J. Physiol.* 262 (2 Pt 2): F306-F314, 1993

NISHIUCH Y, SASAKI M, NAKAYASU, ET AL. Cytotoxicity of cysteine in culture media. *In Vitro* 12: 635, 1976

OLNEY JW, HO OL, RHEE V. Cytotoxic effect of acid and sulphur containing amino acids on the infant mouse central nervous system. *Brain Res.* 14: 61-76, 1971

O'RIORDAIN MG, DE BEAUX A, FEARON KC. Effect of glutamine on immune function in the surgical patient. *Nutrition* 12(11-12 Suppl):S82-S84, 1996

PABLOS MI, AGAPITO MP, GUTIERREZ R, ET AL. Melatonin stimulates the activity of the detoxifying enzyme glutathione peroxidase in several tissues of chicks. J. *Pineal Research* 19: 111-115, 1995

PABLOS MI, CHUANG J, REITER RJ, ET AL. Time course of the melatonin-induced increase in glutathione peroxidase activity in chick tissues. *Biol. Signals* 4: 325-330, 1995

PACKER L, TRITSCHLER HJ, WESSEL K. Neuroprotection by the metabolic antioxidant alpha-lipoic acid. *Free Radic. Biol. Med.* 22: 359-378, 1997

Packer L, Witt EH, Tritschler HJ. Alpha-lipoic acid as a biologic antioxidant. *Free Radic. Biol. Med. 19: 227-250, 1995*

Porta P, Aebi S, Summer K, et al. L-2-Oxothiazolidine-4-carboxylic acid, a cysteine prodrug: Pharmacokinetics and effects on thiols in plasma and lymphocytes in human. *J. Pharmacol. Exp. Ther. 257: 331-334, 1991*

Puri R, Meister A. Transport of glutathione, as gamma-glutamylcysteinylglycyl ester, into liver and kidney. *Proceedings of the National Academy of Science USA 80:5258-60. 1983*

Redman C, Scott JA, Baines AT, et al. Inhibitory effect of selenomethionine on growth of three selected human tumor cell lines. *Cancer Lett. 125: 103-110, 1998*

Reiter RJ, Tang L, Garcia JJ, Munoz-Hoyos A. Pharmacological actions of melatonin in oxygen radical pathophysiology. *Life Sci. 60: 2255-2271, 1997*

Reiter RJ, Tang L, Cabrera J, et al. The oxidant/antioxidant network: role of melatonin. *Biol. Signals Recept. 8: 56-63, 1999*

Roederer M, Staal FJ, Ela SW, Herzenberg LA, Herzenberg LA. N-acetylcysteine: potential for AIDS therapy. *Pharmacology 46: 121-129, 1993*

Rouse K, Nwokedi E, Woodliff JE, Epstein J, Klimberg JS. Glutamine enhances selectivity of chemotherapy through changes in glutathione metabolism. *Ann. Surg. 221: 420-426, 1995*

Saez G, Thornally PJ, Hill HAO, et. al. The production of free radicals during the oxidation of cysteine and their effects on isolated rat hepatocytes. *Biochem Biophys Acta 719:24-31, 1982*

Selhub J, Jacques PF, Bostom HG, D'Agostino RB, Wilson PWF, Belanger AJ, O'Leary DH, Wolf PA, Schaefer EJ, Rosenberg IH. Association between plasma homocysteine concentrations and extracranial carotid-artery stenosis. *The New England Journal of Medicine 332:286-291, 1995*

Shear NH, Malkiewicz IM, Klein D, et al. Acetaminophen-induced toxicity to human epidermoid cell line A431 and hepatoblastoma cell line Hep G2, in vitro, is diminished by silymarin. *Skin Pharmacol. 8: 279-291, 1995*

Shug AL, Madsen DC. Protection of the ischemic rat heart by procysteine and amino acids. *J. Nutr. Biochem. 5: 356-359, 1994*

Souba WW. Glutamine and cancer. *Ann. Surg. 218: 715-728, 1993*

Stadtman TC. Specific occurrence of selenium in enzymes and amino acid tRNAs. *FASEB J. 1: 375-379, 1987*

Stone J, Hinks LJ, Beasly R, et al. Reduced selenium status of patients with asthma. *Clin. Sci. 77: 495-500, 1989*

Vale JA, Buckley BM. Asthma associated with N-acetyl cysteine infusion and paracetamol poisoning. *British Medical Journal 287:1223, 1983*

Vale JA, Wheeler DC. Anaphylactoid reactions to N-acetyl cysteine. *Lancet 2(8305):988, 1982*

Valenzuela A, Aspillaga M, Vial S, Guerra R. Selectivity of silymarin on the increase of the glutathione content in different tissues of the rat. *Planta Med. 55: 420-422, 1989*

Valenzuela A, Garrido A. Biochemical bases of the pharmacological action of the flavonoid silymarin and of its structural isomer silibinin. *Biol. Res. 27: 105-112, 1994*

Van Zandwijk N. N-acetylcysteine for lung cancer prevention. *Chest 107: 1437-1441, 1995*

Walton NG, Mann TAN, Shwa KM. Anaphylactoid reactions to N-acetyl cysteine. *Lancet 2(8155):1298, 1979*

Witschi A, Reddy S, Stofer B, Lauterberg B. The systemic availability of oral glutathione. *European Journal of Clinical Pharmacology 43:667-9, 1992*

Yoshida S, Kaibara A, Yamasaki K, et al. Effect of glutamine supplementation on protein metabolism and glutathione in tumor-bearing rats. J. Parenter. *Enteral Nutrition 19: 492-497, 1995*

PART TWO
GSH IN HEALTH AND HEALING
[CHAPTERS 5 TO 23]

The fifteen chapters of part two describe
glutathione's activity in a wide variety of diseases
and show how it plays specific roles
in pathologies related to oxidative stress, toxicology
and immune dysfunction.

CHAPTER 5
CANCER

Few words strike as much fear and loathing in a doctor's office as 'cancer.' More than one hundred types are known, of varying levels of aggression. Many are treatable or even curable. Still, cancer is the second greatest cause of death in North America, after cardiovascular disease. One third of Americans will eventually die of some form of cancer. It must be emphasized that many cancers can be prevented through the threefold regimen of diet, avoidance of carcinogens and reinforced bodily defenses.

The most common cancers are of the prostate (for men) and breast (for women), followed by lung and colorectal cancers. Next is bladder cancer for men, uterine cancer for women, lymphoma for men and ovarian cancer for women. See figure 15.

CARCINOGENESIS

Healthy cells have a built-in mechanism that only allows cellular replication for three purposes: normal growth, healing of injured tissue and replacement of cells lost in normal metabolism. But cells can lose their ability to regulate growth, replicating uncontrollably and eventually forming a clump of cancerous tissue. This tumor can grow sufficiently to crowd out normal tissue, sometimes releasing diseased cells that spread the cancer into other parts of the body by the process of metastasis. Symptoms develop when the growth begins to interfere with bodily functions or deplete energy resources.

It is not clear precisely how and why these cells lose their self-regulation, although many possible causes have been singled out. Certain environmental carcinogens will predictably initiate cancerous growth, including a variety of chemicals and high radiation levels. Other factors are less predictable.

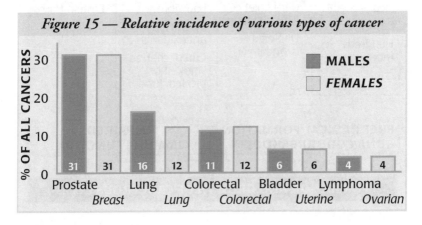

Figure 15 — Relative incidence of various types of cancer

Differences in our genetic makeup or immune systems apparently protect some people better than others. We also know that susceptibility to certain cancers is sometimes inherited from the family or racial gene pool, but the triggering factors are still unknown.

Apart from genetic factors, we can identify the following causal factors: the pollution of cigarette smoke, fossil fuel exhaust, heavy metals, pesticides and others; the ionizing radiation of X-rays, nuclear waste, ultraviolet (UV) radiation from the sun intensified by a depleted ozone layer; poor diet is an important factor; finally, certain viruses can contribute to the development of cancer: AIDS, hepatitis C, Epstein-Barr disease and papilloma (see figure 16).

The American Cancer Society makes the following suggestions to minimize the risk of cancer: maintain appropriate body weight, eat a varied diet including daily fruits and vegetables, eat more high-fiber foods (whole grains, cereals, legumes, etc.), cut down on total fat intake and limit consumption of alcoholic beverages and salt-cured, smoked and nitrate-preserved foods (see also figure 16).

Cancer starts with a mutation in the genetic code of the cell—a reprogramming of developmental patterns that results in uncontrolled growth. A combination of genetic and environmental factors including diet may contribute to

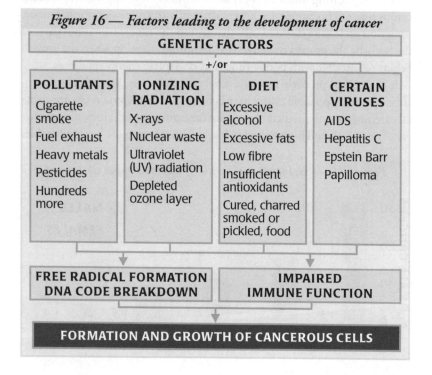

Figure 16 — Factors leading to the development of cancer

GENETIC FACTORS

+/or

POLLUTANTS	IONIZING RADIATION	DIET	CERTAIN VIRUSES
Cigarette smoke	X-rays	Excessive alcohol	AIDS
Fuel exhaust	Nuclear waste	Excessive fats	Hepatitis C
Heavy metals	Ultraviolet (UV) radiation	Low fibre	Epstein Barr
Pesticides	Depleted ozone layer	Insufficient antioxidants	Papilloma
Hundreds more		Cured, charred smoked or pickled, food	

FREE RADICAL FORMATION DNA CODE BREAKDOWN — **IMPAIRED IMMUNE FUNCTION**

FORMATION AND GROWTH OF CANCEROUS CELLS

this aberrant replication. One theory suggests that when free radicals form in the cell nucleus, its DNA code may be damaged. Another theory suggests that factors such as poor diet and cigarette smoke compromise the immune system and weaken bodily defenses which might otherwise destroy a newly cancerous cell at the outset, when it is still vulnerable. Regardless of theory, we owe it to ourselves to pay attention to all possible factors, and take advantage of any way to minimize the danger of cancer. One of these is by maintaining GSH levels.

GSH AND CANCER

Hundreds of medical articles have been written describing the role of GSH in cancer prevention and cancer treatment. They fall into three main groups: 1) prevention, including detoxification of carcinogens, antioxidation and heightened immune response; 2) therapeutic possibilities, such as anti-tumor methodologies and the treatment and prevention of malnutrition and wasting, and 3) a special role for GSH in chemotherapy and radiotherapy whereby it enhances the effectiveness of these arduous treatments while minimizing their side-effects. See figure 17.

CANCER PREVENTION

A 1996 article in the European Journal of Cancer actually suggested that free radicals be listed as an important class of carcinogens. Because of its great capacity as the cell's major antioxidant (see chapter 1) GSH can soak up oxyradicals and other free radicals as they form in the cell. This prevents subsequent damage to various parts of the cell, particularly to the DNA in its nucleus. GSH has the additional benefit of enhancing the effect of other antioxidants such as vitamin C, vitamin E and selenium. This further strengthens the body's ability to destroy free radicals. To top it off, GSH also plays an important role in the synthesis and repair of DNA.

There is no doubt that a well-functioning glutathione enzyme system wards off cancer. This is clearly illustrated by a study published in the Journal of the National Cancer Institute. It focused on people deficient in the

Figure 17 — Potential roles of GSH in cancer

CANCER PREVENTION	THERAPEUTIC POSSIBILITIES	INTERACTION/ TREATMENT OF SIDE-EFFECTS
❏ Detoxification of carcinogens ❏ Antioxidation ❏ Heightened immune response	❏ Anti-tumor characteristics ❏ Treatment/ prevention of malnutrition, wasting	❏ Chemotherapy ❏ Radiotherapy

Figure 18 — American Cancer Society guidelines, diet & nutrition

- ❏ Maintain appropriate body weight
- ❏ Eat a varied diet
- ❏ Include a variety of fruits and vegetables in your daily diet
- ❏ Eat more high fiber foods (whole grains, cereals, legumes, etc.)
- ❏ Cut down on total fat intake
- ❏ Limit consumption of alcoholic beverages
- ❏ Limit salt-cured, smoked and nitrate-preserved foods

enzyme glutathione-S tranferase-mu-1 (GSTM1). GSTM1 is an important antioxidant that also detoxifies common bladder cancer carcinogens such as tobacco smoke. Approximately one person in two inherits two defective copies of the GSTM1 gene, impairing the function of this enzyme. It was found that 25% of all bladder cancers occurred in people missing this enzyme. Heavy smokers missing this gene were six times more likely to develop bladder cancer.

There is a link between the loss of glutathione activity and the development of prostate cancer. Another glutathione enzyme, glutathione-S-transferase-pi-1 (GSTP1) almost always disappears in both cancerous and precancerous prostate lesions. It seems that prostate cancer begins with the inactivation of this glutathione enzyme. Many studies have made the connection between GSTP1 loss and malignant transformation of prostatic tissues. Similar studies have linked GSH-defective genes to breast and lung cancer as well, especially in smokers. Several scientists have suggested that people should be screened for these genetic or enzymatic defects as a way to determine their risk level.

GSH also plays a specific role in the detoxification of numerous well-known carcinogens and mutagens in our environment. Some of the most important ones are:

- ❏ Aflatoxin B1
- ❏ N-acetyl-2-aminofluorine
- ❏ Benzanthracene
- ❏ Benzapyrene
- ❏ Benzidine
- ❏ Dimethylhydrazine
- ❏ Dimethylnitrosamine
- ❏ Ethyl methane sulfonate
- ❏ N-methyl-4-aminoazobenzine
- ❏ 7-methyl-benzanthracene
- ❏ 3-methyl-cholanthracene
- ❏ 1-nitropyrene

These cancer-causing substances are conjugated or neutralized by GSH and rendered into a form the body can eliminate. The role of GSH in detoxification simply can't be overstated. Since the liver is the body's principal detoxifying organ it is not surprising that it carries the highest concentrations of GSH in the body.

The Chemoprevention Branch of the National Cancer Institute (USA) has for the last decade been developing drugs to diminish the incidence of this dreaded disease. Substances that raise GSH levels, such as NAC and the selenium derivative selenomethionine (see chapter 4), are on their short list of useful therapies. One of the major successes of their research efforts is their statistical demonstration that selenium protects against prostate cancer (see chapter 23). Other studies have identified selenium as protecting against colon, rectal and lung cancers as well as colonic polyps. R.B. Balansky, C.C. Conaway, H. Witschi, and other American and European researchers have successfully shown that NAC can slow the growth of cancers induced by toxins including urethane, nitrosamines, doxorubicin, ethylnitrosourea and other cancer-causing agents.

NAC apparently protects against the carcinogenic properties of cigarette smoke. N. Van Zandwijk from the Cancer Institute of the Netherlands writes, "NAC has emerged as a most promising cancer chemopreventive agent." S. De Flora summarized a very large chemoprevention trial sponsored by Project Euroscan and described the many positive effects of NAC as a cancer prevention agent. It reviewed potential uses against lung, breast, bowel, and skin cancers, and the actual mechanisms by which NAC and GSH exert these protective effects.

One of glutathione's effects upon the immune system is to control and balance the growth of T-cell lymphocytes (a type of white blood cell), thereby strengthening the immune response. Immuno-depressed individuals are often more prone to cancer, a good example being Karposi's sarcoma, a cancer found mostly in AIDS patients. Cancer specialists have recently developed a strategy called immunotherapy—an attempt to optimize the body's natural defenses against the cancer. Immunotherapy consists of tools to stimulate the immune system. A Japanese team from Kyoto University showed that adding NAC to cytokines—a class of immunotherapeutic agents—stimulated immune cells and their biochemical products. They suggest that this may be an effective complement for the treatment of primary liver cancer.

Other anti-cancer substances produced naturally by the immune system are TNF (tumor necrosis factor) and IL-2 (inter-leukin 2). Glaxo Wellcome Research and Development scientists showed that NAC acts against tumors by elevating TNF. In the laboratory NAC halted tumor growth in more than one third of mice injected with cancer cells. C.Y. Yim and J.B. Hibbs at the University of Utah had similar success in suppressing tumor growth by using NAC to stimulate IL-2 (a promoter of white blood cell activity) in lymphokine killer cells, a type of T-cell lymphocyte.

Therapeutic possibilities

Surgical removal of cancer is only feasible if the tumor is not widespread and is accessible. Radiation and/or chemical therapy can help, but both inflict great damage on normal as well as cancerous cells. A cornerstone of recent research has been the search for ways to limit the damage to normal cells by such anti-cancer treatments.

Chemotherapy is a controlled poisoning of the patient based on the idea that rapidly growing cancer cells are more sensitive to the poison than are normal cells. Many but not all chemotherapeutic agents produce particularly unpleasant side effects. Radiation therapy works in a similar way. The cancerous area is targeted and bombarded with radiation. The tumor is theoretically more sensitive to the radiation than the surrounding healthy tissue, but this treatment can also produce severe side-effects.

Recent experiments show that the GSH content of both normal and cancerous cells makes them more or less susceptible to damage. High GSH levels clearly help protect cells from chemotherapy, low levels make them vulnerable. It would be ideal if GSH levels were high in normal cells and low in tumorous cells, but many human cancer cells have particularly high GSH levels. Cancer is the only known condition under which the otherwise tightly regulated GSH levels are exceeded. It is characteristic of cancer cells to bypass normal regulatory controls.

Tumor cells high in GSH often show resistance to chemotherapy, so there has been some effort to reduce GSH levels in cancerous cells with GSH-depleting drugs like BSO. The trouble is, BSO reduces GSH levels in healthy cells too, magnifying the already intolerable side-effects of chemotherapy. So this approach is impractical.

Nevertheless, there may be a way to diminish GSH in cancer cells alone. Paradoxically, the precursors that raise glutathione levels in normal cells trigger the opposite reaction in cancerous cells. When GSH production is overstimulated in cancer cells, they shut down glutathione production in a process called negative feedback inhibition, making them more susceptible to destruction. Meanwhile, normal tissue uses the precursors to make glutathione, leaving it with better defenses.

This paradox was described as early as 1986 by A. Russo's team in the journal Cancer Research. When the GSH-promoting drug OTZ was added to human lung cancer cells, their glutathione level did not increase even though GSH levels in surrounding normal cells did. McGill University researchers Sylvain Baruchel, Gerry Batist and their team in Montreal showed that OTZ could deplete GSH in breast cancer cells while enhancing it in normal cells. This team later worked with Dr. Gustavo Bounous and published similar results in the journal Cancer Research, using the whey protein isolate Immunocal to provide dietary GSH precursors.

Studies with the same product were also carried out on patients with metastatic carcinoma—cancer that is spreading through the body. They were fed Immunocal for six months. Although it did not cure the cancer, a significant proportion showed either tumor regression or stabilization. Most also experienced the advantage of normalized hemoglobin and white blood cell counts. The same researchers showed that elevated GSH levels may enhance the anti-cancer action of certain chemotherapeutic agents.

Another Canadian team—this one from the University of Saskatchewan —conducted trials on patients with advanced progressive cancer. They were given toxic doses of acetaminophen as chemotherapy, plus NAC to raise glutathione levels. They hoped that NAC would raise GSH in normal cells only, and their results bear them out. More than half the patients showed either improvement or stabilization.

Nevertheless, cancer specialists are still concerned that elevating GSH non-selectively might in certain cases diminish the advantages of chemotherapy. Any GSH therapy should be an integral part of the whole cancer treatment. Cancer patients should never initiate it on their own and must first talk to their treating physician.

Additional studies have investigated the effects of nutritional proteins on cancer-causing chemicals in animals. Researchers doing similar experiments in Canada and Australia subjected rodents to the powerful carcinogen dim-ethylhydrazine—which causes colonic cancer similar to humans—and fed them a variety of proteins. Animals fed on undenatured whey protein concentrate showed fewer tumors and a reduced tumor load. The scientists found that this protein offered "considerable protection to the host," more so than any other protein.

It is accepted as a fact of life that the incidence and mortality rates of cancer increase with age. Certain cancers may in fact be considered diseases of aging, especially cancer of the prostate gland (see chapter 23). Specific changes of aging render patients more susceptible to cancer. They also have less protection against oxidative damage, and diminished immune response (see chapter 6). The protective effect of GSH diminishes with age. We generally lose from 20 to 40% of GSH after age 65.

A recent study convincingly showed that normal levels of androgens (male sex hormones) in older men lead to decreased GSH levels in the prostate gland. Anti-androgen therapy—also known as chemical castration—is a common treatment for prostate cancer. Androgens are known to act as oxidative stressors and can upset the prooxidant-antioxidant balance. Lowered GSH levels lead to loss of antioxidant function and may trigger the mechanism of prostatic carcinogenesis.

The prostate specific antigen (PSA) blood test is used to screen for prostate cancer and to track the progress of men suffering from this cancer. Higher PSA levels usually indicate progression of the disease, while falling levels show the success of treatment. Studies following PSA levels in patients taking GSH-promoting substances are in progress. GSH therapy has minimal toxic potential and one hopes it will become a standard treatment.

PREVENTION/TREATMENT OF SIDE-EFFECTS

Chemotherapy and radiotherapy lead to huge increases in free radical formation and a build-up of toxic metabolites. If the problem is not addressed, the side effects grow worse. Numerous studies have shown that when patients eat well—especially when their diets include vitamins and supplements—their tolerance of these unpleasant therapies improves. Patients with higher intracellular GSH levels experience far fewer chemotherapeutic side effects and cells with higher levels of GSH carry more protection against radiation damage, thereby lessening the side effects of radiotherapy.

Radiotherapists studying the protective role of GSH have correlated higher pretreatment glutathione levels with fewer subsequent radiation burns. Pretreatment or simultaneous treatment with products that raise and maintain GSH levels gives patients greater tolerance to therapy. Chapter 2 contains more details on GSH and radiation toxicity.

Women with cancer were treated at the University of California (San Diego) with the standard chemotherapy cisplatin and supplemented with intravenous glutathione. This enabled them to take higher doses of chemotherapy while experiencing fewer side-effects. A similar but much larger study was carried out at the Western General Hospital in Edinburgh, Scotland. Over one hundred and fifty patients being treated for ovarian cancer with cisplatin and glutathione were monitored for side effects, quality of life, and outcome. They were compared to another group receiving no glutathione. The first group showed statistically less depression, vomiting, hair loss, shortness of breath and neurotoxicity. Their mental concentration and kidney function improved measurably and there was a distinct trend toward better outcome.

The hair loss that often results from chemotherapy may not be life-threatening but it can be extremely distressing to patients, especially at a time when they don't need additional stress. Hair loss may also suggest damage inflicted on other cells that regenerate quickly, like those lining the intestine. Researcher J.J. Jimenez at the University of Miami and others have demonstrated that NAC can protect from the baldness caused by common chemotherapy agents like cyclophosphamide.

Evidence suggests that glutathione-enhancing strategies may make certain chemotherapy agents more efficient. These include Adriamycin, cyclophosphamide, cisplatin and others. However, patients absolutely must talk to their treating physician before beginning any GSH-enhancing therapy. There are theoretical instances when non-specific glutathione elevation may interfere with the anti-cancer treatment, although this is less of a risk after the course of chemotherapy or radiotherapy is complete.

MALNUTRITION/WASTING

Anti-cancer treatment is often accompanied by loss of weight, appetite, energy and strength. Good nutrition is critical and should include appropriate dietary supplements. The cancer itself, the anti-cancer treatment and the resulting state of nutritional compromise all decrease intracellular GSH levels. This greatly weakens antioxidant and immune defenses rendering patients more susceptible to other diseases and opportunistic infections. Well-known German immunologist and researcher Wulf Droge has studied weight and muscle loss in cancer, AIDS, sepsis and other diseases. He has noted the similarities among them and points to a common cause—GSH depletion. He and others have gone on to test the possibility that glutathione enhancing therapy may slow or halt this process of degeneration.

Increased GSH synthesis depends on the intake of cysteine-containing foods. Rich sources of this GSH-precursor are very hard to come by and often are not well tolerated by the patient. Cysteine is available as a free amino acid and may be taken, but it has toxic qualities and is not recommended. The drugs NAC and OTC (see chapter 4) can raise GSH levels but their effects are short-lived. These pharmaceutical drugs also have little nutritional value. Whey proteins have excellent nutritional value but usually lack GSH-precursors. The ideal source of dietary cysteine should be natural, nutritional, bioactive and undenatured. The patented whey protein Immunocal fits these criteria. It is biologically active, sustains elevated GSH levels and has great nutritional value (see chapter 4).

CASE HISTORIES

Quebecer Ivy-Marie is a very active thirty-seven year-old breast cancer survivor. After undergoing her initial surgery, the pathologist's report suggested she undergo a dozen sessions of chemotherapy and radiotherapy. She experienced many side-effects, including profound weakness and fatigue—a new experience for her. After ten sessions of therapy and many visits to her doctor to treat side-effects, she was put on 30 gm/day of the whey protein concentrate Immunocal. Her strength and sense of well-being improved within a week and she tolerated her last two sessions of chemotherapy with few side-effects. She is back to her usual routine, and remains disease-free.

Complaining of abdominal pain, Louisa from Alberta was 54 when she found out she had ovarian cancer. While awaiting surgery, she fell ill with a persistent cough and malaise which turned out to be a metastasis (spreading cancer) which had traveled to her lung. She ultimately needed pelvic surgery to relieve her discomfort, but decided not to undergo treatment for her lung metastasis. She started taking Immunocal and multivitamins daily and noticed a great improvement after several weeks. Four months later, repeat chest x-rays showed no increase in tumor size. Nine months later the radiographs revealed a decrease in tumor size. Louise continues to enjoy tending to her family and household.

CONCLUSION

There are many types of cancer, and perhaps hundreds of potential causes, but most cases are accompanied by poor antioxidant defenses. To make matters worse, most anti-cancer therapies place an enormous burden on the body and may deplete whatever natural defenses remain. Cancer sufferers must place themselves in best possible medical hands, but must also take special care of their nutrition. Patients are heavily dosed with pharmaceutical drugs and suffer from poor appetite and low energy, especially while undergoing chemical or radiation therapy. A natural source of energy that can also reinforce antioxidant defenses may make all the difference for people undergoing this distressing disease and its noxious treatment. Undenatured, bioactive whey proteins are an ideal way to increase GSH levels and simultaneously address protein requirements. Elevated glutathione replenishes antioxidant defenses, contributes to synthesis and repair of DNA and helps detoxify numerous carcinogens and mutagens.

CANCER

AMES BN. Understanding the causes of aging and cancer. *Microbiologia 11: 305-308, 1995*

BALANSKY RB, D'AGOSTINI F, ZANACCHI P, ET AL. Protection by N-acetylcysteine of the histopathological and cytogenetic damage produced by exposure of rats to cigarette smoke. *Cancer Lett. 64: 123-131, 1992*

BALANSKY RM, DE FLORA S. Chemoprevention by N-acetylcysteine of urethane-induced clastogenicity and lung tumors in mice. *Int. J. Cancer 77: 302-305, 1998*

BARUCHEL S, VIAU G. In vitro selective modulation of cellular GSH by a humanized native milk protein isolate in normal cells and rat mammary carcinoma model. *Anticancer Res. 16: 1095-1100, 1996*

BARUCHEL S, VIAU G, OLIVIER R, BOUNOUS G, WAINBERG M. Nutriceutical modulation of GSH with a humanized native milk serum protein isolate, Immunocal: application in AIDS and cancer. In: *Oxidative Stress in Cancer, AIDS, and Neurodegenerative Diseases.* EDITORS L. MONTAGNIER, R. OLIVIER, C. PASQUIER. Institute Pasteur. Pub. Marcel Dekker Inc. 1996

BARTA O, BARTA VD, CRISMAN MV, AKERS RM. Inhibition of blastogenesis by whey. *American J. Vet. Res. 52: 247-253, 1991*

BELL DA, TAYLOR JA, PAULSON DF, ET AL. Genetic risk and carcinogen exposure: a common inherited defect of the carcinogen-metabolism gene glutathione S-transferase M1 (GSTM1) that increases susceptibility to bladder cancer. *J. Natl. Cancer Inst. 85: 1159-1164, 1993*

BEUTLER E, GELBART T. Plasma glutathione in health and in patients with malignant disease. *Journal of Laboratory and Clinical Medicine 105: 581-584, 1985*

BHATTATHIRI VN, SREELEKHA TT, SEBASTIAN P, ET AL. Influence of plasma GSH level on acute radiation mucositis of the oral cavity. *Int. J. Radiat. Oncol. Biol. Phys. 29: 383-386, 1994*

BONGERS V, DE JONG J, STEEN I, ET AL. Antioxidant-related parameters in patients treated for cancer chemoprevention with N-acetylcysteine. *Eur. J. Cancer 31: 921-923, 1995*

BOONE CW, KELLOFF GJ. Biomarker endpoints in cancer chemoprevention trials. *IARC Sci. Publ. 142: 273-280, 1997*

BOUNOUS G, BATIST G, GOLD P. Whey proteins in cancer prevention. *Cancer Letters 57:91-94, 1991*

BOUNOUS G, PAPENBURG R, KONGSHAVN P, GOLD P, FLEISZER D. Dietary Whey protein inhibits the development of dimethylhydrazine induced malignancy. *Clinical and Investigative Medicine 11:213-217, 1988*

BOURTOURAULT M, BULEON R, SAMPEREZ S, ET AL. Effect of proteins from bovine milk serum on the multiplication of human cancerous cells. *C. R. Seances Soc. Biol. Fil. 185: 319-323, 1991*

BRAY TM, TAYLOR CG. Enhancement of tissue GSH for antioxidant and immune functions in malnutrition. *Biochemical Pharmacology 47:2113-2123, 1994*

BURT RW. Cohorts with familial disposition for colon cancers in chemoprevention trials. *Journal of Cellular Biochemistry – Supplement 25: 131-135, 1996*

CLARK LC, COMBS GF JR, TURNBULL BW, ET AL. Effects of selenium supplementation for cancer prevention in patients with carcinoma of the skin. A randomized controlled trial. *Nutritional Prevention of Cancer Study Group. JAMA 277: 1520, 1997*

CLARK LC, DALKIN B, KRONGRAD A, ET AL. Decreased incidence of prostate cancer with selenium supplementation: results of a double-blind cancer prevention trial. *Br. J. Urol. 81: 730-734, 1998*

CLARK LC, HIXSON LJ, COMBS GF JR, ET AL. Plasma selenium concentration predicts the prevalence of colorectal adenomatous polyps. *Cancer Epidemiol. Biomarkers Prev. 2: 41-46, 1993*

COMBS GF JR, CLARK LC, TURNBULL BW. Reduction of cancer mortality and incidence by selenium supplementation. *Med. Klin. 92 (Suppl 3): 42-45, 1997*

CONAWAY CC, JIAO D, KELLOFF GJ, ET AL. Chemopreventive potential of fumaric acid, N-acetylcysteine, N-(4-hydroxyphenyl) retinamide and beta-carotene for tobacco-nitrosamine-induced lung tumors in A/J mice. *Cancer Lett. 124: 85-93, 1998*

D'AGOSTINI F, BAGNASCO M, GIUNCIUGLIO D, ET AL. Inhibition by oral N-acetylcysteine of doxorubicin-induced clastogenicity and alopecia, and prevention of primary tumors and lung micrometastases in mice. *Int. J. Oncol. 13: 217-224, 1998*

DE FLORA S, ET AL. Antioxidant activity and other mechanisms of thiols involved in chemoprevention of mutation and cancer. *The American Journal of Medicine 91:3c-122s-3c-130s, 1991*

DE FLORA S, CESARONE CF, BALANSKY RM, ET AL. Chemopreventive properties and mechanisms of N-Acetylcysteine. The experimental background. *J. Cell Biochem. Suppl. 22: 33-41, 1995*

DELNESTE Y, JEANNIN P, POTIER L, ET AL. N-acetyl-L-cysteine exhibits antitumoral activity by increasing tumor necrosis factor alpha-dependent T-cell cytotoxicity. *Blood 90: 1124-1132, 1997*

DREHER D, JUNOD AF. Role of oxygen free radicals in cancer development. *Eur. J. Cancer 32: 30-38, 1996*

DROGE W, GROSS A, HACK V, KINSCHERF R, SCHYKOWSKI M, BOCKSTETTE M, MIHM S, GALTER D. Role of cysteine and GSH in HIV infection and cancer cachexia: Therapeutic intervention with n-acetylcysteine. *Advances in Pharmacology 38: 581-600, 1997*

GUENGERICH FP, THEIR R, PERSMARK M, ET AL. Conjugation of carcinogens by theta class glutathione s-transferases: mechanisms and relevance to variations in human risk. *Pharmacogenetics 5 Spec. No: S103-107, 1995*

HARRIES LW, STUBBINS MJ, FORMAN D, ET AL. Identification of genetic polymorphisms at the glutathione S-transferase Pi locus and association with susceptibility to bladder, testicular and prostate cancer. *Carcinogenesis 18: 641-644, 1997*

HECKBERT SR, WEISS NS, HORNUNG SK, ET AL. Glutathione S-transferase and epoxide hydrolase activity in human leukocytes in relation to risk of lung cancer and other smoking-related cancers. *J. Natl. Cancer Inst. 84: 414-422, 1992*

HIETANEN E, BARTSCH H, BEREZIAT JC, ET AL. Diet and oxidative stress in breast, colon and prostate cancer patients: a case-control study. *Eur. J. Clin. Nutr. 48: 575-586, 1994*

IZZOTTI A, ORLANDO M, GASPARINI L, ET AL. In vitro inhibition by N-acetylcysteine of oxidative DNA modifications detected by 32P postlabeling. *Free Radic. Res. 28: 165-178, 1998*

JIMENEZ JJ, HUANG HS, YUNIS AA. Treatment with ImuVert/N-acetylcysteine protects rats from cyclophosphamide/cytarabine-induced alopecia. *Cancer Invest. 10: 271-276, 1992*

KENNEDY RS, KONOK JP, BOUNOUS G, BARUCHEL S, LEE TDG. The use of a whey protein concentrate in the treatment of patients with metastatic carcinoma: A phase I-II clinical study. *Anticancer Research 15:2643-2650, 1995*

KETTERER B, HARRIS JM, TALASKA G, ET AL. The human glutathione S-transferase supergene family, its polymorphism, and its effects on susceptibility to lung cancer. *Environmental Health Perspectives 98: 87-94, 1992*

KOBRINSKY NL, HARTFIELD D, HORNER H, ET AL. Treatment of advanced malignancies with high-dose acetaminophen and N-acetylcysteine rescue. *Cancer Invest. 14: 202-210, 1996*

LENTON KJ, THERRIAULT H, FULOP T, ET AL. Glutathione and ascorbate are negatively correlated with oxidative DNA damage in human lymphocytes. *Carcinogenesis 20: 607-613, 1999*

MCINTOSH GH, REGESTER GO, LELEU RK, ROYLE PJ, SMITHERS GW. Dairy proteins protect against dimethyl-hydrazine induced intestinal cancers in rats. *Journal of Nutrition 125:809-816, 1995*

MOHANDAS J, MARSHALL JJ, DUGGIN GG, ET AL. Low activities of glutathione-related enzymes as factors in the genesis of urinary bladder cancer. *Cancer Res. 44: 5086-5091, 1984*

MULDERS TMT, KEIZER HJ, BREIMER DD, MULDER GJ. In Vivo characterization and modulation of the glutathion/glutathione S-transferase system in cancer patients. *Drug Metab. Rev. 27: 191-229, 1995*

NAKANISHI Y, MATSUKI H, TAKAYAMA K, ET AL. Glutathione derivatives enhance Adriamycin cytotoxicity in a human lung adenocarcinoma cell line. *Anticancer Res. 17: 2129-2134, 1997*

O'Dwyer PJ, Hamilton TC, Yao KS, Tew KD, Ozols RF. Modulation of GSH and related enzymes in reversal of resistance to anticancer drugs. *Hematology / Oncology Clinics of North America 9(2):383-396, 1995*

PAPENBURG R, BOUNOUS, DR. GUSTAVO BOUNOUS G, FLEISZER D, GOLD P. Dietary milk proteins inhibit the development of dimethyl-hydrazine induced malignancy. *Tumor Biology 11:129-136, 1990*

PLAXE S, FREDDO J, KIM S, ET AL. Phase I trial of cisplatin in combination with glutathione. *Gynecologic Oncology 55: 82-86, 1994*

REDMAN C, SCOTT JA, BAINES AT, ET AL. Inhibitory effect of selenomethionine on the growth of three selected human tumor cell lines. *Cancer Lett. 125: 103-110, 1998*

RICHIE JP JR. The role of GSH in aging and cancer. *Experimental Gerontology 27:615-626, 1992*

RIPPLE MO, HENRY WF, RAGO RP, WILDING G. Prooxidant-antioxidant shift induced by androgen treatment of human prostate carcinoma cells. *Journal of the National Cancer Institute 89:40-48. 1997*

ROSS RK, JONES PA, YU MC. Bladder cancer epidemiology and pathogenesis. *Seminars in Oncology. 23: 536-545, 1996*

ROSS DA, KISH P, MURASZKO KM, ET AL. Effect of dietary vitamin A or N-acetylcysteine on ethylnitrosourea-induced rat gliomas. *J. Neurooncol. 40: 29-38, 1998*

ROTSTEIN JB, SLAGA TJ. Effect of exogenous glutathione on tumor progression in the murine skin multistage carcinogenesis model. *Carcinogenesis 9: 1547-1551, 1988*

RUSSO A, DEGRAFF W, FRIEDMAN N, ET AL. Selective modulation of glutathione levels in human normal versus tumor cells and subsequent differential response to chemotherapy drugs. *Cancer Res. 46: 2845-2848, 1986*

SCHRODER CP, GODWIN AK, O'DWYER PJ, Tew KD, Hamilton TC, Ozois RF. GSH and drug resistance. *Cancer Investigation 14:158-168, 1996*

SCHWARTZ JL, SHKLAR G. Glutathione inhibits experimental oral carcinogenesis, p53 expression, and angiogenesis. *Nutrition & Cancer 26: 229-236, 1996*

SHKLAR G, SCHWARTZ J, TRICKLER D, CHEVERIE SR. The effectiveness of a mixture of beta-carotene, alpha-tocopherol, GSH, and ascorbic acid for cancer prevention. *Nutrition and Cancer 20:145-151, 1993*

SINGH DK, LIPPMAN SM. Cancer chemo-prevention. Part 1: Retinoids and carotenoids and other classic antioxidants. *Oncology (Huntingt.)* 12: 1643-1653, 1657-1660, 1998

SINGH DK, LIPPMAN SM. Cancer chemoprevention. Part 2: hormones, nonclassic antioxidant natural agents, NSAIDs, and other agents. *Oncology (Huntingt.)* 12: 1787-1800, 1998

SMYTH JF, BOWMAN A, PERREN T, WILKINSON P, PRESCOTT RJ, QUINN KJ, TEDESCHI M. GSH reduces the toxicity and improves the quality of life of women diagnosed with ovarian cancer treated with cisplatin: results of a double blind, randomized trial. *Annals of Oncology* 8:569-573, 1997

TRICKLER D, SHKLAR G, SCHWARTZ J. Inhibition of oral carcinogenesis by glutathione. *Nutr. Cancer* 20: 139-144, 1993

TSUYUKI S, YAMAUCHI A, NAKAMURA H, ET AL. Possible availability of N-acetylcysteine as an adjunct to cytokine therapy for hepatocellular carcinoma. *Clin. Immunol. Immunopathol.* 88: 192-198, 1998

VAN ZANDWIJK N. N-acetylcysteine for lung cancer prevention. *Chest* 107: 1437-1441, 1995

VAN ZANDWIJK N. N-acetylcysteine (NAC) and glutathione (GSH): antioxidant and chemopreventive properties, with special reference to lung cancer. *J. Cell Biochem. Suppl.* 22: 24-32, 1995

VOS O, ROOS-VERHEY WS. Endogenous versus exogenous thiols in radioprotection. *Pharmacological Therapeutics* 39:169-177, 1988

WANG T, CHEN X, SCHECTER RL, BARUCHEL S, ALAOUI-JAMALI M, MELNYCHUK D, BATIST G. Modulation of GSH by a cysteine pro-drug enhances in vivo tumor response. Journal of Pharmacology and *Experimental Therapeutics* 276:1169-1173, 1996

WEISBURGER JH. Nutritional approach to cancer prevention with emphasis on vitamins, antioxidants and carotinoids. American *Journal of Clinical Nutrition* 53:226s-237s, 1991

WHITE EL, ROSS LJ, STEELE VE, ET AL. Screening of potential cancer preventing chemicals as antioxidants in an in vitro assay. *Anticancer Res.* 18: 769-773, 1998

WITSCHI H, ESPIRITU I, YU M, ET AL. The effects of phenethyl isothiocyanate, N-acetylcysteine and green tea on tobacco smoke-induced lung tumors in strain A/J mice. *Carcinogenesis* 19: 1789-1794, 1998

YIM CY, HIBBS JB Jr, McGREGOR JR, et al. Use of N-acetylcysteine to increase intracellular glutathione during the induction of antitumor responses by IL-2. *J. Immunol.* 152: 5796-5805, 1994

CHAPTER 6
AGING

The rules for aging are definitely being broken. In 1900 a North American's life expectancy was 49 years. By year 2000 it was 78 and climbing. With scientific and medical advances a new breed of physician is emerging—the longevity specialist. Doctors may now write certified board exams to obtain their specialty in anti-aging. Dr. Ronald Klatz, founder and president of the American Academy of Anti-Aging Medicine (A⁴M), representing over 8500 members in 1999, states "These health professionals believe aging is not inevitable… Fifty years from now when millions of baby boomers start reaching the century mark, we will look back on the medical science of today as though it were the dark ages." Duke University demographer James Vaupel says, "There is no evidence that human life expectancy is anywhere close to its ultimate limit." Many believe that 100-120 years is an obtainable goal. See figure 19.

Twentieth century improvements in sanitation, occupational health and life-style as well as advances in antibiotics, vaccines and medical care have helped to extend the human life span. We all want to maintain our health during these senior years. A practical knowledge of GSH can help us ensure they bring a good quality of life. More than 12% of North Americans are over 65 and occupy a growing proportion of the population as baby boomers age. Most will suffer from heart disease, stroke, certain cancers, arthritis, Alzheimer's, Parkinson's, cataracts and other debilitating diseases (see figure 20). Oxidative stress is common to all these diseases, and the free-radical theory of aging based on oxidative damage underlies most anti-aging treatments.

GSH & AGING
The GSH antioxidant system is the body's powerhouse for diffusing and disposing of free radicals that threaten cell, tissue and organ damage, thus slowing the approach of aging. John T. Pinto of Sloan Kettering Cancer Center in

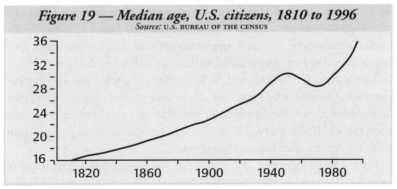

Figure 19 — Median age, U.S. citizens, 1810 to 1996
Source: U.S. BUREAU OF THE CENSUS

Figure 20 — Diseases of aging discussed in this book

Heart Disease	chapter 9	Parkinson's Disease	chapter 7
Stroke	chapter 9	Prostate Disease	chapter 23
Certain Cancers	chapter 5	Macular degeneration	chapter 17
Rheumatoid Arthritis	chapter 6	Cataracts	chapter 17
Alzheimer's Disease	chapter 8	Immune Deficiency	chapter 6

New York proclaims GSH "The master antioxidant." Jean Carper in her bestseller Stop Aging Now! highlights the same point: "You must get your levels of GSH up if you want to keep your youth and live longer. High blood levels of GSH predict good health as you age and a long life. Low levels predict early disease and death." These opinions result from convincing, fascinating research and experimentation. Age-specific decreases in GSH are seen in all tissues, including liver, kidney, lung, heart, spleen and the brain. Laboratory studies on the role of GSH in aging show GSH deficiency in all aging creatures, from mosquitoes and houseflies to rats and mice (see figure 21).

Similar findings in humans indicate that elderly subjects bear increased risk of disease and impairment. Blood-GSH concentrations in younger people (20-40 years) are 20 to 40% higher than in those aged 60-80 years. Studies by leading experts on aging (C.A. Lang, M. Julius and others) suggest that elevated GSH levels give elderly individuals a physical, psychological and sociological advantage over those with lower levels.

Researchers Mara Julius and Calvin Lang measured glutathione concentrations in community-based individuals over 60 years of age, mapping these values to health, number of illnesses and risk factors for chronic disease (tobacco, alcohol, cholesterol, blood pressure and obesity). Higher glutathione levels corresponded to lessened effects of aging and better general health. Those with 20% higher levels experience about one-third the rate of arthritis, high blood pressure, heart disease, circulatory difficulties and other maladies.

Dr. Lang also looked at glutathione levels in age groups: 20-40, 40-60, 60-80 and 80-100 years. The youngest group had acceptable levels but 14% of the 40-60 year olds and 53% of the 60-80 year olds had critically low levels. Interestingly, only 24% of the 80-100 year olds had low levels, perhaps explaining how they reached such a ripe old age in the first place.

The Italians G. Paolisso and M.R. Tagliamonte went one step further, comparing adults under age 50 with those over 50. Both the GSH and antioxidant function were depressed in the older group. However, those over 100 years old had higher GSH levels than the other over-50 group. Again, this may explain their unusual longevity.

Several researchers over the years have also shown that life span can be extended by restricting diet and maintaining low body weight. No satisfactory explanation has emerged for this phenomenon, but some scientists have demonstrated that glutathione levels rise in these longer-living individuals. They suggest that glutathione may be involved in a molecular mechanism that contributes to longevity.

S.L. Nuttal and his British team published a revealing study in The Lancet, comparing GSH levels in individuals of different ages and states of health. The healthy young had the highest levels, ahead of the healthy elderly. The lowest levels were found in sick, elderly patients. The results clearly showed that GSH levels fall as we age and as we become ill. The more severe the illness, the more evident the decrease.

Back in the laboratory, scientists are trying to find out whether elevated GSH levels can actually extend the life span. Aging-expert John Richie Jr. thinks that glutathione deficiency may be a biochemical cause of the aging process. In some of his experiments MgTC—a GSH promoting drug similar to OTC—was fed to mosquitoes. GSH levels were found to be 50 to 100% higher, and life span was increased by almost 40%. In another experiment, Diane Birt at the University of Nebraska fed hamsters the whey-protein concentrate lactalbumin—a GSH-precursor. These animals also lived longer. Interestingly, control hamsters on a diet including casein and cysteine, or methionine did not benefit. In fact high cysteine loads proved harmful, showing how the bioactivity of these amino acids changes when part of a larger protein, rather than free amino acids.

Dr. Gustavo Bounous and other researchers at McGill University demonstrated this anti-aging effect using a natural product to elevate GSH levels. They fed mice a specially developed whey protein isolate—later trademarked Immunocal—and compared their GSH levels and lifespan to mice on a standard diet. Not only were the tissue GSH levels found to be higher, the whey-fed mice had an average life span of 27 months (corresponding to a human age of 80 years) as compared to the control diet average of 21 months (human equivalent of 55 years). This is an astonishing increase of 30%. Further experiments using both cysteine and caseine (another milk protein) neither increased longevity nor raised GSH levels.

AGING & DETOXIFICATION

As we age, GSH levels fall and we become increasingly susceptible to the toxic threats of many drugs and pollutants. Older people usually have enough health challenges without the additional load of drugs and toxins. Well-known aging researchers T.S. Chen, J.P. Ritchie and C.A. Lang suggest that

Figure 21 — GSH decrease in older mice [Richie JP Jr., 1992]					
Liver	29%	Kidney	22%	Spleen	22%
Lung	39%	Heart	27%	Brain	33%

lower GSH levels in aging livers diminish the body's ability to detoxify poisons, including toxic doses of acetaminophen. Considering the widespread use of prescription drugs in the geriatric population, this is highly significant.

AGING & EXERCISE

Increased physical activity as a way of life clearly corresponds to longevity and improved health. There are many reasons, and some researchers have focused on the role of antioxidants and GSH. H.M. Allessio and E.R. Blasi at the Department of Physical Education at Miami University, summed it up by saying that exercise can elevate antioxidant enzymes and cofactors and that antioxidant levels are inversely related to mortality.

The Germans M. Kretzschmar and D. Muller suggest in a series of reports that the elderly can compensate for the decline in glutathione levels through exercise. The resultant increase in GSH levels can protect against many of the diseases common to older people. The Israelis A.Z. Reznick and E.H. Witt went one step further, suggesting that raised antioxidant function enables aging people to tolerate more exercise without the ill-effects of over-training.

Chapter 24 discusses glutathione and athletic performance, explaining how glutathione levels increase with exercise and how it wards off some of the ill effects of excessive exercise. It has been suggested several times that physical activity promotes longevity by increasing glutathione levels.

IMMUNITY, AGING AND GSH

Aging is characterized by a decline in the immune system, accounting in part for increased incidence of cancer and other diseases, especially the infections common among aging individuals. R.K. Fidelius and M.F. Tsan from the Veterans Administration Research Service have linked low GSH levels with this increased susceptibility. By both raising and depleting glutathione levels they were able to significantly alter immune responsiveness.

As the immune system ages T-cell lymphocytes (see chapter 3) undergo the most significant changes, leaving us less able to respond to viruses, bacteria and other threats. The same T-cell insufficiency has also been identified in certain autoimmune diseases such as rheumatoid arthritis (RA) and systemic lupus erythematosus (SLE).

Separate study groups were able to enhance immune responsiveness in aging laboratory animals using GSH or GSH-promoting drugs like OTC (ornithine decarboxylase) or 2ME (2-mercapto-ethanol), and these tests were carried into human studies. Tufts University researchers Drs. Simin Meydani & Dayang Wu showed that by adding GSH to the white blood cells of elderly people, immune activity approached the levels of much younger individuals. The same team went on to do an *in vitro* study in humans, feeding subjects supplements to raise their GSH levels. These test had equally positive results in immune response. These leading researchers in aging and immunology conclude that increased oxidative stress and/or lower consumption of antioxidants contribute to the decline of white-blood cell function and weakened immune response in the aged.

RHEUMATOID ARTHRITIS

Rheumatoid arthritis (RA) is a common chronic inflammatory joint disease that progresses with aging. Although its exact cause is unknown, several factors have been identified. Strong evidence shows that many of the changes in RA-affected joints result from oxidation and free radical damage. Some researchers have also implicated poor T-cell and overactive B-cell activity. Scientists have also demonstrated that T-cell GSH content in rheumatoid joints are much lower than in peripheral T-cells of the same patients. GSH modulation may play a role—a team of rheumatologists from Leiden University Medical Center in the Netherlands diminished inflammation at a cellular level by using NAC to raise glutathione in these tissues.

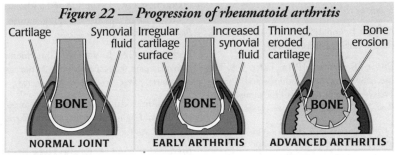

Figure 22 — Progression of rheumatoid arthritis

Cartilage · Synovial fluid · Irregular cartilage surface · Increased synovial fluid · Thinned, eroded cartilage · Bone erosion

BONE — BONE — BONE

NORMAL JOINT · EARLY ARTHRITIS · ADVANCED ARTHRITIS

CONCLUSION

There is little doubt that cellular oxidative damage contributes to aging and its many diseases. It has been documented that those who live to 100 years or more have unusually high levels of glutathione, and we know that oxyradicals are very destructive. Given that GSH is a powerful antioxidant, it seems reasonable to expect a connection between longevity and GSH. It may at least improve our immune defenses and quality of life at a time when many people experience one health problem after another. Although we are not mice, the extension of this rodent's life span by 30 to 50% suggests that GSH may reduce the wear and tear of aging on overall health. Quite apart from the process of aging, good health in general is associated with high GSH levels. And GSH helps the liver deal with the toxic effects of medications used by the elderly. It may also improve the value of exercise, in turn elevating the GSH system and contributing to better overall health and well-being. GSH can enhance our immune response at a time when it normally begins to decline, ward off diseases of aging, and improve T-cell function—a critical part of the immune system.

AGING

Alessio HM, Blasi ER. Physical activity as a natural antioxidant booster and its effect on a healthy life span. *Res. Q. Exerc. Sport.* 68:292-302, 1997

Benzi G, Pastoris O, Marzatico F, Villa RF. Age-related effect induced by oxidative stress on the cerebral glutathione system. *Neurochem. Res. 14:473-481, 1989*

Birt DF, Schuldt GH, Salmasi S. Survival of hamsters fed graded levels of two protein sources. *Lab. Animal Sci. 32:363-366, 1982*

Bounous G, Gervais F, Amer V, Batist G, Gold P. The influence of dietary whey protein on tissue GSH and the diseases of aging. *Clin. & Investig. Med. 12: 343-349, 1989*

Carper J. Stop Aging Now! New York, NY, Harper Collins Publishers, 1995

Chen TS, Richie JP Jr, Lang CA. The effects of aging on glutathione and cysteine levels in different regions of the mouse brain. *Proc. Soc. Exp. Biol. Med. 190:399-402, 1989*

Chen TS, Richie JP Jr, Lang CA. Life span profiles of glutathione and acetaminophen detoxification. *Drug Metab. Dispos. 18:882-887, 1990*

Fidelus RK, Tsan MF. GSH and lymphocyte activation: a function of aging and autoimmune disease. *Immunology 61:503-508, 1987*

Fletcher RH, Fletcher SW. GSH and Aging: Ideas and evidence. *Lancet 344:1379-1380, 1994*

Furukawa T, Meydani SN, Blumberg JB. Reversal of age associated decline in immune responsiveness by dietary GSH supplementation in mice. *Mechanisms of Aging and Development 38:107-117, 1987*

Gringhuis SI, Leow A, Papendrecht-Van Der Voort EA, et al. Displacement of linker for activation of T cells from the plasma membrane due to redox balance alterations results in hyporesponsiveness of synovial fluid T lymphocytes in rheumatoid arthritis. *J. Immunol. 164:2170-2179, 2000*

Gutteridge JM. Aging and free radicals. *Med. Lab. Sci. 49:313-318, 1992*

Harman D. Free radicals in aging. *Mol. Cell. Biochem. 84:155-161, 1988*

Harman D. Free radical theory of aging. *Mutat. Res. 275:257-266, 1992*

Hazelton GA, Lang CA. Glutathione contents of tissues in the aging mouse. *Biochem. J. 188:25-30, 1980*

Hazelton GA, Lang CA. Glutathione peroxidase and reductase activities in the aging mouse. *Mech. Aging Dev. 29:71-81, 1985*

Ji, LL. Antioxidant enzyme response to exercising and aging. *Med. Sci. Sports Exerc. 25:225-231, 1993*

Julius M, Lang CA, Gleiberman L, et al. GSH and morbidity in a community based sample of elderly. *Journal of Clinical Epidemiology 47: 1021-1026, 1994*

Khanna SC, Garg SK, Sharma SP. Antioxidant-influenced alterations in glutathione reductase activity in different age groups of male mice. *Gerontology 38:9-12, 1992*

Klatz R. Grow young with HGH [ISBN 0-06-098434-1]. *Harper Perennial. 1997*

Knight JA. Free radicals: their history and current status in aging and disease. *Ann. Clin. Lab. Sci. 28:331-346, 1998*

Kretzschmar M, Muller D. Aging, training and exercise. A review of effects on plasma glutathione and lipid peroxides. *Sports Med. 15:196-209, 1993*

KRETZSCHMAR M, MULLER D, HUBSCHER J, ET AL. Influence of aging, training and acute physical exercise on plasma glutathione and lipid peroxides in man. *Int. J. Sports Med. 12, 218-222, 1991*

LANG CA, NARYSHKIN S, SCHNEIDER DL, MILLS BJ, LINDEMAN RD. Low blood GSH in healthy aging adults. *Journal of Laboratory & Clinical Medicine 120:720-725, 1992*

LANG CA, WU WK, CHEN T, MILLS BJ. Blood glutathione: a biochemical index of life span enhancement in the diet restricted Lobund-Wistar rat. *Prog. Clin. Biol. Res. 287:241-246, 1989*

MAURICE MM, VAN DER VOORT EAM, VILET AI, TAK PP, BREEDVELD FC, VERWEIJ CL. Chronic oxidative stress in rheumatoid arthritis: Implications for T-cell function. Oxidative Stress in Cancer, AIDS and Neurodegenerative Diseases. *Institute Pasteur.* EDITORS MONTAGNIER L, OLIVIER R, PASQUIER C. MARCEL DEKKER, *1998*

MERRY P, WINYARD PG, MORRIS CJ, GROOTVELD M, BLAKE DR. Oxygen-free radicals, inflammation, and synovitis: the current status. *Annals of Rheumatic Disease 48:864-870, 1989*

MEYDANI SN, WU D, SANTOS MS, HAYEK MG. Antioxidants and immune response in aged persons: overview of present evidence. *American Journal of Clinical Nutrition 62(s):1462-1476, 1995*

MICHELET F, GUEGUEN R, LEROY P, ET AL. Blood and plasma glutathione measured in healthy subjects by HPLC: relation to sex, aging, biological variables, and life habits. *Clin. Chem. 41:1509-1517, 1995*

NOHI H. Involvement of free radicals in aging: a consequence or cause of senescence. *Br. Med. Bull. 49:653-667, 1993*

NUTALL SL, MARTIN U, SINCLAIR AJ, KENDALL MJ. Glutathione in sickness and in health. *Lancet 351: 645-646, 1998*

PAOLISO G, TAGLIAMONTE MR, RIZZO MR, ET AL. Oxidative stress and advancing age: results in healthy centenarians. *J. American Geriatric Soc. 46:833-838, 1998*

POOT M. Oxidants and antioxidants in proliferative senescence. *Mutat. Res. 256:177-189, 1991*

REMACLE J, MICHIELS C, RAES M. The importance of antioxidant enzymes in cellular aging and degeneration. *EXS. 62:99-108, 1992*

REZNICK AZ, WITT EH, SILBERMANN M, PACKER L. The threshold of age in exercise and antioxidants action. *EXS. 62:423-427, 1992*

RICHIE JP JR. Correction of a GSH deficiency in the aging mosquito increases its longevity. Proc. of the Society for *Experimental Biology and Medicine 184:113-117, 1987*

RICHIE JP JR. The role of GSH in aging and cancer. *Experimental Gerontology 27:615-626, 1992*

SALMON M, GASTON JSH. The role of T-cell lymphocytes in rheumatoid arthritis. *British Medical Bulletin 51:332-345, 1995*

VINA J, SASTRE J, ANTON V, ET AL. Effect of aging on glutathione metabolism. Protection by antioxidants. *EXS. 62:136-144, 1992*

WU D, MEYDANI SN, SASTRE J, HAYEK M, MEYDANI M. In vitro GSH supplementation enhances interleukin-2 production and mitogenic response of peripheral blood mononuclear cells from young and old subjects. *Journal of Nutrition 124: 655-663, 1994*

CHAPTER 7

PARKINSON'S DISEASE

Also known as shaking palsy, Parkinson's disease is one of North America's most common debilitating illnesses. It is often thought of as a disease of old age—one person in a hundred will develop it by retirement age, but half of them may have it by age 40.

Parkinson's disease develops progressively. Nerve cells slowly degenerate in the part of the mid-brain that controls movement (the substantia nigra layer of the basal ganglia). In normal health, messages from the motor cortex to the reticular formation initiate free movement, and neurotransmitters released from the basal ganglia in response to the same messages slow or dampen movement, providing the suppleness and dexterity we take for granted. These two neurotransmitters are dopamine, which stimulates the damping effect, and acetylcholine, which inhibits it.

SYMPTOMS AND CAUSES

Its exact cause is usually unknown, but Parkinson's disease is characterized by cell damage in the basal ganglia. Production of dopamine slows down and the characteristic symptoms appear. It begins with weakness or stiffness accompanied by a slight tremor of the hands or head. Over time the shaking increases, muscles stiffen further and there is a visible deterioration in balance and coordination. In advanced stages, symptoms include generalized rigidity, drooling, loss of appetite, stooped posture, a shuffling walk and a fixed facial expression. Eventually, communication skills may be impaired. Dementia, depression and other emotional problems are common.

Genetic factors play a role too, but there are other contributing causes including certain medications, pesticides, carbon monoxide, cyanide, manganese, street heroin, specific viruses and the type of repetitive head trauma suffered by boxer Mohammed Ali (dementia pugilistica). Researchers at the National Institute of Health in Bethesda have recently identified a gene programmed for the production of a protein called alpha synuclein. There is hope that this clue will open the door to further discoveries about Parkinson's disease and innovative ways to treat it.

TREATMENT

There is so far no definitive cure for Parkinson's disease but it is treatable—most effectively at its outset. Therefore, early diagnosis is best. For the time being, conventional treatments include medication that attempts to restore neurochemical balance by replacing or supplementing the body's production of dopamine. Neurosurgical techniques and fetal tissue implants have had some success. Some scientists are developing implantable electrodes into the brain to stimulate specific neural pathways. Drugs such as selegiline have shown promise. A team headed by researchers P. Jenner and C.W. Olanow from the Neurodegenerative Disease Research Centre in London have shown that selegiline may increase GSH activity. Recently, newer drugs like pramipexole and ropenerole have emerged as more effective treatments.

PARKINSON'S DISEASE AND GLUTATHIONE

Recent research has revealed two important findings: first, biochemical analysis of the affected brain tissue shows damage consistent with extensive oxidative stress and the circulation of free radicals that follows it; second, GSH levels in these tissues are particularly low. A striking feature of Parkinson's is an approximate 40% decrease during the early stages of the disease. A group of researchers from the University of Southern California led by J.D. Adams Jr. were able to show that in advanced Parkinson's Disease glutathione levels fall to a mere 2% of normal. Whether the drop in GSH is a cause or a symptom of this damage remains unclear. But there is good news—elevated GSH levels slow brain tissue damage. Some symptoms may even be reversed.

Since damage caused by free radicals is an invariable component of Parkinson's Disease, researchers have experimented with a variety of high-dose antioxidants. In addition to the more well-known antioxidants, glutathione therapy has also been used. Not only is GSH an exceptional antioxidant, the substantia nigra of Parkinson's patients is especially deficient in it, so their need is particularly great. M. Gabby's research team in Israel showed that elevated GSH levels more effectively reduce dopaminergic toxicity than the antioxidant vitamins C and E. Paradoxically, while brain cells need dopamine to function, dopamine at certain times is actually toxic to the same tissues. This may be why drugs which raise L-dopa levels, like Sinemet, only work for a few years before the effects wear off and the patient subsequently deteriorates.

Dr. P. Jenner and his team at the Parkinson's Disease Experimental Research Laboratories in London have extensively examined the role of GSH in the progression of this disease. They found that glutathione levels fall consistently at the onset of Parkinson's Disease and believe that elevated GSH levels can help prevent neural damage.

D. Offen's team at the Beilinson Medical Center in Israel experimented on the actual neurons involved in dopamine metabolism. They investigated the cell-death associated with the Parkinsonian decline in dopamine. To slow down this decline they used antioxidants, and found that the thiol (sulfur-containing) antioxidants GSH, NAC and dithioleitol worked well. In the cautious language of medical science, they described them as "markedly protective" of brain cells. This corroborated the findings of M. Gabby's work (above), further supporting the theory that GSH may prevent or delay dopamine-induced cell death.

G. Sechi and his team in Italy studied a group of untreated Parkinson's patients in the early stages of the disease who received intravenous GSH therapy twice a day for a month. All patients improved significantly with more than 40% decrease in their disability. The improvement faded away two to four months after the last GSH treatment.

Other authors have drawn attention to the role of GSH-enhancing drugs in the treatment of this disease. There is much evidence to support the usefulness of elevated glutathione levels. Today, however, there are ways to raise GSH levels without the use of pharmaceutical drugs—see chapter 4.

CASE STUDIES

Glutathione is part of the body's defense system and protects us against the onset of many disease processes. It can also help to reverse certain conditions or symptoms, either temporarily or permanently. The following story illustrates the apparent helpfulness of GSH supplementation in one particular case.

Wally, a seventy-four year-old baseball fan, was diagnosed with Parkinson's disease in May 1997. His disease progressed quickly and his doctors placed him on Sinemet (carbidopa/levodopa). In November he began to experience severe headaches—presumably from the medication—and he discontinued it. Up to this point he had been a very active man, but now he deteriorated to the point where he could not get out of bed or even rise from a chair without help. He says movement felt like 'walking in cement.' He was constantly fatigued and soon needed a wheelchair to go outdoors. The doctors used other medications including Eldepryl (selegiline hydrochloride) and Requip (ropinirole hydrochloride). They helped slightly. In March 1998 he started taking Immunocal, a natural protein which raises GSH levels. After five days his headaches were gone. Within two weeks his fatigue had lessened. Two months later Wally was walking well again and was eventually able to visit the new Angels baseball stadium, Edison Field, and jog around the block. There was no other therapeutic intervention and seven months later his active lifestyle continued.

62 year-old Carol maintained an active legal practice until 1990. After a diagnosis of Parkinson's disease in 1986, she was able for a while to continue her career as a lawyer, but eventually had to quit. The

stress was aggravating her symptoms and the symptoms were in turn increasing her stress levels. She was treated with a number of different medications but her health continued to deteriorate until she eventually needed help at home to carry out day-to-day tasks. She quit driving her car and stopped taking her daily walks, which she loved. Then, within days of starting to take a bioactive whey protein isolate she noticed her strength returning. Weeks afterwards she was once more exploring her neighborhood and nine months later she was driving again.

CONCLUSION

Parkinson's disease is characterized by a loss of the brain cells that regulate dopamine. Significant evidence points to the role of oxidative stress and dramatically low GSH levels as critical contributing causes of this damage. Studies have demonstrated that protecting these cells from damage and death by raising GSH levels can succeed both in the laboratory and in patients and is a welcome addition to conventional medical treatments.

PARKINSON'S DISEASE

ADAMS JD JR, KLAIDMAN LK, ODUNZE IN, SHEN HC, MILLER CA. Alzheimer's and Parkinson's disease. Brain levels of glutathione, glutathione disulfide, and vitamin E. *Molecular Chemical Neuropathology 14(3):213-226, 1991*

ADAMS JD JR, ODUNZE IN. Oxygen free radicals and Parkinson's disease. *Free Radical Biol Med 10(2):161-169, 1991*

DI MONTE DA, CHAN P, SANDY MS. Glutathione in Parkinson's disease: a link between oxidative stress and mitochondrial damage? *Annals of Neurology 32(suppl): SIII-115, 1992*

EBADI M, SRINIVASAN SK, BAXI MD. Oxidative stress and antioxidant therapy in Parkinson's disease. *Progress in Neurobiology 48(1):1-19, 1996*

GABBY M, TAUBER M, PORAT S, SIMANTOV R. Selective role of glutathione in protecting human neuronal cells from dopamine-induced apoptosis. *Neuropharmacology 35(5):57—578, 1996*

JENNER P. Oxidative damage in neurodegenerative disease. *The Lancet 344:796-798, 1994*

JENNER P. Oxidative stress in Parkinson's disease and other neurodegenerative disorders. *Pathologie Biologie 44(1):57-64, 1996*

JENNER P, OLANOW CW. Oxidative stress and the pathogenesis of Parkinson's disease. *Neurology 47(6 suppl 3):S161-170, 1996*

OWEN AD, SCHAPIRA AHV, JENNER P, MARSDEN CD. Oxidative stress and Parkinson's disease. *Annals of the New York Academy of Science 786:217-223, 1996*

OFFEN D, ZIV I, STERNIN H, MELAMED E, HOCHMAN A. Prevention of dopamine-induced cell death by thiol antioxidants: possible implications for treatment of Parkinson's disease. *Experimental Biology 141(1):32-39, 1996*

PERRY TL, GODIN DV, HANSEN S. Parkinson's disease: a disorder due to nigral glutathione deficiency? *Neuroscience Letter 33(3):305-310, 1982*

REIDERER P, SOFIC E, RAUSCH WD, SCHMIDT B ET AL. Transition metals, ferritin, glutathione, ascorbic acid in Parkinsonian Brains. *Journal of Neurochemistry 52: 515-520, 1989*

SECHI G, DELEDDA MG, BUA G, SATTA WM, DEIANA GA, PES GM, ROSATI G. Reduced intravenous glutathione in the treatment of early Parkinson's disease. *Progress in Neuro-Psychopharmacology & Biological Psychiatry 20(7):1159-70, 1996*

SIAN J, DEXTER DT, LEES AJ, DANIEL S, JENNER P, MARSDEN CD. Glutathione-related enzymes in brain in Parkinson's disease. *Annals of Neurology 36(3):356-361, 1994*

SIAN J, DEXTER DT, LEES AJ, DANIEL S, AGID Y, JAVOY-AGID F, JENNER P, MARSDEN CD. Alterations in glutathione levels in Parkinson's disease and other neurodegenerative disorders affecting basal ganglia. *Annals of Neurology 36(3): 348-355, 1994*

SIMONIAN NA, COYLE JT. Oxidative stress in neurodegenerative diseases. *Annual Review of Pharmacology & Toxicology 36:83-106, 1996*

SPENCER JPE, JENNER P, HALLIWELL B. Superoxide-dependent depletion of reduced glutathione by L-Dopa and dopamine. Relevance to Parkinson's disease. *Neuroreport 6(11):1480-84, 1995*

ZHANG F, DRYHURST G. Effects of L-cysteine on the oxidation chemistry of dopamine: new reaction pathways of potential relevance to idiopathic Parkinson's disease. *Journal of Medical Chemistry 37(8):1084-98, 1994*

CHAPTER 8

ALZHEIMER'S DISEASE

Alzheimer's disease (AD) is the most common form of dementia in North America and currently afflicts more than four million people. Studies estimate that as many as five to ten percent of adults over the age of 65 will be affected. Over age 80 this figure can rise to one in three. Given the change in our population demographics towards longer life spans, this represents an enormous future burden. Alzheimer's disease follows heart disease, cancer and stroke as the fourth most common cause of death.

Alzheimer's is a neurodegenerative disease with progressive deterioration of memory, comprehension, intellectual function and behavior. It may have a subtle onset with a slow progression over twenty years or the patient may deteriorate rapidly with a devastating decline in mental capacity over a short period of time. The average duration is about seven years.

Not to be confused with the simple forgetfulness of normal aging, Alzheimer's leads to significant memory lapses, dramatic mood changes, emotional outbursts, childish behavior, inability to retain new information and general confusion or disorientation, particularly at night. Health and abilities decline until one is unable to care for oneself and eventually dies.

Causes

Alzheimer's disease is characterized by a degeneration of brain nerve cells and a shrinkage of brain mass. Although its exact cause has yet to be determined, certain changes in the brain have been well identified. Patients have decreased or altered levels of certain neurotransmitters such as ACh and GABA which relay messages from neuron to neuron. Two other striking features are neurofibrillary tangles and neural plaque formation.

Several theories attempt to explain these changes. Alzheimer's was once thought to be a variant of the normal aging process. It used to be called 'senile dementia.' It is now clear that Alzheimer's is an abnormal condition

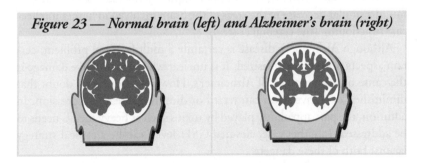

Figure 23 — Normal brain (left) and Alzheimer's brain (right)

but that a number of factors may at least delay or slow its progression. Recent research has identified a blood protein called ApoE which appears to be altered in Alzheimer's patients and leads to nerve cell damage. Other studies point towards the interaction of this protein with heavy metals such as aluminum and mercury, and other elements such as iron, zinc and calcium, leading to plaque formation. A strong argument has been made for the role of oxidative stress and free radical formation in promoting the damage in these tissues.

GSH AND ALZHEIMER'S DISEASE

How and where does GSH fit into this picture? If heavy metals are involved in the progression of Alzheimer's, GSH can play a critical role in their elimination and detoxification. Certain studies have demonstrated that when aluminum is 'pulled' out of the cells using chelators, the symptoms of Alzheimer's can be reduced or delayed. As we outlined in chapter 2, one of our primary defenses against these toxins is an adequate GSH enzyme system. And as researchers further define how free radicals contribute to brain cell destruction, the role of GSH as the primary intracellular antioxidant will come to the forefront.

Much research has focused on the role of antioxidants in alleviating Alzheimer's symptoms and its progression, especially vitamin E because of its availability and low price. But as we saw in chapter 1 the interaction of these antioxidants is complex. Many are dependent on adequate GSH levels for their proper functioning. A large number of post-mortem studies have compared normal with diseased brain tissue. They reveal significant changes in GSH and GSH peroxidase levels as well as elevated levels of the powerful oxidant lipid peroxide, against which GSH is a primary defense. Fibroblast cells cultured from brain tissue affected by Alzheimer's disease are more sensitive to damage by free radicals than normal tissue. The sites of this increased vulnerability likely occur at the mitochondrial level. Adams and his research team found GSH levels diminished in the area of the brain involved in short-term memory (hippocampus). Jenner and his co-workers found a similar decrease in the areas of the brain involved in higher intellectual functioning (the cerebral cortex).

Although Alzheimer's disease is certainly a multifactorial problem, certain aspects must be emphasized. It is unclear whether oxidative damage is the cause or just an effect of Alzheimer's. However, there is no doubt that diminished oxidative stress can retard or diminish disease progression. In addition, the part apparently played by toxins such as heavy metals needs to be addressed. In either case, elevated GSH levels can be a critical strategy against both of these dangers.

Case study

Despite excellent care at home, Max eventually had to be institutionalized for his Alzheimer's disease. His 78-year-old wife's arthritis and heart disease left her unable to give him the high-maintenance care he needed. Previously a gregarious salesman who loved to tell a joke, in his present condition he was even unaware of who was in the room. His history of smoking one to two packs a day left him with chronic bronchitis, requiring frequent inhalation therapy. To treat his ever-thickening secretions, the respiratory therapist started using Mucomyst (N-acetylcysteine—a GSH-promoting drug). After several weeks on the Mucomyst, Max began to smile when his wife entered his room and was visibly pleased by her visits.

Conclusion

In Alzheimer's disease certain proteins seem to react with heavy metals and other elements, leading to plaque formation. Oxidative stress and free radical formation definitely play a role in promoting this damage. When heavy metals are removed by chelators, the symptoms of Alzheimer's can be reduced or delayed.

It is unclear whether oxidative damage is the cause or just an effect of Alzheimer's. Nevertheless, antioxidants such as vitamin E may be useful. Their antioxidant function is maximized by maintaining adequate GSH levels. By diminishing oxidative stress disease the progression of this disease can be retarded or diminished.

ALZHEIMER'S DISEASE

ADAMS JD JR, KLAIDMAN LK, ODUNZE IN, SHEN HC, MILLER CA. Alzheimer's and Parkinson's disease. Brain levels of glutathione, glutathione disulfide, and vitamin E. *Molecular Chemical Neuropathology 14:213-226, 1991*

BALAZS L, LEON M. Evidence of an oxidative challenge in the Alzheimer's brain. *Neurochemical Research 19:1131-1137, 1994*

BENZI G, MORETTI A. Are reactive oxygen species involved in Alzheimer's disease? *Neurobiol Aging 16:661-674, 1995*

CEBALLOS-PICOT I, MERAD-BOUDIA M, NICOLE A, THEVENIN M, HELLIER G, LEGRAIN S, BERR C. Peripheral antioxidant enzyme activities and selenium in elderly subjects and in dementia of Alzheimer's type : place of the extracellular glutathione peroxidase. *Free Radical Biology and Medicine 20:579-587, 1996*

CONNOR RJ, MENZIES SL, ST. MARTIN SM, MUFSON EJ. A histochemical study of iron, transferrin, and ferritin in Alzheimer's diseased brains. *Journal of Neuroscience Research 31: 75-83, 1992*

JENNER P. Oxidative damage in neurodegenerative disease. *Lancet 344:796-798, 1994*

LOHR JB, BROWNING JA. Free radical involvement in neuropsychiatric illnesses. *Psychopharmacological Bulletin 31:159-165, 1995*

LOVELL MA, EHMANN WD, BUTLER SM, MARKESBERY WR. Elevated thiobarbituric acid-reactive substances and antioxidant enzyme activity in the brain in Alzheimer's disease. *Neurology 45:1594-1601, 1995*

TREPANIER G, FURLING D, PUYMIRAT J, MIRAULT ME. Immunocytochemical localization of seleno-glutathione peroxidase in the adult mouse brain. *Neuroscience 75:231-243, 1996*

CHAPTER 9
HEART DISEASE, STROKE AND CHOLESTEROL

ARTERIOSCLEROSIS

Heart disease and stroke are the main cause of death in North America. Both result from the same process—arteriosclerosis, also called atherosclerosis or hardening of the arteries. This is such a common disease in the developed world that it has been considered a normal part of the aging process. In fact, overwhelming evidence links it closely to diet and life-style issues such as smoking and lack of exercise, suggesting that this major cause of mortality and morbidity is preventable, or that its progress may be slowed down or even reversed.

Although it is more common in older people, the early stages of this disease is sometimes found in children, and people in their thirties can suffer significant damage.

The consequences of arteriosclerosis are disastrous—heart failure, heart attack, stroke, kidney failure, high blood pressure, impaired circulation and many other ailments. Additional contributing factors aggravate this condition and must be managed throughout our lives to ensure health and longevity. Some of the high risk factors are listed below and in figure 24, together with suggested ways to deal with them.

LOW FIBER

Dietary fiber adds bulk to the feces, which then pass through the intestines more easily, aiding normal bowel function. Low-fiber diets affect fat absorption and increase cholesterol levels. A high-fiber diet is critical. Adequate fiber can be found by eating a variety of fruits, vegetables and grains every day.

To understand how GSH can help prevent and treat this disease, let's look at how arteriosclerosis develops. An artery wall has three layers (see figure 25)—a tough epithelium, a thick muscular mesothelium and a delicate endothelium. The endothelial lining is especially prone to damage, and thin streaks of fatty deposits can build up there. In the healthy artery, this process is combated by several processes, including our natural antioxidant defenses. In arteries damaged by high blood pressure, stress or cigarette smoking, these fatty deposits accumulate. In an attempt to heal the damage, the body lays down platelets, calcium and scar tissue. Plaque thickens and makes the area stickier than normal, encouraging the accumulation of additional lipids. Slowly the artery becomes sufficiently clogged to inhibit blood flow, depriving organs and muscles of oxygen.

Heart disease

Poor circulation affects all organ systems including the brain, kidneys, eyes and extremities, but its main burden is heart disease. When blood flow to areas of the heart through the coronary arteries is cut off, a heart attack results. The pain of angina comes from heart tissue that cannot get enough oxygen because of insufficient blood flow. A heart with poor blood flow weakens and leads to heart failure. Hardened arteries often lead to high blood pressure, which further compromises the heart.

Physicians try to prevent this downward spiral with medications that lower blood pressure, thin the blood, decrease cholesterol, strengthen heart muscle contractions and improve arterial blood flow. Surgery can provide a way around blockages. A coronary bypass operation consists of a grafted vein that bypasses the blockage. Angioplasty is a way to squash plaque against the artery wall and make more room for blood to pass through.

Stroke

A stroke is caused by blocked blood flow (ischemia) that deprives the brain of oxygen. All vital organs are prone to ischemia when arteries become narrow and hard. In these cases it is important to thin the blood and manage

---

Figure 24 — How to avoid arteriosclerosis

FIBER
A high-fiber diet is critical. Include a variety of fruits, vegetables and grains.

FAT
Eat high-fat foods only occasionally. These include fried food, junk food, meat products, butter, lard, margarine and rich dairy products.

COOKING OIL
Use pure, cold-pressed olive oil or unrefined canola oil. Heating any oil increases its damaging effects.

FAMILY HISTORY
If your family has a history of cardio-vascular disease, see your

STRESS
Reduce stress levels and use relaxation techniques.

EXERCISE
Take regular, moderate exercise, at least three times weekly for 30-45 minutes.

BLOOD PRESSURE
Monitor and maintain normal blood pressure.

TOBACCO
Avoid smoking and second-hand smoke. This is a powerful source of oxidation.

WEIGHT
Maintain an appropriate body weight.

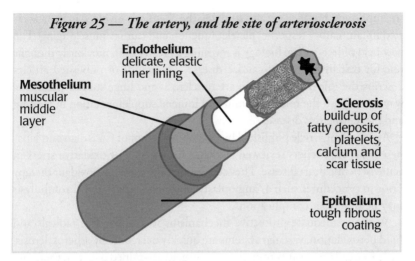

Figure 25 — The artery, and the site of arteriosclerosis

Endothelium
delicate, elastic
inner lining

Mesothelium
muscular
middle
layer

Sclerosis
build-up of
fatty deposits,
platelets,
calcium and
scar tissue

Epithelium
tough fibrous
coating

cholesterol levels. Occasionally, surgery is performed to remove the buildup of plaque in the arteries leading to the brain.

Both the deprivation of oxygen from brain tissue and its subsequent re-introduction (see reperfusion injury, below) cause significant damage. Neurologists from the University of California (San Francisco) showed the importance of glutathione in protecting the brain from such attack. Animals whose glutathione levels were artificially lowered suffered significantly greater brain damage after a stroke. Neurosurgeons at the University of Washington went further, demonstrating that glutathione depletion also leads to further narrowing of the critical arteries serving those oxygen-starved areas.

CHOLESTEROL AND PLAQUE FORMATION

The process of plaque formation is complex and it takes years to reach the point of causing symptoms. However it is clear that certain types of fatty substances are more dangerous than others. LDL, bad cholesterol, leads to plaque formation, while HDL—good cholesterol—prevents it. Other factors increase the danger of these fats, especially oxidative stress.

Oxidation makes fat rancid. In our blood stream this chemical change is called lipid peroxidation and causes fatty deposits to stick to the artery walls. The corresponding formation of free radicals leads to further lipid peroxidation and subsequent hardening of the arteries. Cigarette smoke releases large amounts of free radicals into the blood stream, explaining why more smokers die of cardiovascular disease than of lung cancer. For similar reasons diabetics are also prone to vascular damage.

Researchers have identified many causes of cardiovascular disease. The biochemical changes that result in oxidation of fat, especially LDL-cholesterol, are important, but they are also studying the chemicals involved in the associated inflammatory response, platelet function and cardiac muscle aging. The new field of free-radical biology is revealing a greater than previously thought role for oxidative stress in cardiac disease. Thousands of published articles describe the role of oxidation in arteriosclerosis and huge studies are underway to establish the role of vitamin and mineral supplementation in treating and preventing this disease.

An excellent article published by a combined team of Canadian and Japanese heart researchers reviewed evidence for the role of oxidative stress in acute ischemic heart disease. They suggest that the use of antioxidant therapy prior to procedures such as angioplasty, coronary bypass and thrombolysis may help prevent complications.

Without adequate protective mechanisms to combat free radicals and lipid peroxidation, vascular systems are quickly overcome by atherosclerosis. M.J. Kendall's team at Birmingham University examined over two thousand patients with confirmed coronary artery disease in a randomized clinical trial. Patients taking antioxidant supplements reduced their risk of cardiovascular disease by 47%. Some cardiologists argue that well-defined clinical trials have not yet proven beyond doubt that antioxidants are essential, but a poll of cardiologists published in the American Journal of Cardiology found that a full 44% of them take antioxidants themselves.

GSH AND ARTERIOSCLEROSIS

The principal antioxidant in our cells is GSH. This applies to the endothelial cells of the arteries as well as red blood cells and platelets. University of British Columbia researchers led by Kimberly Cheng showed the connection among cholesterol levels, GSH levels and plaque formation in the aorta. L.L. Ji, D. Dillon and E. Wu showed that decreasing GSH levels as we age contribute to the formation of atherosclerosis. Although antioxidants like vitamins C and E are increasingly considered important, the naturally occurring antioxidant in the cell is GSH. GSH also serves to recycle these other antioxidants into their functionally active form. This is described in chapter 1.

In determining cardiovascular risk factors, certain tests or markers can indicate the risk or existence of heart disease. Two of these are lipoprotein-a (Lp[a]) and Homocysteine. D. Gavish, J.L. Breslow and other researchers have shown the GSH-promoting drug NAC to be very effective in lowering Lp[a] levels. They reported a 50 to 70% reduction using two to four grams of NAC per day—a considerable dose. Other researchers using more tolerable amounts were less successful at reducing Lp[a] but have suggested that NAC may influence atherosclerosis in other ways. They include reduc-

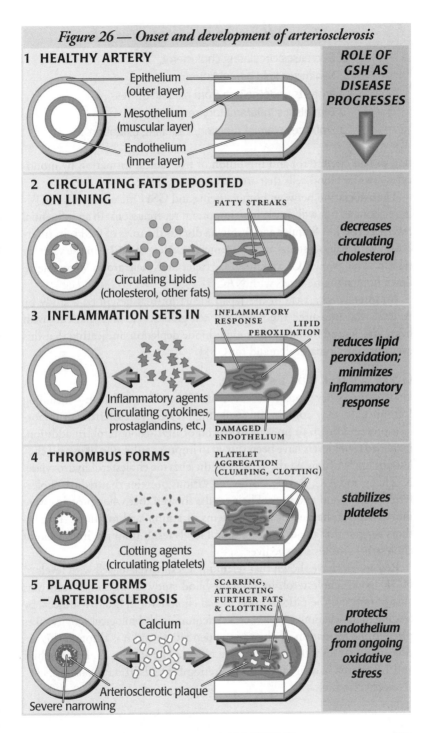

Figure 26 — Onset and development of arteriosclerosis

ROLE OF GSH AS DISEASE PROGRESSES

1 HEALTHY ARTERY

- Epithelium (outer layer)
- Mesothelium (muscular layer)
- Endothelium (inner layer)

2 CIRCULATING FATS DEPOSITED ON LINING

FATTY STREAKS

Circulating Lipids (cholesterol, other fats)

decreases circulating cholesterol

3 INFLAMMATION SETS IN

INFLAMMATORY RESPONSE
LIPID PEROXIDATION

Inflammatory agents (Circulating cytokines, prostaglandins, etc.)

DAMAGED ENDOTHELIUM

reduces lipid peroxidation; minimizes inflammatory response

4 THROMBUS FORMS

PLATELET AGGREGATION (CLUMPING, CLOTTING)

Clotting agents (circulating platelets)

stabilizes platelets

5 PLAQUE FORMS – ARTERIOSCLEROSIS

SCARRING, ATTRACTING FURTHER FATS & CLOTTING

Calcium

Arteriosclerotic plaque

Severe narrowing

protects endothelium from ongoing oxidative stress

Figure 27 — GSH in the fight against arteriosclerosis

- ❏ Decreases circulating cholesterol
- ❏ Minimizes lipid peroxidation
- ❏ Protects endothelium from oxidative stress
- ❏ Diminishes inflammatory response
- ❏ Stabilizes platelet function, inhibiting oxidation

tion of bad cholesterol and inhibition of free radical formation by monocytes—white blood cells that are attracted to platelets.

The association between homocysteine and GSH metabolism is still being elaborated but will clearly have important repercussions. In an influential review article J.S. Stamler and A. Slivka discuss the roles of GSH, its interaction with homocysteine and the protective effect of GSH on the vascular system. The Swedes O. Wiklund, G. Fager and their group were able to lower homocysteine levels with NAC.

An interesting article in the Japan Heart Journal described a study by A. Usal who measured the red blood cell glutathione of 21 patients with heart attacks and found evident glutathione depletion, indicating that this event presents a major demand for GSH.

GSH AND CHOLESTEROL

Undenatured whey proteins raise cellular GSH and some of them—including Immunocal—may contain unusually high levels of lactoferrin, an important protein known to prevent oxidation of LDL-cholesterol. In addition, increased GSH levels have been shown to improve reduction of overall cholesterol levels by raising the activity of the enzyme cholesterol hydroxylase. X. Zhang and A.C. Beynen compared various proteins that reduce cholesterol in the blood and liver. Their results showed that whey proteins were more effective than other milk proteins or amino acid mixtures. The authors suggest that the lower cholesterol levels result from the inhibition of cholesterol synthesis in the liver.

Researchers have shown that selenium levels correlate well with levels of HDL (good) cholesterol. In a double-blind study, P.V. Luoma's team was able to improve the ratio of good to bad cholesterol in healthy subjects by feeding them selenium supplements. Selenium's only biological activity takes place in the formation of glutathione peroxidase and it is through this action that selenium exerts its positive effects. The Italians G. Franceschini and J.P. Werba had similar success altering HDL/LDL ratios using NAC (N-acetylcysteine).

GSH AND REPERFUSION INJURY

If a blood clot deprives tissue of blood and oxygen for more than a very brief period, its ability to produce life-giving energy is compromized. The immune system responds by building up neutrophils, a type of white blood cell, further compounding the damage by releasing even more products of oxidation. When bypass surgery or thrombolytic drugs break down the clot and re-establish oxygen flow, the tissues are said to be "reperfused." But when the fresh blood floods into the starved tissue, it responds with a surge of energy production that places exceptionally heavy oxidative stress on the tissue at the very time that its antioxidant resources have been depleted, paradoxically causing further damage. This condition is called reperfusion injury.

Pharmacologists such as K.S. Kilgore and B.R. Lucchesi from the University of Michigan long ago suggested the antioxidants should be administered alongside thromobolytic therapy. Cardiologists at the University of Brescia in Italy have shown significant glutathione depletion after cardiac ischemia, and the ability of NAC to combat this depletion.

GSH AND CIRCULATION

There are many other ways in which GSH protects blood vessels, but they exceed the scope of this book. They involve the role of GSH in maintaining smooth muscle tone in the vessel wall, the shifts and balance in substances including prostaglandins, leukotrienes, thromboxanes, and platelet factors. For more detailed information consult the references following this chapter.

CONCLUSION

Glutathione has been shown to diminish the oxidation of fats (lipid peroxidation), decrease circulating cholesterol, minimize the inflammatory response around arteriosclerotic plaque, stabilize platelets and protect the sensitive lining of the arteries. These are all important ways to combat hardening of the arteries and subsequent heart disease. Glutathione also diminishes damage to oxygen-deprived tissue during ischemia, and also during the subsequent complications of reperfusion.

Cardiovascular disease has had a huge impact on our population. It is to a great degree preventable, and strategies for raising GSH should go hand-in-hand with a responsible diet and life-style. Such measures can prevent and may even help reverse this all-too-common illness.

REFERENCES TO CHAPTER 9
HEART DISEASE, STROKE & CHOLESTEROL

AMBROSIO G, TRITTO I, GOLINO P. Reactive oxygen metabolites and arterial thrombosis. *Cardiovasc. Research 34:445-452, 1997*

BERENSON GS, Srinivasan SR, Bao W, Newman WP III, Tracy RE, Wattigney WA. Association between multiple, cardiovascular risk factors and atherosclerosis in children and young adults. *New England Journal of Medicine 338: 1650-1656, 1998*

BRESLOW JL, AZROLAN N, BOSTOM A. N-acetylcysteine and lipoprotein. *Lancet 339: 126-127, 1992*

CECONI C, CURELLO S, CARGNONI A, ET AL. The role of glutathione status in the protection against ischaemic and reperfusion damage: effects of N-acetylcysteine. *J. Mol. Cell. Cardiol. 20: 5-13, 1988*

CHENG KM, AGGREY SE, NICHOLS CR, GARNETT ME, GODIN DV. Antioxidant enzymes and atherosclerosis in Japanese quail: Hereditability and genetic correlation estimates. *Canadian Journal of Cardiology 13:669-676, 1997*

DHALLA NS, GOLFMAN L, TAKEDA S, ET AL. Evidence for the role of oxidative stress in acute ischemic heart disease: A brief review. *Can. J. Cardiol. 15: 587-593, 1999*

FRANCHESCHINI G, WERBA JP, SAFA O, ET AL. Dose-related increase of HDL-cholesterol levels after N-acetylcysteine in man. *Pharmacol. Res. 28: 213-218, 1993*

FREI B. Reactive oxygen species and antioxidant vitamins: Mechanisms of action. *American J. Med. 97(suppl 3A): 5S-13S, 1994*

GAVISH D, BRESLOW JL. Lipoprotein[a] reduction by NAC. *The Lancet 337: 203-204, 1991*

GAZIANO JM. Antioxidant vitamins and coronary artery disease risk. *The American Journal of Medicine 97: 3a 18S-3a-21S, 1994*

GAZIANO JM. Randomized trials of dietary antioxidants in cardiovascular disease prevention and treatment. *J. Cardiovascular Risk 3: 368-371, 1996*

HALLIWELL B. Current status review: Free radicals, reactive oxygen species, and human disease: a critical evaluation with special reference to atherosclerosis. *British Journal of Experimental Pathology 70:737-757, 1989*

HANSEN PR. Lipoprotein (a) reduction by N-acetylcysteine. *Lancet 337: 672-673, 1991*

HASSAN AS, HACKLEY JJ, JEFFERY EH. Role of GSH in the regulation of hepatic cholesterol 7a-hydroxylase, the rate-limiting enzyme of bile acid biosynthesis. *Steroids, 44:373-380, 1984*

HENNEKENS CH, GAZIANO JM. Antioxidants and heart disease: Epidemiology and clinical evidence. *Clinical Cardiology 16: I.10-I.15, 1993*

HESS ML, MANSON NH. The oxygen free radical system and myocardial dysfunction. *Advances in Myocardiology 5:177-181, 1985*

HODIS HN, MACK WJ, LABREE L, CASHIN-HEMPHILL L, SEVANIAN A, JOHNSON R, AZEN SP. Serial coronary angiographic evidence that antioxidant vitamin intake reduces progression of coronary artery atherosclerosis. *Journal of the American Medical Association 273: 1849-1854, 1995*

HOFFMAN RM, GAREWAL HS. Antioxidants and the prevention of coronary heart disease. *Archives of Internal Medicine 155: 241-246, 1995*

JI LL, DILLON D, WU E. Myocardial aging: antioxidant enzyme systems and related biochemical properties. *American Journal of Physiology 261:R386-R392, 1991*

KASHIWAGI A, ASAHINA T, NISHIO Y, IKEBUCHI M, TANAKA Y, KIKKAWA R, SHIGETA Y. Glycation, oxidative stress, and scavenger activity: glucose metabolism and radical scavenger dysfunction in endothelial cells. *Diabetes 45: S84-S86, 1996*

KENDALL MJ, NUTTALL SL, MARTIN U. Antioxidant therapy—a new therapeutic option for reducing mortality from coronary artery disease. *J. Clin. Pharm. Ther. 23: 323-325, 1998*

KIDD PM. Cell membranes, endothelia, and atherosclerosis - the importance of dietary fatty acid balance. *Alt. Medicine Reviews 1: 148-167, 1996*

KIDD PM. Glutathione: Systemic protectant against oxidative and free radical damage. *Alternative Medicine Review 2:155-176, 1997*

KILGORE KS, LUCCHESI BR. Reperfusion injury after myocardial infarction: The role of free radicals and the inflammatory response. *Clin. Biochem. 26: 359-370, 1993*

KUBOW S, GOYETTE N, KERMASHA S, STEWART-PHILLIP J, KOSKI K. Effects of dietary lipid and protein composition on serum lipids and tissue lipid peroxidation in the Syrian Hamster. *Inform 3:484, 1992*

LEONCINI G, SIGNORELLO MG, PIANA A, CARRUBBA M, ARMANI U. Hyperactivity and increased hydrogen peroxide formation in platelets of NIDDM patients. *Thrombosis Research 86: 153-160, 1997*

LUOMA PV, SOTANIEMI EA, KORPELA H, KUMPULAINEN J. Serum selenium, glutathione peroxidase activity and high-density lipoprotein cholesterol – effect of selenium supplementation *Res. Commun. Chem. Pathol. Pharmacol. 46: 469-472, 1984*

MEHTA J. Intake of antioxidants among American cardiologists. *American J. Cardiol. 79: 1558-1560, 1997*

MIURA K, ET AL. Cysteine uptake and glutathione level in endothelial cells exposed to oxidative stress. *American Journal of Physiology 262: C50-C58, 1992*

MIZUI T, KINOUCHI H, CHAN PH. Depletion of glutathione by buthionine sulfoximine enhances cerebral ischemic injury in rats. *Am. J. Physiol. 262:H313-H317, 1992*

OCHI H, MORITA I, MUROTA S. Roles of glutathione and glutathione peroxidase in the protection against endothelial cell injury induced by 15-hydroperoxyeicosatetraenoic acid. *Archives of Biochemistry and Biophysiology 294:407-411, 1992*

O'KEEFE JH, LAVIE CJ, MCCALLISTER BD. Insights into the pathogenesis and prevention of coronary artery disease. *Mayo Clinic Proceedings 70: 69-79, 1995*

RIMM EB, STAMPFER MJ. The role of antioxidants in preventive cardiology. *Curr. Opin. Cardiol. 12: 188-194, 1997*

SCANU AM. N-acetylcysteine and immunoreactivity of lipoprotein[a]. *The Lancet 337: 1159, 1991*

STAMLER JS, SLIVKA A. Biological chemistry of thiols in the vasculature and in vascular-related disease. *Nutrition Reviews 54:1-30, 1996*

STAMPFER MJ, MALINOW MR. Can lowering homocysteine levels reduce cardiovascular risk? *The New England Journal of Medicine 332:328-329, 1995*

USAL A, ACARTURK E, YUREGIR GT, ET AL. Decreased glutathione levels in acute myocardial infarction. *Japan Heart J. 37: 177-182, 1996*

WIKLUND O, FAGER G, ANDERSON A, ET AL. N-acetylcysteine treatment lowers plasma homocysteine but not serum lipoprotein(a) levels. *Atherosclerosis 119: 99-106, 1996*

ZHANG X, BEYNEN AC. Lowering effect of dietary milk- whey protein v. casein on plasma and liver cholesterol concentrations in rats. *British Journal of Nutrition 70:139-146, 1993*

ZHOU D, MAYBERG MR, LONDON S, GAJDUSEK C. Reduction of intracellular glutathione levels produces sustained arterial narrowing. *Neurosurgery 39: 991-997, 1996*

CHAPTER 10
DIABETES

Diabetes mellitus or 'sugar diabetes' is the most common glandular condition in North America. It affects 10 to 25 million people, most of whom have yet to be diagnosed. Diabetics run an above-average risk of developing heart disease and stroke, the leading causes of death in the USA and Canada. Given that most types of diabetes and its complications are related to life-style and environment, this is for the most part a preventable problem.

Diabetes mellitus is an insulin disorder that impairs the body's sugar metabolism. The important hormone insulin is responsible for the absorption of sugar into cells for on-demand energy and into the liver and fat cells for energy storage. There are two main types of diabetes mellitus.

In type 1 diabetes mellitus, insulin-producing cells in the pancreas are destroyed. With regular injections of insulin, the patient may lead a normal life. Without it, he or she may lapse into coma and die.

In type 2 diabetes mellitus, pancreatic production of insulin is diminished or the body gradually loses its ability to utilize it. This is by far the most common form of diabetes and is usually linked to bad eating habits, obesity and poor life-style.

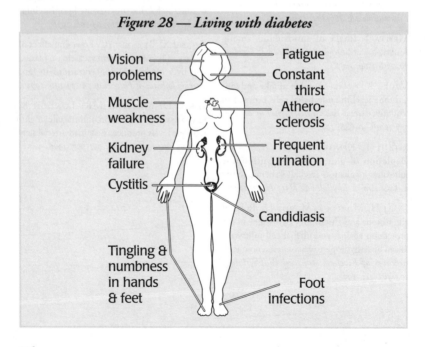

Figure 28 — Living with diabetes

Vision problems
Muscle weakness
Kidney failure
Cystitis
Tingling & numbness in hands & feet
Fatigue
Constant thirst
Athero-sclerosis
Frequent urination
Candidiasis
Foot infections

Both type 1 and type 2 diabetes are generally characterized by high blood sugar (hyperglycemia) but in cases of overmedication or illness/stress during medication blood sugar levels can plummet (hypoglycemia). Both events are potentially serious.

Hyperglycemia produces excessive thirst and urination, fatigue, weight loss, and dehydration. Occasionally, life-threatening illnesses (hyper-osmolar coma or ketoacidosis) may result from excessive sugar levels. These are medical emergencies requiring immediate hospitalization.

Some diabetics take insulin injections or pills to lower sugar levels and are susceptible to the complications of low blood sugar levels. This may happen because they take too much medication, miss a meal, increase their energy expenditures, become sick or febrile, or suffer any sort of stress. This condition too must be treated immediately. Usually, a sweet drink or food is enough and produces rapid results.

Apart from the emergencies resulting from such blood sugar imbalances, most diabetics fall ill from complications of diabetes itself, of which there are two types: reduced ability to fight infection and damage to the circulatory system, including both small and large blood vessels. These complications can cause symptomatic problems with the eyes, muscle, kidneys and bladder. They can also reduce energy levels, promote thirst, and cause tingling in the extremities. Cardiovascular plaque buildup is another result of diabetic complications.

DIABETES AND THE IMMUNE SYSTEM

Diabetics should be considered immune-compromised because they are prone to many more infections than they can normally resist. Their immune systems may be overwhelmed by thrush and other fungal infections of the skin and even of the bloodstream. Bacterial infections are more common and their consequences are serious— gangrene (especially of the toes and foot) and sepsis. Diabetics with any sort of infection must always be treated immediately and aggressively.

Most illness and death in diabetics is due to circulatory damage from heart disease, myocardial infarction, high blood pressure, atherosclerosis, stroke, renal failure, neuropathy, blindness and other effects of impaired blood circulation. In fact, diabetic complications are the major cause of blindness in the USA. Diabetics are also more prone to cataracts and glaucoma (see chapter 17).

GLUTATHIONE'S ROLE IN DIABETES

GSH plays an important role in the fight against diabetes. We have seen that it can prevent circulatory problems such as arteriosclerosis and stroke—

the main causes of diabetic death (see chapter 9). GSH also enhances the immune system. Many visits to the doctor or hospital could be avoided if diabetics were less prone to infection. Elevated GSH levels may help by providing:

❑ Immune system support against infection
❑ Decrease of oxidative stress from hyperglycemia
❑ Decrease of platelet aggregation
❑ Prevention of vascular complications including:
  ■ Atherosclerosis (including heart disease, stroke)
  ■ Nephropathy (kidney damage)
  ■ Retinopathy (retinal damage)
  ■ Neuropathy (nerve damage)

In this way, GSH can help a weakened immune system combat bacterial infection and fungal infection, support compromised circulation against hardening of the arteries (arteriosclerosis), kidney failure (nephropathy), visual loss (retinopathy) and neurological problems (neuropathy). It also retards oxidative stress and anemia in dialysis patients.

It is clear that the small blood vessels of diabetics are subject to accelerated degeneration, but the causes of this particular illness are still being identified. Recent studies demonstrate that diabetics are more prone than others to oxidative stress and free radical formation. In fact, the blood and tissues of diabetics are marked by critically low GSH levels.

R.K. Sundaram's studies suggest that this antioxidant deficiency precedes the subsequent complications of diabetes. K. Yoshida and his research group have shown that low or weak GSH synthesis leads to increased cellular damage and other complications. Going one step further, Thornalley's trials revealed a correspondence between low GSH levels and higher diabetic complications. S.K. Jain and R. McVie suggest that the low GSH levels characteristic of diabetes play a role in impaired insulin secretion in uncontrolled diabetic patients.

Many researchers have established a link between low GSH levels and a higher likelihood of endothelial damage, with increased platelet aggregation.

Other researchers have looked more specifically at the relationship of GSH to isolated complications such as hypertension, diabetic neuropathy and nephropathy, with favorable results. The role of GSH in protecting red blood cells from oxidative damage in the case of renal dialysis is also very promising (see chapter 16).

CASE STUDY

Deana was a motivated, positive entrepreneur who developed a wellness health center even though she suffered from a serious case of diabetes. Increasingly fatigued, this 32 year-old Texan continued to run her center even after receiving and rejecting a kidney transplant, failing eyesight and dialysis treatments. Eventually she developed a chronic foot infection that required weekly debriding of dead tissue. Her doctor feared that amputation might prove necessary. She began taking high doses of the whey protein isolate Immunocal and found her energy levels increased over several weeks. Kidney function tests and hemoglobin levels improved. Medication doses for her anemia and hypertension were decreased or eliminated. Peripheral circulation was better. Five months later the foot was healed. Deana has since married and continues to run her clinic.

CONCLUSION

Circulatory damage contributes substantially to diabetic complications and GSH helps fight the oxidative damage that contributes to this damage. In fact, the blood and tissues of diabetics are marked by critically low GSH levels. These complications could be avoided or minimized if diabetics were less prone to infection, and elevated GSH levels may help accomplish that (see chapter 3).

Bravenboer B, Kappelle AC, Hamers FPT, Van Buren T, Erkelens DW, Gispen WH. Potential use of glutathione for the prevention and treatment of diabetic neuropathy in the streptozotocin-induced diabetic rat. *Diabetologia 35:813-817, 1992*

Ceriello A, Curcio F, dello Russo P, Pegoraro I, Stel G, Amstad P, Cerutti P. The defense against free radicals protects endothelial cells from hyperglycemia-induced plasminogen activator inhibitor 1 over-production. *Blood Coagulation and Fibrinolysis 6:133-137, 1995*

Ceriello A, Giacomello R, Stel G, Motz E, Taboga C, Tonutti L, Pirisi M, Falleti E, Bartoli E. Hyperglycemia-induced thrombin formation in diabetes. The possible role of oxidative stress. *Diabetes 44:924-928, 1995*

Ceriello A, Motz E, Cavarape A, Lizzio S, Russo A, Quatraro A, Giugliano D. Hyperglycemia counterbalances the antihypertensive effect of glutathione in diabetic patients: evidence linking hypertension and glycemia through the oxidative stress in diabetes mellitus. *Journal of Diabetes Complications 11:250-255, 1997*

Ciuchi E, Odetti P, Prando R. Relationship between glutathione and sorbitol concentrations in erythrocytes from diabetic patients. *Metabolism 45:611-613, 1996*

Ciuchi E, Odetti P, Prando R. The effect of acute glutathione treatment on sorbitol level in erythrocytes from diabetic patients. *Diabetes Metabolism 23:58-60, 1997*

Curcio F, Ceriello A. Decreased cultured endothelial cell proliferation in high glucose medium is reversed by antioxidants: new insights on the pathophysiological mechanisms of diabetic vascular complications. *In Vitro Cell Developmental Biology 28A: 787-790, 1992*

Curcio F, Pegoraro I, dello Russo P, Falleti E, Perrella G, Ceriello A. SOD and GSH inhibit the high glucose-induced oxidative damage and the PDGF increased secretion in cultured human endothelial cells. *Thrombolysis and Hemostasis: 74:969-973, 1995*

Di Simplicio P, de Giorgio LA, Cardaioli E, Lecis R, Miceli M, Rossi R, Anichini R, Mian M, Seghieri G, Franconi F. Glutathione, glutathione utilizing enzymes and thioltransferase in platelets of insulin-dependent diabetic patients: relation with platelet aggregation and with microangiographic complications. *European Journal of Clinical Investigation 25:665-669, 1995*

Donnini D, Zambito AM, Perrella G, Ambesi-Impiombato FS, Curcio F. Glucose may induce cell death through a free radical-mediated mechanism. *Biochem Biophys Research Communications 219:412-417, 1996*

Jain SK, McVie R. Effect of glycemic control, race and duration of diabetes on reduced glutathione content in erythrocytes of diabetic patients. *Metabolism 43:306-309, 1994*

Kakkar R, Mantha SV, Radhi J, Prasad K, Kalra J. Antioxidant defense system in diabetic kidney: a time course study. *Life Science 60:667-679, 1997*

Kashiwagi A, Asahina T, Nishio Y, Ikebuchi M, Tanaka Y, Kikkawa R, Shigeta Y. Glycation, oxidative stress, and scavenger activity: glucose metabolism and radical scavenger dysfunction in endothelial cells. *Diabetes 45:S84-S86, 1996*

Low PA, Nickander KK, Tritschler HJ. The roles of oxidative stress and antioxidant treatment in experimental diabetic neuropathy. *Diabetes 46:S38-S42, 1997*

MURAKAMI K, KONDO T, OHTSUKA Y, FUJIWARA Y, SHIMANDA M, KAWAKAMI Y. Impairment of glutathione metabolism in erythrocytes from patients with diabetes mellitus. *Metabolism 38:753-758, 1989*

RUDICH A, KOZLOVSKY N, POTASHNIK R, BASHAN N. Oxidant stress reduces insulin responsiveness in 3T3-L1 adipocytes. *American Journal of Physiology 272:E935-E940, 1997*

SUNDARAM RK, BHASKAR A, VIJAYALINGAM S, VISWANATHAN M, MOHAN R, SHANMUGASUNDARAM KR. Antioxidant status and lipid peroxidation in type II diabetes mellitus with and without complications. *Clinical Science 90:255-260, 1996*

THORNALLEY PJ, MCLELLAN AC, LO TW, BENN J, SONKSEN PH. Negative association between erythrocyte reduced glutathione concentration and diabetic complications. *Clinical Science 91:575-582, 1996*

VIJAYALINGAM S, PARTHIBAN A, SHANMUGASUNDARAM KR, MOHAN V. Abnormal antioxidant status in impaired glucose tolerance and non-insulin-dependent diabetes mellitus. *Diabetic Medicine 13:715-719, 1996*

YOSHIDA K, HIROKAWA J, TAGAMI S, KAWAKAMI Y, URATA Y, KONDO T. Weakened cellular scavenging activity against oxidative stress in diabetes mellitus: regulation of glutathione synthesis and efflux. *Diabetologia 38:201-210, 1995*

CHAPTER 11
THE LIVER AND HEPATITIS

Hepatitis is an inflammation of the liver. The two major types of hepatitis in North America are alcoholic hepatitis (a type of toxic hepatitis) and infectious (viral) hepatitis, usually caused by virus types A, B or C.

Toxic hepatitis

Toxic hepatitis is a non-infectious condition caused by exposure to chemicals that damage the liver. The list of harmful agents is quite extensive, but simple alcohol abuse accounts for the vast majority of cases. Alcoholism tends to be a chronic disease, and this prolonged inflammation often leads to cirrhosis (scarring) of the liver.

Infectious hepatitis

Infectious hepatitis is the most common of all serious infectious diseases in North America. It is estimated that perhaps a half million Americans per year contract the disease. Given the growing prevalence of a relatively new hepatitis virus—type C—this number will likely increase. An accurate count is difficult because most cases of acute hepatitis go undiagnosed or unreported—the illness often feels no more serious than the flu. Other viruses and pathogens can cause hepatitis, but less frequently than hepatitis virus types A, B and C (see figure 29).

The course of the disease is variable. It can range from being totally asymptomatic to causing death in a small percentage of cases. Most people with infectious hepatitis suffer a few weeks of a flu-like illness, consisting of fatigue, aches and pains, mild fever, loss of appetite, abdominal pain, nausea and vomiting. More serious cases exhibit jaundice, dark colored urine, light colored stools, itching, and altered mental states, lapsing occasionally into coma. Most patients experience full recovery, but some progress to chronic hepatitis and possibly cirrhosis.

The extent of liver inflammation determines how poorly the liver works. In hepatic dysfunction it cannot normally filter and eliminate toxins, help digestion, regulate the chemical composition of the blood, process and store nutrients, and other vital functions. The extent of dysfunction can be measured by liver function tests (LFT's), a measure of certain liver enzymes in the blood. LFT's are a sensitive indicator of liver well-being.

Treatment for acute hepatitis usually follows a conservative regimen— lots of rest, good nutrition and plenty of fluids. Special care must be taken to avoid spreading the disease.

Figure 29 — The three main types of viral hepatitis

	HEPATITIS A	HEPATITIS B	HEPATITIS C
Transmission	Fecal contamination of water and food. Feces are infected from two to three weeks before until eight days after onset of jaundice.	Contaminated blood transfusions, sexual exchange of bodily fluids, needle-sharing. Transmission possible from mother to unborn child.	Shared hypodermic needles, unprotected sex and pre-1992 blood transfusions. Transmission possible from mother to unborn child.
Symptoms	Flu-like symptoms such as fatigue, stomach and intestinal pain, appetite loss, nausea, diarrhea, darkened urine and jaundice. Occasionally symptom-free.	Jaundice, fatigue, abdominal pain, joint pain, loss of appetite, nausea and vomiting. May lead to liver cirrhosis or cancer. Most infected people do not develop chronic infection. Occasionally symptom-free.	Usually without acute symptoms. Fatigue, abdominal and joint pain, loss of appetite, jaundice, nausea and vomiting. Can cause chronic liver damage including cirrhosis and cancer.
Traditional treatment	Bed rest, increased fluid intake, Vaccines available. Immunization with immunoglobulin.	Interferon reduces chances of recurrence and is effective in 30-40% of cases. Vaccines available.	Interferon. If not effective, Rebetron, a combination of interferon and ribavirin. No vaccine.
infections per year	Up to 200,000.	From 150,000 to 300,000.	From 28,000 to 180,000.

CHRONIC HEPATITIS

Some cases of toxic or infectious hepatitis turn into chronic hepatitis, which poses a greater problem. Chronic cases are prescribed steroids or interferon. In both cases, benefits need to be weighed against side effects. In toxic hepatitis, the patient must be removed from the offending toxin. This may be challenging when the cause is alcohol.

PREVENTION

The best way to deal with all forms of hepatitis is prevention—proper sanitation and hygiene, screening of blood products, vaccination, avoidance of toxins such as alcohol and intravenous drugs, and avoiding contact with the bodily fluids of infected people.

GSH IN THE LIVER

Hepatologists know that GSH plays a critical role in the liver—it is that organ's most abundant antioxidant enzyme. We have already said that GSH concentrations are higher in the liver than in any other organ. This is because it functions as a substrate for key detoxification processes in the liver (see chapter 2).

Phase I liver detoxification transforms toxins into water-soluble forms. GSH is essential in Phase II, which neutralizes or conjugates these products and helps the body eliminate them through the gut or the kidneys. If these two detoxification phases are impaired for any reason, toxins will accumulate in the body and lead to disease.

Medical science has long known that a GSH deficiency invariably accompanies liver damage. When hepatitis results from acute overdoses of hepatotoxic pharmaceutical drugs such as acetaminophen (Tylenol, Atasol, etc.), the GSH-enhancing drug NAC (N-acetylcysteine) is used to raise GSH levels rapidly. This eliminates the toxic breakdown products of the overdose. The GSH deficiency is critical because it further compounds the illness and can easily lead it on a downward spiral.

Decreased liver production of GSH is seen in alcoholic cirrhosis, sicknesses caused by exposure to hydrocarbons and other toxins, viral hepatitis, fatty livers and even aging individuals. Ongoing research aims to raise GSH levels in an attempt to support liver function in these patients. This approach is even being tried in the treatment of fulminant hepatic failure.

Alcoholic patients with lower GSH levels are more prone to liver damage. This has prompted researchers to try to treat alcoholic liver disease by raising GSH levels, and both clinical symptoms and liver function test results have improved with this method.

GSH IN THE TREATMENT OF VIRAL HEPATITIS

N.S. Weiss and his team at the Max Planck Institute demonstrated the antiviral properties of NAC in human tissue cultures. C. Watanabe found

Figure 30 — Hepatitis C: some important numbers	
Death rate:	10,000 per year and rising. Will triple in next ten years
Prevalence:	4 million Americans; four times more than AIDS
Percentage that will develop chronic hepatitis:	80%
Percentage that will develop cirrhosis:	20%
Percentage that will develop liver cancer:	5%
Success rate of Interferon treatment:	20%

undenatured whey protein, a natural GSH precursor, to be effective in improving liver function abnormalities and immunological parameters in hepatitis B patients. These improvements continued even after the treatment ended, reflecting the long-term benefits of such an approach.

Treatment options for chronic hepatitis C sufferers are far from ideal. G. Barbaro and his team in Italy eloquently described the systemic depletion of GSH in hepatitis C patients, suggesting that this deficiency could explain their resistance to interferon therapy. O. Beloqui's team confirms this in a controlled study of hepatitis C positive individuals. By successfully raising one group's GSH levels with NAC therapy, they showed that interferon therapy was enhanced.

CASE STUDY

When he was young, Roger required multiple blood transfusions for hemophilia, a bleeding disorder. As a young adult his liver was tested for abnormal function and the results revealed that he had acquired hepatitis C, probably from contaminated blood. Worried about the side-effects of antiviral medications and their limited success, he preferred to undergo unconventional treatment. His protocol included milk thistle (silymarin), turmeric (curcuma), alpha lipoic acid, methionine, N-acetylcysteine, and intravenous glutathione as well as a low-meat diet and avoidance of alcohol, acetaminophen and cigarettes. His liver function tests have since normalized.

CONCLUSION

The liver is the largest and most complicated organ in your body. It is intimately linked to a myriad of factors effecting health and illness. GSH is a key constituent of proper liver function. Low GSH levels invite a host of toxicological and immunological diseases. High levels offer protection against these maladies.

REFERENCES TO CHAPTER 11
HEPATITIS

ANKRAH NA, RIKIMARU T, EKUBAN FA, ADDAE MM. Decreased cysteine and glutathione levels: possible determinants of liver toxicity in Ghanaian subjects. *Journal of Int. Medical Research 22:171-176, 1994*

BARBARO G, DI LORENZO G, SOLDINI M, ET AL. Hepatic glutathione deficiency in chronic hepatitis C: quantitative evaluation in patients who are HIV positive and HIV negative and correlations with plasmatic and lymphocytic concentrations and with the activity of the liver disease. *American Journal of Gastroenterology 91:2569-2573, 1996*

BELOQUI O, PRIETO J, SUAREZ M, GIL B, QIAN CH, GARCIA N, CIVEIRA MP. N-acetyl cysteine enhances the response to interferon-α in chronic hepatitis C: a pilot study. *Journal of Interferon Research 13:279-282, 1993*

BRESCI G, PICCINOCCHI M, BANTI S. The use of reduced glutathione in alcoholic hepatopathy. *Minerva Medicine 82:753-755, 1991*

DENTICO P, VOLPE A, BUONGIORNO R, ET AL. Glutathione in the treatment of chronic fatty liver diseases. *Recent. Prog. Med. 86:290-293, 1995*

FARINATI F, CARDIN R, DE MARIA N, ET AL. Iron storage, lipid peroxidation and glutathione turnover in chronic anti-HCV positive hepatitis. *Journal of Hepatology 22:449-456, 1995*

HARRISON PM, WENDON JA, GIMSON AES, ALEXANDER GJM, WILLIAMS R. Improvement by acetylcysteine of hemodynamics and oxygen transport in fulminant hepatic failure. *New England Journal of Medicine 324:1852-1857, 1991*

JEWELL SA, DI MONTE D, GENTILE A, GUGLIELMI A, ALTOMARE E, ALBANO O. Decreased hepatic glutathione in chronic alcoholic patients. *Journal of Hepatology 3:1-6, 1986*

Lieber CS. Susceptibility to alcohol-related liver injury. *Alcohol 2(supple):315-326, 1994*

LOGUERCIO C, TARANTO D, VITALE LM, BENEDUCE F, DEL VECCHIO, BLANCO C. Effect of liver cirrhosis and age on the glutathione concentration in the plasma, erythrocytes, and gastric mucosa. *Free Radical Biology Medicine 20:483-488, 1996*

MULDER TP, JANSSENS AR, DE BRUIN WC, ET AL. Plasma glutathione S-transferase alpha 1-1 levels in patients with chronic liver disorders. *Clin. Chim. Acta 258:69-77, 1997*

NARDI EA, DEVITO R, CECCANTI M. High-dose glutathione in the therapy of alcoholic hepatopathy. *Clinical Ter. 136:47-51, 1991*

PRESSMAN AH. The GSH Phenomenon *St. Martin's Press, New York NY, 1997*

PROCEEDINGS of the 16th International *Congress of Nutrition. Montreal, PR514, 1997*

SAVOLAINEN VT, PJARINEN J, PEROLA M, PENTTILA A, KARHUNEN PJ. Glutathione S-transferase GST M1 "null" genotype and the risk of alcoholic liver disease. *Alcohol Clinical Experimental Research 20:1340-1345, 1996*

WATANABE A, HIGUCHI K, OKADA Y, SHIMIZU Y, KONDO Y, KOHRI H. Treatment of chronic hepatitis using whey protein (non-heated)

WATANABE A, HIGUCHI K, YASUMURA Y, SHIMIZU Y, KONDO Y, KOHRI H. Nutritional modulation of glutathione level and cellular immunity in chronic hepatitis B and C. *Hepatology 24: pt2: 597A*

WEISS L, HILDT E, HOFSCHNEIDER PH. Anti-hepatitis B virus activity of N-acetyl-L-cysteine (NAC): New aspects of a well-established drug. *Antiviral Research 32:43-53, 1996*

CHAPTER 12
AIDS

The spread of AIDS (acquired immune deficiency syndrome) is the most serious health crisis of our time and has reached epidemic proportions worldwide. In many American cities and other areas of the world it is the leading cause of death for 25 to 45 year-olds. Because of widespread AIDS research, the scientific community has learned more about viruses and the immune system in the last few years than in the previous ninety.

Human immunodeficiency virus (HIV)

AIDS is linked to the human immunodeficiency virus (HIV), which is particularly destructive to the victim's T-cell lymphocytes—a type of white blood cell necessary for effective immune response. There are three types—killer T-cells, helper T-cells and suppressor T-cells. Helper cells—which signal the presence of antigens so the body can effectively counter them— are destroyed by HIV, preempting the build-up of killer cells that ordinarily combat viruses. The result is immune-deficiency. The AIDS virus does not kill directly, but leaves the victim defenseless against even the most innocuous disease organisms.

Long-term prospects for AIDS sufferers are slowly improving, and much can be done in the short-term. With good care the worst symptoms can be avoided for years and the patient can lead a productive life. As more is known about the disease and its spread, more effective treatments will emerge. There is widespread hope for a cure within the next decade.

Many pharmacological and naturopathic medications are promoted as possible AIDS therapies, both for treatment and prevention. These have varying levels of success but at a cost—many pharmacological drugs are toxic, and while they help in their own ways to fight the disease, they exact a heavy toll in other ways, both physical and financial. There are certainly no miracle cures. Some therapies help, some are hazardous. Nevertheless, a combination of treatments is more effective than any one alone, so most AIDS patients adopt one of several regimens known as drug cocktails.

The worst aspects of the disease are secondary to HIV itself. Because the immune system has been compromised, it cannot respond adequately to most sorts of infection. These infections, not the HIV, cause disease.

The role of GSH in AIDS

Much attention is therefore paid to the role of GSH in AIDS patients. Among other things, the disease causes chronic inflammatory change and oxidative stress. These activities consume GSH and lead to dysfunction in CD4 helper cells. Once T-cells lose their efficiency, the patient becomes

Figure 31 — Normal immune response (left) and immune response of AIDS patients (right)

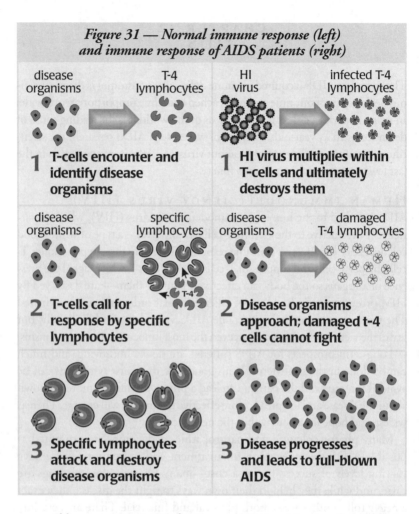

disease organisms — T-4 lymphocytes | HI virus — infected T-4 lymphocytes

1 T-cells encounter and identify disease organisms

1 HI virus multiplies within T-cells and ultimately destroys them

disease organisms — specific lymphocytes | disease organisms — damaged T-4 lymphocytes

2 T-cells call for response by specific lymphocytes

2 Disease organisms approach; damaged t-4 cells cannot fight

3 Specific lymphocytes attack and destroy disease organisms

3 Disease progresses and leads to full-blown AIDS

susceptible to opportunistic infections, such as certain types of pneumonia, diarrhea, candida and unusual cancers—diseases to which healthy individuals are immune. The immuno-deficiency becomes generalized and leads to malnutrition, wasting and death.

Researchers led by M. Roederer have discovered that, among other biochemical changes, AIDS patients experience unusually low GSH concentrations. Some have reported that GSH levels in the blood fall to about 30% of normal. They suggest that this deficiency contributes to the typical feature of HIV infection—progressive weakening of the immune system. Others assign GSH a proactive role, saying that the inflammatory cytokines that make HIV growth possible are inhibited by elevated GSH concentrations. They demonstrated this effect by raising GSH levels with drugs like

NAC (N-acetyl-cysteine). The same team in 1991 showed how the loss of CD4 and CD8 T-cell GSH corresponds to the progression of the disease.

In 1992, a team led by Dr. Gustavo Bounous investigated the properties of milk protein isolates at McGill University, Montreal. They developed a method of extraction that preserved the GSH-enhancing properties of the protein. The product was later patented and named Immunocal.

Dr. Bounous and his colleagues knew that heightened GSH levels seemed to enhance the human immune system. Learning of the correlation between HIV progression and low GSH levels, they studied its effects on AIDS patients. Their milk-protein isolate was given as a dietary supplement. The results were that it often diminished and sometimes reversed the wasting effects of AIDS. These patients also exhibited elevated CD4 T-cell counts and decreased viral load.

The natural availability of GSH precursors was welcome news to the AIDS research community. Immunocal was presented at the Canadian Conference on HIV/AIDS Research in 1994 by Baruchel, Olivier and Mark Wainberg, the incumbent chairman of the International AIDS Research Association. Dr. Luc Montagnier, co-discoverer of the AIDS virus, drew attention to the promising effects of Immunocal in his opening address at the Tenth International AIDS conference in Japan in 1994.

Baruchel, Bounous and Gold's research with Immunocal was significant enough to receive funding from the Canadian HIV Trials Network, and a large multi-center study is in progress.

The Center for Disease Control (CDC), Atlanta reported on their AIDS web page in February 1997:

"...laboratory studies have shown that a new whey protein concentrate, called Immunocal, can inhibit HIV replication while also stimulating the production of GSH, an amino acid that helps control the virus."

In a landmark 1997 paper Herzenberg and Herzenberg clearly stated that GSH deficiency is associated with decreased survival in HIV disease. They improved survival rates by administering NAC (a GSH-promoting drug). Given the growing body of evidence demonstrating the benefits of raising GSH levels in AIDS patients, this represents a welcome addition to complementary therapy.

Case study

The first member of this family of three to be diagnosed with AIDS was the father Bob, who developed pneumonia at age forty-four. His wife Joan who developed swollen glands (lymphadenopathy), tested positive shortly afterwards. Subsequently they discovered that their

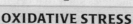

Figure 32 — Role of GSH loss in AIDS

> ## CHRONIC INFLAMMATION
> inflammatory cytokines normally blocked by
> GSH stimulate production of latent virus

➕

> ## OXIDATIVE STRESS
> depletion of antioxidants; cellular damage

⬇

> ## LOSS OF GSH
> ## (GLUTATHIONE)

⬇

> ## T-CELL DYSFUNCTION
> loss of CD-4 lymphocytes

⬇   ⬇

> ## ATYPICAL
> ## CANCERS
> Karposi's sarcoma

> ## OPPORTUNISTIC
> ## INFECTION
> pneumonia,
> encephalitis,
> diarrhea, etc.

⬇   ⬇

> ## MALNUTRITION
> ## WASTING DISEASE

⬇

> ## DEATH

two-year old son Justin was also HIV-positive, although he was asymptomatic. Both Bob and Joan became progressively unwell and Bob quit his job due to fatigue. Both were started on the antiviral drug AZT, but both discontinued this therapy because of intolerable side-effects. Because of her vomiting and profound headaches on the drug, Joan decided not to allow her son to receive this therapy. Bob, Joan and Justin were started on Immunocal. Both husband and wife noticed significant increase in their energy levels within weeks, Monitoring the families' blood tests over the next nine months, improvements in viral load, lymphocyte (white blood cell) count and specific CD4 lymphocyte values were apparent. Bob returned to work, Justin remained symptom-free and Joan wanted another child but was convinced not to pursue this idea.

CONCLUSION

AIDS attacks the immune system and is characterized by decreased GSH levels and a general lack of resistance to pathogens. In fact, glutathione deficiency is associated with decreased survival in HIV disease. Scientific studies have shown that supplementation aimed at maintaining GSH levels can diminish and sometimes reverse the wasting effect of AIDS. The patients studied in these experiments often also exhibit elevated CD-4 lymphocyte cell counts and decreased viral loads. As a result of these and many other AIDS trials, larger studies should establish glutathione supplementation as a mainstay of complementary therapy.

AIDS

BARUCHEL S, BOUNOUS G, GOLD P. Place for an antioxidant therapy in HIV infection *Oxidative Stress, Cell Activation and Viral Infection* C. PASQUIER ED. *1994*

BARUCHEL S, VIAU G, OLIVIER R, BOUNOUS G. Nutriceutical modulation of glutathione with a humanized native milk serum protein isolate, Immunocal. Application in AIDS and cancer in: *Oxidative Stress in Cancer, AIDS and Neurodegenerative Diseases. Institute Pasteur. Editors* MONTAGNIER L, OLIVIER R, PASQUIER C. MARCEL DEKKER, *1998*

BARUCHEL S, WAINBERG MA. The role of oxidative stress in disease progression in individuals infected by HIV. *Journal of Leukocyte Biology 52:111-114, 1992*

BOUNOUS G, BARUCHEL S, FALUTZ J, GOLD P. Whey proteins as a food supplement in HIV-seropositive individuals *Clinical Investigative Medicine 16(3):204-209, 1993*

BUHL R, JAFFE HA, HOLROYD KJ ET AL. Systemic glutathione deficiency in symptom-free HIV seropositive individuals *Lancet ii:1294-1298, 1989*

HARMSEN MC, SWART PJ, DE BETHUNE MP, PAUWELSR, DE CLERCQ E, THE TH, MEIJER DKF. Antiviral effects of plasma and milk proteins: Lactoferrin shows potent activity against both human immunodeficiency virus and human cytomegalovirus replication in vitro. *The Journal of Infectious Diseases 172:380-388, 1995*

HERZENBERG LA, DE ROSA SC, DUBS JG, ROEDERER M, ANDERSON MT, ELA SW, DERESINSKI SC, HERZENBERG LA. Glutathione deficiency is associated with impaired survival in HIV disease. *Proceedings of the National Academy of Science USA 94:1967-1972, 1997*

KALEBIC T, KINTER A, POLI G, ANDERSON ME, MEISTER A, FAUCI A. Suppression of human immunodeficiency virus expression in chronically infected monocytic cells by glutathione, glutathione ester, and N-acetylcysteine. *Proceedings of the National Academy of Science USA 88:986-990, 1991*

KAMEOKA M, OKADA Y, TOBIUME M, KIMURA T, IKUTA K. Intracellular glutathione as a possible direct blocker of HIV type I reverse transcription. *AIDS Research and Human Retroviruses 12(17):1635-1638, 1996*

PALAMARA AT, PERNO CF, AQUARO S, BUE MC, DINI L, GARACI E. Glutathione inhibits HIV replication by acting at late stages of the virus life cycle. *AIDS Research and Human Retroviruses 12(16):1537-1541, 1996*

ROEDERER M, STAAL FJT, OSADA H, HERZENBERG LA, HERZENBERG LA. CD4 and CD8 T cells with high intracellular glutathione levels are selectively lost as the HIV infection progresses. *International Immunology 3(9):993-937, 1991*

ROEDERER M, STAAL FJ, RAJU PA, ELA SW, HERZENBERG LA, HERZENBERG LA. Cytokine-stimulated human immunodeficiency virus replication is inhibited by N-acetyl-L-cysteine. *Proceedings of the National Academy of Science USA 87:4884-4888, 1990*

STAAL FJT, ELA SW, ROEDERER M, ANDERSON MT, HERZENBERG LA, HERZENBERG LA. Glutathione deficiency and human immunodeficiency virus infection *Lancet 339:909-912, 1992*

VALLIS KA. Glutathione deficiency and radiosensitivity in AIDS *patients Lancet 337:918-919, 1991*

CHAPTER 13
MULTIPLE SCLEROSIS

Multiple sclerosis (MS) has in recent times been referred to as "the great crippler of young adults." It usually strikes victims in the prime of their life and is one of the most dreaded degenerative diseases of the nervous system. The symptoms of MS are quite variable, ranging from one or two attacks of weakness in a limb or blurred vision, to a relentless, progressive deterioration of speech, movement and other basic functions.

MS affects various parts of the nervous system by destroying myelin, a fatty sheath that insulates nerve fibers rather as a plastic sheath insulates electrical wire. This destruction leaves scars or *plaques* that short-circuit the electrical signals passing through the nerve fibers. The scarring process is called sclerosis. Figure 33 shows the degeneration of the myelin sheath.

Depending on the nerves affected, patients may suffer localized weakness or stiffness, visual difficulties, diminished bladder or bowel control and other neurological dysfunctions. Attacks may be mild, lasting only days and followed by remission, but most sufferers relapse after months or years. A few experience rapid progression of the disease and are quickly disabled.

The causes of MS are still unclear. However, many theories have been put forward. Some point to environmental and/or genetic factors, and some researchers believe that certain viruses may be involved, or view MS as an autoimmune ailment (in which the immune system mistakenly attacks healthy tissue). Others are investigating dietary factors or exposure to toxins such as lead, mercury, pesticides and carbon monoxide. Yet another theory considers the role of allergies.

Conventional medicine treats the symptoms of MS but cannot cure it. However, some newer drugs show promise in diminishing the rate of relapse. Diets of all sorts have been widely tested without consistent results. Everything about this disease is difficult to study because symptoms vary so widely, patients often recover spontaneously and one can never be sure whether or not a treatment has been instrumental.

Multiple sclerosis is one of a group of nervous system diseases called neurodegenerative disorders that also includes Alzheimer's, Parkinson's and ALS (amyotrophic lateral sclerosis or Lou Gehrig's disease). Although their specific causes are unknown, a number of studies suggest that a large role is played by oxygen-derived free radical formation and/or inadequate antioxidant defenses.

OXIDATION AND MULTIPLE SCLEROSIS
The myelin sheaths destroyed by MS are made of lipids, fatty substances highly sensitive to damage by lipid peroxidation, a particularly agressive

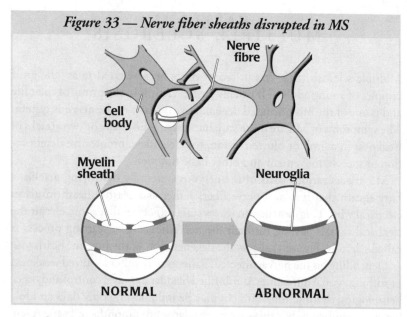

Figure 33 — Nerve fiber sheaths disrupted in MS

Nerve fibre

Cell body

Myelin sheath

Neuroglia

NORMAL   ABNORMAL

type of oxidation. Our key metabolic defenses are GSH and SOD (super-oxide dismutase). It has been shown that elevating these natural defense systems reduces the damage of oxidative stress.

Investigations looking specifically at the breakdown products of oxidation have revealed significantly higher levels in MS patients. Pradlip Toshniwal and Edwin Zarling from Loyola University in Chicago went one step further in their studies. They were able to show that these levels of oxidative stress corresponded to the severity of the MS attack.

Some authors including S.M. LeVine from the University of Kansas suggest that the pathological process leading to the demyelination of nerves is possible because the immune system cooperates with a free radical generating system present within the myelin sheaths. This explanation combines the two hypotheses that describe MS—that it is an autoimmune disease, and is also caused by oxidative stress. He describes how during a demyelination episode, macrophages (cells of the immune system that are supposed to act protectively) seek out myelin and release powerful chemicals (lipases, proteinases, H_2O_2 and others). These biochemicals result in tremendous levels of oxidative stress.

Such a hypothesis leads us to believe that either blunting the immune response or minimizing oxidative stress could help MS patients. Immunosuppressive drugs that blunt the immune response have had only limited success. This has driven researchers to find ways to improve antioxidant protection, glutathione modulation being one of the most promising areas.

Glutathione and multiple sclerosis

Many studies have compared groups of MS patients to healthy individuals. Among other things, they have measured levels of reactive metabolites (breakdown products of oxidation) and of protective enzymes, especially GSH.

An Italian group headed by Vince Calabrese drew samples of cerebrospinal fluid (CSF) through spinal taps. CSF analysis is a good indicator of brain metabolism. They found that GSH-peroxidase levels in the cerebrospinal fluid of MS patients were consistently low. Their conclusion was that in MS, the fundamental activity of anti-oxidation is abnormal and that oxidative stress plays a causative role.

Another study looking at CSF was performed by the Swedes G. Ronquist and G. Frithz who tested spinal taps from a large number of patients including those with stroke, seizures, brain tumors and MS. The cerebrospinal fluid of MS patients was found to be almost entirely lacking in GSH.

There is further evidence of the involvement of free radical elevation and GSH depletion in MS. Helen Langemann in Switzerland measured GSH levels within MS plaques themselves. Without exception, they were depleted.

Researchers led by I. Singh at the University of South Carolina examined the fundamental tissue abnormality in multiple sclerosis. The actual myelin breakdown occurs to a large part because of the release of strong inflammatory chemicals called cytokines. These cytokines generate huge numbers of free radicals. Pre-treating neurological tissues with NAC (N-acetylcysteine) to raise glutathione levels protected these tissues from demyelination. Conversely, when GSH was chemically depleted, the demyelination grew worse.

Simpler studies demonstrating decreased blood levels of GSH peroxidase in MS patients have been repeated by many Scandinavian, Italian and North American researchers. These levels as well can be inversely correlated with the degree of severity of the attack.

Selenium and multiple sclerosis

Some research suggests that low selenium levels are connected to the development of MS. Selenium is an essential part of the GSH peroxidase enzyme and low selenium levels certainly decrease GSH effectiveness. A Danish team led by J. Mai supplied high-dose antioxidant supplements to MS patients made up of 6 mg selenium, 2 g vitamin C, and 480 mg of vitamin E. These patients showed few side effects and glutathione peroxidase activity increased by a factor of five within five weeks.

Conclusion

MS is a difficult disease to study because its spontaneous remissions and relapses make it very unpredictable. It is therefore hard to correlate any sort of intervention with changes in a patient's condition. In order to be statistically significant, prospective trials would have to include hundreds of subjects.

However, certain findings have been demonstrated consistently in multiple sclerosis patients. The breakdown products of oxidative stress are present in large numbers, and the level of free radical formation corresponds to the severity of the MS attack. Furthermore, glutathione activity is clearly impaired in this disease.

Also, individual tissues suffer less free radical damage when antioxidants and glutathione therapy are used. Although not a cure, many authors have suggested that reduced oxidative damage would help MS patients, and suggest in particular the helpful role of elevated GSH levels.

MULTIPLE SCLEROSIS

CALABRESE V, RAFFAELE R, COSENTINO E, RIZZA V. Changes in cerebrospinal fluid levels of malondialdehyde and GSH reductase activity in multiple sclerosis. *International Journal of Clinical Pharmacology Research* 14(4):119-123, 1994

CLAUSEN J, JENSEN GE, NIELSEN SA. Selenium in chronic neurologic diseases. Multiple sclerosis and Batten's disease. *Biological Trace Element Research* 15:179-203, 1988

GUY J, ELLIS EA, HOPE GM, RAO NA. Antioxidant enzymes reduce loss of blood-brain barrier integrity in experimental optic neuritis. *Archives of Ophthalmology* 107(9): 1359-63 1989

JENNER P. Oxidative damage in neurodegenerative disease. *Lancet* 344:796-798, 1994

JENSEN GE, CLAUSEN J. Glutathione peroxidase and reductase, glucose-6-phosphate dehydrogenase and catalase activities in multiple sclerosis. *J. Neurol. Sci.* 63:45-53, 1984

KARG E, KLIVENYI P, NEMETH I, ET AL. Nonenzymatic antioxidants of blood in multiple sclerosis. *J. Neurol.* 246:533-539, 1999

KNIGHT JA. Reactive oxygen species and the neurodegenerative disorders. *Annals of Clinical Laboratory Science* 27(1):11-25, 1997

KORPELA H, KINNUNEN E, JUNTUNEN J, KUMULAINEN J, KOSKENVUO M. Serum selenium concentration, GSH peroxidase activity and lipid peroxides in a co-twin control study on multiple sclerosis. *Journal of the Neurological Sciences* 91(1-2):79-84, 1989

LANGEMANN H, KABIERSCH A, NEWCOMBE J. Measurement of low-molecular-weight antioxidants, uric acid, tyrosine and tryptophan in plaques and white matter from patients with multiple sclerosis. *European Neurology* 32(5):248-252, 1992

LE VINE SM. The role of reactive oxygen species in the pathogenesis of multiple sclerosis. *Medical Hypothesis* 39(3):271-274, 1992

MAI J, SORENSON PS, HANSEN JC. High dose antioxidant supplementation to MS patients. Effects on GSH peroxidase, clinical safety and absorption of selenium. *Biological Trace Element Research* 24(2):109-117, 1990

MAZZELLA GL, SINFORIANI E, SAVOLDI F, ALLEGRINI M, LANZOLA E, SCELSI R. Blood cells GSH peroxidase activity and selenium in multiple sclerosis. *European Neurology* 22(6):442-446, 1983

POLIDORO G, DI ILIO C, ARDUINI A, LA ROVERE G, FEDERICI G. Superoxide dismutase, reduced GSH and TBA-reactive products in erythrocytes of patients with multiple sclerosis. *International Journal of Biochemistry* 16(5):505-509, 1984

RONQUIST G, FRITHZ G. Adenylate kinase activity and GSH concentration of cerebrospinal fluid in different neurological disorders. *European Neurology* 18(2):106-110, 1979

SHUKLA VK, JENSEN GE, CLAUSEN J. Erythrocyte GSH peroxidase deficiency in multiple sclerosis. *Acta Neurology Scandinavia* 56(6):542-550, 1977

SIMONIAN NA, COYLE JT. Oxidative stress in neurodegenerative diseases. *Annual Review of Pharmacology & Toxicology* 36:83-106, 1996

SINGH I, PAHAN K, KHAN M, SINGH AK. Cytokine-mediated induction of ceramide production is redox-sensitive. Implications to proinflammatory cytokine-mediated apoptosis in demyelinating diseases. *J. Biol. Chem.* 273:20354-20362, 1998

SZEINBERG A, GOLAN R, BEN EZZER J, SAROVA-PINHAS I, SADEH M, BRAHAM J. Decreased erythrocyte GSH peroxidase activity in multiple sclerosis. *Acta Neurology Scandinavia* 60(5):265-271, 1979

TOSHNIWAL PK, ZARLING EJ. Evidence for increased lipid peroxidation in multiple sclerosis. *Neurochemistry Research* 17(2):205-207, 1992

CHAPTER 14
LUNG DISEASE

One of the most distressing symptoms that anyone can experience is short-ness of breath—dyspnea. Patients describe themselves as 'not getting enough air.' This triggers a series of physiological and behavioral reactions that in-clude increased heart rate, blood pressure and hormonal secretions accom-panied by a feeling of general panic. Shortness of breath is a common symp-tom of many respiratory illnesses.

Just as the gut separates and absorbs food into the body, the lungs are a passage for the exchange of used air and fresh air. But there's a crucial differ-ence between food and oxygen—we can't store oxygen. We must meet a second-by-second demand for the life-giving element or die within min-utes. The body responds immediately to any interference with this exchange.

Over 30 million Americans are affected by chronic lung disease. Dozens of illnesses can affect the respiratory system, and pulmonary (lung-related) medicine is vast and complicated. It deals with congenital problems like cystic fibrosis, acquired diseases like bronchitis and self-inflicted problems like smoking. The importance of GSH in the respiratory system cannot be overstated. We can't address every known respiratory problem but we will discuss a large number of common and not-so-common ailments, including:

❏ Asthma
❏ Bronchitis, acute and chronic
❏ Chronic obstructive pulmonary disease (COPD)
❏ Emphysema
❏ Adult respiratory distress syndrome (ARDS)

❏ Cystic fibrosis
❏ Pulmonary fibrosis
❏ Cancer
❏ Pneumonia
❏ Toxic exposures
❏ Tobacco abuse

ANTIOXIDANTS AND THE LUNGS

As you will see in the following pages, inflammation of the lung is common to most pulmonary diseases, whether the disorder is acute—like toxic expo-sure—or chronic—like cystic fibrosis. The processes of infection in asthma, bronchitis or pneumonia all lead to inflammation. Many traditional medica-tions attempt to reduce this inflammation. The body's inflammatory response itself generates free radicals, and antioxidants are increasingly used to comple-ment conventional treatments. The researchers P.E. Morris and G.R. Bernard drew attention to this complementary treatment in an article aptly called "Significance of glutathione in lung disease and implications for therapy," in which they reviewed the great weight of evidence that supports such research.

There is a fragile balance in the lungs between oxidants and antioxidants.

Oxidative stress is high in the lungs for many reasons. For a start, this center of oxygen interchange produces very large numbers of oxyradicals. Secondly, white blood cells are highly active in the lining of the lungs, where they release huge quantities of oxidative products, both because of their high metabolic rates and the way they combat biological and chemical invaders. Finally, antioxidants in the fluid lining of the lungs play a large part in our front-line defense against airborne pollutants, many of which are powerful sources of free radicals.

When white blood cells encounter, for example, a bacteria, they release caustic substances like peroxides. This is biochemical warfare, and the white blood cell and the surrounding tissues use GSH to defend themselves. When oxidant levels grow too high or GSH levels too low, the inevitable result is tissue damage. Remember that GSH is the most critical of all naturally-occurring antioxidants (see chapter 1) and that it effectively supports exogenous antioxidants such as vitamins C and E. Unlike glutathione, exogenous antioxidants are derived from the outside environment and are not native to the body, but together they soak up free radicals.

Generally, most tissues and organs must manufacture their own glutathione from dietary or drug-delivered precursors. However, the lining of the respiratory tree— which usually requires high levels of GSH—can absorb GSH directly. To take advantage of this unusual ability, a topical GSH aerosol has been developed and used successfully to treat a number of diseases, including adult respiratory distress syndrome (ARDS), pulmonary fibrosis and HIV

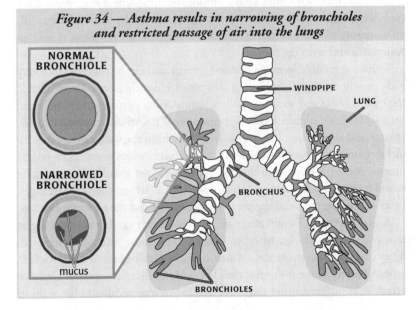

Figure 34 — Asthma results in narrowing of bronchioles and restricted passage of air into the lungs

NORMAL BRONCHIOLE

NARROWED BRONCHIOLE

mucus

WINDPIPE

LUNG

BRONCHUS

BRONCHIOLES

infection. In addition, the topical form of NAC (Mucomist)—a potent GSH precursor—has long been used as a treatment for cystic fibrosis.

Oral and intravenous GSH precursors are receiving a lot of attention from researchers and many papers have been published on the subject. Pulmonologists (lung doctors) are paying increasing attention to lung GSH content and learning a great deal about future applications. O. Ortolani and his team in Italy placed forty intensive care patients with respiratory difficulties on intravenous GSH, then compared their response to an equal number of untreated patients and found significant reductions in oxidative stress levels.

An experiment in preventive medicine was conducted by S. De Flora and his research team at the Institute of Hygiene and Preventive Medicine, University of Genoa. Patients were placed on a course of oral NAC tablets or placebo during the months of the influenza season. Although the number of people infected by the virus was unchanged, subjects receiving NAC experienced significantly fewer and less virulent symptoms.

ASTHMA

Bronchial asthma causes constriction of the bronchioles (airway passages). Figure 34 shows the windpipe and lungs, and cross-sections of normal and narrowed air passages (bronchioles). Asthma is always unpleasant and sometimes even fatal. The intensity of asthma attacks vary, but all are characterized by a feeling of tightness in the chest, shortness of breath, restlessness, coughing and wheezing. Although asthma is reversible and intermittent, it tends to recur and is generally considered a chronic condition. It is one of the most common causes of absenteeism and hospital admission in school-age children, among whom it is most prevalent. It currently affects about 15 million Americans and is on the rise.

Asthma is variable in frequency and severity and can be triggered by a very wide variety of stimuli, including allergens (things that provoke an allergic response). These include dust, pollen, dander (tiny particles of animal skin, fur and feather), certain foods and drugs, viral infections, emotional stress, anxiety and even plain old exercise. Muscles within the walls of the bronchioles flex and go into spasm, the walls thicken, air passages become clogged by mucus, and air is trapped in the deepest airways (the alveoli). The wheezing sound is caused by air passing with difficulty through these narrowed passages. In its severest form, breathing becomes impossible and the patient suffocates.

Asthma sufferers should make an effort to identify and avoid the triggers that cause their attacks, whether allergic, infectious, toxic, or emotional. They can also take preventative medications—antihistamines and sodium cromoglycate. These minimize the effects of the allergic response. Once an attack is in progress other drugs are needed to reopen (dilate) the walls of the bronchioles. These are called bronchodilators and are commonly used in inhalers such as salbutemol or albuterol. Inhaled or ingested steroids are also available. They minimize the swelling and inflammation of the bronchial walls. In any case, once an attack has begun, treatment must be immediate and aggressive. The longer an attack lasts, the more the symptoms advance and the longer they take to reverse. There is little time to waste.

It has been long thought that low levels of glutathione and glutathione peroxidase levels play a role in the onset and progression of asthma. Numerous studies in asthmatics have identified such abnormalities in their red-blood GSH, white-blood cell GSH, serum GSH, platelet GSH and lung-fluid GSH. There is a direct correspondence between low glutathione levels and the severity of the asthma attack.

Dietary, environmental, and genetic factors that diminish the potency of the antioxidant systems in the lung increase the risk of asthma. This relationship between antioxidant levels and asthma is seen in situations of elevated free-radical activity. Examples are lead poisoning, excessive iron stores and G6PD-deficiency, as well as low levels of vitamin C, vitamin E, and selenium (a component of glutathione peroxidase).

The pulmonologist Dr. Carol Trenga recently presented to the American Lung Association an antioxidant cocktail that helped asthmatics particularly sensitive to air pollutants. European physicians have long used GSH precursors in the treatment of asthma, particularly as a mucolytic (phlegm thinner) to break down thick secretions. In a double-blind study, inhaled bronchodilators were tested with and without NAC. The NAC (GSH-enhanced) group experienced greater improvement in lung function than the control group.

CASE STUDY
Jean-Pierre, a financial analyst, suffered from allergies and asthma his whole life. Summers were particularly bad and he often had to leave his native Montreal for weeks in August to escape the ragweed allergy season. In early summer, he was started on a program of NAC (N-acetylcysteine), L-cysteine, selenium, alpha-lipoic acid, multivitamins and stinging nettle (Urtica dioici). That season, he reported having to use his Ventolin inhaler (salbutemol, a bronchodilator for asthma) only two or three times a week, rather than two or three times a day, and his use of antihistamine drugs was at a minimum. He's even ventured to go camping with his girlfriend.

BRONCHITIS, EMPHYSEMA, AND COPD
Bronchitis is an inflammation or obstruction of the bronchi, the larger airways that eventually branch out to become the bronchioles (the site of

asthma). It resembles asthma in some ways, their common symptoms being shortness of breath, a phlegm-producing cough, chest discomfort and occasional wheezing. Bronchitis has two distinct forms—acute or chronic. They differ in important ways.

Acute bronchitis is almost always caused by infection, either viral or bacterial. Coughing, chest pains, fever and chills are common complaints. In the healthy individual, it is usually a short-lived illness that clears up once the infection is overcome. If the infection is bacterial or mycoplasmal, antibiotics may be required. Occasionally, some inflammation remains, leading to a post-inflammatory cough that may persist for weeks. Inhaled steroids are often prescribed for this condition.

Like emphysema (described below), chronic bronchitis is an ongoing illness requiring frequent medical attention. Although it may be exacerbated by infectious disease, chronic bronchitis is usually caused by long-term exposure to lung irritants—toxins, allergens or repeated bouts of acute bronchitis. The most common cause of chronic bronchitis is cigarette smoke.

Lungs exposed to tobacco smoke are subject to several pathological processes. One of the most critical is the dysfunction or loss of cilia lining the airways. Cilia are microscopic hair-like structures that trap and remove dust, mucus and other debris. A single puff of a cigarette can paralyze these hairs, increasing the chances of subsequent lung injury and infection.

As chronic bronchitis progresses. the lung's ability to exchange oxygen and carbon dioxide diminishes. In an attempt to compensate for the loss of pulmonary function, energy demands increase, the chest muscles work harder and the heart pumps faster. This in turn can lead to secondary diseases such as pulmonary hypertension, heart failure and emphysema.

Emphysema progresses slowly over time and is usually the result of prior lung disease. Chronic cough and shortness of breath are typical symptoms. Although it may occasionally be caused by hereditary factors, environmental exposures, chronic asthma or chronic bronchitis, emphysema most often results from years of heavy smoking. It is the most common cause of death from respiratory disease in North America.

Emphysema shares many symptoms with chronic bronchitis. In fact, the two diseases usually overlap to some degree. They are often classed together under the heading COPD (chronic obstructive pulmonary disease). However, they differ anatomically. Emphysema results in irreversible damage to alveoli—tiny sac-like structures where the actual exchange of oxygen and carbon dioxide occurs. Alveoli are counted in the millions, like bubbles in a bubble bath. Emphysema causes them to burst one by one. They then coalesce into fewer, larger sacs. As a result, their total surface area dwindles, decreasing the amount of air that can be exchanged by each breath.

It is well known that most lung diseases are characterized by weak anti-oxidant activity and impaired glutathione-related enzyme systems. Taking advantage of this information, a group of French researchers tested to see whether GSH screening could predict a predisposition to pulmonary diseases. They tested subjects for the absence of a gene (GSTM1) responsible for a specific GSH enzyme. About 47% of the French population lacks this gene. They found that heavy smokers with moderate chronic bronchitis were missing this gene 66% of the time and that smokers with severe chronic bronchitis were deficient in 71% of cases. They concluded that factors diminishing GSH function—in this case a hereditary factor—put individuals at higher risk for respiratory problems.

Other studies determined that COPD patients were very sensitive to low GSH levels after even light exercise, demonstrating the precarious balance of glutathione in these patients and the great importance of maintaining adequate stores of GSH.

N.C. Hansen and his team at Odense University in Denmark conducted a double-blind study of the general well-being of patients with mild chronic bronchitis. They gave them oral NAC during the winter months, and placebo to a similar group. Of the two groups, the GSH-enhanced group did much better on a GHQ (general health questionnaire). Several other research teams have studied the use of oral NAC as a preventative measure. Although it didn't significantly reduce the number of chronic bronchitis attacks, their severity—measured by symptoms and days off work—was greatly reduced.

In a large open study of over two thousand patients, K.P. Volkl and B. Schneider from Hanover Medical School in Germany showed that the use of NAC led to clear improvements in symptoms and pulmonary function. The four-week study included patients with acute and chronic bronchitis, bronchial asthma and emphysema. All groups had similar improvement in their disease.

SMOKING AND GSH

There is no longer any doubt that cigarette smoking is a major risk factor for chronic bronchitis, emphysema, COPD, cancer and cardiovascular disease. One of the ways in which cigarette smoke damages the body is by profoundly raising the extent of oxidative stress in the lungs.

A single puff of cigarette smoke contains billions of free radicals and can literally "burn up" antioxidants. But this isn't the worst of it. A still greater source of oxidative stress results from the lung inflammation resulting from smoking. The total oxidative damage caused by smoke corresponds directly to the degree of lung injury, respiratory compromise, morbidity and mortality found in individual patients.

Pharmacologists are investigating the use of inhaled GSH to prevent the onset or progression of emphysema in smokers. As a GSH precursor, NAC is receiving equal attention. Double blind studies in smokers using NAC demonstrate the enhanced ability of their lungs to clear away thick secretions in their airways.

R.B. Balansky at the Institute of Hygiene and Preventive Medicine in Italy exposed rats to high levels of cigarette smoke. This led to decreased body weight, intense pathological damage of the terminal airways, inflammation of the bronchial and bronchiolar linings, alveolar damage, emphysema, white blood cell abnormalities and pre-cancerous lesions. Rats given daily NAC at the same time suffered significantly less damage, demonstrating the protective role of GSH against lung damage and the onset of cancer.

Smokers are also more prone to the development of infectious bronchitis and pneumonia. Chronic bronchitis in smokers results in increased bacterial colonization. Treatment with NAC has decreased both the frequency of infectious episodes and the virulence of the bacteria.

ADULT RESPIRATORY DISTRESS SYNDROME (ARDS)

ARDS is acute, life-threatening respiratory failure following pulmonary injury. It leads to profound dyspnea (shortness of breath), pulmonary edema (fluid accumulation in the lungs) and hypoxemia (oxygen starvation). This all-too-common medical emergency is caused by a number of different acute processes that directly or indirectly damage the lung. They include bacterial or viral pneumonias, inhalation of stomach contents or other toxins, direct trauma to the chest, sepsis (overwhelming generalized infection), profound circulatory shock, drowning and many other medical conditions. Even with appropriate therapy the survival rate is only about 50%. Long-term complications include the eventual development of pulmonary fibrosis.

ARDS is a very complicated inflammatory process of which edema is only one facet. In the past, physicians treated this disorder aggressively with corticosteroids, because of their well-known anti-inflammatory properties. Unfortunately, randomized trials have shown that steroids are relatively ineffective against this disease. A hunt is on for useful treatments.

For several reasons, ARDS patients experience high levels of oxidative stress and subsequent depletion of antioxidants and glutathione. One cause may be the release of free radicals at the injury site by endotoxins. Endotoxins are produced by certain bacteria, though only released when the bacteria die. However, most of this oxidative stress probably comes from inflammation. Some white blood cells (neutrophils) are very active at sites of inflammation, producing very large amounts of reactive oxygen species, such as free oxygen radicals, hydrogen peroxide, 'hot' oxygen, and others.

Recognizing the severe oxidant-antioxidant imbalance and GSH depletion that comes with this condition, many researchers have put NAC under the spotlight. G.R. Bernard and his team at Vanderbilt University tested the usefulness of intravenous NAC for the lungs. Both in the lab and in clinical trials they found increased oxygen delivery, improved lung compliance (elasticity) and an improvement in the condition of pulmonary edema patients. Trials with another GSH precursor—OTZ (Procysteine)—led to similar results and reduced the duration of lung injury.

In a larger double-blind study, P.M. Suter's group at the University of Geneva used intravenous NAC on intensive care patients. Compared to a control group, the NAC patients showed significant improvement in oxygenation and required less time on mechanical ventilators (life support).

PULMONARY FIBROSIS

Pulmonary fibrosis is called fibrosing alveolitis or interstitial fibrosis, among other things. It is a non-specific condition in which the lungs respond to damage by the production of scar tissue (fibrosis). This leads to stiffness of the lungs and difficulties clearing secretions. It also interferes with gas exchange. Its causes include numerous bacterial, viral or fungal infections and inhaled toxins, dusts (organic and inorganic) and chemicals. Occasionally stomach contents can be inhaled to the detriment of the lungs. Other diseases are involved less often, such as certain autoimmune disorders (mistaken immune response to healthy processes), sarcoidosis (a multi-system inflammatory disorder), or collagen-vascular diseases (rheumatoid arthritis, lupus, polyarteritis nodosa, scleroderma and dermatomytosis). This disease is often an unwanted result of radiation therapy or chemotherapy. The standard treatments have limited success.

Oxidative stress plays an important role in the causes and conditions of many types of pulmonary fibrosis. J. Behr and his group of pulmonologists from the University of Munich studied this phenomenon both in laboratory cultures and in pulmonary fibrosis patients. Because pulmonary fibrosis is an inflammatory disorder, their treatment includes therapy to suppress the immune inflammatory response. With the help of NAC, patients' pulmonary function tests improved and the number of oxidative breakdown products fell. By using aerosolized NAC, Z. Borok from the NIH (National Institute of Health) reversed the oxidant-antioxidant imbalance in pulmonary fibrosis patients. Both NAC and aerosol GSH have shown success in this situation. Clearly, both oral and inhaled NAC can successfully raise pulmonary GSH levels.

In pulmonary fibrosis, fibroblasts—cells in part responsible for the fibrous scar tissue—grow excessively in both number and activity. Tissue cultures made of these cells revealed that the presence of GSH down-regulated their growth, implying that GSH may slow the progress of pulmonary fibrosis.

CASE STUDY

With a background in law from her native France, Nona became actively involved with business and philanthropic pursuits in Canada. She was a 41 year-old mother of three suffering from Hodgkin's disease and requiring both chemotherapy and radiotherapy. Although these treatments cured her of Hodgkin's disease, the treatments left her lungs scarred—the condition of pulmonary fibrosis. Her interests had to be dropped as her breathing deteriorated. She ended up staying at home, using home oxygen and many medications. Despite all interventions, her pulmonary function tests (PFT's) continued to fall. After six weeks of Immunocal 20 grams/day she went back to her pulmonary doctor, claiming she could breath again. Thinking there might be a placebo effect; the physician repeated her pulmonary function tests, which showed her back at about 90% of normal values. To eliminate other possibilities, the Immunocal was withdrawn. She subsequently deteriorated again. Three weeks after reinstating the Immunocal, her PFT's went back up to 95% of normal values. She promised herself never to stop again.

CYSTIC FIBROSIS

Cystic fibrosis affects many organ systems, but particularly the lungs. It is also called mucoviscidosis because it secretes a sticky mucus which neither lubricates nor flows freely in the nose, throat, airways and intestines. Cystic fibrosis is one of the most common inherited diseases in North America and affects some 30,000 people. Survivors live to an age of about 28 years, depending on the extent of pulmonary involvement.

Cystic fibrosis is most often classified as a disorder of the exocrine glands, and primarily affects the pancreas in fibrocystic pancreatic disease, the sweat glands, and pulmonary mucus production in mucoviscidosis. The problem stems from an inherited defect in the gene responsible for secreting certain fluids from these glands.

The disease often appaars early in life. Cystic fibrosis babies have very frequent digestive difficulties since the pancreas cannot provide enough digestive juice. This leads to malabsorption (poor ability to use nutrients) and malnutrition. Their skin loses large amounts of salt and they may sweat profusely. The lungs secrete a very thick (viscous) mucus that can obstruct airways, causing coughing, wheezing, and recurrent lung infections. Comprehensive and intensive therapy with health workers specialized in nursing, nutrition, physical therapy and respiratory therapy is essential for this problem.

Dr. Larry Lands, director of the cystic fibrosis clinic at McGill University in Montreal, aptly points out that inflammation is central to cystic fibrosis, that inflammation always precedes lung infection, and that lung infection almost inevitably follows severe inflammation. Continued inflammation depletes antioxidants and GSH even more and a vicious circle ensues.

GSH decrease in cystic fibrosis is noticeable in the fluid lining of the lungs (epithelial lining fluid), and also in blood serum, red blood cells and elsewhere. This points to whole-body depletion as a result of ongoing oxidative stress.

Cystic fibrosis patients are at further risk of antioxidant depletion because of pancreatic involvement leading to digestive difficulties and poor absorption of essential nutrients. Many researchers are investigating the use of supplemental antioxidants in this disease, including Lands' team investigating Immunocal, the whey-based GSH precursor. Immunocal is described in chapter 4.

NAC has long been utilized in an aerosol form to break down mucus accumulation in cystic fibrosis patients. It can be used in the same way for asthma, bronchitis, COPD, emphysema, pneumonia and other situations where thick secretions impair pulmonary function.

CASE STUDY

Eight year-old Zach, a cystic fibrosis patient, loved baseball. He was smaller than the rest of the kids, but it was shortness of breath and recurrent respiratory problems, not height, that kept him off the team. He took more care of his nutritional needs and was good about taking his additional vitamin and antioxidant supplementation. His parents learned how to provide him with home aerosol treatments by mask. He has been using both oral and nebulized (by mask) Mucomyst (N-acetylcysteine). Although primarily used as a "bench-warmer," Zach is back on the team.

CONCLUSION

An impressive amount of research has clarified the critical importance of antioxidants and GSH in all these pulmonary diseases. Unlike most other tissues, the lungs can use GSH as-is—through direct contact—rather than having to first absorb its precursors and then manufacture it. There are many ways to elevate pulmonary GSH, including oral, intravenous and inhaled therapies. In the next few years we will see increased use of these products to raise glutathione levels in acute, chronic and critical care patients.

LUNG DISEASE

BALANSKY RM, DE FLORA S. Chemoprevention by N-acetylcysteine of urethane-induced clastogenicity and lung tumors in mice. *Int. J. Cancer 77: 302-305, 1998*

BALANSKY RB, D'AGOSTININ F, ZANNACCHI P, DE FLORA S. Protection of N-acetylcysteine of the histopathological and cytogenetical damage produced by exposure of rats to cigarette smoke. *Cancer Lett. 64: 123-131, 1992*

BARANOVA H, PERRIOT J, ALBUISSON E, ET AL. Peculiarities of the GSTM1 o/o genotype in French heavy smokers with various types of chronic bronchitis. *Human Genetics 99: 822-826, 1997*

BEHR J, DEGENKOLB B, MAIER K, ET AL. Increased oxidation of extracellular glutathione by bronchoalveolar inflammatory cells in diffuse fibrosing alveolitis. *Eur. Respir. J. 8: 1286-1292, 1995*

BEHR J, MAIER K, DEGENKOLB B, ET AL. Antioxidative and clinical effects of high-dose N-acetylcysteine in fibrosing alveolitis. Adjunctive therapy to maintenance immunosuppression. *American J. Respir. Crit. Care Med. 156: 1897-1901, 1997*

BERNARD GR. Potential of N-acetylcysteine as treatment for the adult respiratory distress syndrome. *Eur. Respir. J. Suppl. 11: 496S-498S, 1990*

BERNARD GR. N-acetylcysteine in experimental and clinical acute lung injury. *American J. Med. 91:(3c): 54S-59S, 1991*

BERNARD GR, WHEELER AP, ARONS MM, ET AL. A trial of antioxidants N-acetylcysteine and procysteine in ARDS. The antioxidant in ARDS Study Group. *Chest 112: 164-172, 1997*

BIBI H, SCHLESINGER M, TABACHNIK E, ET AL. Erythrocyte glutathione peroxidase activity in asthmatic children. Ann. *Allergy 61: 339-340, 1988*

BOROK Z, BUHL R, GRIMES GJ, ET AL. Effect of glutathione aerosol on oxidant-antioxidant imbalance in idiopathic pulmonary fibrosis. *Lancet 338: 215-216, 1991*

BRIGHAM KL. Oxidant stress and adult respiratory distress syndrome. *Eur. Respir. J. Suppl. 11: 482s-484s, 1990*

BROWN RK, KELLY FJ. Evidence for increased oxidative damage in patients with cystic fibrosis. *Pediatr. Res. 36: 487-493, 1994*

BUHL R, MEYER A, VOGELMEIER C. Oxidant-protease interaction in the lung. Prospects for antioxidant therapy. *Chest 110 (6 Suppl): 267S-272S, 1996*

BUHL R, VOGELMEIER C. Therapy of lung diseases with anti-oxidants. *Pneumologie 48: 50-56, 1994*

BUHL R, VOGELMEIER C, CRITINDEN, ET AL. Augmentation of glutathione in the fluid lining the epithelium of the lower respiratory tract by directly administering glutathione aerosol. *Proc. Natl. Acad. Sci. USA 87: 4063-4067, 1990*

BUNNEL E, PACHT ER. Oxidized glutathione is increased in the alveolar fluid of patients with the adult respiratory distress syndrome. *American Rev. Respir. Dis. 148: 1174-1178, 1993*

CANTIN A, CRYSTAL RG. Oxidants, antioxidants and the pathogenesis of emphysema. *Eur. J. Dis. Suppl. 139:7-17, 1985*

CANTIN A, HUBBARD RC, CRYSTAL RG. Glutathione deficiency in the epithelial lining fluid of the lower respiratory tract in idiopathic pulmonary fibrosis. *American Rev. Respir. Dis. 139: 370-372, 1989*

CANTIN A, LARIVEE P, BEGIN RO. Extracellular glutathione suppresses human lung fibroblast proliferation. *American J. Respir. Cell. Mol. Biol. 3: 79-85, 1990*

CATO A, GOLDSTEIN I, MILLMAN. A double-blind parallel study of acetylcysteine-isoproterenol and saline-isoproterenol in patients with chronic obstructive lung disease. *J. Int. Med. Res. 5: 175-183, 1977*

CONAWAY CC, JIAO D, KELLOFF GJ, ET AL. Chemopreventive potential of fumaric acid, N-acetylcysteine, N-(4-hydroxyphenyl) retinamide and beta-carotene for tobacco-nitrosamine-induced lung tumors in A/J mice. *Cancer Lett. 124: 85-93, 1998*

Cotgreave IA, Moldeus P. Lung protection by thiol-containing antioxidants. *Bull. Eur. Physiopathol. Respir. 23: 272-277, 1987*

D'Agostini F, Bagnasco M, Giunciuglio D, et al. Inhibition by oral N-acetylcysteine of doxorubicin-induced clastogenicity and alopecia, and prevention of primary tumors and lung metastasis in mice. *Int. J. Oncol. 13: 217-224, 1998*

Davreux CJ, Soric I, Nathens AB, et al. N- acetyl cysteine attenuates acute lung injury in the rat. *Shock 8: 432-438, 1997*

De Flora S, Grassi C, Carati L. Attenuation of influenza-like symptomatology and improvement of cell-mediated immunity with long-term N-acetylcysteine treatment. *Eur. Respir. J. 19: 1535-1541, 1997*

Demling R, Ikegami K, Lalonde C. Increased lipid peroxidation and decreased antioxidant activity correspond with death after smoke exposure in the rat. *J. Burn Care Rehabil. 16(2 Pt 1): 104-110, 1995*

Demling R, Lalonde C, Picard L, Blanchard J. Changes in lung and systemic oxidant and antioxidant activity after smoke inhalation. *Shock 1: 101-107, 1994*

Eiserich JP, van der Vliet, et al. Dietary antioxidants and cigarette smoke-induced biomolecular damage: a complex interaction. *American J. Clin. Nutr. 62(6 Suppl): 1490S-1500S, 1995*

Goldstein RH, Fine A. Potential therapeutic initiatives for fibrogenic lung diseases. *Chest 108: 848-855, 1995*

Greene LS. Asthma and oxidant stress: nutritional, environmental and genetic risk factors. *J. American Coll. Nutr. 14: 317-324, 1995*

Gressier B, Lebegue S, Gosset P, et al. Protective role of glutathione on alpha ! proteinase inhibitor inactivation by the myeloperoxidase system. Hypothetic study for the therapeutic strategy in the management of smoker's emphysema. *Fundam. Clin. Pharmacol. 8: 518-524, 1994*

Hansen NC, Skriver A, Brorsen-Riis L, et al. Orally administered N-acetylcysteine may improve general well-being in patients with mild chronic bronchitis.

Respir. Med. 88: 531-515, 1994

Hasselmark L, Malmgren R, Unge G, Zetterstrom O. Lowered platelet glutathione peroxidase activity in patients with intrinsic asthma. *Allergy 45: 523-527, 1990*

Hull J, Vervaart P, Grimwood K, Phelan P. Pulmonary oxidative stress response in young children with cystic fibrosis. *Thorax 52: 557-560, 1997*

Hunninghake GW, Kalica AR. Approaches to the treatment of pulmonary fibrosis. *American J. Respir. Crit. Care Med. 151(3 Pt 1): 915-918, 1995*

Ikegami K, Lalonde C, Young YK, et al. Comparison of plasma reduced glutathione and oxidized glutathione with lung and liver tissue oxidant and antioxidant activity during acute inflammation. *Shock 1: 307-312, 1994*

Kadrabova J, Mad'aric A, Kovacikova Z, et al. Selenium status is decreased in patients with intrinsic asthma. *Biol. Tr. Elem. Res. 52: 241-248, 1996*

Kelly FJ, Cotgrove M, Mudway IS. Respiratory lining tract fluid antioxidants: the first line of defense against serious gaseous pollutants. *Cent. Eur. J. Public Health 4 Suppl: 11-14, 1996*

Lands LC, Grey VL, Grenier. Total plasma antioxidant capacity in cystic fibrosis. *Pediatr. Pulmonol. 29: 81-87, 2000*

Laurent T, Markert M, Feihl F, et al. Oxidant-antioxidant balance in granulocytes during ARDS. Effect of N-acetylcysteine. *Chest 109: 163-166, 1996*

Lothian B, Grey V, Kimoff RJ, Lands LC. Treatment of obstructive airway disease with a cysteine donor protein supplement: A case report. *Chest: 117:914-916, 2000*

MacNee W. Chronic obstructive pulmonary disease from science to the clinic: the role of glutathione in oxidant-antioxidant balance. *Monaldi. Arch. Chest Dis. 52: 479-485, 1997*

MacNee W, Bridgeman MM, Marsden M, et al. The effects of N-acetylcysteine and glutathione on smoke-induced changes in lung phagocytes and epithelial cells. *American J. Med. 91(3C): 60S-66S, 1991*

MEYER A, BUHL R, KAMPF S, MAGNUSSEN H. Intravenous N-acetylcysteine and lung glutathione of patients with pulmonary fibrosis and normals. *American J. Respir. Crit. Care Med. 152: 1055-1060, 1995*

MEYER A, BUHL R, MAGNUSSEN H. The effect of oral N-acetylcysteine on lung glutathione levels in idiopathic pulmonary fibrosis. *Eur. Respir. J. 7: 431-436, 1994*

MISSO NL, POWERS KA, GILLON RL, ET AL. Reduced platelet glutathione peroxidase activity and serum selenium concentration in atopic asthmatic patients. *Clin. Exp. Allergy 26: 838-847, 1996*

MORRIS PE, BERNARD GR. Significance of glutathione in lung disease and implications for therapy. *American J. Med. Sci. 307: 119-127, 1994*

NOVAK Z, NEMETH I, GYURKOVITS K, ET AL. Examination of the role of oxygen free radicals in bronchial asthma in childhood. *Clin. Chim. Acta. 201: 247-251, 1991*

OLIVIERI D, MARISCO SA, DEL DONNO M. Improvement of mucociliary transport in smokers by mucolytics. *Eur. J. Respir. Dis. Suppl. 139: 142-145, 1985*

ORTOLANI O, GRATINO F, LEONE D, ET AL. Usefulness of the prevention of oxygen radical damage in the critical patient using the parental administration of reduced glutathione in high doses. *Boll. Soc. Ital. Biol. Sper. 68: 239-244, 1992*

PACHT ER, TIMERMAN AP, LYKENS MG, MEROLA AJ. Deficiency of alveolar fluid glutathione in patients with sepsis and the adult respiratory distress syndrome. *Chest 100: 1397-1403, 1991*

PARR GD, HUITSON A. Oral Fabrol (oral N-acetylcysteine) in chronic bronchitis. *Br. J. Dis. Chest 81: 341-348, 1987*

PATTERSON CE, RHOADES RA. Protective role of sulfhydryl reagents in oxidant lung injury. *Exp. Lung Res. 14 Suppl: 1005-1019, 1988*

PEARSON DJ, SUAREZ-MENDEZ VJ, DAY JP, MILLER PF. Selenium status in relation to reduced glutathione peroxidase activity in aspirin-sensitive asthma. *Clin Exp. Allergy 21: 203-208, 1991*

PORTAL BC, RICHARD MJ, FAURE HS, ET AL. Altered antioxidant status and increased lipid peroxidation in children with cystic fibrosis. *American J. Clin. Nutr. 61: 843-847, 1995*

POWELL CV, NASH AA, POWERS HJ, PRIMHAK RA. Antioxidant status in asthma. *Pediatr. Pulmonol. 18: 34-38, 1994*

RAHMAN I, MACNEE W. Role of oxidants/antioxidants in smoking-induced lung diseases. *Free Radic. Biol. Med. 21: 6669-681, 1996*

RASMUSSEN JB, GLENNOW C. Reduction in days of illness after long-term treatment with N-acetylcysteine controlled-release tablets in patients with chronic bronchitis. *Eur. Respirol. J. 4:351-355, 1988*

RIISE GC, LARSSON S, LARSSON P, ET AL. The intrabronchial microbial flora in chronic bronchitis patients: a target for N-acetylcysteine therapy? *Eur. Respir. J. 7: 94-101, 1994*

ROGERS DF, JEFFERY PK. Inhibition by oral N-acetylcysteine of cigarette smoke-induced "bronchitis" in the rat. Exp. *Lung Res. 10: 267-283, 1986*

ROUM JH, BUHL R, MCELVANEY, ET AL. Systemic deficiency of glutathione in cystic fibrosis. *J. Appl. Physiol. 75: 2419-2424, 1993*

SALA R, MORIGGI E, CORVASCE G, MORELLI D. Protection by N-acetylcysteine against pulmonary endothelial cell damage induced by oxidant injury. *Eur. Respir. J. 6: 440-446, 1993*

SIMON LM, SUTTORP N. Lung cell oxidant injury: decrease in oxidant mediated cytotoxicity by N-acetylcysteine. *Eur. J. Dis. Suppl. 139: 132-135, 1985*

SUTER PM, DOMENIGHETTI G, SCHALLER, ET AL. N-acetylcysteine enhances recovery from acute lung injury in man. A randomized, double-blind, placebo-controlled clinical study. *Chest 105: 190-194, 1994*

TANSWELL AK, FREEMAN BA. Antioxidant therapy in critical care medicine. *New Horiz. 3: 330-341, 1995*

TATTERSALL AB, BRIDGMAN KM, HUITSON A. Irish general practice study of acetylcysteine (Fabrol) in chronic bronchitis. *J. Int. Med. Res. 12: 96-101. 1984*

TERAMOTO S, FUKUCHI Y, UEJIMA Y, ET AL. Superoxide anion formation and glutathione metabolism of blood in patients with idiopathic pulmonary fibrosis. *Biochem. Mol. Med. 55: 66-70, 1995*

VAN ZANDWIJK N. N-acetylcysteine (NAC) and glutathione: antioxidant and chemopreventative properties, with special reference to lung cancer. *J. Cell. Biochem. Suppl. 22: 24-32, 1995*

VAN ZANDWIJK N. N-acetylcysteine for lung cancer protection. *Chest 107: 1437-1441, 1995*

VINA J, SERVERA E, ASENI M, ET AL. Exercise causes blood glutathione oxidation in chronic obstructive pulmonary disease: prevention by O2 therapy. *J. Appl. Physiol. 81: 2198-2202. 1996*

VOLKL KP, SCHNEIDER B. Therapy of respiratory tract diseases with N-acetylcysteine. An open therapeutic observation study of 2,512 patients. *Fortschr. Med. 110: 346-350, 1992*

WAGNER PD, MATHIEU-COSTELLO O, BEBOUT BE, ET AL. Protection against pulmonary O2 toxicity by N-acetylcysteine. *Eur. Respir. J. 2: 116-126, 1989*

WHITE CW, REPINE JE. Pulmonary antioxidant defense mechanisms. *Exp. Lung Res. 8: 81-96, 1985*

WINKLHOFER-ROOB BM. Oxygen free radicals and antioxidants in cystic fibrosis: the concept of an oxidant-antioxidant imbalance. *Acta. Paediatr. Suppl. 83: 49-57, 1994*

WITSCHI H, ESPIRITU I, YU M, WILLITS NH. The effects of phenethyl isothianate, N-acetylcysteine and green tea on tobacco smoke-induced lung tumors in strain A/J mice. *Carcinogenesis 19: 1789-1794, 1998*

CHAPTER 15

DIGESTIVE DISEASES

The digestive tract is a string of connected organs stretching from the mouth to the bowels. With it we eat, digest and eliminate waste. The many digestive disorders are caused by such factors as genetics, stress, toxins, infectious diseases and pharmaceutical drugs. This chapter discusses the latest research on glutathione in the digestive tract.

GSH helps protect the mouth and salivary organs from periodontal disease, stomatitis and gingivitis and the esophagus from inflammation. In the stomach, it protects against gastritis, peptic ulcer and cancer and in the liver, hepatitis and organ failure. GSH also defends the pancreas against inflammation and the large intestine (bowel) against colitis, inflammatory bowel disease, ulcerative colitis, Crohn's disease and cancer.

GASTRITIS
Gastritis is an inflammation of the stomach lining (gastric mucosa). Acute gastritis produces a short-lived inflammation with symptoms of pain, heart-

Figure 35 — The digestive tract: organs and their disorders	
ORGAN	**COMMON DISORDERS**
Mouth and salivary organs	periodontal disease stomatitis, gingivitis, parotitis
Esophagus	esophagitis cancer hiatus hernia
Stomach	gastritis peptic ulcer cancer
Liver	hepatitis liver failure
Gall bladder	gallstones (cholelithiasis)
Pancreas	pancreatitis cancer
Small intestines	gastroenteritis
Large intestines (bowel)	colitis inflammatory bowel disease ulcerative colitis Crohn's disease cancer, polyps malabsorption syndromes

burn, occasional nausea, vomiting and loss of appetite. Chronic gastritis is more prolonged. It has fewer symptoms but more readily progresses to serious illnesses such as anemia, stomach ulcer and stomach cancer. As the population ages gastritis is becoming so common that some scientists consider it a part of the aging process.

One of many possible causes of gastritis is generalized stress. It may be a psychological reaction to daily life or be physically induced by trauma—the result of major illness, head injury or burns. A long list of toxins has also been implicated with this ailment, the most common ones being coffee, alcohol, tobacco, over-spiced foods and certain infectious diseases. Some common pharmaceutical drugs may also induce gastritis, notably aspirin, corticosteroids, and anti-inflammatory medications. Mixing these drugs may be especially damaging. Consult your physician before you use them in combination.

Stomach ulcers

Stomach ulcers—also called peptic ulcers—are spots where the lining of stomach has been eroded leaving an open wound. This can vary in depth and may lead to an actual hole right through the stomach wall (a perforated ulcer). Most ulcers occur in the stomach or duodenum and are rarely found elsewhere along the digestive tract. About one in ten North Americans will suffer at some point in their life from an ulcer, leading to symptoms like those seen in gastritis—abdominal pain, heartburn, and even melena (black or maroon-colored stools caused by oxidized blood leaking into the digestive tract) and anemia (a low hemoglobin or red blood count) if the ulcer is bleeding.

Ulcers develop when the stomach lining loses its ability to protect itself from the acids produced in the digestive juices. This was once thought to be caused by high acid levels, but it is now known that many ulcer patients have normal acid levels. We know that for various reasons, the lining's defense mechanism against these acids is insufficient, enabling ulcers to develop. Some of the risk factors for developing ulcers are:

- ❏ Stress and anxiety
- ❏ Trauma, burns
- ❏ Aspirin
- ❏ Anti-inflammatories
- ❏ Corticosteroids
- ❏ Caffeine
- ❏ Alcohol
- ❏ Vitamin C
- ❏ Extreme foods
- ❏ Tobacco
- ❏ Blood type O
- ❏ Helicobacter pylori

Several factors contribute to the protective nature of this lining. Mucus production, biochemical cellular barriers and adequate replacement of damaged mucosal cells all play a role in the maintenance of a healthy stomach. Immunological factors are only just now being understood. For example, they seem to explain why blood type 'A' individuals are likely to develop stomach cancer whereas those with blood type 'O' are more prone to duodenal ulcers.

Many factors can disrupt the protective lining. Over-secretion or overproduction of stomach acids has already been mentioned. The same drugs that cause gastritis may also lead to ulcers, either by increasing acid production or by modifying the protective factors. These drugs include corticosteroids, aspirin, and dozens of anti-inflammatories known by various brand names.

As with gastritis, other risk factors include cigarette smoking, alcohol abuse, high caffeine intake, overindulgence in fatty foods and consumption of highly spiced foods like whole chili peppers. Even high-dose vitamin C (ascorbic acid) intake has been implicated with ulcers. Stress and anxiety have traditionally been identified as causes, but now seem less significant than previously thought.

Medical science has recently discovered an infectious agent involved with ulcer formation—the bacteria Helicobacter pylori, found in 70-90% of ulcer cases. A short course of antibiotics often but not always cures the infection. A significant portion of the population have H. pylori in their digestive tract yet never develop problems. Apparently, other immunological or physiological factors must come into play for this organism to become pathological.

CASE STUDY

Kurt was a 53 year-old vice-president of sales for a large manufacturing company. Among the seventy-hour weeks, two-martini lunches, coffees well into the night, a pack-and-a-half-a-day cigarette habit, and the stress of a poor sales quarter, he developed severe stomach pains. He was lucky. Medical investigation determined that he only had a gastritis (stomach inflammation) but that if his present lifestyle continued, he would likely develop an ulcer. Unwilling to quit smoking or working so much, he agreed to a reduction in alcohol and coffee and also to visit a nutritionist. After three weeks on silymarin, melatonin, glutamine, chamomile, selenium, multiple vitamins including B-complex, C and E, he felt "infinitely better," even though sales were still down. He laughs about this now and is thinking of quitting smoking and starting regular exercise. He now believes that if he feels better in his body, his performance at work will improve.

STOMACH CANCER

Stomach cancer—gastric carcinoma—often begins at the site of a stomach ulcer. It is generally believed that that ulcers do not necessarily cause stomach cancer, but that this cancer is often preceded by a particular type of ulcer. In America, it is the seventh most common cause of cancer death. However, incidence of stomach cancer varies enormously around the world; in Japan, Chile, and Iceland, it is one of the most common causes of mortality. Scientists have suggested that this may be due to differences in diet or environment. The theory is supported by the fact that certain occupational hazards such as exposure to coal dust or heavy metals like mercury and lead increase one's chances of contracting this disease.

Other risk factors include the consumption of certain types of prepared food and moulds. Moldy foods may include a carcinogen called aflatoxin. This byproduct of fungi can be found growing in nuts, seeds, corn and other dried foods.

The H. pylori bacteria has also been implicated in stomach cancer. Chronic gastritis (stomach inflammation) and polyps (abnormal protruding growth of tissue) may also become cancerous. Medical conditions such as stomach ulcer, chronic gastritis, stomach polyps, toxins like alcohol, tobacco, aflatoxins and foods that are barbecued, smoked, pickled and highly salted may all contribute to the development of cancer.

GSH AND THE STOMACH

Glutathione's ability to protect the stomach is being widely researched. Its therapeutic role is promising and it has been shown to protect the stomach in several different ways. It is a primary shield against oxidative stress, detoxifies potentially harmful or even carcinogenic substances and mediates the immune mechanisms, ensuring a more effective immune response.

ACUTE GASTRITIS

It has recently been shown that when the lining of the stomach faces a toxic challenge GSH levels rise. Several groups of researchers demonstrated this using alcohol to provoke an anti-toxic response by the body. Low to moderate levels of alcohol led to an adaptive elevation in GSH levels, but high levels of alcohol overwhelmed this system, causing subsequent damage. An

Figure 36 — Some potential causes of stomach cancer

MEDICAL CONDITIONS	TOXINS	FOODS
❏ Stomach ulcer	❏ Alcohol	❏ Barbecued
❏ Chronic gastritis	❏ Tobacco	❏ Smoked
❏ Stomach polyps	❏ Aflatoxins	❏ Pickled
	❏ Heavy metals	❏ Highly salted

even more direct clinical application of glutathione's protective role in the stomach was brought to light by G.A. Balint in Hungary. His team studied an all-too-common problem—the gastric side-effects of anti-inflammatory drugs such as indomethacin and piroxicam (Indocid, Feldene, etc.). Subjects given small amounts of glutathione or cysteine at the time of drug ingestion had significantly fewer side-effects. This is a great example of a natural therapy and traditional medicine being used to complement each other.

The increase in free-radical damage and GSH turnover is well known in patients suffering from chronic inflammation of the stomach lining (gastritis) and those carrying the bacteria Helicobacter Pylori. Both of these conditions may progress to ulcer disease and probably increase the risk of stomach cancer.

Ulcer disease may also be caused in part by high levels of lipid peroxidation and disruption of the antioxidant defense mechanisms in the lining of the stomach. There is certainly a close relationship between GSH-dependent enzymes and the progress of gastric ulcers. Glutathione and its related enzymes are found in very low concentrations within the ulcer, but often rise again when ulcerated tissues heal. When laboratory animals were given drugs to lower their GSH levels, oxidative damage to the stomach lining (gastric mucosa) was significantly higher.

Traditionally, Helicobacter Pylori-related ulcers are treated with antibiotics (Amoxicillin, Biaxin, Flagyl, etc.) and proton-pump inhibitors (Losec, Pantoloc, etc.). This treatment is more effective when used in conjunction with antioxidants. A new medication called Rebamipide developed in Japan works partly as a free radical scavenger. It also slows depletion of GSH. Studies using Rebamipide along with conventional drugs show improved healing.

A Swiss group from the University of Zurich recently studied smokers suffering from ulcers. They combined conventional treatment with the potent GSH precursor NAC (n-acetylcysteine), with good results. This is understandable since smokers in general suffer from much higher levels of oxidative stress than non-smokers and benefit more obviously from high antioxidant levels. Davydenko's team in the Ukraine believe that antioxidant therapy should continue even after conventional treatment has stopped.

When we look at cancer cells in the stomach as well as the immediately surrounding normal cells, we find several recurring characteristics—cells are heavily damaged by oxidative stress, their antioxidant defenses are diminished and the power-plants of each cell (the mitochondria) are defective—possibly due to free radical damage. Notably, GSH-related enzyme systems are impaired. There is little doubt that low glutathione levels go hand-in-hand with increased risk of cancer. The following research results speak for themselves.

T. Katoh at the National Institute of Environmental Health Sciences in

North Carolina showed a particular relationship between GSH levels and the development of gastric cancer. For various reasons some people have inactive or inefficient sub-types of GSH enzymes. They have at greater risk of contracting both stomach and bowel cancer.

A group from Italy studied glutathione levels in patients with stomach cancer and came to the unequivocal conclusion that the 'decrease of this tripeptide' was 'dramatical.' Their work suggests that any therapeutic approach should include GSH precursors such as cysteine.

A Japanese team reached similar conclusions while investigating gastric ulcers. They found that levels of gastric mucosal GSH 'are closely related to the etiology and course of gastric ulcer.' Various researchers and theorists have suggested that the antioxidant capacity of the cancerous tissues has been impaired and, even more significantly, that the body's entire antioxidant defense mechanism may be breaking down.

PANCREATITIS

The pancreas is an organ involved in several important functions, the two most crucial are to secrete digestive enzymes that help prepare food for intestinal absorbtion and to produce hormones such as insulin and glucagon that are critical to the metabolism of sugars and carbohydrates.

Pancreatitis is an inflammation of the pancreas that leads to pain (often severe), and digestive and metabolic abnormalities. It can be potentially life-threatening and if chronic may lead to other illnesses like diabetes. Acute pancreatitis is an abrupt onset of pancreatitis most commonly caused by blockage of the passage to the intestines. This usually happens when gallstones are lodged there, or sometimes at the site of a tumor. The pancreatic juices contain powerful digestive enzymes which may back up when blocked and start to digest the pancreas itself.

Other causes of acute pancreatitis include certain viral and bacterial infections, specific drugs, high fat levels in the blood including cholesterol or triglycerides (hyperlipidemia), abdominal trauma, and critically low blood pressure (severe hypotension). Chronic pancreatitis develops over months or years, usually after repeated bouts of acute pancreatitis. The most common trigger by far for this type is alcoholism. Chronic pancreatitis may impair normal functions such as insulin secretion and lead among other potential problems to secondary diabetes.

Many studies suggest that oxyradicals and free radicals are involved in the development of all types of pancreatitis. The importance of glutathione in the pancreas' antioxidant defense cannot be overstated. J.M. Braganza and his team at the Royal Infirmary in Manchester, UK, have found GSH depletion in all early stages of acute pancreatitis. They surmise that low levels may predict the vulnerability of other organs to pancreatitis. M.H. Schoenberg from the University of Ulm in Germany suggests that GSH supplementation may be a way to avoid extra-pancreatic complications.

Other researchers at the Royal Infirmary developed the 'Manchester oxidant stress hypothesis' to describe the development of pancreatitis. They think that oxidant stress (caused mainly by toxins) opens the door to chronic pancreatitis because diminishing GSH levels allow the eventual breakdown of cells. This team developed a combination of antioxidants: methionine, vitamin C and selenium and tested them in placebo controlled and retrospective cross-sectional trials.

Oxothiazolidine carboxylate (OTC)—a potent GSH-enhancing drug— was successfully used by R. Luthen at the University of Dusseldorf in Germany to decrease the severity of pancreatitis. He found a critical loss of glutathione content in biliary pancreatitis (pancreatitis due to blockage by a gall stone). He and his researchers think that glutathione depletion has something to do with the early activation of auto-digestive enzymes, because the defense against oxidative stress is weakened. M.A. Walling says that GSH depletion is key to the evolution of chronic pancreatitis caused by external toxins.

The most common cause of chronic pancreatitis is alcoholic pancreatitis. Sufferers of this disease are particularly deficient in levels of vitamins E and A, selenium, and glutathione peroxidase. Researchers have suggested that these patients required higher daily requirements to ward off this oxidative stress.

Another variety of this disease is known as hereditary pancreatitis, an inherited disease which was examined at the Cleveland Clinic Foundation. A correlation was found between the disease and diminished antioxidant defenses, most notably GSH, selenium and vitamin E. The relationships among these three antioxidants are described in chapters 1 and 4. The researchers at Cleveland propose supplementation therapy with natural products to decrease the frequency of attacks.

The major complication leading to death from pancreatitis is multiple organ failure. This is partly because the integrity of cell membranes breaks down, leading to leakages both in and out of these cells. X.D. Wang and his team at Lund University in Sweden successfully used N-acetylcysteine, a potent GSH-raising drug, to prevent damage to most tissues. I. Gukovsky at the University of California, also found significant improvement in acute pancreatitis patients using NAC.

INFLAMMATORY BOWEL DISEASES
Inflammatory bowel disease occurs in several forms, including ulcerative colitis and Crohn's Disease, both described here.

ULCERATIVE COLITIS

Colitis is a general term for inflammation of the bowel. Ulcerative colitis (UC) is a chronic inflammatory disease of the large bowel (colon) leading to ulcers in the mucous membranes lining it and causing pain, bloody diarrhea, gas, bloating and many other symptoms. Fever, weight loss, joint pains and even visual symptoms may accompany the digestive problems.

Most patients develop this disease early on in life, usually between the ages of 15 and 30. This disease ranges in severity from a single brief attack to a progressive course complicated by severe blood loss (hemorrhaging), perforated bowel or the spread of infection into the bloodstream (sepsis). Ulcerative colitis patients bear a higher risk of subsequent colon cancer. However the ulcerative colitis is rarely fatal and the majority of those affected lead fairly normal lives.

The cause of this disease is still unclear but it has a small tendency to run in families. Various possible causes have been proposed, including infectious agents, immunological abnormalities, dietary factors, toxins, allergies and stress. However, these hypotheses remain unproven.

The large and small intestines are located in the lower abdomen like a loosely-folded fire hose that leads a long and winding path from the stomach to the anus. Ulcerative colitis is marked by the formation of ulcers that eat away at the intestinal wall. Crohn's Disease is an inflammation that

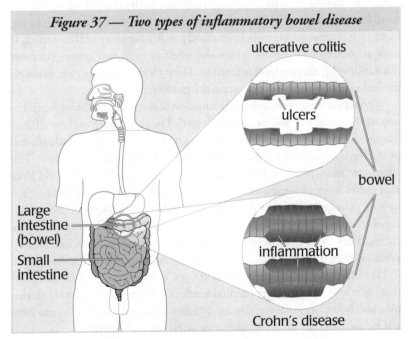

Figure 37 — Two types of inflammatory bowel disease

ulcerative colitis

ulcers

bowel

Large intestine (bowel)

Small intestine

inflammation

Crohn's disease

leads to swelling and tenderness in the intestinal wall. Figure 37 shows the location of these diseases and the different ways they affect the intestines.

CASE STUDY

28 year-old Debbie, a massage therapist, had ulcerative colitis but had so far managed to avoid any surgery. She maintained a sensible diet, continued the medications her doctor had prescribed, and avoided foods that disagreed with her. However, the previous few years had been fraught with repeated bouts of cramps, diarrhea and occasional bloody stool. Eventually, she could not make it through her workday without numerous visits to the washroom. A dietary consultant added to her diet a high-dose antioxidant mixture, selenium, L-glutamine, and— when her stool was firmer—psyllium husks. Her blood loss has abated, and she now visits the washroom at lunchtimes only.

CROHN'S DISEASE

Crohn's disease (CD) is similar in many ways to ulcerative colitis (see above). Its differences, however, make this a potentially more severe disease. In ulcerative colitis small ulcers are scattered in the lining of the large bowel. Crohn's disease is less selective and may affect any part of the digestive system, from mouth to anus. It is most common in the ileum (the end of the small intestine where it joins the large intestine). The disease occurs in heavy patches, but areas between these diseased patches are also mildly affected. It is most common in the gut where the intestine wall may grow extremely thick following repeated inflammation. Deep ulcers may pass right through the lining and completely penetrate the gut tissues.

With repeated or prolonged inflammation of the intestine the entire thickness of the intestinal wall becomes affected. The thickening of the wall may narrow the intestinal passage and obstruct it. Symptoms can include spasms of abdominal pain, diarrhea, appetite loss, anemia and weight loss. The elderly are more prone to inflammation of the rectum. Young and old alike may suffer from chronic abscesses, deeps fissures (cracks) and fistulas (abnormal passageways) in the anus. Because the entire digestive system is susceptible, complications are more profound than those following ulcerative colitis. They include bowel obstruction, infection, malabsorption, and elevated cancer risk—as much as 20 times greater than healthy individuals.

Like ulcerative colitis, the exact cause of Crohn's disease is unknown, but there tends to be a stronger familial tendency. Some researchers think this may also be an autoimmune disease. Studies suggest that sufferers may benefit by avoiding certain food additives, allergens and cigarettes.

It is clear from observing patients with inflammatory bowel disease that inflamed cells in the lining of the intestines are a hotbed of free radicals. However, there is still debate as to whether the free radicals cause or result from the damage characterizing these diseases. Samples of tissue inflamed by ulcerative colitis and Crohn's disease show consistent evidence of severe oxidative stress. The degree of oxidative damage can even be correlated to the degree of inflammation. Of all the antioxidants that can prevent or retard this damage, GSH is the central one.

Researchers from all over the world—including L. Bhaskar from India and G.D. Buffington from Australia have looked at tissues affected by inflammatory bowel disease and Crohn's disease. All have identified a significant depletion of glutathione and alteration of its enzymes. In the past, most researchers believed that GSH depletion was more likely to be a consequence of ongoing inflammation and oxidative stress than a contributing cause of the problem. But today, opinions may be changing. More recent findings by B. Sido of the University of Heidelberg in Germany have found not only diminished GSH levels but also diminished activity of the enzymes involved with GSH production. This implies that declining GSH production may actually contribute to the development of the disease.

Antioxidant therapy has thus emerged as a treatment for inflammatory bowel disease. One of the more traditional groups of medications applied to these diseases are the aminosalicylates (sulfasalazine, Asacol, Dipentum, etc.) These are potent antioxidants, but are also pharmaceutical drugs, and the hunt for less toxic, more natural products is on.

T. Cruz and J. Galvez and their team from the University of Granada in Spain, were able to protect inflamed bowels with a flavonoid called rutoside—flavonoids are a variety of crystalline compounds found in plants. This worked with both acute and chronic disease. They explained their success by pointing to rutoside's tendency to maintain or increase GSH content in the gut.

Malnutrition results more often from Crohn's disease (CD) than from ulcerative colitis. The reasons are complex but are summarized by the fact that CD is more deeply involved in the bowel. The nutritional status of those suffering from this disease has been investigated at great length and reveals a generalized GSH depletion throughout the body. These findings have also been reported in children with CD, possibly resulting from ongoing oxidative stress.

Numerous scientists have suggested oral GSH supplementation as a treatment for UC and CD. It is clear from the information we presented in chapters 1 and 4 that oral glutathione is not very effective in raising total body GSH. However, these digestive tissues seem able to make use of locally supplemented GSH. The tissues most positively affected by oral GSH are those in direct contact with it. The intestinal lining (mucosa) provides such an opportunity. In fact Alton Meister—often called the father of GSH research—suggests that both oral GSH and GSH excreted in the bile can protect the intestinal mucosa from injury. Experimental depletion of gut glutathione leads to severe damage of this sensitive lining.

CONCLUSIONS

GSH AND STOMACH DISEASE
Research evidence suggests that glutathione defends the stomach lining against various threats, including toxins, oxidative stress and carcinogenesis. The results have prompted others to seek ways to raise glutathione levels in humans for both preventive and curative purposes. Elevated glutathione levels may protect against gastritis, ulcer and cancer and can certainly complement conventional treatments for these diseases.

PANCREATITIS
The high levels of oxidative stress and the depletion of glutathione in pancreatitis is well documented and scientists are investigating the role of antioxidant therapy in the treatment of pancreatitis and prevention of recurrent bouts. Even though antioxidant therapy is a safe complementary treatment for chronic pancreatitis, its wider adoption as a standard healthcare tool will take time. The lynchpin of this new approach is the search for tools to enhance (modulate) intracellular glutathione levels. As these tools emerge, further research will be needed to use them effectively.

INFLAMMATORY BOWEL DISEASE
An imbalance in the formation of free radicals and a poor supply or availability of antioxidant micronutrients may cause or encourage tissue injury in inflammatory bowel disease. Levels of glutathione and its related compounds are significantly lower in these diseases. Different antioxidants including GSH, GSH monoesters, NAC (N-acetylcysteine), vitamin C (ascorbate), vitamin E (tocopherol), SOD (superoxide dismutase) and others have been used with varying success. It may not be clear whether GSH loss is a cause or consequence of these inflammatory disorders, but in either case, they are positively affected by therapies that raise or sustain GSH levels. Recent research suggests that raising glutathione levels may be a novel approach to the treatment of ulcerative colitis and Crohn's disease.

REFERENCES TO CHAPTER 15
DIGESTIVE DISEASES

STOMACH DISEASE

ALTOMARE E, GRATTAGLIANO I, DIDONNA D, ET AL. Gastric and intestinal ethanol toxicity in the rat. Effect on glutathione level and role of alcohol and acetaldehyde metabolisms. *Ital. J. Gastroenterol. Hepatol. 30:82-90, 1998*

ARIVAZHAGA S, KAVITHA K, NAGINI S. Erythrocyte lipid peroxidation and antioxidants in gastric cancer patients. *Cell. Biochem. Funct. 15:15-18, 1997*

BALINT GA. A novel approach to reduce the unwanted gastric side-effects of orally administered non-steroidal anti-inflammatory drugs in rats. *Exp. Toxicol. Pathol. 49:61-63, 1997*

DAVYDENKO OM, KOLOMOIETS MIU, DAVYDENKO IS. Free-radical oxidation, the glutathione system and the status of the gastric mucosa in peptic ulcer in adolescents and young people under dynamic restorative treatment. *Lik Sprava 7-8:60-64, 1994*

EAPEN CE, MADESH M. BALASUBRAMANIAN KA, ET AL. Mucosal mitochondrial function and antioxidant defenses in patients with gastric carcinoma. *Scand. J. Gastroenterol. 33:957-981, 1998*

FARINATI F, DELLA LIBERA G, CARDIN R, ET AL. Gastric antioxidant, nitrites, and mucosal lipoperoxidation in chronic gastritis and Helicobacter pylori infection. *J. Clin. Gastroenterol. 22:275-281, 1996*

GIORGI G, MICHELI L, SEGRE G, PECCHI A. Glutathione (GSH) in human stomach mucosa. *Riv. Eur. Sci. Med. Farmacol. 11:163-167, 1989*

HAHM KB, LEE KJ, KIM YS, ET AL. Augmented eradication rates of Helicobacter pylori by new combination therapy with lansoprazole, amoxicillin, and rebamipide. *Dig. Dis. Sci. 43:235-240, 1998*

HIROKAWA K, KAWASAKI H. Changes in glutathione in gastric mucosa of gastric ulcer patients. *Res. Commun. Mol. Pathol. Pharmacol. 88: 163-176, 1995*

KATOH T, NAGATA N, KURODA Y, ET AL. Glutathione S-transferase M1 (GSTM1) and T1 (GSTT1) genetic polymorphism and susceptibility to gastric and colorectal adenocarcinoma. *Carcinogenesis 17:1855-1859, 1996*

KUROKAWA T, JOH T, IKAI M, ET AL. Rebamipide protects against oxygen radical-mediated gastric mucosal injury in rats. *Dig. Dis. Sci. 43 (9 Suppl): 113S-117S, 1998*

MOGHADASIAN MH, GODIN DV. Ethanol-induced gastrointestinal damage. Influence of endogenous antioxidant components and gender. *Digestive Disease Sci. 41:791-797, 1996*

PASECHNIKOV VD, MOSIN VI, VIGRANSKII AO. Lipid peroxidation and the antioxidant enzyme system of the gastric mucosa in peptic ulcer. *Ter. Arkh 60: 30-33, 1988*

SAKURI K, OSAKA T, YAMASAKI K. Protection by rebamipide against acetic acid-induced colitis in rats: relationship with its antioxidative activity. *Dig. Dis. Sci. 43 (9 Suppl): 125S-133S, 1998*

YOSHIKAWA T, MINAMIYAMA Y, ICHKAWA H, ET AL. Role of lipid peroxidation and antioxidants in gastric mucosal injury induced by the hypoxanthine-xanthine oxidase system in rats. *Free Radic. Biol. Med. 23: 243-250. 1997*

ZALA G, FLURY R, WUST, ET AL. Omeprazole/amoxicillin: improved eradication of Helicobacter pylori in smokers because of N-acetylcysteine. *Schweiz. Med. Wochenschr. 124: 1391-1397, 1994*

PANCREATITIS

BRAGANZA JM, SCOTT P, BILTON D, ET AL. Evidence of early oxidative stress in acute pancreatitis. Clues for correction. *Int. J. Pancreatol. 17:69-81, 1995*

GUKOVSKY I, GUKOVSKAYA AS, BLINMAN TA, ET AL. Early NF-kappa B activation is associated with hormone-induced pancreatitis. *American J. Physiol. 275(6 pt 1): G1402-1414, 1998*

LUTHEN R, GRENDELL JH, HAUSSINGER D, NIEDERAU C. Beneficial effects of L-2-oxothiazolidine-4-carboxylate on cerulein pancreatitis in mice. *Gastroenterology 112:1681-1691, 1997*

LUTHEN R, GRENDELL JH, NIEDERAU C, HAUSSINGER D. Trypsinogen activation and glutathione content are linked to pancreatic injury in models of biliary acute pancreatitis. *Int. J. Pancreatol. 24: 193-202, 1998*

LUTHEN R, NIEDERAU C, GRENDELL JH. Intrapancreatic zymogen activation and levels of ATP and glutathione during caerulein pancreatitis in rats. *Am. J. Physiol.* 268(4 pt 1): G592-604, 1995

MATHEW P, WYLLIE R, VAN LENTE F, ET AL. Antioxidants in hereditary pancreatitis. *American J. Gastroenterology* 91: 1558-1562, 1996

McCLOY R. Chronic pancreatitis at Manchester UK. Focus on antioxidant therapy. *Digestion 59 (Suppl 4): 36-48, 1998*

SCHOENBERG MH, BIRK D, BERGER HG. Oxidative stress in acute and chronic pancreatitis. *American J. Clin. Nutr. 62(Supl 6): 1306S-1314S, 1995*

SCHOENBERG MH, BUCHLER M, YOUNES M, ET AL. Effect of antioxidant treatment in rats with acute hemorrhagic pancreatitis. *Dig. Dis. Sci. 39: 1034-1040, 1994*

WALLING MA. Xenobiotic metabolism, oxidant stress and chronic pancreatitis> Focus on glutathione. *Digestion 59(Supl 4): 13-24, 1998*

WANG XD, DENG XM, HARALDSON P, ET AL. Antioxidant and calcium channel blockers counteract endothelial barrier injury induced by acute pancreatitis in rats. *Scand. J. Gastroenterol. 30:1129-1136, 1995*

INFLAMM. BOWEL DISEASE

AHNFELT-RANNE I, NIELSEN OH, CHRISTENSEN A, ET AL. Clinical evidence supporting the radical scavenger mechanism of 5-aminosalicylic acid. *Gastroenterology 98:1162-1169, 1990*

BHASKAR L, RAMAKRISHNA BS, BALASUBRAMANIAN KA. Colonic mucosal antioxidant enzymes and lipid peroxide levels in normal subjects and patients with ulcerative colitis. *J. Gastroent. Hepatol. 10:140-143, 1995*

BUFFINGTON GD, DOE WF. Depleted mucosal antioxidant defenses in inflammatory bowel disease. *Free Radic. Biol. Med. 19: 911-918, 1995*

BULGER EM, HELTON WS. Nutrient antioxidants in gastrointestinal diseases. *Gastrenterol. Clin. North America 27: 403-419, 1998*

CRUZ T, GALVEZ J, OCETE MA, ET AL. Oral administration of rutoside can ameliorate inflammatory bowel disease in rats. *Life Sci. 62:687-695, 1998*

GEERLING BJ, BADART-SMOOK A, STOCKBRUGGER RW, BRUMMER RJ. Comprehensive nutritional status in patients with long-standing Crohn's disease currently in remission. *American J. Clin. Nutr. 67: 919-926, 1998*

GRISHAM MB. Oxidants and free radicals in inflamm. bowel disease. *Lancet 344(8926): 859-861, 1994*

GROSS V, ARNDT H, ANDUS, ET AL. Free radicals in inflammatory bowel diseases pathophysiology and therapeutic implications. *Hepatogastroenterology 41: 320-327, 1994*

HAGEN TM, WIERZBIKA GT, BOWMAN BB, ET AL. Fate of dietary glutathione: disposition in the gastrointestinal tract. *American J. Physiol. 259:G530-G535, 1990*

HARRIS ML, SCHILLER HJ, REILLY PM, ET AL. Free radicals and other reactive oxygen metabolites in inflammatory bowel disease: cause, consequence, or epiphenomenon? *Pharmac. Ther. 53:375-408, 1992*

HOFFENBER EJ, DEUTSCH J, SMITH S, SOKOL RJ. Circulating antioxidant concentrations in children with inflammatory bowel disease. *American J. Clin. Nutr. 65:1482-1488, 1997*

HOLMES EW, YONG SL, EIZENHAMER D, KESHAVARIAN A. Glutathione content of colonic mucosa: evidence for oxidative damage in active ulcerative colitis. *Dig. Dis. Sci. 43:1088-1095, 1998*

IANTOMASI T, MARRACCINI P, FAVILLI F, ET AL. Glutathione metabolism in Crohn's disease. *Biochem. Med. Metab. Biol. 53: 87-91, 1994*

LIH-BRODY L, POWELL SR, COLLIER KP, ET AL. Increased oxidative stress and decreased antioxidant defenses in mucosa of inflammatory bowel disease. *Digestive Diseases and Sciences, 41:2078-2086, 1996*

MARTENSSON J, JAIN A, MEISTER A. Glutathione is required for intestinal function. *Proc. Natl. Acad. Sci. USA 87: 1715-1719, 1990*

SIDO B, HACK V, HOCHLEHNERT A, ET AL. Impairment of intestinal glutathione synthesis in patients with inflammatory bowel disease. *Gut 42: 485-492, 1998*

SOKOL RJ, HOFFENBERG EJ. Antioxidants in pediatric gastrointestinal disease. *Pediatr. Clin. North America 43: 471-488, 1996*

CHAPTER 16
KIDNEY FAILURE AND DIALYSIS

The kidney (renal) system is responsible for filtering the blood and disposing of waste products, toxins and excess fluid in the form of urine. It also maintains water balance and regulates various chemical levels and blood pressure. If the kidneys cannot do their job, waste products and toxins accumulate in the blood. This affects other organ systems, often producing neurological symptoms and circulatory problems. Any sort of acute (sudden) or chronic (gradual/prolonged) illnesses can interfere with kidney function and lead to long-term disease. Kidney disease may shorten life expectancy.

Acute kidney failure can be triggered by all sorts of conditions. For example, a massive hemorrhage, heart attack or overwhelming infection (sepsis) can severely and suddenly restrict blood flow, quickly injuring the sensitive kidney tissues. The most common medical conditions leading to chronic renal failure are hardening of the arteries (atherosclerosis), high blood pressure and diabetes. These long-term diseases damage the circulation involved with the kidneys. Serious damage is also caused by organic and inorganic toxins, such as poisonous mushrooms, solvents, wood alcohol, antifreeze and heavy metals, either inhaled or ingested. There are many other causes of kidney failure, including chronic toxic exposure, inherited kidney diseases, vascular diseases and autoimmune disease.

Kidney disease and renal failure are often triggered by other disorders, so the initial or potential cause must be identified. Diabetics should carefully control their sugar levels. Hypertensive patients must keep blood pressure down, and we all need to eliminate ongoing exposure to toxins. Some drugs help manage chemical imbalances, circulatory problems and accumulation of waste products. Proper nutrition and dietary management are particularly important, and reduced protein intake is often advised in cases of renal failure.

If these measures do not sufficiently limit renal failure, a kidney transplant may be necessary. A less traumatic but very intrusive alternative is dialysis— the use of artificial devices to perform the kidney's functions. Two types of dialysis are commonly used today—hemodialysis and peritoneal dialysis. Like chemical and radiation therapy for cancer patients, these procedures are life-saving but exact a heavy toll on the body's antioxidant defenses.

HEMODIALYSIS
In hemodialysis, blood is shunted out of the body to a mechanical filtering device, cleansed, chemically balanced, and returned to the person's circulatory system. The procedure is repeated several times a week. Each session takes

several hours, during which the patient is physically attached to the machine.

PERITONEAL DIALYSIS

Peritoneal dialysis cleans blood without removing it from the body by using the peritoneal membrane (inner lining of the abdomen) as a filter. This membrane has many of the characteristics of the kidney's filtering system. Once a plastic tube has been implanted in the abdominal wall, patients usually carry out the procedure for themselves. A special dialysis solution (dialysate) is passed through the tube and into the abdomen. Waste material from the blood filters through the small vessels of the peritoneal membrane and is trapped by the fluid. After a few hours, the dialysate is drained and discarded. This procedure may be repeated several times a day.

GSH AND RENAL FAILURE

One cause of renal toxicity and kidney failure is exposure to heavy metals such as mercury, cadmium and lead (see chapter 2). The body detoxifies these substances principally through GSH-related enzymes. Glutathione molecules bind themselves to these metals by the process of chelation, after which they are easily and safely removed from the body. The cells of the kidney are protected by high levels of GSH. In treatment for severe mercury toxicity, tests in laboratory trials and with kidney patients show that adding NAC (a GSH-enhancing drug) to the dialysate helps chelate inorganic mercury and remove it from the solution.

Acute renal failure occurs most commonly when the kidneys suffer inadequate blood flow (ischemia). Laboratory studies at the University of Texas and elsewhere have shown that damage suffered during ischemic renal failure is lessened by the infusion of NAC. This appears to result from an improved supply of antioxidants to the tissue, the detoxification of noxious metabolites like nitric oxide, or both.

Many pharmaceutical drugs are implicated in kidney failure. Such common medications as ibuprofen, acetaminophen and even vitamin D put a high demand on the kidneys, and can damage them. Many anti-cancer agents used in chemotherapy do the same. Cyclosporin—an immuno-suppressant used after organ transplantation and in certain kidney diseases such as the nephrotic syndrome—can also damage the kidneys. Research indicates that elevated antioxidant defenses help protect the body from cyclosporin toxicity.

A rarer cause of kidney failure is polycystic kidney disease—the growth of cysts within the kidneys, eventually impairing their function. Experiments were carried out to artificially lower GSH levels with the drug BSO. This led to worsening of the disease and suggests that the presence of GSH plays a protective role.

The most common cause of poor blood flow is atherosclerosis—the build-up of plaque and other blockages in blood vessels. While GSH detoxifies pharmaceutical drugs and heavy metals, and fights such threats as polycystic kidney disease, it also fights plaque formation by inhibiting lipid peroxidation.

GSH AND DIALYSIS

Renal failure patients suffer from a profound imbalance of oxidants and antioxidants that grows worse as the kidney fails—and dialysis only compounds the problem. In spite of their life-saving action, peritoneal dialysis and especially hemodialysis worsen this aspect of kidney malfunction by increasing oxidative stress levels. Because dialysis is not optional for these patients, its side-effects must be addressed.

Some researchers think that dialysis damages the anti-oxidant system and leads to a dramatic fall in levels of the GSH enzymes that protect us from lipid peroxidation. The result is long-term complications such as accelerated atherosclerosis. In fact, cardiovascular disease is the major cause of morbidity and mortality in patients with end-stage renal failure. Abundant evidence shows that antioxidant support might benefit these patients. A strong link between kidney function and glutathione availability has led some scientists to suggest that glutathione peroxidase levels may be a measure of kidney function.

To test this hypothesis, elderly patients undergoing continuous peritoneal dialysis were studied to determine nutritional status and oxidative stress levels. The former was measured by their ability to absorb and process certain nutrients, especially serum albumin and iron. Test results were well below normal. As for antioxidant defenses, glutathione peroxidase levels were even lower. Clearly, the ability of kidney patients to fight oxidation is profoundly and progressively compromised. Unchallenged oxidative stress leads to untold damage.

To get a clearer picture of the process, the cells of the peritoneal membrane of peritoneal dialysis patients were examined. Researchers found that when the patients were exposed to the life-saving dialysate fluid, GSH levels fell significantly. To counteract this decline, OTZ (a pharmaceutical precursor of GSH) was added to the dialysate fluid. This helped restore GSH to protective levels in these tissues.

The link between GSH status and oxidative stress in dialysis patients is not only widely accepted, it is also considered highly significant. In patients with renal failure oxidative stress damages the circulating red blood cells (erythrocytes) causing low hemoglobin levels (anemia). This damage is normally kept to a minimum by glutathione—the principal antioxidant in this struggle. GSH acts on the surface of the wall of the red blood cell to preserve its integrity. Since hemodialysis causes significant oxidative changes and damages red blood cells, it is important that patients undergoing this procedure maintain high GSH levels. Drugs like NAC and OTZ effectively raise glutathione levels and improve the ability of patients to fight oxidative stress, but there are also safer, dietary ways to raise GSH levels. These are described in chapter 4.

Many dialysis patients are treated for their anemia (shortage of red blood cells) with erythropoietin. This drug is intended to stimulate the production of red blood cells, but provides an additional benefit. It turns out that younger cells have higher levels of GSH and are thus more resistant to lipid peroxidation and cell-wall breakdown. Studies have shown that antioxidants given to patients on erythropoietin may enhance the effectiveness of the drug, making it possible to lower dosage. This was demonstrated by giving patients intravenous GSH during dialysis sessions.

Another important study of hemodialysis patients was conducted by C. Costagliola's team in Italy. In this double-blind study some patients were given intravenous GSH while others received placebo. To test for anemia, doctors measured red blood cell, hemoglobin and hematocrit levels—all known to fall in dialysis patients. Those receiving GSH maintained higher levels than those on placebo. Their levels of oxidative stress also fell. Similar but separate Italian studies led by M. Usberti also resulted in lower levels of anemia. These findings show that elevated GSH levels help manage the anemia to which dialysis patients are particularly prone.

CASE STUDY

Since poor antioxidant and detoxification defenses are implicated in kidney disease and the complications of dialysis, there is reason to believe that GSH supplementation may help individuals like George, a 62 year old former country and western singer.

George had struggled with diabetes for over thirty years. Following only moderate success controlling his sugar levels, he developed progressive kidney failure and subsequent anemia. In a few short years he went from an active, gregarious entertainer to a listless, sofa-ridden recluse. His energy level and concentration deteriorated more and more and the local hospital clinic in Hawaii where he lived was obliged to monitor his condition closely. His levels of biliary urea nitrogen (BUN) and creatinine crept higher and higher—signs of diminishing kidney function—and his red blood cell (hemoglobin) value continued to fall. His physician placed him on a waiting list to undergo preparation for dialysis.

After hearing about GSH, George started taking 20 grams per day of a whey protein isolate high in GSH precursors. Within three weeks his BUN and creatinine levels started to fall—a sign of improving kidney function. After a further three weeks his hemoglobin climbed by one full gram per deciliter (g/dL) of blood and he was again singing at his friends' parties. His wife was uncomfortable about his exposure to alcohol and cigarettes but three months later his renal function tests and hemoglobin levels had improved so much his physician put plans for dialysis on hold.

PROTEIN INTAKE AND RENAL FAILURE

Diseased kidneys already have trouble clearing away breakdown products, many of which come from the digestion of dietary protein. Large quantities of protein leave high levels of urea-nitrogen in the blood, a condition called uremia that leads to further health problems. Therefore, protein intake is restricted and carefully monitored. Renal failure patients are encouraged to eat plenty of carbohydrates, but protein is an important nutrient and cannot be avoided. Since kidney failure patients often can consume it only in limited quantities, its quality is of great importance.

A measure of food protein quality is biological value (BV). It rates the usefulness and quantity of biochemicals made available to the body by a particular food protein. BV especially reflects the proportion of essential to non-essential amino acids. We must have a continuous supply of essential amino acids in our diet. We need non-essential amino acids too, but don't necessarily have to eat them—our body can manufacture them from the essential ones. For dialysis patients, proteins rich in essential amino acids are preferable because of their higher biological value. Some patients undergoing dialysis become protein deficient (hypoalbuminemic). For them, the quality of dietary protein is even more important.

The natural protein with the highest biological value is whey protein, which is ideal for kidney patients. Also, the amino acids found in some whey proteins are GSH precursors (building blocks). Their presence depends principally on how the whey protein is prepared and stored. See chapter 4 for more about whey protein.

CONCLUSION

GSH plays important roles in the prevention and treatment of renal failure, the anemia that often accompanies kidney failure and dialysis, and the cardio-vascular complications of kidney disease. GSH-modifying agents offer promising treatments for both short and long-term complications of kidney failure. GSH acts as both a detoxifier and as an antioxidant, preventing lipid peroxidation. Because some whey proteins contain additional nutritional benefits and act as glutathione precursors, they are a useful complement to traditional therapy.

ANDREOLI SP. Reactive oxygen molecules, oxidant injury and renal disease. *Pediatr. Nephrol.* 5: 733-742, 1991

BONNEFONT-ROUSSELOT D, JAUDON MC, ISSAD B, ET AL. Antioxidant status of elderly chronic renal patients treated by continuous ambulatory peritoneal dialysis. *Nephrol. Dial. Transplant.* 12: 1399-1405, 1997

BREBOROWICZ A, RODELA H, MARTIS L, OREOPOULOS DG. Intracellular glutathione in human peritoneal mesothelial cell exposed in vitro to dialysis fluid. *Int. J. Artif. Organs* 19: 268-275, 1996

CANESTRARI F, GALLI F, GIORGINI A, ET AL. Erythrocyte redox state in uremic anemia: effects of hemodialysis and relevance of glutathione metabolism. *Acta. Haematol.* 91: 187-193, 1994

CAVDAR C, CANSARI T, SEMIN I, ET AL. Lipid peroxidation and antioxidant activity in chronic hemodialysis patients treated with recombinant human erythropoietin. *Scand. J. Urol. Nephrol.* 31: 371-375, 1997

CEBALLOS-PICT I, WITKO-SARSAT V, MERAD-BOUDIA M, ET AL. Glutathione antioxidant system as a marker of oxidative stress in chronic renal failure. *Free Radic. Biol. Med.* 21:845-853, 1996

CHEN CK, LIAW JM, JUANG JG, LIN TH. Antioxidant enzymes and trace elements in hemodialyzed patients. *Biol. Trace Elem. Res.* 58: 140-157, 1997

COSTAGLIOLA C, ROMANO L, SCIBELLI G, ET AL. Anemia and chronic renal failure: a therapeutic approach by reduced glutathione parenteral administration. *Nephron* 61: 404-408, 1992

COSTAGLIOLA C, ROMANO L, SORICE P, DI BENEDETTO A. Anemia and chronic renal failure: the possible role of the oxidative state of glutathione. *Nephron* 52: 11-14, 1989

CRISTOL JP, BOSE JY, BADIOU S, ET AL. Erythropoietin and oxidative stress in haemodialysis: beneficial effects of vitamin E supplementation. *Nephrol. Dial. Transplant.* 12: 2312-2317, 1997

DIAMOND GL, ZALUPS RK. Understanding renal toxicity of heavy metals. *Toxicol. Pathol.* 26: 92-103, 1998

DiMARI J, MEGYESI J, UDVARHELYI N, ET AL. N-acetyl cysteine ameliorates ischemic renal failure. *American J. Physiol.* 272(3 Pt 2): F292-F298, 1997

DURAK I, KARABACAK HI, BUYUKKOCAK S, ET AL. Impaired antioxidant defense system in the kidney tissues from rabbits treated with cyclosporin. Protective effects of vitamins E and C. *Nephron* 78: 207-211, 1998

EPPERLEIN MM, NOUROOZ-ZADEH J, JAYASENA SD, ET AL. Nature and biological significance of free radicals generated during bicarbonate hemodialysis. *J. American Soc. Nephrol.* 9: 457-463, 1998

FERGUSON CL, CANTILENA LR JR. Mercury clearance from human plasma during in vitro dialysis: screening systems for chelating agents. *J. Toxicol. Clin. Toxicol.* 30: 423-441, 1992

LUND ME, BANNER W JR, CLARKSON TW, BERLIN M. Treatment of acute methylmercury ingestion by hemodialysis with N-acetylcysteine (Mucomyst) infusion and 2,3-dimercaptopropane sulfonate. *J. Toxicol. Clin. Toxicol.* 22: 31-49, 1984

MARTIN-MATEO MC, DEL CANTO-JAFIEZ E, BARRERO-MARTINEZ MJ. Oxidative stress and enzyme activity in ambulatory renal patients undergoing continuous peritoneal dialysis. *Renal Failure* 20: 117-124, 1998

Martin-Mateo MC, Sanchez-Portugal M, Iglesias S, et al. Oxidative stress in chronic renal failure. *Renal Failure 21: 155-167, 1999*

Mimic-Oka J, Simic T, Elkmescic V, Dragicevic P. Erythrocyte glutathione peroxidase and superoxide dismutase activities in different stages of chronic renal failure. *Clin Nephrol. 44: 44-48, 1995*

Moberly JB, Logan J, Borum PR, et al. Elevation of whole-blood glutathione in peritoneal dialysis patients by L-2-oxothiazolidine-4-carboxylate, a cysteine prodrug (Procysteine). *J. American Soc. Nephrol. 9: 1093-1099, 1998*

Ong-awyooth L, Ong-ajyooth S, Tiensong K, et al. Reduced free radical scavengers and chronic renal failure. *J. Med. Assoc. Thai. 80: 101-108, 1997*

Pasaoglu H, Muhtaroglu S, Gunes M, Utas C. The role of the oxidative state of glutathione and glutathione-related enzymes in anemia of hemodialysis patients. *Clin. Biochem. 29: 567-572, 1996*

Ross EA, Koo LC, Moberly JB. Low whole blood and erythrocyte levels of glutathione in hemodialysis and peritoneal dialysis patients. *American J. Kidney Disease 30: 489-494, 1997*

Roxborough HE, Mercer C, McMaster D, et al. Plasma glutathione peroxidase activity is reduced in haemodialysis patients. *Nephron 81: 278-283, 1999*

Salom MG, Ramirez P, Carbonell LF, et al. Protective effect of N-acetyl-L-cysteine on the renal failure induced by inferior cava occlusion. *Transplantation 65: 1315-1321, 1998*

Schiavon R, Biasioli S, De Fanti E, et al. The plasma glutathione peroxidase enzyme in hemodialyzed subjects. *ASAIO J 40:968-971, 1994*

Schiavon R, Guidi GC, Biasioli S, et al. Plasma glutathione peroxidase activity as an index of renal function. *Eur. J. Clin. Chem. Clin. Biochem. 32: 759-765, 1994*

Torres VE, Bengal RJ, Litwiller RD, Wilson DM. Aggravation of polycystic kidney disease in Han:SPRD rats by buthionine sulfoxamine. *J. American Soc. Nephrol. 8: 1283-1291, 1997*

Usberti M, Lima G, Arisi M, et al. Effect of exogenous reduced glutathione on the survival of red blood cells in hemodialyzed patients. *J. Nephrol. 10: 261-265, 1997*

Whitin JC, Tham DM, Bhamre S, et al. Plasma glutathione peroxidase and its relationship to renal proximal tubule function. *Mol. Genet. Metab. 65: 238-245, 1998*

Yoshimura S, Suemizu H, Nomoto Y, et al. Plasma glutathione peroxidase deficiency caused by renal dysfunction. *Nephron 73: 207-211, 1996*

Zachee P, Ferrant A, Daelmans R, et al. Reduced glutathione for the treatment of anemia during hemodialysis: a preliminary communication. *Nephron 71: 343-349, 1995*

CHAPTER 17

EYES, EARS, NOSE, THROAT AND TEETH

It's well known that glutathione is important for the normal functioning of the eye. Some of the earliest studies with GSH focused on its role in preventing cataracts, and GSH is relatively well known among ophthalmologists. Specialists in ear, nose and throat (ENT) and in dentistry have only recently become aware of the role of glutathione in the diseases they treat. Given the critical roles of GSH as the body's most important naturally occurring antioxidant, its ability to detoxify substances encountered in the environment and its immune-sustaining abilities, glutathione research is now finally picking up in these fields as well.

OPHTHALMOLOGY

Cataracts

Cataract is a clouding (opacification) that takes place in the lens of the eye. It is the leading cause of morbidity and functional impairment among the elderly and leads to more than one million operations per year in the United States.

The lens of the eye is composed of deceptively simple tissue. This completely transparent part of the eye has the job of focusing light on the retina, which it does by changing shape to adjust its focal length. Scientists believe that any damage to the lens, no matter how small, contributes to opacification. This usually results from physical injury, repeated exposure to ionizing radiation (such as sunlight) or any of a host of different illnesses. Over time the damage accumulates and the lens begins to cloud.

Oxidative stress plays a role in the aging of the lens, so antioxidants are an important defense against cataracts. The researcher M.A. Babizhaev in Russia measured the breakdown products of lipid peroxidation as cataracts developed. He found that as the cataract worsened, oxidative stress increased. An Italian team at the University of Bari went a step further and demonstrated that in people with cataracts the loss of GSH paralleled the increase in oxidative breakdown products.

It is known that cataract in humans usually shows significant, extensive oxidation of lens proteins. With this in mind, researchers experimented on cataracts by stimulating them with various chemicals. They showed that cataract formation could be delayed or prevented by elevated GSH levels. Clearly, the key defense in the lens against oxidation is glutathione.

The legendary GSH expert, Alton Meister and a team at Cornell University in New York, used the drug BSO to deplete glutathione levels in the eyes of laboratory animals. The animals subsequently developed cataracts. Meister's team was then able to prevent cataract formation by reestablishing glutathione levels with GSH-monoester and suggested that this strategy may be effective in delaying cataract formation.

Diabetics are more prone to cataract than non-diabetics. E. Altomare's team in Italy measured glutathione status in the lenses of four groups of patients: diabetics with and without cataracts and non-diabetics with and without cataracts. As expected, both cataract groups showed impaired glutathione defenses, but the diabetic groups fared worse in all cases.

CASE STUDY

Edgar loved to paint. Now retired, he could pursue this hobby full-time if he so pleased. Over the previous few years, his wife had commented that the color in his landscapes was too loud. At first he did not believe he had changed his techniques, but a side-by-side comparison with earlier works proved him wrong. Still, he felt the colors in previous paintings were "weak." A routine check revealed cataracts. One eye required surgery, the other was "not yet ripe." After surgery he eventually recovered excellent vision, but post-operative complications left him hesitant about having the same treatment on the other eye. His wife did some homework, learning about glutathione and cataracts. She started him on Immunocal. One year later, his ophthalmologist was baffled by the unusual observation that the cataract was less dense.

MACULAR DEGENERATION

Macular degeneration is a progressive loss of sight due to breakdown of the macula—the portion of the retina responsible for fine vision. Figure 38 shows its location on the back of the eye. Age-related macular degeneration (ARMD) is a leading cause of visual loss in people over 65. Although susceptibility to this disease may be predominantly genetic, contributing factors such as smoking and atherosclerosis can make it worse. This disease is thought to result from the cumulative damage of free radicals primarily released by exposure to ultraviolet (UV) sunlight, but other sources of oxidative stress may play a role.

Because elderly people generally have low GSH levels, they are predisposed to oxidative damage. Researchers have shown that low GSH levels go along with poor eye health in ARMD patients compared to normal control groups. Experiments have been conducted to test glutathione's antioxidant

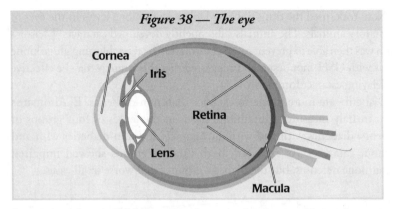

Figure 38 — The eye

Cornea

Iris

Retina

Lens

Macula

function in the whole body and in the eyes of patients suffering from macular degeneration. S.M. Cohen and his team at the University of California (Davis) found significantly altered GSH activity in blood samples of macular degeneration patients. It appears that high GSH levels correspond to healthy eyes and suggests a possible role for GSH in the protection against or delay of this disease.

GLAUCOMA

Glaucoma is a serious condition in which fluid pressure within the eye rises. A certain amount of pressure is necessary to maintain the shape of the eyeball. Too much pressure compresses and obstructs the small blood vessels within the eye. This damages the surrounding areas, most importantly the optic nerve. Glaucoma is one of the leading causes of visual loss. It becomes more common as we age, runs in certain families, and is often seen in conjunction with diabetes, hypertension (high blood pressure) and severe myopia (nearsightedness). Traditional therapy aims to relieve the pressure in the eye either surgically or with drugs.

The Russians A.I. Bunin, A.A. Filina and V.P. Erichev measured GSH levels in the eyes of hundreds of patients undergoing surgery for all sorts of reasons. The lowest GSH levels were found among cataracts patients and in patients with open angle glaucoma. They noticed this fall even at the earliest stages of the disease and suggested that reestablished glutathione levels would help prevent or delay this process, and used the nutritional supplement lipoic acid to do so (see chapter 4).

A Harvard University group investigated different GSH-related compounds to increase the outflow of fluid from the eye and reduce pressure within it. In combination with the topical form of ethacrynic acid (a diuretic) they found that cysteine, glutathione and N-acetylcysteine all benefited eye pressure and even lessened the side effects of the drug.

EAR, NOSE & THROAT

GLUTATHIONE IN THE UPPER RESPIRATORY TRACT

All the food we eat, fluids we drink and air we breathe pass through the nose, mouth and throat that make up the upper respiratory tract. The importance of GSH in the lower respiratory tract (lungs) is well known. Since the upper tract is our front-line contact with the external environment, it seems fitting that glutathione would protect us here against xenobiotics (infections and toxins).

The respiratory tract is lined with a fluid made up of a complicated mixture of biochemicals and cells of the immune system, called the respiratory tract lining fluid (RTLF). Glutathione is the main antioxidant in this fluid and provides our initial defense against inhaled toxins. Institutions like the Inhalation and Toxicology Research Institute in Albuquerque, New Mexico started researching the role of antioxidant enzyme activities in RTLF in the early 1990's. More recent work at the University of California (Davis) elaborates further on the role of antioxidants in this fluid.

This research project is only one of several focusing on the importance of glutathione in respiratory tract lining fluids, where it protects us from xenobiotics and infection. In severe or prolonged illness, these GSH levels may become depleted and enable the disease to progress and cause further complications. Furthermore, N.S. Krishna and his team at the University of Kentucky showed that this glutathione defense system weakens with aging, and more quickly in men than women.

B. Testa and M. Mesolella from the Institute of Otolaryngology, University of Naples, used a GSH nasal aerosol spray in their studies. Statistics from the experiments show that this treatment significantly improved nasal obstruction, rhinorrhea (runny nose) and ear fullness. The lining of the nose is one of few human tissues that readily absorb glutathione. Most other tissue can only use the glutathione it manufactures for itself from GSH precursors.

SINUSITIS

Infection or inflammation of the sinus cavities in the bones of the face is one of the most common reasons people go to the doctor. As many as 50 million Americans are affected each year, most commonly by bacterial or viral infection, allergies and impaired mucus flow. Most treatments are designed to either destroy the infection or improve drainage of mucus from the sinuses. The sinus cavities are near the front of the head, behind the forehead, nose region and cheeks, as shown in figure 39.

Physicians have long used the drug NAC for the treatment of disorders involving thickened lung secretions (cystic fibrosis, chronic bronchitis). It is now being used for upper airway problems such as sinusitis. NAC breaks down mucus and raises glutathione levels at the same time. American, French,

Italian, Korean and Scandinavian research teams have all studied the efficacy of NAC and other antioxidants in the treatment of sinusitis.

The Amsterdam group led by G.J. Westerveld showed the glutathione levels fall during chronic sinusitis and concluded that this drop is part of a generally decreased antioxidant defense, which subsequently worsens the disorder.

EAR INFECTION

Infection of the middle ear is an extremely common cause of illness, especially among children. It is caused mostly by a combination of fluid buildup in the middle ear and infection. The triggering event often is a viral infection, but the site is commonly superinfected (one infection on top of another) by bacteria. Treatment for many years was with antibiotics, but doctors are increasingly reluctant to over-prescribe these drugs nowadays, especially for ear infections. Decongestants can help drain fluid from the middle ear, through the eustachian canal and into the throat.

More and more evidence shows that free radicals play a large part in the development of inflammation leading to middle-ear infections. Studies examining GSH levels in these tissues show that they fluctuate according to how infected or inflamed the site is. Scientists have examined the effects of both ways of raising glutathione levels—topical and ingested, and have found both to be effective ways to address oxidative stress in these tissues.

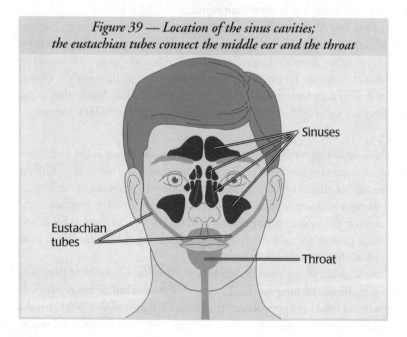

Figure 39 — Location of the sinus cavities; the eustachian tubes connect the middle ear and the throat

Patients with middle-ear infections are sometimes treated by placing tubes through the eardrum to drain accumulated fluid and prevent subsequent infection. This does the job but has its downside. In response to this intrusion by a foreign object the body sets up an inflammatory process. The procedure also encourages a high oxygen state in the middle ear. Both of these factors lead to free radical and oxyradical formation, causing changes in the cells lining the middle ear that lead to scarring and fibrosis. T. Ovesen and his team of ENT researchers at the Aarhus University in Denmark instilled liquid NAC through these small tubes. The drug reduced inflammation and prevented the long-term scarring that normally follows this condition.

DEAFNESS AND HEARING LOSS

Almost 30 million North Americans experience sufficient hearing loss to interfere with their ability to converse. This is almost one person in ten. One percent of our population cannot hear at all and is considered deaf. Almost a third of individuals over the age of 65 have some form of hearing loss and this figure increases with age.

There are many causes of impaired hearing, all of which broadly fit into two categories: conductive hearing loss caused by a mechanical problem in the middle ear or external ear canal and sensorineural hearing loss, a problem of the inner ear or auditory nerve. In the latter category the problem may be sensory—in the cochlea, the essential organ of hearing—or neural—affecting the auditory nerve itself. Causes of hearing loss include physical trauma, exposure to repeated loud noise, infection, tumors and malignancies, obstruction of the ear canal, genetic defects, toxins and drugs, various neurological diseases and the aging process in general.

NOISE EXPOSURE

Exposure to noise accounts for about one third of all hearing loss cases. It's particularly unfortunate because most cases are avoidable. All it takes is appropriate caution. Teenagers often enjoy and are fed damaging levels of noise. Preventive aids such as earplugs can help. So can turning down the volume.

People working in noisy environments and those with noisy hobbies all risk their hearing. Most of us have experienced that buzzing, ringing or hissing in our ears after leaving a concert or construction site. Hearing is sometimes diminished temporarily. This can last minutes or days and is generally followed by a return to normal. This is a 'temporary threshold shift' and is caused by injury to the sensitive hair cells in the cochlea—the spiral shaped organ in the middle ear. Severe, repeated or prolonged exposure to excessive noise can destroy these neurological hair cells and lead to permanent hearing damage.

Interestingly enough, the cochlea can be trained to withstand greater noise levels and suffer less damage. This is known as 'sound conditioning' or 'toughening'. Priming the ear to low level noise before the higher levels seems to protect from hearing loss. Researchers at the Albert Einstein College of Medicine in New York examined the biochemical changes found in sound conditioning. They saw that certain enzymes which raise GSH levels or keep glutathione in a reduced (non-oxidized) state were stimulated by low noise exposure. This suggests that whatever protects or increases the glutathione system in the cochlea also protects against noise-induced hearing loss.

Other studies of glutathione and noise exposure lend support to this model. A team at the Kresge Hearing Research Institute at the University of Michigan chemically depleted glutathione levels using the drug BSO, with the result that noise-induced hearing loss was more profound. The same team went on to raise GSH levels with OTC, with the result that hearing loss was minimized.

Dr. Denis McBride, from the Office of Naval Research in Arlington, Virginia, found that delivering antioxidants directly to the cochlea through a small tube could prevent permanent damage following noise exposure. This treatment must be delivered within six hours of exposure. Other researchers suggest that workers with prolonged noise exposure would gain long-term benefits from elevated glutathione levels.

HEARING LOSS INDUCED BY DRUGS OR TOXINS

Exposure to all sorts of pharmaceutical chemicals may lead to sensorineural hearing loss. They include high doses of aspirin, several different antibiotics, a number of diuretics (high blood pressure medication), quinine, and several chemotherapy agents.

One of these chemotherapy drugs is cisplatin. It is a common cancer treatment that can also damage auditory neurons (hearing nerve cells). Researchers have shown that this damage is caused by free radicals in the tissue. Studies lowering GSH levels show increased damage, those raising GSH decreased the damage. It seems that raising glutathione levels could protect patients from both the hearing and the kidney damage that may result from this treatment.

Similar studies have been conducted in relation to aminoglycoside antibiotics (gentamycin, kanamycin, amikacin, others) and loop diuretics (lasix, furosemide, ethacrynic acid, others). Research teams from the USA (University of Michigan, Southern Illinois University), Japan (Hiroshima General Hospital), and Germany (Universitats HNO) all found that substances used to raise glutathione activity have a protective effect against the hearing loss than can be provoked by these drugs. Dr. C.P. Maruzi from the Houston Medical Center even suggests that deafness following acute meningitis may be caused by free radicals in the inflamed tissue, and that antioxidants preventing lipid peroxidation in the auditory nerve would protect the patient.

DENTISTRY

A fact little known by doctors but common knowledge to dentists is that dental and periodontal (gum) disease is the most common illness in America. Even more importantly, periodontal disease has recently been linked to more serious systemic diseases that may be encouraged by poor oral hygiene. Robert Genco, editor-in-chief of the Journal of Periodontology has said, "It seems clear that gum disease, far from being just an oral health problem, actually represents a significant health risk to millions of people."

It goes beyond unsightly smiles and bad breath. Infections and toxins in the mouth have been linked to heart disease, stroke, bacteremia, prosthetic device infection, diabetes, pulmonary disease, impairment of fetal growth and other systemic disease. Dr. Charles Mayo, founder of the Mayo Clinic is purported to have said, "Preventive dentistry can extend your life expectancy 10 years."

One of the most impressive of all studies is the Veteran Administration's Normative Aging Study in Boston. They followed the medical history of over 1000 outwardly healthy men, starting in the 1960's. Those who started out with any sign of gum disease suffered about twice the death rate— mostly from cardiovascular disease—than those with healthy gums. At a recent conference on the subject, Dr. Raul Garcia, one of the researchers, stated, "Gum disease kills. Floss or die!"

Links have been made between the infective and inflammatory processes of periodontitis and free radicals. Research will show whether elevated glutathione levels combat the formation of free radicals and bolster the immune system's defenses. Immunotec Research Ltd. has developed a toothpaste with glutathione precursors. Direct application to these tissues may combat the disease.

CONCLUSION

Scientists studying the eye have long recognized the importance of glutathione as an ocular antioxidant. Practical applications are now available for the prevention and treatment of disorders like cataract and macular degeneration.

GSH plays three roles in the upper respiratory tract. Its suppression of free radicals, detoxification of environmental xenobiotics and reinforcement of the immune system give us tools against airway irritation from pollution, sinusitis, otitis and other infections and inflammations of our ears, nose and throat. Having long utilized NAC in pulmonary disease, the medical profession is now pursuing its use in ear, nose and throat diseases. An interesting clinical application of elevated GSH is the treatment and prevention of noise-induced hearing loss as well as that caused by certain ototoxic drugs.

Dentistry's importance in total health care is now acknowledged. Periodontal disease is as a risk factor for heart disease, stroke and other systemic disease, and enhanced glutathione levels should be part of a good oral hygiene program.

EYES, EARS, NOSE, THROAT & TEETH

ALTOMARE E, VENDEMIALE G, GRATTAGLIANO I, ET AL. Human diabetic cataract: role of lipid peroxidation. *Diabetes. Metab. 21: 173-179, 1995*

BABIZHAEV MA. Accumulation of lipid peroxidation products in the human lens during cataract maturation. *Vopr. Med. Khim. 31: 100-104, 1985*

BABIZHAEV MA, SHVEDOVA AA, ARKHIPENKO IV, KAGAN VE. Accumulation of lipid peroxidation products in cataractous lenses. *Biull. Eksp. Biol. Med. 100: 299-301, 1985*

BEBEAR JP, DARROUZET V. Efficacy of N-acetylcysteine by oral route in chronic sinusitis. *Rev. Laryngol. Otol. Rhinol. 109: 185-186, 1988*

BECK J, GARCIA R, HEISS G, ET AL. Periodontal disease and cardiovascular disease. *J. Periodont. 67(10 Suppl): 1123-1137, 1996*

BONER AL, VALLETTE EA, ANDRIOLI A, ET AL. A combination of cefuroxime and N-acetylcysteine for the treatment of maxillary sinusitis in children with respiratory allergy. *Int. J. Clin. Pharmacol. Ther. Toxicol. 22: 511-514, 1984*

BOWLES WH, BURNS H JR. Catalase/peroxidase activity in dental pulp. *J. Endod. 18: 527-534, 1992*

BUNIN AI, FILINA AA, ERICHEV VP. A glutathione deficiency in open-angle glaucoma and the approaches to its correction. *Vestn. Oftalmol. 108: 13-15, 1992*

CHAPPLE IL. Reactive oxygen species and antioxidants in inflammatory diseases. *J. Clin. Periodontol. 24: 287-296, 1997*

CROSS CE, VAN DER VILET A, O'NEIL CA, ET AL. Oxidants, antioxidants, and respiratory tract lining fluids, *Environ. Health Perspect. 102(Suppl 10): 185-191, 1994*

COHEN SM, OLIN KL, FEUER WJ, ET AL. Low glutathione reductase and peroxidase activity in age-related macular degeneration. *Br. J. Ophthalmol. 78: 791-794, 1994*

DAHL AR, HADLEY WM. Nasal cavity enzymes involved in xenobiotic metabolism: effects on the toxicity of inhalants. *Crit. Rev. Toxicol. 21: 345-372, 1991*

DE LA PAZ MA, ZHANG J, FRIDOVITCH I. Antioxidant enzymes of the human retina: effect of age on enzyme activity of macula and periphery. *Curr. Eye Res. 15: 273-278, 1996*

EPSTEIN DL, HOOSHMAND LB, EPTEIN MP. Thiol adducts of ethacrynic acid increase outflow facility in enucleated calf eyes. *Curr. Eye Res. 11:253-258, 1992*

FILINA AA, DAVYDOVA NG, KOLOMOITSEVA EM. The effect of lipoic acid on the components of the glutathione system in the lachrymal fluid of patients with open-angle glaucoma. *Vestn. Oftalmol. 109: 5-7, 1993*

GABAIZADEH R, STAECKER H, LIU W, VAN DE WATER TR. BDNF protection of auditory neurons from cisplatin involves changes in intracellular levels of both reactive oxygen species and glutathione. *Brain Res. Mol. Brain Res. 50: 71-78, 1997*

GARCIA RI, KRALL EA, VOKONAS PS. Periodontal disease and mortality from all causes in the VA Dental Longitudinal Study. *Ann. Periodontol. 3: 339-349, 1998*

GARETZ SL, ALTSHULER RA, SCHACHT J. Attenuation of gentamycin ototoxicity by glutathione in the guinea pig in vivo. *Hearing Research 77: 81-87, 1994*

GERVASI PG, LONGO V, NALDI F, ET AL. Xenobiotic-metabolizing enzymes in human respiratory nasal mucosa. *Biochem. Pharmacol. 41: 177-184, 1991*

GRAU AJ, BUGGLE F, ZEIGLER C, ET AL. Association between acute cerebrovascular ischemia and chronic and recurrent infection. *Stroke 28: 1724-1729, 1997*

HAMAGUCHI Y, JUHN SK, SAKAKURA Y. Recurrence of antigen-induced otitis media by thiol compound. *American J. Otolaryngol. 9: 111-116, 1988*

HOFFMAN DW, WHITWORTH CA, JONES KL, RYBAK LP. Nutritional status, glutathione levels, and ototoxicity of loop diuretics and aminoglycoside antibiotics. *Hearing Research 31: 217-222, 1987*

HOFFMAN DW, WHITWORTH CA, JONES KL, RYBAK LP. Potentiation of ototoxicity by glutathione depletion. *Ann. Otol. Laryngol. 97: 36-41, 1988*

JACONO AA, HU B, KOPKE RD, ET AL. Changes in cochlear antioxidant enzyme activity after sound conditioning and noise exposure in the chinchilla. *Hearing Research 117: 31-38, 1998*

KEINER S, ZIMMERMANN U. Glutathione-SH as protection from cytotoxic side effects of gentamycin. Studies with isolated outer hair cells. *HNO 43: 492-497, 1995*

KILIC F, HANDELMAN GJ, TRABER K. ET AL. Modeling cortical cataractogenesis XX. In vitro effect of alpha-lipoic acid on glutathione concentrations in lens in model diabetic cataractogenesis. *Biochem. Mol. Biol. Int. 46: 585-595, 1998*

KRISHNA NS, GETCHALL TV, DHOOPER N, ET AL. Age- and gender-related trends in the expression of glutathione S-transferases in human nasal mucosa. *Ann. Otol. Rhinol. Laryngol. 104: 812-822, 1995*

LAUTERMANN J, MCLAREN J, SCHACHT J. Glutathione protection against gentamycin ototoxicity depends on nutritional status. *Hearing Research 86: 15-24, 1995*

LINETSKY M, RANSON N, ORTWERTH BJ. The aggregation in human lens proteins blocks the scavenging of UVA-generated singlet oxygen by ascorbic acid and glutathione. *Arch. Biochem. Biophys. 351: 180-188, 1998*

MARTENSSON J, STEINHERZ R, JAIN A, MEISTER A, Glutathione ester prevents buthionine sulfoxamine-induced cataracts and lens epithelial cell damage. *Proc. Natl. Acad. Sci. USA 86: 8727-8731, 1989*

MATTILA KJ, VALTONEN VV, NIEMINEN M, HUTTUNEN JK. Dental infection and the risk of new coronary events: prospective study of patients with documented coronary artery disease. *Clin. Infect. Dis. 20: 588-592, 1995*

MAURIZI CP. Could antioxidant therapy reduce the incidence of deafness following bacterial meningitis? *Med. Hypotheses 52: 85-87, 1999*

MENDEZ MV, SCOTT T, LAMORTE W, ET AL. An association between periodontal disease and peripheral vascular disease. *American J. Surgery 176: 153-157, 1998*

MICELLI-FERRARI T, VENDEMIALE G, GRATTAGLIANO I, ET AL. Role of lipid peroxidation in the pathogenesis of myopic and senile cataract. *Br. J. Ophthalmol. 80: 840-843, 1996*

NISHIDA I, TAKUMIDA M. Attenuation of aminoglycoside ototoxicity by glutathione. *ORL J Otorhinolaryngol. Relat. Spec. 58: 68-73, 1996*

OFFENBACHER S, KATZ V, FERTIK G, ET AL. Periodontal infection as a possible risk factor for pre-term low birth weight. *J. Periodont. 67: 1103-1113, 1996*

OVESEN T, PAASKE PB, ELBROEND O. Local application of N-acetylcysteine in secretory otitis media in rabbits. *Clin. Otolaryngol. 17: 327-331, 1992*

PARKS RR, HUANG CC, HADDAD J JR. Middle ear catalase distribution in an animal model of otitis media. *Eur. Arch. Otorhinolaryngol. 253: 445-449, 1996*

PAU H, GRAF P, SIES H. Glutathione levels in human lens: regional distribution in different forms of cataract. *Exp. Eye Res. 50: 17-20, 1990*

Potter DW, Finch L, Udinsky JR. Glutathione content and turnover in rat nasal epithelia. Toxicol. appl. *Pharmacol. 135: 185-191, 1995*

Prashar S, Pandav SS, Gupta A, Nath R. Antioxidant enzymes in RBC's as a biological index of age-related macula degeneration. *Acta. Ophthalmol. (Copnh) 71: 214-218, 1993*

Rao GN, Sadasivudu B, Cotlier E. Studies on glutathione S-transferases, glutathione peroxidase and glutathione reductase in human normal and cataractous lenses. *Ophthalmic Res. 15: 173-179, 1983*

Ravi R, Somani SM, Rybak LP. Mechanism of cisplatin ototoxicity: antioxidant system. Pharmacol. *Toxicol. 76: 386-394, 1995*

Rhee CS, Majima Y, Cho JS, et al. Effects of mucokinetic drugs on rheological properties of reconstituted human nasal mucus. *Arch. Otolaryngol. Head Neck Surg. 125: 101-105, 1999*

Scannapieco FA. American Academy of Periodontology, Position Paper Periodontal disease as a potential risk factor for systemic diseases. *J. Periodontol. 69: 841-850, 1998*

Scannapieco FA, Papandonatos GD, Dunford RG. Associations between oral conditions and respiratory disease in a national sample survey population. *Ann. Periodontol. 3: 251-256, 1998*

Schmidt AM, Weidman E, Lalla E, et al. Advanced glycation end-products (AGE's) induce oxidant stress in the gingiva: a potential mechanism underlying accelerated periodontal disease associated with diabetes. *J. Periodontal. Res. 31: 508-515, 1996*

Simonelli F, Nesti A, Pensa M, et al. Lipid peroxidation and human cataractogenesis in diabetics and severe myopia. *Exp. Eye Res. 49: 181-187, 1989*

Sweeney MP, Bagg J, Fell GS, Yip B. The relationship between micronutrient depletion and oral health in geriatrics. *J. Oral Pathol. Med. 23: 168-171, 1994*

Testa B, Mesolella M, Teata D, et al. Glutathione in the upper respiratory tract. *Ann. Otol. Rhinol. Laryngol. 104: 117-119, 1995*

Tingey DP, Schroeder A, Epstein MP, Epstein DL. Effects of topical ethacrynic acid adducts on intraoccular pressure in rabbits and monkeys. *Arch. Ophthalmol. 110: 699-702, 1992*

Van der Vilet A, O'Neil CA, Cross CE, et al. Determination of low-molecular mass antioxidant concentrations in human respiratory tract lining fluids. *American J. Physiol. 276(2 Pt 1): L289-L296, 1999*

Westerveld GJ, Dekker I, Voss HP, et al. Antioxidant levels in the nasal mucosa of patients with chronic sinusitis and healthy controls. *Arch. Otolaryngol. Head Neck Surg. 123: 201-204, 1997*

Yamasoba T, Harris C, Shoji F, et al. Influence of intense sound exposure on glutathione synthesis in the cochlea. *Brain Research 804: 72-78, 1998*

Yamasoba T, Nuttall AL, Harris C. Role of glutathione in protection against noise-induced hearing loss. *Brain Research 784: 82-90, 1998*

Zeiger RS. Prospects for ancillary treatment of sinusitis in the 1990's. *J. Allergy Immunol. 90: 478-495, 1992*

CHAPTER 18
PREGNANCY, LACTATION AND CHILDBIRTH

Women undergo drastic physiological changes during pregnancy. More so, in fact, than at any other time except for their own birth. Pregnancy is challenging at the best of times. It is fraught with hazards and potential complications. The mother and child are at the mercy of their genetic makeup, which may be the main cause of some of these challenges. However, they are also susceptible to the environment—mainly the air, food and liquids they consume. It is especially important to avoid or limit exposure to toxins and teratogens (substances causing birth defects). Good general health and nutrition are important for both mother and child. Vitamins and antioxidants naturally have an important role to play. GSH wears several hats in this scenario and proves itself indispensable.

The list of pregnancy-related illnesses is very long. We cannot describe them all in this chapter but will cover those in which the role of GSH has particular relevance. Since the newborn's GSH levels greatly depend on the mothers' glutathione status, we will also discuss the brief but eventful stages of childbirth and the neonatal period (from birth to six weeks).

Many pregnant women are susceptible to hypertension (high blood pressure). This is caused by hormonal shifts and changes in blood volume and circulation. Some women are always hypertensive and some experience this problem only during pregnancy. About one in twenty have a more serious condition called pre-eclampsia.

PRE-ECLAMPSIA, ECLAMPSIA & HYPERTENSION OF PREGNANCY

Symptoms of pre-eclampsia are hypertension, proteinurea (protein in the urine) and edema—accumulation of water in the tissues leading to swelling, particularly of the hands, feet and face. It usually occurs between the 20th week of gestation and the week following birth. Its exact cause is unknown but most obstetricians (pregnancy and delivery doctors) consider it a vascular disease. It occurs most often in first-time pregnancies and in women who already have high blood pressure.

If left unchecked, one in 200 cases of pre-eclampsia progresses to eclampsia, a very serious condition featuring convulsive seizures and coma. If not dealt with promptly eclampsia is usually fatal, so it must be treated aggressively. Another major complication of pre-eclampsia is the HELLP syndrome: Hemolysis (red blood cell breakdown), Elevated Liver enzymes (indicator of liver damage), and Low Platelet count (impaired blood clotting).

Treatment for a mild case of eclampsia includes bed rest, increased fluid intake and nutritional support. Attempts to stimulate urination and stabilize fluid levels with diuretics and salt restriction have no effect. Blood pressure and neurological symptoms are best controlled with intravenous magnesium sulfate and hydralazine. The definitive solution for eclampsia patients is childbirth, which is often induced or cesarean.

Pre-eclampsia and GSH

Many scientists have noticed that when pregnancy is complicated by pre-eclampsia, there is a precipitous drop in the patient's antioxidant function. This has been linked to the oxidation of circulating fats (lipid peroxidation) which damages the sensitive endothelium (lining of the blood vessels—see chapter 9). Subsequent constriction of the muscles in the artery wall leads to narrowing of the passageways and decreased blood flow. Combined with the demands of gestation, this triggers a complex cascade of events that can lead to full-blown eclampsia.

Researchers have consistently found glutathione levels of hypertensive pregnant mothers to be very low. G. Chen and his team at the University of Glasgow believe this depletion might account for some of the important features of pregnancy-induced hypertension—elevated intracellular calcium, decreased red blood cell deformability and endothelial damage. D.W. Branch's team at the University of Utah think the lipid peroxidation that follows may be part of the pathological process in cells of pre-eclamptic placentas—the foam-cell formation of decidua. It also seems that measuring GSH levels may be a good way to determine the severity of this disease.

The HELLP syndrome is a serious complication of pre-eclampsia. Patients suffer liver damage, breakdown of red blood cells and loss of blood-clotting cells. GSH loss is particularly pronounced. Researchers have established a threefold correlation—severity of the pre-eclampsia, cell fragility and the level of GSH-oxidation.

C. Lees' obstetrical team in London, England attempted to control symptoms in a test-group of pre-eclampsia patients. Women with severe cases not responding to traditional therapy were given S-nitroso-glutathione. Arterial pressure, platelet activation, and uterine artery resistance all improved without further compromise of fetal well-being. In other words, it slowed or reversed the symptoms of the disorder.

Gestational diabetes & diabetes in pregnancy

Some women enter pregnancy with a long history of diabetes while others only suffer the disease's high blood-sugar levels when becoming pregnant. This is called 'gestational diabetes' and occurs in one to three percent of pregnancies. A number of gestational diabetics will develop true diabetes later in life.

The main cause of death among newborn children of diabetic pregnancies is abnormality of the child in the uterus (congenital malformation). The causes can be traced to inadequate control of the mother's diabetes during pregnancy. Diabetic mothers run the risk of larger babies and tougher deliveries. As a result, births are usually induced if they haven't occurred by the forty-second week of pregnancy. Aside from developmental defects these babies are also at higher risk for developing jaundice, respiratory difficulties, blood sugar abnormalities, low blood calcium and other metabolic abnormalities.

GSH AND DIABETES IN PREGNANCY

All diabetic patients are subject to higher levels of free radical production and lipid peroxidation (see chapter 10). In a diabetic environment, embryos develop a higher incidence of malformations and developmental problems. This phenomenon is called 'embryotoxicity.' The exact mechanism of embryotoxicity in diabetes has yet to be elaborated, but it is clear that oxidative damage to cells plays an important role. Low GSH levels in these patients' embryos place the fetus at risk from the ravages of free radicals.

A Japanese study confirmed that restoring GSH status in embryo cultures normalized the growth retardation and embryo malformations seen with untreated mothers. A Swedish group had similarly positive results treating embryo cultures with NAC (N-acetylcysteine), a potent GSH-enhancing precursor.

TOXINS AND TERATOGENS IN PREGNANCY

We are all exposed to toxins from our environment. They come from the food we eat, the water we drink, the air we breath, the medications we take, the jobs we hold and bad habits like drinking and smoking. The embryo is exposed to the same toxins as its pregnant mother, but is at much higher risk because they affect its fundamental growth and development.

The consequences range from low birth weight to malformations or even fetal death. Sometimes the consequences are so subtle that they may not appear for years—such as diminished IQ scores in later childhood. The mother is the only one who can keep these risks to a minimum. Above all, she must ensure that her built-in detoxification processes are working well.

GSH AND TOXICOLOGY IN PREGNANCY

According to recent research, the fetus seems to be low in antioxidant defenses. Perhaps it depends on its mother's good health, in which case anything that further depresses these levels could compromise fetal development. After all, the fetus grows from the embryo, and GSH levels are very high in the embryo's conceptual tissue. Conceptual tissue is the extraordinary mass of cells that differentiates and grows into the organs and systems of a human fetus. The process of organ development (organogenesis) is extremely sensitive, but at this stage is especially well protected by higher GSH levels. Researchers in toxicology are studying the possibility that elevated GSH levels may protect unborn children from foreign substances (xenobiotics). If this proves so, measuring GSH in early pregnancy may also be a way to identify possible risks of toxicity.

Some pediatric researchers have tried to match levels of antioxidant defense systems to the frequency and severity of birth defects, W.D. Graf and his associates at the University of Washington compared the frequency of neural tube defects with GSH enzyme levels and established just such a connection. In a very significant Ukrainian study, scientists collected the placentas of women from around the country. All lived in areas affected to a greater or lesser extent by radioactive pollution. As expected, the placentas from the most polluted areas had the lowest GSH levels. They were simply depleted by the overwhelming demands of an ongoing radiation threat. This group was able to show that placentas with low GSH levels were associated with more difficult pregnancies, harder deliveries and poor postnatal health. They concluded that "glutathione status [is] a prerequisite of the detoxifying activity of the feto-placental barrier." In other words, without placental GSH the fetus is largely unprotected from toxins and other xenobiotics.

The two most common toxins found in pregnancy are alcohol and tobacco. Although most pregnant women can and do choose to avoid them, abuse of these drugs is not uncommon. The mother may have a habitual dependence on these drugs or may simply be exposed to second-hand smoke. In either case, GSH plays an important role in protecting mother and child against such toxic threats.

ALCOHOL AND TOBACCO

Most drug-induced malformations of the fetus result from alcohol abuse during pregnancy. Fetal alcohol syndrome is a clinical condition leading to a long list of possible abnormalities, the most serious being severe mental retardation. In tests on laboratory mammals, the presence of alcohol drained GSH from the liver much more quickly in the fetus than in the mother. Other studies combined alcohol with cocaine, which further magnified the fall in GSH. At the University of New Mexico researchers gave test animals GSH-depleting drugs. This increased the severity of fetal alcohol syndrome. On a more positive note, G.I. Henderson and his team at the University of Texas used antioxidants on their test animals and showed that much of the damage of fetal alcohol exposure could be avoided by maintaining adequate GSH levels.

Women who smoke during pregnancy risk many complications, including early labor, premature rupture of membranes and premature delivery. A possible cause was identified by researchers who demonstrated that cigarette smoke interferes with signals between certain white blood cells and blood platelets, thus interfering with normal blood clotting. The same researchers were able to stop this interference by raising GSH levels. More detailed discussions on smoking can be found in chapters 2 and 14.

OTHER TOXINS

Many other studies have shown that antioxidant defense systems—notably the GSH system—play an indispensable role in detoxifying the newborn of numerous xenobiotics, including heavy metals such as mercury, lead, cadmium and arsenic, drugs such as hydantoin, phenytoin, and various poisons. In the lab, GSH-enhancing drugs like NAC actually diminish the toxic effects of mercury on congenital abnormalities and death. NAC is in fact recommended as an emergency measure for pregnant women who have overdosed on acetaminophen.

GSH, CHILDBIRTH, AND THE PERINATAL PERIOD

One of the major complications around childbirth (the perinatal period) is inadequate oxygen supply to the baby (hypoxia). Before the separation, the baby is dependent for its oxygen on umbilical supplies, but this can be compromised during delivery. For a number of reasons the baby might also suffer respiratory difficulties. In either case, the consequences of hypoxia are problematic and every effort is made to avoid it.

When the baby does not get enough oxygen individual cells are unable to maintain energy levels. This results in hypoxic damage. One molecule—adenosine triphosphate (ATP)—is responsible for carrying energy from the power generators (mitochondria) of individual cells. Because GSH stimulates ATP-production it can be considered anti-hypoxic. Another complication of the hypoxic child is lipid peroxidation, which is also addressed by GSH. And there is every reason to believe it would also help infants suffering from diminished liver function (jaundice).

OXYGEN—SOURCE OF LIFE & OXIDATIVE STRESS

Premature infants often need oxygen therapy. This brings energy production up but also increases oxidative stress, explaining why visual problems are often encountered by premature infants. Excessive oxygenation causes immature tissue such as that at the margin of the retina to shut down their blood vessels. This condition is called retrolental fibroplasia or retinopathy of prematurity, and has such serious consequences as retinal detachment. Antioxidants may be a potential antidote to this side effect of oxygen therapy. A. Papp from Hungary suggests that giving mothers sulfur-containing amino acids sustains GSH levels and helps prevent this problem.

Other problems relating to high oxygen levels include developmental changes to the nervous system and oxidative lung injury. Newborn animals depleted of glutathione with BSO (a GSH inhibitor) experienced a dramatic increase in these types of damage. J. Sastre and his group from Spain conducted laboratory test to demonstrate NAC's ability to lessen oxidative stress in newborns. The NAC was administered to the mothers. L.A. Brown of Emory University in Atlanta was able to prevent oxygen-induced lung injury in mammals with GSH supplementation. There is every reason to believe that elevated GSH levels in the mother will counteract the negative effects of many perinatal complications.

GSH AND LACTATION

Lactation and breast-feeding are usually discussed alongside pregnancy and childbirth. In this context, GSH is particularly interesting. One could say it plays a starring role.

It is impossible to overestimate the benefits of mother's milk on the health and development of newborns, especially considering its long-term effects on the immune system. Compared with bottle-fed children, those who are breast-fed suffer from fewer infectious diseases, especially ear infections and pneumonia, fewer problems with allergies, and fewer cases of childhood cancer, including leukemia, lymphoma and bone and brain tumors.

Compared to the milk of other mammals, human milk has the lowest proportion of protein. But the protein make-up is also very different. The two major protein constituents of milk are whey and casein. The whey to casein ratio is much higher in human milk, and these predominant whey proteins contain the critical precursors of glutathione, including beta-lactoglobulin, alpha-lactalbumin, serum albumin, and lactoferrin. These proteins are high in sulfur-containing amino acids such as cysteine and cystine. The structure of these proteins as well as their content is very important. Because the cysteine and cystine are integrated into these larger proteins, they can survive the rigors of digestion and arrive intact in the cells of the infant. There, they are subsequently used to manufacture GSH. Breast-feeding therefore profoundly affects the baby's immune function by giving it high levels of glutathione precursors.

It is possible to extract these proteins intact from cow's milk. The extraction of whey must be carried out carefully, because these proteins are extremely fragile. Their structure easily changes to a form that is biologically inactive. In spite of its unchanged food value, denatured protein loses its capacity to deliver GSH precursors. New technologies have been developed to extract these proteins from mammalian milk without denaturization. In a sense, this is mother's milk protein for adults—a natural way to raise GSH levels. Immunocal is one such whey protein. See chapter 4.

Conclusion

Glutathione's role in embryonic, fetal and placental development is crucial. It is constantly at work as a scavenger of free radicals and as a detoxifying enzyme of dozens of foreign substances and toxins. Without GSH, these substances can push the child towards an unnerving variety of developmental and health problems. Once past the stage of organogenesis, the unborn child's principal GSH protection comes from outside its own body—the placenta. There is an interesting similarity between the placenta and the liver. Among their many other functions, both act as filters for toxins and both have high levels of GSH within their tissues. It is no coincidence.

Many common complications of pregnancy including high blood pressure, pre-eclampsia and gestational diabetes coincide with low glutathione levels. Decreased GSH can cause many difficulties in pregnancy. A great deal of research is being carried out using GSH enhancing strategies to combat these problems. There is already some success and much optimism.

REFERENCES TO CHAPTER 18
PREGNANCY, LACTATION & CHILDBIRTH

ADDOLORATO G, GASPARININ A, MARCOCCIA S, ET AL. Prenatal exposure to ethanol in rats: effects on liver energy level and antioxidant status in mothers, fetuses, and newborns. *Alcohol 14: 569-573, 1997*

AFIFI NM, ABDEL-RAHMAN MS, NASSAR AM. Effect of alcohol and/or cocaine on blood glutathione and the ultrastructure of the liver of pregnant CF-1 mice. *Toxicol. Lett. 98: 1-12, 1998*

AYDIN A, SAYAL A, ISIMIR A. Plasma glutathione peroxidase activity and selenium levels of newborns with jaundice. *Biol. Trace Elem. Res. 58: 85-90, 1997*

BOHLES H. Antioxidative vitamins in prematurely and maturely born infants. *Int. J. Vitamin Nutr. Res. 67: 321-328. 1997*

BOUNOUS G, KONGSHAVN PAL, TAVEROFF A, GOLD P. Evolutionary traits in human milk proteins. *Medical Hypothesis 27: 133-140, 1988*

BRANCH DW, MITCHELL MD, MILLER E, ET AL. Pre-eclampsia and serum antibodies to oxidized low-density lipoprotein. *Lancet 343; 645-646, 1994*

BROWN LA, PEREZ JA, HARRIS FL, CLARK RH. Glutathione supplements protect pre-term rabbits from oxidative lung injury. *American J. Physiol. 270(3 Pt 1): L446-L451, 1996*

CHANDRA RK. Prospective studies of the effect of breast-feeding on incidence of infection and allergy. *Acta. Paed. Scand. 68:691, 1987*

CHEN G, WILSON R, CUMMING G, ET AL. Intracellular and extracellular antioxidant buffering levels in erythrocytes from pregnancy-induced hypertension. *J. Human Hypertension 8: 37-42, 1994*

DATTA K, ROY SK, MITRA AK, ET AL. Glutathione S-transferase mediated detoxification and bioactivation of xenobiotics during early human pregnancy. *Early Human Development 37: 167-174, 1994*

DAVIDGE ST, HUBEL CA, BRAYDEN RD, ET AL. Sera antioxidant activity in uncomplicated and preeclamptic pregnancies. *Obstetrics and Gynecology 79: 897-901, 1992*

DUNCAN B, EY J, HOLBERG CJ, ET AL. Exclusive breast-feeding for at least 4 months protects against otitis media. *Paediatrics 91: 867-872, 1993*

FRANK AL, TABER LN, GLEZEN WP, ET AL. Breast-feeding and respiratory virus infection. *Paediatrics 70: 239-245, 1982*

GRAF WD, OLEINUK OE, PIPPENGER CE, ET AL. Comparison of erythrocyte antioxidant activities and embryologic level of neural tube defects. *Eur. J. Pediatr. Surg. 5(Suppl 1): 8-11, 1995*

GUPTA A, GUPTA A, SHUKLA GS. Development of brain free radical scavenging system and lipid peroxidation under the influence of gestational and lactational cadmium exposure. *Human Exp. Toxicol. 14: 428-433, 1995*

HENDERSON GI, DEVI BG, PEREZ A, SCHENKER S. In utero ethanol exposure elicits oxidative stress in the rat fetus. *Alcohol Clin. Exp. Res. 19: 714-720, 1995*

KAMRIN MA, CARNEY EW, CHOU K, CUMMINGS A, ET AL. Female reproductive and developmental toxicology: overview and current approaches. *Toxicol. Lett. 74: 99-119, 1994*

KNAPEN MF, MULDER TP, VAN ROOIJ IA, ET AL. Low whole blood glutathione levels in pregnancies complicated by preeclampsia or the hemolysis, elevated liver enzymes, low platelets syndrome. *Obstetrics and Gynecology 92: 1012-1015, 1998*

Korneev AA, Komissarova IA, Nartissov IR. The use of glutathione as a protector agent in hypoxic exposure. *Biull. Eksp. Biol. Med. 116: 261-263, 1993*

Langley SC, Kelly FJ. N-acetylcysteine ameliorates hyperoxic lung injury in the preterm guinea pig. *Biochem. Pharmacol. 45: 841-846, 1993*

Lees C, Langford E, Brown AS, et al. The effects of S-nitrosoglutathione on platelet activation, hypertension, and uterine and fetal doppler in severe preeclampsia. *Obstetrics and Gynecology 88: 14-19, 1996*

Liu CS, Wu HM, Kao SH, Wei YH. Phenytoin-mediated oxidative stress in serum of female epileptics: a possible pathogenesis in the fetal hydantoin syndrome. *Human Exp. Toxicol. 16: 177-181, 1997*

Mather G, Gupta N, Mather S, et al. Breast-feeding and childhood cancer. Ind. *Paediatrics 30: 652-657, 1993*

Menegola E, Broccia ML, Prati M, et al. Glutathione status in diabetes-induced embryopathies. *Biol. Neonate 69: 293-297, 1996*

Narahara H, Johnston JM. Smoking and preterm labor: effect of cigarette smoke extract on the secretion of platelet activating factor-acetylhydrolase by human decidual macrophages. *American J. Obstet. Gynecol. 169: 1321-1326, 1993*

Obolenskaya MY, Tschaikovskaya TL, et al. Glutathione status of placentae from differently polluted regions of Ukraine. *Eur. J. Obstet. Gynecol. Reprod. Biol. 71: 23-30, 1997*

Obolenskaya MY, Chaikovska TL, et al. Detoxicating function of the placenta of childbearing women from ecologically unfavorable regions of the Ukraine. *Ukr. Biokhim. Zh. 70: 89-97, 1998*

Ornaghi F, Ferrini S, Prati M, Giavini E. The protective effects of N-acetylcysteine against methyl mercury embryotoxicity in mice. *Fundam. Appl. Toxicol. 20: 437-445, 1993*

Papp A, Nemeth I, Pelle Z, Tekulic P. Prospective biochemical study of the antioxidant defense capacity in retinopathy of prematurity. *Orv. Hetil. 138: 201-205, 1997*

Reyes E, Ott S. Effects of buthionine sulfoxamine on the outcome of the in utero administration of alcohol on fetal development. *Alcohol Clin. Exp. Res. 20: 1243-1251, 1996*

Riggs BS, Bronstein AC, Kulig K, et al. Acute acetaminophen overdose during pregnancy. *Obstet. Gynecol. 74: 247-253, 1989*

Sastre J, Aseni M, Rodrigo F, et al. Antioxidant administration to the mother prevents oxidative stress associated with birth in the neonatal rat. *Life Science 54: 2055-2059, 1994*

Schmidt H, Gruner T, Muller R, et al. Increased levels of lipid peroxidation products malondialdehyde and 4-hydroxynonenal after perinatal hypoxia. *Pediatr. Res. 40: 15-20, 1996*

Simsek M, Naziroglu M, Simsek H, et al. Blood plasma levels of lipoperoxides, glutathione peroxidase, beta carotene, vitamin A and E in women with habitual abortion. *Cell. Biochem. Funct. 16: 227-231, 1998*

Spickett CM, Reglinski J, Smith WE, et al. Erythrocyte glutathione balance and membrane stability during preeclampsia. *Free Radic. Biol. Med. 24: 1049-1055, 1998*

Tabacova S, Baird DD, Balabaeva L, et al. Placental arsenic and cadmium in relation to lipid peroxides and glutathione levels in maternal-infant pairs from a copper smelter area. *Placenta 15: 873-881, 1994*

Tabacova S, Balabaeva L, Little RE. Maternal exposure to exogenous nitrogen compounds and complications of pregnancy. *Arch. Environ. Health 52: 341-347, 1997*

Tabacova S, Little RE, Balabaeva L. Complications of pregnancy in relation to maternal lipid peroxides, glutathione, and exposure to metals. *Reprod. Toxicol. 8: 217-224, 1994*

TAGLIALATELA G, PEREZ-POLO JR, RASSIN DK. Induction of apoptosis in the CNS during development by the combination of hyperoxia and inhibition of glutathione synthesis. *Free Radic. Biol. Med.* 25: 936-942, 1998

TROCINO RA, AKAZAWA S, ISHIBASHI M, ET AL. Significance of glutathione depletion and oxidative stress in early embryogenesis in glucose-induced rat embryo culture. *Diabetes 44: 992-998, 1995*

UOTILA JT, TUIMALA RJ, AARNIO TM, ET AL. Findings on lipid peroxidation and antioxidant function in hypertensive complications of pregnancy. *Br. J. Obstet. Gynaecol. 100: 270-276, 1993*

UOTILA JT, TUIMALA RJ, PYYKKO K. Erythrocyte glutathione peroxidase activity in hypertensive complications of pregnancy. *Gynecol. Obstet. Invest. 29: 259-262, 1990*

WAGNER PD, MATHIEU-COSTELLO O, BEBOUT DE, ET AL. Protection against pulmonary O_2 toxicity by N-acetylcysteine. *Eur. Respir. J. 2: 116-126, 1989*

WALSH SW, WANG Y. Deficient glutathione peroxidase activity in preeclampsia is associated with increased placental production of thromboxane and lipid peroxidases. *American J. Obstet. Gynecol. 169: 1456-1461, 1993*

WARSHAW JB, WILSON CW, SAITO K, PROUGH RA. The responses of glutathione and antioxidant enzymes to hyperoxia in the developing lung. *Pediatr. Res. 8: 819-823, 1985*

WENTZEL P, THUNBERG L, ERIKSSON UJ. Teratogenic effect of diabetic serum is prevented by supplementation of superoxide dismutase and N-acetylcysteine in rat embryo culture. *Diabetologia 40: 7-14, 1997*

WOODS JR JR, PLESSINGER MA, FANTEL A. An introduction to reactive oxygen species and their possible roles in substance abuse. *Obstet. Gynecol. Clin. North America 25:219-236, 1998*

CHAPTER 19
TRAUMA AND BURNS

Trauma is any sort of injury, including the emotional trauma of divorce or the physical trauma of a broken hip. In this chapter, we will talk mostly of physical trauma even though emotional trauma is also known to deplete glutathione. Motor vehicle accidents, work injuries and falls are common examples of accidental trauma. Intentional trauma includes everything from gunshot wounds to surgical procedures. Burns may be caused by heat, chemicals or radiation. Radiation burns are discussed in chapter 2, and sunburn and UV (ultraviolet) burns in chapter 22.

Glutathione, antioxidant protection, immune defenses, and oxidative stress play an important role in all of these conditions. High or low levels of GSH have a significant effect on the susceptibility, tolerance and degree of injury, as well as the recovery time and outcome.

PHYSICAL TRAUMA

Until this century, traumatic injury was the major cause of death in human beings. In North America today, trauma has fallen to third place behind heart disease/stroke and cancer, but in some economic groups—especially poor urban male populations—trauma remains at the forefront.

Any critical illness depletes glutathione reserves. In a recent article from the journal Critical Care Medicine, F. Hammarqvist showed that intensive care patents suffered an approximate 40% loss of glutathione compared with healthy individuals. M. Kretzschmar from Germany followed patients with multiple injuries in an intensive care unit, from admission to discharge or death. He found the more severe the injuries, the higher the degree of oxidative stress and depletion of glutathione defenses. An Irish team led by C. Kilty suggests the measurement of glutathione S-transferases could be a useful indicator of general organ damage.

A Harvard Medical School team led by M.K. Robinson showed that lab animals artificially depleted of glutathione were dramatically more prone to death and complications of blood loss (hemorrhagic shock). Their results suggest that treatment of trauma should include some way to maintain glutathione levels. This would decrease the likelihood of multi-system organ failure in the event of shock.

The role of oxidative stress and glutathione metabolism in brain and neurological tissue injuries has been the focus of much research. Head injuries often damage the crucial blood-brain barrier, and subsequent circulatory problems lead to swelling and fluid buildup in the brain. Free radicals mediate some of the complex "secondary injuries" seen in this type of trauma.

Efforts to prevent post-injury complications are a crucial part of treatment in emergency and critical care management.

Glutathione metabolism counteracts the damage caused by these oxyradicals. Increases in glutathione peroxidase activity following neurological trauma have been well documented. If injury is severe or complicated, these resources may become eventually depleted. Canadians B.H. Juurlink and P.G. Paterson of the University of Saskatchewan suggest that nutritional interventions with GSH-precursors can maximize antioxidant defenses, and that such strategies should be pursued aggressively.

E.F. Ellis's team at the Department of Pharmacology and Toxicology, Medical College of Virginia, tested NAC on concussion after trauma to the brain. NAC given prior to or soon after the injury prevented some consequences of oxidative circulatory compromise. At Ohio State University, J.H. Lucas and D.G. Wheeler showed similar effects using glutathione on spinal cord injury. Using the GSH-precursors gamma-glutamyl-cysteine and OTZ (see chapter 4) elevated glutathione levels increased spinal neuron survival after ph4ysical trauma.

R. Wagner and R.R. Myers of the University of California developed an interesting therapy for nerve injury and sciatic inflammation and presented it in the journal "Pain." They were able to decrease the pathological consequences of sciatic nerve injury by using the drug NAC to raise GSH levels. Pre-treated subjects responded best. The longer the delay in administering NAC after injury, the less effective was the treatment.

Surgery is intrusive and disrupts a patient's anatomy. It leads to a host of physiological adjustments. Although from the surgeon's point of view this is a controlled procedure with end-point objectives, from the body's point of view, it is traumatic. Just like recovery from accidental trauma, the outcome of the operation depends on the patient's prior defenses, fitness, and immune status.

Surgery releases billions of free radicals into the body. These severely tax the patient's antioxidant defenses and poor surgical outcomes seem to go hand-in-hand with low antioxidant levels. As the cell's primary intracellular antioxidant, glutathione is drawn from stores in the liver and skeletal muscles and dispersed to reduce the damage. The result of major surgery may be whole-body glutathione depletion. Articles from the American Journal of Physiology as well as the Annals of Surgery describe a fall in glutathione levels of 40% after abdominal surgery. This may increase the patient's susceptibility to cellular oxidative injury.

A relatively new surgical device—the laparoscope—is a tube with a fiberoptic cable through which the surgeon can see into and work within a body cavity. Tools are attached to the end of the laparoscope and procedures are performed through small surgical holes in the patient's body. This reduces cutting, recovery time and hospital stays for many patients. The difference in trauma induced by conventional surgery and laparoscopic surgery is measurable. A team of Hungarian surgeons noted oxidative stress and GSH levels in two such groups of patients undergoing gall-bladder removal. The laparoscopic group showed significantly lower values of oxidation and less depletion of GSH-systems than the open-surgery group.

Glutathione not only protects us from oxidative stress, it also bolsters immune response, controls and balances the inflammatory response and helps synthesize and repair proteins involved in the healing process. This knowledge has stimulated research into the use of GSH enhancing strategies to improve and accelerate wound repair.

Plastic surgeons from the University of Michigan, Ann Arbor showed that depleted glutathione levels lead to delayed wound healing and poor repair. Biochemists from the Max Plank Institute in Germany showed that while healing, skin wounds initially increase their production of glutathione peroxidase in order to fight free radical formation. As healing progresses GSH levels fall. Pharmacologists from the Central Drug Research Institute in India demonstrated a 60-70% depletion of glutathione peroxidase and glutathione S-transferase levels in skin wounds after several days healing. Understanding these mechanisms at play, Van der Laan described in an article in the Journal Of Surgical Research how NAC infusion could reduce tissue injury and shorten the repair period of crush injuries.

An important consideration in all surgery is disruption of blood flow to tissues (ischemia). When blood flow is re-established (reperfusion) there is a burst of free radical formation in the affected region that may affect the survival of those tissues. The Australians K.R. Knight and K. MacPhadden found that NAC, the glutathione precursor was able to decrease the amount of reperfusion injury in skin flaps. Potential applications are being investigated in cardiac surgery to avoid reperfusion injury (see chapter 9).

Burns

Heat or thermal burns consist of a complex series of events involving initial injury, physiological adjustments to circulatory and fluid changes, hematological and immunological responses, and an elaborate healing process. Death from heat burns is often delayed. Days after a burn, patients may die from circulatory shock, a result of loss of fluids from the burn. Weeks after a burn, patients may succumb to overwhelming infection (sepsis) because of the breakdown in their immune defenses.

Burn specialists know oxidative stress to be dramatic in severe burn patients. Consistently high lipid peroxide levels, a good measure of free radical damage, and impaired activity of glutathione and its related enzyme activities have prompted researchers to use antioxidants to protect from further damage.

A German team of pediatric surgeons conducted a two-year study on children with burns and severe inflammatory diseases. They managed to correct parameters of oxidative stress in these patients using selenium substitution (see chapter 4), which raised glutathione peroxidase. They found this a valid supportive therapy for such conditions. Other nutritionists have increased selenium delivery through TPN (Total Parenteral Nutrition or intravenous nutrition) or through tube feeding, where food is supplied directly to the stomach or intestines.

One phenomenon of the early post-burn period is a drop in hemoglobin (red blood cell count). Scientists have questioned why. A team from Varna Medical University showed that burns depleted the glutathione and antioxidant defenses of the red blood cell itself. Oxidative byproducts accumulated, leading to destruction of these cells. They suggest that adequate antioxidant therapy might prevent this complication, as long as it is begun early enough.

A Japanese team led by Y. Kasanuma from the Environmental Health Sciences Division of Tohuku University of Medicine investigated the effects of mild heat injury on oxidative stress. Rather than burning tissue, they exposed animals to mild chronic heat exposure (35°C, 95°F). They showed that chronic exposure to high temperatures causes oxidative damage and that GSH-related anti-oxidative systems play an important role in defending against this damage.

A recent study published in the journal "Burns" by D. Konukoglu was aimed at the use of NAC to treat burns. Researchers were able to decrease levels of lipid peroxidation and increase GSH levels. Using antioxidant supplementation (GSH, vitamin C and NAC) to raise glutathione levels, several Boston studies published in the Journal of Burn Care Rehabilitation and in Shock, showed that they could reduce mortality from 60% to zero in animals suffering third degree burns. This is strong evidence that oxidation contributes to post-burn mortality.

CONCLUSION

Surgery, burns, trauma and shock are all complex events, consisting of a series of biochemical, anatomical, physiological and immune responses. Oxidative stress and the release of free radicals are inevitable in the initial injury, the subsequent inflammatory reactions and the healing processes. Glutathione, an integral part of our body's mechanism to minimize damage and promote healing, acts both as an antioxidant and to support the immune system.

The value of antioxidant supplementation and nutritional support has been underestimated in the past, but new approaches to this problem are being developed and attitudes are changing. Strategies to maintain or increase glutathione enzyme systems have been beneficial in preliminary trials and show promise in the treatment of major trauma, surgery and burn management protocols.

TRAUMA & BURNS

ADAMSON B, SCHWARZ D, KLUGSTON P, ET AL. Delayed repair: the role of glutathione in a rat incisional wound model. *J. Surg. Res. 62: 159-164, 1996*

BEKYAROVA G, YANKOVA T, MARINOV M. Lipofuscin product accumulation, insufficient antioxidant defense in erythrocytes and plasma and enhanced susceptibility to oxidative haemolysis after thermal trauma. *Acta Chir. Plast. 39: 60-64, 1997*

BIENKOWSKI W, GROMADZINSKA J, POWLOWICZ Z, ET AL. Concentrations of selenium and lipid peroxides and glutathione peroxidase activities in plasma of thermally injured pigs. *Acta Chir. Plast. 33: 126-132, 1991*

BORNER J, ZIMMERMANN T, ALBRECHT S, ET AL. Selenium administration in severe inflammatory surgical diseases and burns in childhood. *Med. Klin. 92 (Suppl 3): 17-19, 1997*

ELLIS EF, DODSON LY, POLICE RJ. Restoration of cerebrovascular responsiveness to hyperventilation by the oxygen radical scavenger n-acetylcysteine following experimental traumatic brain injury. *J. Neurosurg. 75: 774-779, 1991*

Gal I, Roth E, Lantos J, et al. Inflammatory mediators and surgical trauma regarding laparoscopic access: free radical mediated reactions. *Acta Chir. Hung. 36: 97-99, 1997*

GIDDAY JM, BEETSCH JW, PARK TS. Endogenous glutathione protects cerebral endothelial cells from traumatic injury. *J. Neurotrauma. 16: 27-36, 1999*

GILMONT RR, DARDANO A, YOUNG M, ET AL. Effects of glutathione depletion on oxidant-induced endothelial cell injury. *J. Surg. Res. 80: 62-68, 1998*

GOSS JR, TAFFE KM, KOCHANEK PM, ET AL. The antioxidant enzymes glutathione peroxidase and catalase increase following traumatic brain injury in the rat. *Exp. Neurol. 146: 291-294, 1997*

HAMMARQVIST F, LUO JL, COTGREAVE IA, ET AL. Skeletal muscle glutathione is depleted in critically ill patients. *Crit. Care Med. 25: 78-84, 1997*

HUNT DR, LANE HW, BEESINGER D, ET AL. Selenium depletion in burn patients. *JPEN J. Parenter. Enterel. Nutr. 8: 695-699, 1984*

JUURLINK BH, PATERSON PG. Review of oxidative stress in brain and spinal cord injury: suggestions for pharmacological and nutritional management strategies. *J. Spinal Cord Med. 21: 309-334, 1998*

KASANUMA Y, WATANABE C, KIM CY, ET AL. Effects of mild chronic heat exposure on the concentrations of thiobarbituric acid reactive substances, glutathione, and selenium, and glutathione peroxidase activity in the mouse liver. *Tohoku J. Exp. Med. 185: 79-87, 1998*

KILTY C, DOYLE S, HASSETT B, ET AL. Glutathione S-transferases as biomarkers of organ damage: applications of rodent and canine GST enzyme immunoassays. *Chem. Biol. Interact. 111: 123-135, 1998*

KNIGHT KR, MACPHADYEN K, LEPORE DA, ET AL. Enhancement of ischaemic rabbit skin flap survival with the antioxidant and free-radical scavenger N-acetylcysteine. *Clin. Sci. (Colch) 81: 31-36, 1991*

KONUKOGLU D, CETINKALE O, BULAN R. Effects of N-acetylcysteine on lung glutathione levels in rats after burn injury. *Burns 23: 541-544, 1997*

KRETZSCHMAR M, PFEIFFER L, SCHMIDT C, ET AL. Plasma levels of glutathione, alpha-tocopherol and lipid peroxides in polytraumatized patients; evidence for a stimulating effect of TNF alpha on glutathione synthesis. *Exp. Toxicol. Pathol. 50: 477-483, 1998*

LaLonde C, Hennigan J, Nayak U, et al. Energy charge potential and glutathione levels as predictors of outcome following burn injury complicated by endotoxemia. *Shock 9: 27-32, 1998*

LaLonde C, Nayak U, Hennigan J, et al. Excessive liver oxidant stress causes mortality in response to burn injury combined with endotoxin and is prevented with antioxidants. *Burn Care Rehabil. 18: 187-192, 1997*

LaLonde C, Nayak U, Hennigan J, et al. Antioxidants prevent the cellular deficit produced in response to burn injury. *J. Burn Care Rehabil. 17: 379-383, 1996*

Lucas JH, Wheeler DG, Emery DG, et al. The endogenous antioxidant glutathione as a factor in the survival of physically injured mammalian spinal cord neurons. *J. Neuropathol. Exp. Neurol. 57: 937-954, 1998*

Luo JL, Hammarqvist F, Andersson K, et al. Surgical trauma decreases glutathione synthetic capacity in human skeletal muscle tissue. *Am. J. Physiol. 275: E359-365, 1998*

Luo JL, Hammarqvist F, Andersson K, et al. Skeletal muscle glutathione after surgical trauma. *Ann. Surg. 223: 420-427, 1996*

Munz B, Frank S, Hubner G, et al. A novel type of glutathione peroxidase: expression and regulation during wound repair. *Biochem. J. 326: 579-585, 1997*

Robinson MK, Rounds JD, Hong RW, et al. Glutathione deficiency increases organ dysfunction after hemorrhagic shock. *Surgery 112: 140-147, 1992*

Sabeh F, Baxter CR, Norton SJ. Skin burn injury and oxidative stress in liver and lung tissues of rabbit models. *Eur. J. Clin. Chem. Clin. Biochem. 33: 323-328, 1995*

Shi EC, Fisher R, McEvoy M, et al. Factors influencing hepatic glutathione concentrations: a study in surgical patients. *Clin. Sci. 62: 279-283, 1982*

Shukla A, Rasik AM, Patnaik GK. Depletion of reduced glutathione, ascorbic acid, vitamin E and antioxidant defense enzymes in a healing cutaneous wound. *Free Radic. Res. 26: 93-101, 1997*

Sies H, Graf P. Hepatic thiol and glutathione efflux under the influence of vasopressin, phenylephrine and adrenaline. *Biochem. J. 226: 545-549, 1985*

Steiling H, Munz B, Werner S, et al. Different types of ROS-scavenging enzymes are expressed during cutaneous wound repair. *Exp. Cell. Res. 247: 484-494, 1999*

van der Laan L, Oyen WJ, Verhofstad AA, et al. Soft tissue repair capacity after oxygen-derived free radical-induced damage in one hindlimb of the rat. *J. Surg. Res. 72: 60-69, 1997*

Wagner R, Heckman HM, Myers RR. Wallerian degeneration and hyperalgesia after peripheral nerve injury are glutathione-dependent. *Pain 77: 173-179, 1998*

CHAPTER 20
PSYCHONEUROBIOLOGY

As our understanding of the brain has evolved, we have begun to appreciate the intricate interweave of psychiatry, neurology and biochemistry. These fields have overlapped and melded into psychoneurobiology, an integrated medical science that has already yielded important advances in the recognition and treatment of many brain disorders.

Free radicals and oxyradicals have been recognized by psychoneurobiologists as playing an important role in the development and progression of many of these disorders. The brain is particularly susceptible to free radical attack because it generates more oxidative by-products per gram of tissue than any other organ. The brain's main antioxidant is glutathione—it's importance cannot be overstated. Oxidative stress and glutathione are important factors in such various disorders as brain injury, neurodegenerative disease, schizophrenia, Down syndrome and other pathologies dealt with here and in other chapters. A more complete list is shown in figure 40.

Psychosocial stress has also been shown to increase oxidative stress. An interesting experiment studying lipid peroxidation levels in older people, some of whom practiced transcendental meditation, showed that meditators suffered less stress and suffered significantly lower levels of lipid peroxidation.

SCHIZOPHRENIA

The Greek translation of schizophrenia is "split mind," and may be misleading. The disorder should not be confused with split personality or multiple personality disorder. It is a different illness characterized by psychosis—a severe disturbance of normal thought, perception, speech and behavior. In mood disorders like anxiety and depression, the ability to discern the real from the imagined is relatively intact. A schizophrenic patient on the

Figure 40 — Disorders of the brain and nervous system that are linked to oxidative stress may benefit from raised GSH levels

Brain Injury	Neurodegenerative disease	Others
Brain Injury	Parkinson's disease	Schizophrenia
Trauma	Alzheimer's dementia	Down syndrome
Stroke	Multiple sclerosis (MS)	Tardive dyskinesia
Ischemia	Lou Gehrig's disease (ALS)	Sleep deprivation
Toxicity of lead, mercury, etc.	Lipofuscinosis (Batten's disease.)	Huntington's chorea

other hand often suffers from delusions, auditory or visual hallucinations and paranoid thoughts not based on reality.

Although there is no consensus as to the causes of schizophrenia, most specialists will agree that the symptoms stem from a disturbance of normal brain chemistry. The tendency seems to run in families, but no single schizophrenia gene has been identified. Psychotherapy by itself is of little value but antipsychotic drugs have been able to reduce relapses by 50% and considerably shorten periods of hospitalization. However, these drugs have significant side effects and long-term complications.

It has long been known that glutathione levels are lower in schizophrenic patients. Researchers have consistently demonstrated an increase in their oxidative stress and a decrease in their glutathione status. GSH levels even correspond to the severity of the disease. The Russians N.V. and A.V. Govorin further demonstrated that schizophrenics undergoing an acute phase of their disease had higher levels of lipid peroxidation than when in remission. Research scientists such as J.K. Yao and R.D. Reddy of the Veteran's Administration Healthcare System, University of Pittsburgh, suggest that oxidative stress plays an important pathophysiological role in schizophrenia.

A group of neurochemicals called catecholamines are produced normally by the body. They seem to be over-produced in both schizophrenia and Parkinson's disease. The catecholamines break down into ortho-quinones—a group of powerful oxidants. S. Baez's team at the Department of Biochemical Toxicology in Stockholm University examined glutathione's ability to detoxify these metabolites. They concluded that GSH enzymes provided critical protection against the neurodegenerative diseases that are caused or conditioned by these dangerous oxyradicals.

T.D. Buckman and A.S. Kling at UCLA School of Medicine conducted a fascinating study. CT-scans of schizophrenic patients revealed brain atrophy (shrinkage), suggesting damage to nerve tissue. They linked the extent of atrophy to the degree of glutathione peroxidase deficiency. This suggests a unique function of GSH in preserving the brain from tissue damage in schizophrenics. These findings were corroborated by other centers such as Hahnemann University in Philadelphia.

Antipsychotic drugs require long term use and cause a number of side-effects. Haldol, Thorazine and other neuroleptics cause a movement disorder called tardive dyskinesia. This results in involuntary puckering of the lips and writhing of the arms and legs and disfigures a large number of patients. It is possible that lipid peroxidation accounts for neuronal damage in this disorer, and scientists have put this theory to the test.

The Scottish team led by K. Brown and A. Reid measured oxidative breakdown products and antioxidant depletion in diskenetic patients and confirmed the relationship between lipid peroxidation and tardive diskinesia. Other researchers have shown that lipid peroxidation and GSH depletion are aggravated by antipsychotic drugs. Y. Sagara at the Salk Institute in La Jolla, California said that treatments resulting in decreased intracellular GSH would aggravate haloperidol (a neuroleptic antipsychotic) toxicity and may increase a tendency towards tardive dyskinesia.

Researchers J.L. Cadet and L.A. Kahler from the National Institute of Health in Baltimore, S.P. Mahadik and R.E. Scheffer from the Department of Health Behavior, Medical College of Georgia and others have suggested that antioxidants should be used to prevent side effects in patients taking antipsychotics. The Georgia team also showed that oxidative injury increases and GSH-peroxidase levels fall even at the earliest stages of psychosis, and that antioxidants may prevent or slow deterioration.

It appears that sustained GSH levels may slow the progress of schizophrenia and decrease the side effects of some of the drugs used against this disease.

DOWN SYNDROME

Down syndrome is also known as trisomy 21, and inappropriately as mongoloidism because of the distinctive facial characteristics. Ironically, certain areas in the Far East refer to it as 'caucausianism.' This congenital disorder occurs during fetal development, when chromosomes divide mistakenly, producing a third 21st chromosome when there should only be two. It is not an inherited trait and is found more frequently in pregnancies of older women. It is relatively common, occurring once in about every 700 births.

Down syndrome leads to several easily recognizable traits including moderate to severe mental retardation, typically flattened facial features, slanted eyes, low-set ears and a large tongue. Less obvious is a tendency toward congenital heart defects, poor vision, leukemia and susceptibility to infectious disease. In a proper environmental setting, Down syndrome patients may lead happy, productive, but generally shorter lives.

Oxidative stress and free radical formation have been studied in Down syndrome. Although there is still debate, certain factors are clear. The gene for an enzyme involved in oxidation/antioxidation reactions called 'superoxide dismutase' (SOD) is located on chromosome 21. Increased SOD activity may overproduce hydrogen peroxide and thus release free radicals. Researchers have observed the heightened demand this places on antioxidant defenses.

Down syndrome patients that make it to an older age seem more prone to the development of Alzheimer's dementia, another neurodegenerative disease. Scientists including those working at the University of California (San Diego) think this is due to changes in free radical metabolism, causing increased destruction of nerve cells. Simple experiments measuring blood serum levels of glutathione reveal significant alterations in GSH activity. More elaborate studies compare GSH activity in Down patients with and without Alzheimer's disease, demonstrating that the already abnormal glutathione defense is further impaired in Down syndrome patients who also suffer from Alzheimer's disease.

An interesting animal experiment published in the August 1997 issue of Brain Research showed that in brain cells affected by Down syndrome, those with lowered GSH died more quickly. By chemically lowering GSH even further, cell death rates increased. There is no doubt that low GSH levels accelerate brain cell death and that elevated levels slow down neurodegeneration. Intervention with glutathione-enhancing therapies seem helpful.

GSH AND SLEEP

Certain tissues are more susceptible to GSH depletion than others. Measuring glutathione levels in specific areas of the brain of sleep-deprived animals reveals that the thalamus and hypothalamus are particularly susceptible. The vulnerability of these tissues may contribute to some of the functional effects of sleep deprivation.

Oxidized glutathione (GSSG) is an active component of the neurochemical SPS (sleep promoting substance). Researchers at the Tokyo Medical University showed that high levels of oxidized glutathione promote sleep and affect other hypothalamic functions, such as temperature control. The same team also suggests that GSH detoxifies neuronal tissues more actively during certain periods of sleep. This may explain why those taking GSH-enhancing products like Immunocal often report less need for sleep yet feel more energetic.

CASE STUDY

Benjamin, a 44 year-old physician, always wanted a 36-hour day so he'd have time to see his patients, do his research, practice his music, stay in shape and spend more time with his wife and children. Like many other professionals, time and energy were at a premium. Aware of the effects of GSH on the immune system, he took a course of vitamins, selenium and amino acids in the hope of more easily fighting off the viral illnesses to which he was exposed daily. He incorporated Immunocal in to his regimen, wishing to take advantage of its GSH precursors and was soon waking up from 30 to 60 minutes before his alarm went off, and he felt just as refreshed. Now he regularly works later into the evening.

HUNTINGTON'S DISEASE

Huntington's disease, also known as Huntington's chorea, hereditary chorea, or chronic progressive chorea, is an inherited neurodegenerative movement disorder with progressive intellectual deterioration. It strikes people between the ages of 35 and 50 and advances relentlessly, leading eventually to a physical and mental inability to look after oneself. The term "chorea" refers to the rapid, complex, jerky motions of the face, trunk, and limbs. The associated dementia is accompanied by psychiatric disturbances as well. Traditional treatments are symptomatic and only minimally effective.

These patients seem to be less able than others to deal with oxidative stress. They suffer from increased free radical generation and decreased GSH defenses. Studies depleting glutathione from affected tissue show increased damage to and death of these cells. In the laboratory, antioxidants help cells survive. The neurochemical 3-hydroxykynurenine (3-HK) is found in excessive levels in the brains of Huntington's patients and strongly promotes oxidation. Lab experiments using the GSH-enhancing drug NAC seem to reduce the damage done by 3-HK.

O. Bandmann and a team of neurobiologists at the Institute of Neurology in London, think that an inherent defect in the brain's ability to detoxify neurotoxins may be at the root of Huntington's and Parkinson's diseases. Given the importance of glutathione as an antioxidant, its deficiency in these patients will stimulate many more studies.

CONCLUSION

Many neurological and psychiatric disease processes are characterized by high levels of oxidative stress and free radical formation, as well as abnormalities in glutathione metabolism and antioxidant defenses. Even mental stress has been shown to destabilize oxidant/antioxidant balance in the brain.

Both schizophrenia and the drugs used to treat it lead to GSH abnormalities. Supporting and sustaining glutathione levels may prevent or slow the damage to brain cells typical of this disease. Tardive diskinesia, a long-term side-effect of antipsychotic drug usage, has also been linked to free radical production and depletion of glutathione defense mechanisms. Researchers have proposed that elevated GSH levels may slow the progression of schizophrenia and ease the side effects of medications used to treat it.

Down syndrome patients have an inherent chromosomal abnormality that causes overproduction of abnormal SOD (superoxide dismutase), leading to high levels of oxidative stress that may compound the death of brain cells typical of this congenital disease. The increased rates of Alzheimer's disease in older Down syndrome patients seem to support this theory. Glutathione is the major naturally-occurring antioxidant in the brain and helps combat these oxyradicals.

Other applications of GSH in neurodegenerative disease are discussed elsewhere in this book. See the chapters on Alzheimer's disease (chapter 8), Parkinson's disease (chapter 7) and multiple sclerosis (chapter 13).

PSYCHONEUROBIOLOGY

ANTILA E, WESTERMARK T. On the etiopathogenesis and therapy of Down syndrome. *Int. J. Dev. Biol. 33: 183-188, 1989*

BAEZ S, SEGURA-AGUILAR J, WIDERSTEN M, ET AL. Glutathione transferases catalyze the detoxification of oxidized metabolites (o-quinones) of catecholamines and may serve as an antioxidant system preventing degenerative cellular processes. *Biochem J. 324(Pt. 1): 25-28, 1997*

BANDMANN O, VAUGHEN J, HOLMANS P, ET AL. Association of slow acetylator genotype for N-acetyltransferase 2 with familiar Parkinson's disease. *Lancet 350: 1136-1139, 1997*

BERRY T. A selenium transport protein model of a sub-type of schizophrenia. *Med. Hypothesis 43: 409-414, 1994*

BROWN K, REID A, WHITE T, ET AL. Vitamin E, lipids, and lipid peroxidation products in tardive dyskinesia. *Biol. Psychiatry 43: 863-867, 1998*

BRUGGE KL, NICHOLS S, DELIS D, ET AL. The role of alterations in free radical metabolism in mediating cognitive impairments in Down syndrome. *EXS 62: 190-198, 1992*

BUCKMAN TD, KLING AS, EIDUSON S, ET AL. Glutathione peroxidase and CT scan abnormalities in schizophrenia. *Biol. Psychiatry 22: 1349-1356, 1987*

BUCKMAN TD, KLING AS, SUTPHIN MS, ET AL. Platelet glutathione peroxidase and monoamine oxidase activity in schizophrenics with CT scan abnormalities: relation to psychosocial variables. *Psychiatry Res. 31: 1-14, 1990*

CADET JL, KAHLER LA. Free radical mechanisms in schizophrenia and tardive diskinesia. *Neurosci. Biobehav. Rev. 18: 457-467, 1994*

CLAUSEN J, JENSON GE, NIELSEN SA. Selenium in chronic neurological diseases. Multiple sclerosis and Batten's disease. *Biol. Trace Elem. Res. 15: 179-203, 1988*

D'ALMEIDA V, LOBO LL, HIPPOLIDE DC, ET AL. Sleep deprivation induces brain region-specific decreases in glutathione levels. *Neuroreport 9: 2853-2856, 1998*

DAVEY GP, PEUCHEN S, CLARK JB. Energy thresholds in brain mitochondria. Potential involvement in neurodegeneration. *J. Biol. Chem. 273: 12753-12757, 1998*

EVANS PH. Free radicals in brain metabolism and pathology. *Br. Med. Bull. 49: 577-587, 1993*

FEKKES D, BODE WT, ZIJLSTRA FJ, PEPPLINKHUIZEN L. Eicosanoid and amino acid metabolism in transient acute psychoses with psychedelic symptoms. *Prostaglandins Leukot. Essent. Fatty Acids 54: 261-264, 1996*

GOVORIN NV, GOVORIN AV, SKAZHUTIN SA. Significance of disorders of the processes of lipid peroxidation in patients with persistent paranoid schizophrenia resistant to the treatment. *Zh. Nevropatol. Psikhiatr. Im. S. S. Korsakova 91: 121-124, 1991*

HONDA K, KOMODA Y, INOUE S. Oxidized glutathione regulates physiological sleep in unrestrained rats. *Brain Res. 636: 253-258, 1994*

INOUE S, HONDA K, KOMODA Y. Sleep as neuronal detoxification and restitution. Behav. *Brain Res. 69: 91-96, 1995*

KIMURA M, KAPAS L, KRUEGER JM. Oxidized glutathione promotes sleep in rabbits. *Brain Res. Bull. 45: 545-548, 1998*

JAIN A, MARTENSSON J, STOLE E, ET AL. Glutathione deficiency leads to mitochondrial damage in brain. *Proc. Natl. Acad. Sci. USA 88: 1913-1917, 1991*

JENNER P. Oxidative stress in Parkinson's disease and other neurodegenerative disorders. *Pathol. Biol. (Paris) 44: 57-64, 1996*

JENSEN GE, CLAUSEN J. Leukocyte glutathione peroxidase activity and selenium level in Batten's disease. *Scand. J. Clin. Lab. Invest. 43: 187-196, 1983*

LOHR JB. Oxygen radicals and neuropsychiatric illness. Some speculations. *Arch. Gen. Psychiatry 48: 1097-1106, 1991*

LOHR JB, BROWNING JA. Free radical involvement in neuropsychiatric illnesses. *Psychpharmacol. Bull. 31: 159-165, 1995*

MAHADIK SP, SCHEFFER RE. Oxidative injury and potential use of antioxidants in schizophrenia. *Prostaglandins Leukot. Essent. Fatty Acids 55:45-54, 1996*

MAHADIK SP, MUKHERJEE S, SCHEFFER RE, ET AL. Elevated plasma lipid peroxidases at the onset of non-affective psychosis. *Biol. Psychiatry 43: 674-679, 1998*

MAERTENS P, DYKEN P, GRAF W, ET AL. Free radicals, anticonvulsants, and the neuronal ceroid-lipofuscinoses. *American J. Med. Genet. 57: 225-228, 1995*

MAY PC, GRAY PN. The mechanism of glutamate-induced degeneration of cultured Huntington's disease and control fibroblasts. *J. Neurol. Sci. 70: 101-112, 1985*

MUKHERJEE S , MAHADIK SP, SCHEFFER RE, ET AL. Impaired antioxidant defense at the onset of psychosis. *Schizophr. Res. 19: 19-26, 1996*

NAKAGAMI Y, SAITO H, KATSUKI H. 3-Hydroxykynurenine toxicity on the rat striatum in vivo. *Jpn. J. Pharmacol. 71: 183-186, 1996*

PAI BN, JANAKIRAMAIAH N, GANGADHAR BN, RAVINDRANATH V. Depletion of glutathione and enhanced lipid peroxidation in the CSF of acute psychotics following haloperidol administration. *Biol. Psychiatry 36: 489-491, 1994*

PAL SN, DANDIYA PC. Glutathione as a cerebral substrate in depressive behavior. *Pharmacol. Biochem. Behav. 48: 845-851, 1994*

PERCY ME, DALTON AJ, MARKOVIC VD, ET AL. Red cell superoxide dismutase, glutathione peroxidase and catalase in Down syndrome patients with and without manifestations of Alzheimer's disease. *American J. Med. Genet. 35: 459-467, 1990*

REDDY R, SAHEBARAO MP, MUKHERJEE S, MURTHY JN. Enzymes of the antioxidant defense system in chronic schizophrenic patients. *Biol. Psychiatry 30: 409-412, 1991*

REDDY RD, YAO JK. Free radical pathology in schizophrenia: a review. *Prostaglandins Leukot. Essent. Fatty Acids 55: 33-43, 1996*

REITER RJ. Oxidative processes and antioxidative defense mechanisms in the aging brain. *FASEB 9: 526-533, 1995*

ROTROSEN J, ADLER L, EDSON R, LAVORI P. Antioxidant treatment of tardive dyskinesia. *Prostaglandins Leukot. Essent. Fatty Acids 55: 77-81, 1996*

SAGARA Y. Induction of reactive oxygen species in neurons by haloperidol. *J. Neurochem. 71: 1002-1012, 1998*

SCHNEIDER RH, NIDICH SI, SALERNO JW, ET AL. Lower lipid peroxidase levels in practitioners of the *Transcendental Meditation* program. *Psychosom. Med. 60: 38-41, 1998*

SMYTHIES JR. Oxidative reactions and schizophrenia: a review-discussion. *Schizophrenic Res. 24: 357-364, 1997*

STABEL-BUROW J, KLEU A, SCHUCHMANN S, HEINEMANN U. Glutathione levels and nerve cell loss in hippocampal cultures from trisomy 16 mouse – a model of Down Syndrome. *Brain Res. 765: 313-318, 1997*

TABRIZI SJ, CLEETER MW, XUEREB J, ET AL. Biochemical abnormalities and excitotoxicity in Huntington's disease brain. *Ann. Neurol. 45: 25-32, 1999*

TEKSEN F, SAYLI BS, AYDIN A, ET AL. Antioxidative metabolism in Down syndrome. *Biol. Trace Elem. Res. 63: 123-127, 1998*

WESTERMARCK T, SANDHOLM M. Decreased erythrocyte glutathione peroxidase activity in neuronal lipofuscinosis (NCL) – corrected with selenium supplementation. *Acta Pharmacol. Toxicol. (Copenh.) 40: 70-74, 1977*

YAO JK, REDDY R, McELHINNY LG, VAN KAMMEN DP. Effects of haloperidol on antioxidant defense system enzymes in schizophrenia. *J. Psychiatr. Res. 32: 385-391, 1998*

YAO JK, REDDY R, McELHINNY LG, VAN KAMMEN DP. Reduced status of plasma total antioxidant capacity in schizophrenia. *Schizophrenic. Res. 32: 1-8, 1998*

YAO JK, REDDY R, VAN KAMMEN DP. Human plasma glutathione peroxidase and symptom severity in schizophrenia. *Biol. Psychiatry 45: 1512-1515, 1999*

ZANELLA A, IZZO C, MEOLA G, ET AL. Metabolic impairment and membrane abnormality in red cells from Huntington's disease. *J. Neurol. Sci. 47: 93-103, 1980*

CHAPTER 21
SEIZURES

Seizures are a group of neurological disorders typified by muscle contractions, twitching and partial or complete loss of consciousness. Specific symptoms depend on the precise location in the brain of chaotic bursts of electrical activity. Seizures range from violent, uncontrollable contractions of the whole body to a subtle and momentary 'loss of contact' that may appear to be little more than daydreaming.

Seizures have been referred to as convulsions, fits and epilepsy, as well as by other names that do not accurately reflect the various disorders. Types of seizures include tonic-clonic (grand mal), absence (petit mal), complex-partial (psychomotor, temporal lobe), focal (Jacksonian), and status epilepticus (intractable fits). Not all seizures are epileptic. The most common type of seizure in very young children are called febrile seizures, cause by the rapid onset of fever. Other causes of seizures include stroke or may be a result of injury, tumors, meningitis, hypoglycemia, alcohol withdrawal or other health complications.

Epilepsy—a specific type of seizure with recurrent, unprovoked attacks—is however the most common type, affecting close to three million North Americans—about one in a hundred people, half of them children or adolescents. Of these, one-half fortunately grows out of the disorder.

TREATMENT

Recurrent seizures usually require medication with such oral anticonvulsants as phenobarbital, valproic acid, phenytoin and carbamazine. Patients may need to take these drugs indefinitely. Unfortunately they are not a cure and can have many side-effects, some severe.

Nutritional supplements are used in both conventional and complementary medicine. B-vitamins, particularly B6 (pyridoxine), are effective against certain seizures. Magnesium is also useful, especially in seizures related to high blood pressure. Selenium is used in epileptics, since deficiency of this mineral may intensify the frequency and severity of seizures.

FREE RADICAL DAMAGE IN SEIZURES

Seizures are typified by tremendous bioelectrical activity in the affected area of the brain that generates free radicals in large numbers. Convulsions that provoke loss of consciousness may be accompanied by breathing abnormalities and subsequent oxidative stress. When frequent and/or prolonged, this oxidative stress can damage brain cells. Many studies show that lipid peroxidation (a result of free radical formation) can lead to neuronal damage or destruction of these neurological cells. Moreover, the higher the level of oxidative stress in these tissues, the harder it is to treat. Patients respond less effectively to medication when the ongoing injury and nerve damage provokes further epileptic activity. Canadian researchers at the University of Calgary have even suggested that this continual free radical damage may even result in certain brain tumors.

GLUTATHIONE LEVELS IN SEIZURES

Considerable research has demonstrated that glutathione levels fall significantly in seizure conditions. What is less clear is whether this glutathione deficiency causes seizures, results from them, or both. Nevertheless, the total body glutathione levels of seizure patients are measurably lower than those of normal individuals, and this GSH deficiency is even more noticeable in the affected areas of the brain.

Swiss scientists led by S.G. Mueller studied three groups: patients with active epilepsy, those with controlled epilepsy and non-epileptics. They determined that low glutathione levels more often lead to seizures than result from them. Other research supports this theory by showing how seizures are more frequent or severe when glutathione levels are experimentally lowered. Whatever the specific mechanism, the overall picture shows that glutathione levels fall lower and lower as seizures progress.

Worse still, not only are glutathione levels lowered by seizure activity, the drugs used to treat seizures themselves reduce glutathione levels even further. Japanese researchers H. Ono, A. Sakamoto and N. Sakura showed that both carbamazepine and phenytoin—popular anti-seizure medications—diminish glutathione and leave cells even more susceptible to oxidative damage. Turkish physiologists found the same of valproic acid, another anti-seizure drug.

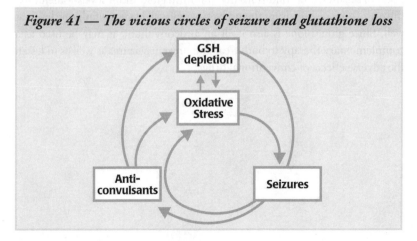

Figure 41 — The vicious circles of seizure and glutathione loss

However, scientists studying childhood seizures at Harvard University found that glutathione levels improved after anticonvulsants were halted and patients were given selenium.

GLUTATHIONE PROTECTS FROM SEIZURES

Since glutathione directly affects the activity of brain cells, it is called a neuromodulator. Japanese scientists K. Abe, K. Nakanishi and H. Saito protected animals from drug-induced seizures by injecting glutathione directly into the fluid of the brain and spinal cord. Canadians at Toronto Western Hospital showed that combined vitamin E and glutathione reduced the number of brain cells damaged after seizure activity. In Texas S.G. Jenkinson, J.M. Jordan and C.A. Duncan were able to protect laboratory animals from seizures and death by injecting them with glutathione, and Italians at the University of Milan successfully prevented seizures caused by isoniazid—a tuberculosis medication—by administering patients with glutathione beforehand.

Several scientists have used n-acetylcysteine (NAC, see chapter 4), a powerful glutathione precursor, to treat seizures, and Swedish researchers led by E. Ben-Menachem applied it to patients suffering from progressive myoclonic epilepsy—a particularly hard-to-treat disease that gradually destroys the nervous system. Patients given a daily dose of 6 grams showed marked improvements, and an American team from Gainesville, Florida used NAC, vitamin E, B2, zinc and selenium to treat this type of seizure, obtaining similar improvements.

CONCLUSION

Free radical formation and oxidative stress can be seen as both a cause and a result of seizures, and conditions that diminish glutathione levels—including the use of anti-seizure drugs themselves—may well lower glutathione levels as well. Since glutathione is also itself an anticonvulsant, it may be used as a complementary therapy to both treat and prevent seizures as well as to lessen the adverse effects of conventional drugs.

SEIZURES

ABBOTT LC, NEJAD HH, BOTTJE WG, HASSAN AS, Glutathione levels in specific brain regions of genetically epileptic (tg/tg) mice, *Brain Res Bull 1990 Oct;25(4):629-31*

ABE K, NAKANISHI K, SAITO H, The anticonvulsive effect of glutathione in mice, *Biol Pharm Bull 1999 Nov;22(11):1177-9*

ABE K, NAKANISHI K, SAITO H, The possible role of endogenous glutathione as an anticonvulsant in mice, *Brain Res 2000 Jan 31;854(1-2):235-8*

BELLISSIMO MI, AMADO D, ABDALLA DS, FERREIRA EC, CAVALHEIRO EA, NAFFAH-MAZZACORATTI MG, Superoxide dismutase, glutathione peroxidase activities and the hydroperoxide concentration are modified in the hippocampus of epileptic rats, *Epilepsy Res 2001 Aug;46(2):121-8*

BEN-MENACHEM E, KYLLERMAN M, MARKLUND S, Superoxide dismutase and glutathione peroxidase function in progressive myoclonus epilepsies, *Epilepsy Res 2000 Jun;40(1):33-9*

BEUTLER E, CURNUTTE JT, FORMAN L, Glutathione peroxidase deficiency and childhood seizures, *Lancet 1991 Sep 14;338(8768):700*

CENGIZ M, YUKSEL A, SEVEN M, The effects of carbamazepine and valproic acid on the erythrocyte glutathione, glutathione peroxidase, superoxide dismutase and serum lipid peroxidation in epileptic children, *Pharmacol Res 2000 Apr;41(4):423-5*

COCK HR, TONG X, HARGREAVES IP, HEALES SJ, CLARK JB, PATSALOS PN, THOM M, GROVES M, SCHAPIRA AH, SHORVON SD, WALKER MC, Mito-chondrial dysfunction associated with neuronal death following status epilepticus in rat, *Epilepsy Res 2002 Feb;48(3):157-68*

ERAKOVIC V, ZUPAN G, VARLJEN J, RADOSEVIC S, SIMONIC A, Electroconvulsive shock in rats: changes in superoxide dismutase and glutathione peroxidase activity, *Brain Res Mol Brain Res 2000 Mar 29;76(2):266-74*

FRANTSEVA MV, PEREZ VELAZQUEZ JL, TSORAKLIDIS G, MENDONCA AJ, ADAMCHIK Y, MILLS LR, CARLEN PL, BURNHAM MW, Oxidative stress is involved in seizure-induced neurodegeneration in the kindling model of epilepsy, *Neuroscience 2000;97(3):431-5*

FRANTSEVA MV, VELAZQUEZ JL, HWANG PA, CARLEN PL, Free radical production correlates with cell death in an in vitro model of epilepsy, *Eur J Neurosci 2000 Apr;12(4):1431-9*

GLUCK MR, JAYATILLEKE E, SHAW S, ROWAN AJ, HAROUTUNIAN V, CNS oxidative stress associated with the kainic acid rodent model of experimental epilepsy, *Epilepsy Res 2000 Mar;39(1):63-71*

HIRAMATSU M, MORI A, Brain glutathione and seizures, *Folia Psychiatr Neurol Jpn 1980;34(3):363*

HIRAMATSU M, MORI A, Reduced and oxidized glutathione in brain and convulsions, *Neurochem Res 1981 Mar;6(3):301-6*

HURD RW, WILDER BJ, HELVESTON WR, UTHMAN BM, Treatment of four siblings with progressive myoclonus epilepsy of the Unverricht-Lundborg type with N-acetylcysteine, *Neurology 1996 Nov;47(5):1264-8*

JENKINSON SG, JORDAN JM, DUNCAN CA, Effects of selenium deficiency on glutathione-induced protection from hyperbaric hyperoxia in rat, *Am J Physiol 1989 Dec;257(6 Pt 1):L393-8*

JIANG D, AKOPIAN G, HO YS, WALSH JP, ANDERSEN JK, Chronic brain oxidation in a glutathione peroxidase knockout mouse model results in increased resistance to induced epileptic seizures, *Exp Neurol 2000 Aug;164(2):257-68*

KUREKCI AE, ALPAY F, TANINDI S, GOKCAY E, OZCAN O, AKIN R, ISIMER A, SAYAL A, Plasma trace element, plasma glutathione peroxidase, and superoxide dismutase levels in epileptic children receiving antiepileptic drug therapy, *Epilepsia 1995 Jun;36(6):600-4*

Liu CS, Wu HM, Kao SH, Wei YH, Serum trace elements, glutathione, copper/zinc superoxide dismutase, and lipid peroxidation in epileptic patients with phenytoin or carbamazepine monotherapy, *Clin Neuropharmacol 1998 Jan-Feb;21(1):62-4*

Lores Arnaiz S, Travacio M, Llesuy S, Rodriguez de Lores Arnaiz G, Regional vulnerability to oxidative stress in a model of experimental epilepsy, *Neurochem Res 1998 Dec;23(12):1477-83*

Louw DF, Bose R, Sima AA, Sutherland GR, Evidence for a high free radical state in low-grade astrocytomas, *Neurosurgery 1997 Nov;41(5):1146-50; discussion 1151*

Mueller SG, Trabesinger AH, Boesiger P, Wieser HG, Brain glutathione levels in patients with epilepsy measured by in vivo (1)H-MRS, *Neurology 2001 Oct 23;57(8):1422-7*

Ogita K, Kitayama T, Okuda H, Yoneda Y, Effects of glutathione depletion by 2-cyclohexen-1-one on excitatory amino acids-induced enhancement of activator protein-1 DNA binding in murine hippocampus, *J Neurochem 2001 Mar;76(6):1905-15*

Ono H, Sakamoto A, Sakura N, Plasma total glutathione concentrations in epileptic patients taking anticonvulsants, *Clin Chim Acta 2000 Aug;298(1-2):135-43*

Peacock MD, Schenk DA, Lawrence RA, Morgan JA, Jenkinson SG, Elimination of glutathione-induced protection from hyperbaric hyperoxia by acivicin, *J Appl Physiol 1994 Mar;76(3):1279-84*

Pinelli A, Trivulzio S, Colombo-Zefinetti G, Tofanetti O, Anti-convulsant effects by reduced glutathione and related aminoacids in rats treated with isoniazid, *Toxicology 1988 Jan;48(1):103-7*

Ramaekers VT, Calomme M, Vanden Berghe D, Makropoulos W, Selenium deficiency triggering intractable seizures, *Neuropediatrics 1994 Aug;25(4):217-23*

Ravikumar A, Arun P, Devi KV, Augustine J, Kurup PA, Isoprenoid pathway and free radical generation and damage in neuropsychiatric disorders, *Indian J Exp Biol 2000 May;38(5):438-46*

Santavuori P, Heiskala H, Westermarck T, Sainio K, Moren R, Experience over 17 years with antioxidant treatment in Spielmeyer-Sjogren disease, *Am J Med Genet Suppl 1988;5:265-74*

Singh R, Pathak DN, Lipid peroxidation and glutathione peroxidase, glutathione reductase, superoxide dismutase, catalase, and glucose-6-phosphate dehydrogenase activities in FeCl3-induced epileptogenic foci in the rat brain, *Epilepsia 1990 Jan-Feb;31(1):15-26*

Sudha K, Rao AV, Rao A, Oxidative stress and antioxidants in epilepsy, *Clin Chim Acta 2001 Jan;303(1-2):19-24*

Tupeev IR, Kryzhanovskii GN, Nikushkin EV, Bordiukov MM, Iuzefova SM, The antioxidant system in the dynamic combined treatment of epilepsy patients with traditional anticonvulsant preparations and an antioxidant—alpha-tocopherol, *Biull Eksp Biol Med 1993 Oct;116(10):362-4*

Weber GF, Maertens P, Meng XZ, Pippenger CE, Glutathione peroxidase deficiency and childhood seizures, *Lancet 1991 Jun 15;337(8755):1443-4*

Wei YH, Lu CY, Wei CY, Ma YS, Lee HC, Oxidative stress in human aging and mitochondrial disease-consequences of defective mitochondrial respiration and impaired antioxidant enzyme system, *Chin J Physiol 2001 Mar 31;44(1):1-11*

Yuksel A, Cengiz M, Seven M, Ulutin T, Erythrocyte glutathione, glutathione peroxidase, superoxide dismutase and serum lipid peroxidation in epileptic children with valproate and carbamazepine monotherapy, *J Basic Clin Physiol Pharmacol 2000;11(1):73-81*

Yuksel A, Cengiz M, Seven M, Ulutin T, Changes in the antioxidant system in epileptic children receiving antiepileptic drugs: two-year prospective studies, *J Child Neurol 2001 Aug;16(8):603-6*

CHAPTER 22
SKIN DISORDERS

What is the largest organ in the body? Most people think it's the liver or even the intestine, but in fact it's the skin. Besides providing a protective barrier against the environment, the skin performs a large number of important functions, endocrinological, thermoregulatory, immunological, toxicological and circulatory.

The skin can host a huge variety of diseases and disorders and about one third of North Americans will experience some sort of skin problem. Skin disorders also affect patients differently, especially in their psychological reaction to the disease. Firstly, the fact that they can actually see the problem makes it hard to forget; secondly they are often nervous about the actual or perceived reaction of others, and the social or interpersonal consequences.

GSH AND SKIN DISEASE

Given the number of functions served by the skin, it is no surprise that glutathione is involved in many skin problems. The role of GSH in detoxification and prevention of radiation damage in other tissues is well-known. It plays just as vital a role here. Low levels of GSH have been documented in many types of skin disease, including:

❑ Psoriasis
❑ Eczema
❑ Vasculitis
❑ Mycosis fungoides
❑ Polymyositis
❑ Scleroderma
❑ SLE (lupus)

❑ Atopic dermatitis
❑ Seborrheic dermatitis
❑ Contact dermatitis
❑ Dermatitis herpetiformis
❑ Pemphigoid
❑ Acne conglobata
❑ Acne vulgaris

This chapter focuses on psoriasis, dermatitis and ultra-violet radiation damage.

PSORIASIS

Psoriasis is a common, chronic recurrent skin condition characterized by scaly white or red patches of skin on the legs, knees, arms, elbows, ears, scalp or back. It may consist of one or two inconspicuous small patches or cover the whole body. This can affect the joints and occasionally even lead to disabling arthritis. However, such extreme cases are rare and general health for most psoriatic patients is good. Lesions are typified by an overgrowth of skin cells which multiply up to ten times faster than normal skin cells. This overgrowth continues and leads to the classic raised, silvery, flaky appearance of the condition.

The actual cause of psoriasis remains unknown. It may be triggered by different factors in different people. Fair-skinned individuals in particular may have a genetic predisposition to it. It certainly has something to do with the immune response itself. Attacks or flare-ups can be triggered by emotional or physical stress, illness, injury, infection, drug and alcohol abuse, obesity, and many different chemicals. The other chapters of this book describe the critical role of glutathione in many of these processes.

One source of relief for psoriatic patients is travel to a healing environment. The Dead Sea in Israel is particularly popular. A medical facility—The Dead-Sea Psoriasis Treatment Center—has been set up specifically for this purpose. Researchers have tried to understand why this particular area seems to help. High levels of sunlight seem to affect psoriasis positively. Most interestingly, the drinking water in the area is very high in selenium. A local research team explains that the best indicator of selenium bioactivity is patients' glutathione peroxidase levels. Compared to a control group and to their own initial GSH levels, patients spending weeks in this treatment center increased GSH peroxidase levels, often as much as 50%.

Psoriasis patients suffer from abnormal glutathione enzyme activities, and researchers have linked the disease to high levels of free radicals. Lowered GSH activity results in greater damage. The clinical results of raising GSH in this disease are promising and more studies are underway.

CASE STUDY

Roland is a 44 year-old energetic and sociable business entrepreneur who suffered from psoriasis for ten years. Itchy, scaly eruptions often covered his entire body, and aggressive scratching led to bleeding and scabbing. His dermatologist tried many different treatments including strong topical corticosteroids and methotrexate tablets, which he had to discontinue due to side-effects. Ultraviolet light therapy was suggested, but having the financial means, Roland preferred frequent trips to Mexico and the Caribbean to sitting in artificial light. Having done significant homework on his condition, he concluded that the psoriasis was caused by an immune dysfunction. He started taking 40 grams/day of Immunocal to raise his glutathione levels. Within two weeks he was free of bleeding and scabs and described his scaling as 75% improved.

DERMATITIS

Dermatitis is a general term meaning inflammation of the skin. It is caused by a wide range of different ailments. Toxins or irritants can lead to contact dermatitis. Allergies can lead to allergic or atopic dermatitis. Many intestinal or immunological diseases can lead to such forms as dermatitis herpetiformis. Overproduction of oils in the skin can lead to seborrheic dermatitis. Dermatitis can be triggered by stress or illness. Overly hot, dry, cold or wet environments also promote dermatitis. All are characterized by red itchy skin and in extreme cases blistering, crusty or oozing lesions. Almost all of these conditions have been linked to abnormal glutathione activity.

In both irritant contact dermatitis and allergic contact dermatitis glutathione levels fall both in the skin and the whole body. A group of Japanese dermatologists inhibited GSH production with BSO and found that both allergic and irritant contact dermatitis rashes became more severe. They link this both to the detoxification abilities of GSH, and to its effect on the immune system.

Several research teams have shown that GSH-precursors help the immune system respond to contact sensitivity. A Swedish team using the GSH enhancing drugs NAC and DiNAC demonstrated significnt results with contact and delayed-hypersensitivity reactions. G. Senaldi of the University of Geneva successfully used both topical and oral NAC to experimentally treat contact and irritant dermatitis. His team suggested that a similar approach may benefit cancer patients suffering from skin inflammation secondary to TNF-alpha (tumor necrosis factor-alpha), an inflammatory side-effect of cancer.

Contact dermatitis often arises from the use of cosmetics, including make-up, skin creams, eyeliners and other products. One particular culprit is a group of preservatives/sanitizers known as MCI/MI (methyl-chloro-isothiazolinone/methyl-isothiolinone). A group of Swedish occupational and environmental dermatologists found that the addition of as little as 2% GSH to these emollients deactivates the MCI/MI.

Thimerosol is another popular preservative used in toiletries, including contact lens solutions. It is known to cause skin and eye reactions, probably because of its organomercury content. At Rome's Dermatological Institute, B. Santucci showed that adding l-cysteine or glutathione to solutions containing thimerosol reduced or prevented reactions to this chemical.

AIDS patients are more prone to skin disease than others. These conditions include Karposi's sarcoma, seborrheic dermatitis and others. As we discussed in chapter 12, most AIDS patients are glutathione-deficient, a factor that contributes to these skin conditions. S. Passi and A. Morrone in Italy and other teams have shown a deficiency of glutathione peroxidase activity both in HIV-positive patients and in otherwise healthy individuals with seborrheic dermatitis.

An interesting experiment was carried out at the Welsh School of Pharmacy. They examined the dermatitis-inducing chemicals of plants such as poison ivy and poison oak and found that most inflammation was due to free radicals. Using the GSH-precursor OTZ they were able to reduce the irritation and sensitizing effect of these noxious compounds.

Sun and ultraviolet radiation skin damage

By far the most common cause of abnormal aging, wrinkling and cancer of the skin is sun exposure and ultraviolet radiation. We may pay later in life for the 'healthy' bronzed glow of our youth. The skin-aging consequences of tanning lead many people to plastic surgery. But most face-lifts would be unnecessary if these patients had avoided tanning when they were younger. Many skin cancers that appear in adult life may actually be initiated by severe sunburn as a child.

The well-known ozone layer in the atmosphere blunts the damaging effects of ultraviolet A and B radiation found in sunlight. The ozone depletion which has so concerned scientists in recent years has already increased the number of skin cancer patients. We may yet witness an even more dramatic increase in the years to come. Physicians are treating sunburn in more and more patients who claim they have never before been so dramatically affected by sun exposure.

Radiation releases high levels of hydroxyl-radicals in the skin. These are the most toxic free radicals known to man. Such radiation comes from sunlight UV-A and UV-B, sun lamps, radiotherapy treatment and X-rays. The damaging radicals are normally neutralized by glutathione, but overexposure overwhelms this protective system and GSH levels can fall, resulting in even more damage. For this reason, doctors have considered using antioxidant supplementation to protect the skin. Studies using various antioxidants have had mixed results. Research into elevated GSH levels has been much more encouraging.

P. Baas and his team at The Netherlands Cancer Institute used halogen lamps to sensitize their patients to light, and showed that sensitivity decreased when the patients were pretreated with NAC to raise glutathione levels. Another Dutch team at the Department of Medicinal Photochemistry, Leiden University looked at various oral and topical products and their capacity to decrease UV skin damage. They found that NAC, whether ingested or applied to the skin was a practical means of protecting from UV-B radiation damage.

French researchers at Joseph Fourier University in Grenoble examined how effectively various GSH precursors could limit UV-A radiation damage. These products included NAC, OTZ, CIT, and selenium. Most are described in detail in chapter 4. To various degrees, all GSH-enhancing substances inhibited the deleterious effects of UV-A radiation. The researchers conclude that elevated GSH levels protect against UV-A damage.

Similar studies at Harvard University and Hirosaki University in Japan investigated the way UV-B radiation causes sunburn. Using animal subjects they first showed that glutathione depletion resulted in significantly greater sunburn damage. Further studies with orally administered esterfied glutathione raised GSH levels and resulted in less damage. Other Japanese experiments using higher doses of UV-radiation on their animals showed that pre-treatment with glutathione esters could actually decrease the number of skin tumors that developed much later on.

A German team at the University of Berlin studied the effect of UV-B damage on people with an inherited defect in a glutathione enzyme called GSH S-transferase. The GSH-impaired group suffered significantly more intense damage than the control group, so it seems that inherited GSH-transferase deficiencies determine how sensitive an individual is to sunlight.

UV-B exposure not only damages skin, at high doses it affects the immune system itself by suppressing the local and general functioning of T-cell lymphocytes. Substances that deplete GSH levels decrease this response even more, and substances that elevate glutathione levels protect it. D.P. Steenvoorden and his team at the Amsterdam Center for Drug Research used BSO to lower glutathione levels and NAC or GSH-esters to raise them, demonstrating that elevated GSH levels provide protection against UV-B immunosuppression.

CASE STUDY

The 61 year-old Canadian Charles loved boating. His dream was to retire and spend most of his time on the water, travelling the coasts. Tall, handsome and fair-skinned, he was unfortunately prone to sunburn. Despite sunscreens and hats, being on the water often left him unprotected and his complexion grew ruddy and inflamed. His physician was worried about the possible development of pre-cancerous sun-induced lesions on his face. Charles had already started taking Immunocal for a potential prostate problem. After several weeks he noticed that his tendency to burn was significantly decreased, despite some "accidental" exposures. In two months his in-the-sun complexion was no longer so different from his winter complexion.

CONCLUSION

Low glutathione levels characterize many skin diseases. Practical applications with GSH-raising substances have been studied in the treatment of several diseases. There has been success in some but not all cases of psoriasis. This may reflect the multiple and various causes of this disease. Many of the diseases that fall under the very general definition of dermatitis may be positively affected by raised glutathione levels. GSH is of extreme importance as a protective agent against ultraviolet radiation of the sun.

REFERENCES TO CHAPTER 22
SKIN DISORDERS

ACETO A, MARTINI F, DRAGANI B, ET AL. Purification and characterization of glutathione transferase from psoriatic skin. *Biochem. Med. Metab. Biol. 48: 212-218, 1992*

BAAS P, VAN MANSOM I, VAN TINTEREN H, ET AL. Effect of N-acetylcysteine on Photoprin-induced skin photosensitivity in patients. *Lasers Surg. Med. 16: 359-367, 1995*

EMERIT I. Free radicals and aging of the skin. *EXS 62: 328-341, 1992*

EMONET N, LECCIA MT, FAVIER A, ET AL. Thiols and selenium: protective effect on human skin fibroblasts exposed to UVA radiation. *J. Photochem. Photobiol B. 40: 84-90, 1997*

FAIRRIS GM, PERKINS PJ, LLOYD B, ET AL. The effect on atopic dermatitis of supplementation with selenium and vitamin E. *Acta. Derm. Venereol. 69: 359-362, 1989*

GREENSTOCK CL. Radiation and aging: free radical damage, biological response and possible antioxidant intervention. *Medical Hypotheses 41: 473-482, 1993*

GRUVBERGER B, BRUZE M. Can glutathione-containing emollients inactivate methylchloroisothiazolinone/methylisothiazolone? *Contact Dermatitis 38: 261-265, 1998*

HANADA K, GANGE RW, CONNOR MJ. Effect of glutathione depletion on sunburn cell formation in the hairless mouse. *J. Invest. Dermatol. 96: 838-40, 1991*

HANADA K, SAWAMURA D, TAMAI K, ET AL. Photoprotective effect of esterified glutathione against ultraviolet B-induced sunburn cell formation in the hairless mouse. *J. Invest. Dermatol. 108: 727-730, 1997*

HIRAI A, MINAMIYAMA Y, HAMADA T, ET AL. Glutathione metabolism in mice is enhanced more with hapten-induced allergic contact dermatitis than with irritant contact dermatitis. *J. Invest. Dermatol. 109: 314-318, 1997*

JUHLIN L, EDQVIST LE, EKMAN LG, ET AL. Blood glutathione peroxidase levels in skin diseases: effect of selenium and vitamin E treatment. *Arch. Derm. Venereol. 62: 211-214, 1982*

KERB R, BROCKMOLLER J, REUM T, ROOTS I. Deficiency of glutathione S-transferases T1 and M1 as heritable factors of increased cutaneous UV sensitivity. *J. Invest. Dermatol. 108: 229-232, 1997*

KIMURA J, HAYAKARI M, KUMANO T, ET AL. Altered glutathione transferase levels in rat skin inflamed due to contact hypersensitivity: induction of the alpha-class subunit 1. *Biochem J. 335 (Pt 3): 605-610, 1998*

KOBAYASHI S, TAKEHANA M, TOHYAMA C. Glutathione isopropyl ester reduces UVB-induced skin damage in hairless mice. *Photochem. Photobiol. 63: 106-110, 1996*

LJUNGHALL K, JUHLIN L, EDQVIST LE, PLANTIN LO. Selenium, glutathione peroxidase and dermatitis herpetiformis. *Acta. Derm. Venereol. 64: 546-546. 1984*

PASCHE-KOO F, ARECHALDE A, ARRIGHI JF, HAUSER C. Effect of N-acetylcysteine, an inhibitor of tumor necrosis factor, on irritant contact dermatitis in the human. *Curr. Prob. Dermatol 23: 198-206, 1995*

PASSI S, MORONNE A, DE LUCA C, ET AL. Blood levels of vitamin E, polyunsaturated fatty acids of phospholipids, lipoperoxides and glutathione peroxidase in patients affected with seborrheic dermatitis. *J. Dermatol. 2: 171-178, 1991*

SANTUCCI B, CANNISTRACI C, CRISTAUDO A, ET AL. Thimerosal positivities: the role of SH groups and divalent ions. *Contact Dermatitis 39: 123-126, 1998*

SARNSTRAND B, JANSSON AH, MATUSEVICIENE G, ET AL. N, N'-Diacetyl-L-cysteine - the disulfide dimer of N-acetylcysteine - is a potent modulator of contact sensitivity / delayed type hypersensitivity reactions in rodents. *J. Pharmacol. Exp. Ther. 288: 1174-1184, 1999*

SCHMIDT RJ, KHAN L, CHUNG LY. Are free radicals and not quinones the haptic species derived from urushiols and other contact allergenic mono- and dihydric alkylbenzines? The significance of NADH, glutathione, and redox cycling in the skin. *Arch. Dermatol. Research 282: 56-64, 1990*

SENALDI G, POINTAIRE P, PIGUET PF, GRAU GE. Protective effect of N-acetylcysteine in hapten-induced irritant and contact hypersensitivity reactions. *J. Invest. Dermatol. 102: 934-937, 1994*

SEUTTER E, COLSON ML, VAN DE STAAK WJ, ET AL. Analysis in blood of dermatological patients. 1. Glutathione and glutathione reductase. *Dermatologica 151: 193-198, 1975*

SHANI J, LIVSHITZ T, ROBBERECH H, ET AL. Increased erythrocyte glutathione peroxidase activity in psoriatics consuming high-selenium drinking water at the Dead-Sea Psoriasis Treatment Center. *Pharmacol. Res. Commun. 17: 479-488, 1985*

STEENVOORDEN DP, BEIJERBERGEN VAN HENEGOUWEN GM. Cysteine derivatives protect against UV-induced reactive intermediates in human keratinocytes: the role of glutathione synthesis. *Photochem. Photobiol. 66: 665-671, 1997*

STEENVOORDEN DP, BEIJERBERGEN VAN HENEGOUWEN GM. Glutathione ethylester protects against local and systemic suppression of contact hypersensitivity induced by ultraviolet B radiation in mice. *Radiation Research 150: 292-297, 1998*

STEENVOORDEN DP, HASSELBAINK DM, BEIJERBERGEN VAN HENEGOUWEN GM. Protection against UV-induced reactive intermediates in human cells and mouse skin by glutathione precursors: a comparison of N-acetylcysteine and glutathione ethylester. *Photochem. Photobiol. 67: 651-666, 1998*

VAN DEN BROEKE LT, BEIJERBERGEN VAN HENEGOUWEN GM. Thiols as potential UV radiation protectors: an in vitro study. *J. Photochem. Photobiol. B. 17: 279-286, 1993*

VAN DEN BROEKE LT, BEIJERBERGEN VAN HENEGOUWEN GM. The effect of N-acetylcysteine on the UVB-induced inhibition of epidermal DNA synthesis in rat skin. *J. Photochem. Photobiol. B. 26: 271-276, 1994*

VAN DEN BROEKE LT, BEIJERBERGEN VAN HENEGOUWEN GM. Topically applied N-acetylcysteine as a protector against UVB-induced systemic immunosuppression. *J. Photochem. Photobiol. B. 27: 61-65, 1995*

CHAPTER 23
GLUTATHIONE IN THE HUMAN MALE

PROSTATE PROBLEMS

Of the hundreds of animal species with a prostate gland, only humans and dogs are known to suffer from prostate cancer and prostatic hyperplasia (an overgrowth of prostate tissue). The prostate is a walnut-sized gland that surrounds the urethra, the tube that drains the bladder through the penis (see figure 41). It is responsible for the production of fluid that carries the sperm when ejaculating. Other prostate problems include infection—both acute and chronic prostatitis. The majority of men will have some sort of prostate problem in their lifetimes.

PROSTATIC HYPERTROPHY (ENLARGED PROSTATE GLAND)

Not all prostate enlargement is cancerous. In fact most enlarged prostates are benign. Hypertrophy of the prostate is caused by an enlargement of the cells in the gland, unlike cancer, which is enlargement caused by an increase in the number of cells. This condition is age related and increases from an incidence of 8% in 30 to 40 year olds, to over 80% in men over 80. Enlargement of the gland often leads to impaired flow from the bladder. Symptoms are frequent and difficult urination, a weak urinary stream, straining, dribbling, incomplete emptying and recurrent urinary infections.

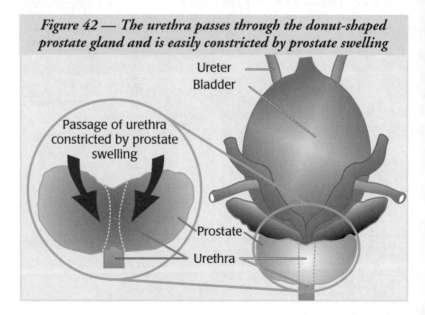

Figure 42 — The urethra passes through the donut-shaped prostate gland and is easily constricted by prostate swelling

Traditional treatments include surgical removal of all or part of the prostate, widening of the urethral passage by such means as scraping or laser surgery, and a number of drugs that either relax the muscles at the neck of the bladder or actually shrink the prostate. Saw palmetto is an herbal therapy that is greatly valued by alternative practitioners and is now also gaining acceptance by conventional doctors as an adjunct to shrink prostate tissues.

In prostatic hypertrophy and prostate cancer the prostate overgrows for several reasons. Male hormones (androgens) have considerable influence on this growth. Physicians may prescribe anti-androgens as an antidote.

Researchers have found that abnormal growth in these tissues often corresponds to deficiencies in glutathione enzymes. One is glutathione S-transferase, which has several sub-types. The balance of these sub-types varies from normal prostate tissue to hypertrophic prostates to cancerous prostates. Several researchers propose that deficiencies in this GSH enzyme system increase the likelihood of developing both an enlarged prostate and prostate cancer.

Prostate cancer

Well-known nutritional specialist Bonnie Liebman writes about "Death, taxes…and prostate cancer…," a poignant comment on the prevalence of prostate cancer in our population. When researchers include in their statistics individuals with pre-cancerous cells, they claim that more than three-quarters of men over the age of 80 show evidence of cancer in their prostate glands. Some scientists are of the opinion that if a man lives long enough, he will eventually get prostate cancer. By this definition, prostate cancer would certainly be a disease of aging (see chapter 6).

Nevertheless, the vast majority of men easily outlive prostate cancer, and may not even suffer significant symptoms. Although the average age at which men are diagnosed is 72, it is usually with a slow-growing tumor that may have begun thirty or forty years earlier. It is by far the most common type of cancer in men, but death by prostate cancer is less frequent than death by either lung cancer or cancer of the colon, the two most frequent cancer killers.

Screening for prostate cancer is pursued aggressively, usually by digital rectal exam or a blood test called a PSA (prostate specific antigen). Rectal exams are a simple way to check for swelling and sensitivity. PSA levels rise in the presence of prostate cancer and are a good screening tool for this cancer. They may also indicate the effectiveness of anti-cancer treatment. Traditional treatments include surgical removal, heat therapy, laser therapy, radiotherapy, chemotherapy, hormonal therapy and benign neglect.

Alternative therapy focuses more on slowing down the process than on curing it. Diet is important since prostatic cancer has been linked with high-fat, low-fiber diets. The use of antioxidants such as vitamin A or selenium is popular for reasons we describe below. Recently, a carotenoid called lycopene that gives certain fruits and vegetables their rich color has been linked to the prevention of prostate cancer. It seems that men who eat lycopene-rich foods (tomato sauces, dark grapes) have lower rates of prostatic disease. This theory is still under investigation.

One of the more significant series of papers to be published on glutathione and prostate cancer comes from the University of Wisconsin. Researchers there describe male hormones (androgens) as a source of oxidative stress, particularly in cancerous prostate cells. An article in the Journal of the National Cancer Institute claims that androgens stimulate free radical damage and also deplete glutathione. Given the natural decline of glutathione levels in males as they age, the article suggests that "unopposed androgen pro-oxidant stress" contributes to prostate cancer. Natural defense against oxidative stress is weakened by the decline of GSH enzymes. This is an interesting model for the development of prostate cancer.

Another finding links the loss of glutathione activity to prostate cancer. The function of a particular glutathione enzyme—glutathione-S-transferase-pi-1 (GSTP1)—is almost universally lost in both cancerous and pre-cancerous prostate cells. The inactivation of this glutathione enzyme is an early event in the development of prostate cancer. Many studies have linked the loss of GSTP1 to malignant transformation of prostatic tissues.

Medical discoveries are often a matter of chance. A very large study was undertaken by the National Cancer Institute (USA) to determine whether selenium could bring down the rate of skin cancer, notoriously caused by strong exposure to sunlight. Researchers L.C. Clarke and G.F. Combs from Cornell University and the University of Arizona already knew of selenium's ability to raise glutathione levels (see chapter 4) and to oppose cancer-causing free radical damage from ultraviolet light. As it turned out, selenium supplementation did not affect the incidence of skin cancer, but did surprisingly and dramatically diminish the incidence of prostate cancer in the selenium supplementation group.

A more recent study from Harvard University confirms that higher selenium levels go hand-in-hand with a decreased risk of prostate cancer. It measured selenium levels in the toenail clippings of over 51,000 male health professionals between 40 and 75 years of age. Those with the highest selenium levels had the lowest chance of developing advanced prostate cancer. Note that selenium is only biologically active—and only has health benefits—when it is part of the enzyme glutathione peroxidase, through which selenium expresses its positive health benefits (see chapter 4).

Studies using undenatured whey protein isolates to raise glutathione levels are underway at several research centers including McGill and Harvard Universities, where its usefulness in the treatment of prostate cancer is being weighed.

CASE STUDY
Franklin was a semi-retired general practitioner who at age 68 scored a PSA reading of over 8 micrograms/liter on a routine screening exam, suggesting a high possibility of prostate cancer. In continued tests, a urologist took a cystoscopic biopsy and confirmed the diagnosis. Four out of Franklin's six biopsy sites tested positive for high-grade tumor. For personal and practical reasons, Franklin delayed aggressive treatment and opted to take 30 grams/day of Immunocal, a protein isolate that raises glutathione levels. Bimonthly PSA levels showed a gradual decline, his latest reading being 3.8 u/L. He is still being closely followed by his urologist, and his decision to undergo chemotherapy, radiotherapy or surgery will be deferred unless his PSA levels rise again.

MALE INFERTILITY

Many complicated factors play a part in the infertility that affects about one fifth of American couples. Ovulatory dysfunction accounts for 20%, tubal dysfunction for 30% and abnormal cervical mucus for 5%. These are all female problems. But male sperm disorders account for 35% of cases. The problem may be low sperm count or another abnormality of the sperm, such as impaired swimming ability.

A growing body of evidence implies that oxidative stress may cause loss of sperm function. Sperm generate an excess amount of oxyradicals and these reactive oxygen molecules may lead to lipid peroxidation (oxidation of fatty substances) in the cell wall of the sperm itself. This leads to poor movement characteristics of the sperm and their impaired ability to fuse with the female's ova or egg. This understanding has opened doors for the development of innovative techniques in the treatment of male infertility.

Patients with idiopathic male infertility were compared to fertile volunteers by measuring oxidative stress, antioxidant activity and glutathione levels. Urologist I. Alkan and his team found significant differences among all parameters of both groups, suggesting that oxidation may cause infertility. Similar studies conducted by F.R. Ochsendorf at the Center of Dermatology and Andrology in Germany support these findings.

A group of reproductive biology scientists led by D.S. Irvine in Edinburgh, Scotland, is raising GSH contents in male infertility patients. In a paper entitled 'Glutathione for male infertility,' he showed that GSH seems to act at the epididymis and during sperm formation as well as improving the function of ejaculated spermatozoa. Another German team headed by T. Oeda experimented with NAC (N-acetylcysteine) and showed that it reduced oxidative stress and improved impaired sperm function.

A. Lenzi's team at the University Laboratory of Seminology and Reproduction in Rome has published many papers on the use of injectable GSH in a variety of infertile males. These studies were human double-blind, crossover studies and the therapy had consistently positive effects on sperm motility, morphology (structure), and semen quality.

BALDING & HAIR LOSS

Human hair varies widely in texture, color, thickness and distribution. It is a sensitive tissue, prone to loss or balding (alopecia). Alopecia universalis is a rare condition of total body hair loss. Alopecia areata is loss of hair in patches. Toxic alopecia is a common cause of hair loss, usually temporary and following serious illness, fever, pregnancy, various drugs (especially those used in chemotherapy) or overdoses of vitamin A. The most common cause of hair loss is androgenic alopecia or male-pattern baldness, which varies in pattern and severity.

Normal hair grows in cycles. Anagen is the active growing phase, catagen is a brief phase when growth slows down, and telogen is a resting dormant phase, where hair falls out, hopefully to be replaced in the next anagen phase. Research shows a positive correlation between GSH content and the percentage of anagen hairs present in a scalp sample, concluding that glutathione helps maintain the hair growth cycle. Researchers theorize that free radical formation plays a role in male pattern baldness. It is possible to measure the breakdown products of oxidative stress in bald and hairy areas of the scalp. The values are doubled in the balding areas. And correspondingly, hairy areas have almost three times as much glutathione.

In male-pattern baldness, androgens (male hormones) target hair follicles, which convert them into even stronger hormones. The unfortunate result is that hair growth slows or stops. M.E. Sawaya at the University of Miami showed that the conversion of these hormones can be influenced by glutathione, suggesting that GSH plays a protective role.

Age-related GSH losses in human hair follicles is part of the total body glutathione depletion described in chapter 6 on aging. Working at the L'Oreal research lab, M. Kermici measured follicular GSH activity in men and women ranging in age from 19 to 102 years and found a significant decline up until about age seventy, then a slower second decline.

For many patients one of the more distressing side effects of cancer chemotherapy is hair loss. Rapidly growing cells such as hair cells and intestinal lining cells are the most sensitive to chemo-toxins, which quickly lead to temporary hair loss, and also cause diarrhea and cramps. Elevated GSH levels help protect these cells from chemotherapeutic agents and diminish their unfortunate side-effects.

The GSH precursor NAC enhances the tumor-killing effect of the drug doxorubicin on skin cancer in the lab, but also completely prevents the hair loss that normally accompanies this treatment. Other researchers have produced similar hair protective effects using NAC in cyclophosphamide and cytarabine chemotherapy.

CONCLUSION

Oxidative damage and low glutathione levels has been implicated in the onset and development of many prostate problems, including cancer. GSH supplementation may provide protection against carcinogenesis in this gland, or at least slow the development of the disease. Male infertility is associated with increased oxidative stress and low GSH levels. Elevated GSH levels may enhance the quality of sperm and increase fertility. And GSH also feeds hair follicles and may prevent or delay hair loss, especially that suffered as a side-effect of chemotherapy.

BALDING

D'AGOSTINI F, BAGNASCO M, GIUNCIUGLIO D, ET AL. Inhibition by oral N-acetylcysteine of doxorubicin-induced clastogenicity and alopecia, and prevention of primary tumors and lung metastases in mice. *International J. Oncology 13: 217-224, 1998*

GIRALT M, CERVELLO I, NOGUES MR, ET AL. Glutathione, glutathione S-transferase and reactive oxygen species of human scalp sebaceous glands in male pattern baldness. *J. Investig. Dermatol. 107: 154-158, 1996*

JIMINEZ JJ, HUANG HS, YUNIS AA. Treatment with ImuVert/N-acetylcysteine protects rats from cyclophosphamide/cytarabine-induced alopecia. *Cancer Investig. 10: 271-276, 1992*

KERMICI M, PRUCHE F, ROGUET R, PRUNIERAS M. Evidence for an age-correlated change in glutathione metabolism enzyme activities in human hair follicle. *Mech. Aging Dev. 53: 73-84, 1990*

PUERTO AM, NOGUES MR, CERVELLO I, ET AL. Glutathione S-transferase in normal human anagen hair follicles. *Rev. Esp. Fisiol. 50: 103-108, 1994*

SAWAYA ME. Purification of androgen receptors in human sebocytes and hair. *J. Investig. Dermaotol. 98 (6 Suppl.): 92S-96S, 1992*

MALE INFERTILITY

AITKEN RJ. A free radical theory of male infertility. *Reprod. Fertil. Dev. 6: 19-23, 1994*

ALKAN I, SIMSEK F, HAKLAR G, ET AL. Reactive oxygen species production by the spermatozoa of patients with idiopathic infertility: relationship to seminal plasma antioxidants. *J. Urology 157: 140-143, 1997*

GOPALAKRISHNAN B, ARAVINDA S, PAWSHE CH, ET AL. Studies on glutathione S-transferees important for sperm function: evidence for catalytic activity-independent func-

tions. *Biochem. J. 15: 231-241, 1998*

GRIVEAU JS, LE LANNOU D. Reactive oxygen species and human spermatozoa: physiology and pathology. *Int. J. Androl. 20: 61-69, 1997*

IRVINE DS. Glutathione as a treatment for male infertility. *Rev. Reprod. 1:6-12, 1996*

LENZI A, CULASSO F, GANDINI L, ET AL. Placebo-controlled, double blind, cross-over trial of glutathione therapy in male infertility. *Human Reproduction 8: 1657-1662, 1993*

LENZI A, GANDINI L, PICARDO M. A rationale for glutathione therapy. *Human Reproduction 13: 1419-1422, 1998*

LENZI A, LOMBARDO F, GANDINI L, ET AL. Glutathione therapy for male infertility. *Arch. Androl. 29: 65-68, 1992*

LENZI A, PICARDO M, GANDINI L, ET AL. Glutathione treatment of dyspermia: effect on the lipoperoxidation process. *Human Reproduction 9: 2044-2050, 1994*

OCHSENDORF FR, BUHL R, BASTLEIN A, BESCHMANN H. Glutathione in spermatozoa and seminal plasma of infertile men. *Human Reproduction 13: 353-359, 1998*

OEDA T, HENKLE R, OHMORI H, SCHILL WB. Scavenging effect of N-acetyl-L-cysteine against reactive oxygen species in human semen: a possible therapeutic modality for male factor infertility? *Andrologia 29: 125-131, 1997*

SIKKA SC. Oxidative stress and role of antioxidants in normal and abnormal sperm function. *Front. Biosci. 1:e78-86, 1996*

SIKKA SC, RAJASEKARAN M, HELLSTROM WJ. Role of oxidative stress and antioxidants in male infertility. *J. Androl. 16: 464-481, 1995*

STOREY BT. Biochemistry of the induction and prevention of lipoperoxidative damage in human spermatozoa. *Mol. Human Reproduction 3: 203-213, 1997*

ZALATA A, HAFEZ T, COMHAIRE F. Evaluation of the role of reactive oxygen species in male infertility. *Human Reproduction 10: 1444-1451, 1995*

THE PROSTATE

BELL DA, TAYLOR JA, PAULSON DF, ET AL. Genetic risk and carcinogen exposure: a common inherited defect of the carcinogen-metabolism gene glutathione S-transferase M1 (GSTM1) that increases susceptibility to bladder cancer. *J. Natl. Cancer Inst. 85: 1159-1164, 1993*

CLARK LC, COMBS GF JR, TURNBULL BW, ET AL. Effects of selenium supplementation for cancer prevention in patients with carcinoma of the skin. A randomized controlled trial. Nutritional Prevention of Cancer Study Group. *JAMA 276: 1957-1963, 1996*

CLARK LC, DALKIN B, KRONGRAD A, ET AL. Decreased incidence of prostate cancer with selenium supplementation: results of a double-blind cancer prevention trial. *Br. J. Urol. 81: 730-734, 1998*

COMBS GF JR, CLARK LC, TURNBULL BW. Reduction of cancer risk with an oral supplement of selenium. *Biomed. Environ. Sci. 10: 227-234, 1997*

COMBS GF JR, CLARK LC, TURNBULL BW. Reduction of cancer mortality and incidence by selenium supplementation. *Med. Klin. 92 (Suppl 3): 42-45, 1997*

COOKSON MS, REUTER VE, LINKOV I, ET AL. Glutathione S-transferase PI (GST-pi) class expression by immunohistochemistry in benign and malignant prostate tissue. *J. Urol. 157: 673-676, 1997*

DE MARZO AM, COFFEY DS, NELSON WG. New concepts in tissue specificity for prostate cancer and benign prostatic hyperplasia. *Urology 53 (3 Suppl 3a): 29-39, 1999*

HARRIES LW, STUBBINS MJ, FORMAN D, ET AL. Identification of genetic polymorphisms at the glutathione S-transferase Pi locus and association with susceptibility to bladder, testicular and prostate cancer. *Carcinogenesis 18: 641-644, 1997*

JUNG K, SEIDEL B, RUDOLPH B, ET AL. Antioxidant enzymes in malignant prostate cell lines and in primary cultured prostatic cells. *Free Radic. Biol. Med. 23: 127-133, 1997*

LIEBMAN B. Clues to prostate cancer. *Nutr. Action Lett. 3: 10-12, 1996*

MOSKALUK CA, DURAY PH, COWAN KH, ET AL. Immunohistochemical expression of pi-class glutathione S-transferase is down-regulated in adenocarcinoma of the prostate. *Cancer 79: 1595-1599, 1997*

MURAKOSHI M, TAGAWA M, INADA R, ET AL. Inhibition of steroid-induced prostatic hyperplasia in rats by treatment with anti-androgen (TZP-4238). *Endocr. J. 40: 479-488, 1993*

RIPPLE MO, HENRY WF, RAGO RP, WILDING G. Prooxidant-antioxidant shift induced by androgen treatment of human prostate carcinoma cells. *J. Natl. Cancer Instit. 89: 40-48, 1997*

TAGUCHI Y. Current strategies in managing prostate cancer. *Can. J. CME. :107-115, 1997*

TEW KD, CLAPPER ML, GREENBERG RE, ET AL. Glutathione S-transferases in human prostate. *Biochim. Biophys. Acta 926: 8-15, 1987*

WINTER ML, LIEHR JG. Possible mechanism of induction of benign prostatic hyperplasia by estradiol and dihydrotestosterone in dogs. *Toxicol. Appl. Pharmacol. 136: 211-219, 1996*

YOSHIZAWA K, ET AL. Study of prediagnostic selenium level in toenails and the risk of advanced prostate cancer. *J. Natl. Cancer Inst. 90: 1219-1224, 1998*

PART THREE

GLUTATHIONE
AND
HEALTH MAINTENANCE
[CHAPTERS 24 & 25]

These two chapters describe how glutathione works in the healthy individual and how it can be used to enhance general health.

CHAPTER 24
EXERCISE & ATHLETIC PERFORMANCE

EXERCISE AND HEALTH

Statistics tell us that a sedentary lifestyle without exercise is as bad for health and longevity as smoking a pack of cigarettes a day. Countless studies show the health benefits of regular physical activity. Recent research suggests that moderate but consistent exercise may actually be more beneficial than intense workouts. The trouble is, most North Americans are not even doing enough to reach this plateau. The U.S. Surgeon General reports that 75% of American adults are physically inactive, and 25% get virtually no exercise at all. Such people are at increased risk for the most common ailments and causes of death of our times. Inactivity as a lifestyle leads to heart disease, obesity, high blood pressure, diabetes, osteoporosis, stroke, depression and certain cancers.

Fortunately, in the last decade interest in preventive health care has skyrocketed. Many people are discovering the benefits of exercise: weight control, muscle strength, bone mass and strength, increased energy, reduced stress, greater endurance, more self esteem and longevity. The fitness industry is growing quickly. Enrollment in gyms and aerobic classes, and sales of fitness supplements, bicycles, skates and blades have all reached new heights. This raises new questions, especially about how much exercise is enough and whether there is such a thing as too much. How far can we push the limits of exercise? And of course amateur and professional athletes want to know how to enhance their performance.

Even moderate exercise has a measurable impact on health and longevity. The Norwegian researcher G. Erikssen followed patients over a 22-year period and found that middle-aged men benefited from moderate fitness improvements and experienced lower risks of mortality from all causes. And it doesn't take extreme exertion to improve fitness. University of Washington doctor Rozenn Lemaitre recently showed that walking for at least one hour per week reduces the risk of heart attacks as much as high-intensity physical activity.

An hour three to five times per week of light, moderate or vigorous effort is all that's needed. A light workout can provides the same benefits as a strenuous one if it lasts longer. An hour of light walking, volleyball, easy gardening, stretching and baseball, thirty to sixty minutes of brisk walking, biking, raking leaves, swimming and dancing, or twenty to thirty minutes of jogging, aerobics, hockey, basketball or fast dancing provide similar health benefits.

AGING AND EXERCISE

Aging is associated with major alterations in body composition and exercise tolerance. Muscle mass, immune defense, antioxidant function and GSH levels all decrease. As our immune system ages, exercise workouts tax us more and more. Performance suffers. So does our ability to recover. Older women and men who participate in regular exercise therefore require more antioxidants in general and GSH in particular. Chapter 1 discusses the antioxidant role of GSH. Chapter 6 discusses GSH and aging.

EXERCISE AND THE IMMUNE SYSTEM

Exercise appears to strengthen the immune system, but too much may have just the opposite effect. Many elite athletes come down with viral illnesses when they train intensely. A widespread virus ravaged the athletic community prior to the 1996 Atlanta Olympic Games, upsetting years of hard work. However, few of us will push our immune resources to the limit. By using it in good measure, exercise can bolster our defenses against disease.

Statistical studies show that adults who exercise are ill less often than non-exercisers. The mechanisms of this increased resistance are very revealing. Many studies have found enhanced activity of various white blood cells—our front-line defense against infection. Fit people have a greater count of natural killer cells, macrophages and T-cell lymphocytes—crucial workers in the immune system—and higher levels of virus-fighting immune factors in their blood. Some studies have shown that the saliva of athletes contains higher levels of viral antibodies, offering greater resistance to disease. This is particularly relevant since many upper respiratory infections enter though the mouth. After several well-designed studies D.C. Nieman's team of exercise physiologists at the Department of Health and Exercise, Appalachian State University have said that people who exercise can double resistance to viral illness.

Although it is clear that the immune system responds positively to moderate activity, it has been repeatedly shown that too much leads to a winding down of the immune system—immunosuppression. After a certain time the increase in immune factors and white cell activity initiated by exercise becomes blunted. This period depends on the intensity of the activity and the condition of the athlete's defenses. Dozens of articles have documented a temporary immune deficiency following exhaustive training. Test conducted on marathon runners revealed that those running over 60 miles per week were twice as likely to catch a cold than those running 20. Some of these effects can be avoided by balancing and regulating nutrition and training levels.

OVER-TRAINING SYNDROME

Besides the obvious possibility of physical injury, serious athletes run the risk of contracting all sorts of sickness. Their weakened immune response following exhaustive training is only one aspect of 'over-training syndrome.' Adjectives like 'burn-out,' 'staleness' and 'plateauing' are used by athletes to describe the physical sensation. Some respond stubbornly by pushing even harder, with increasingly negative effects. Some exercise scientists have shown that decreasing the intensity of workouts may actually improve performance.

The over-trained athlete experiences a host of physiological effects that contribute to poor performance and illness. They include fluctuations in insulin secretion, alterations in glucocorticoid and hormone levels, inhibition of glucose uptake to tissues, catabolic (breakdown) effects on protein and nitrogen excretion and lactic acid over-production.

Oxidative stress

While working out, athletes may consume ten to fifteen times more oxygen than usual, so oxidative stress is a major factor in exercise. Physical activity increases oxygen consumption and intensifies numerous metabolic processes. The result is the creation and circulation of liberated oxidative breakdown products free radicals (see chapter 1).

Some scientists believe that that free radicals might play a significant role in the events leading up to muscle inflammation and damage. More and more evidence supports this theory. When cells need more energy their mitochondria (power plants) work harder. In addition to increasing energy, this also boosts production of unhealthy by-products and results in lipid peroxidation—the harmful oxidation of fats. Bad cholesterol and fats, for example, are rendered even more harmful by peroxidation. Another consequence of increased mitochondrial activity is electron transport flux—the chain reaction of atoms snatching each other's electrons and gradually destabilizing cellular structure (see chapter 1). These two threats can be countered both by exogenous antioxidants—derived like vitamins C and E from food sources—and endogenous ones—those produced within the body. The most critical of these in-house antioxidants is GSH.

The body is not entirely defenseless. Exercise also increases the level and activity of many antioxidants. A well-trained body will adapt to increased oxidative stress by developing improved physiological mechanisms, but the drive for better performance can overtake these adaptations and lead to increased muscular fatigue, injury and recovery time. And antioxidants can easily be depleted by over-training. We therefore strongly encourage the use of oral antioxidant supplements.

GSH and athletic performance

Because antioxidants are especially critical to those who exercise, researchers have spent considerable time observing and testing them. This research has two possible goals—to avoid the negative potential of over-training and to explore the possibility of improving performance. A great deal has been written about the role of antioxidants in sports physiology. As you might imagine, much of this research is focused on the body's most important endogenous antioxidant—glutathione. Elevated glutathione levels provide better immune defenses and reduced susceptibility to infectious disease. They also help decrease recovery time from workouts, reduce muscle fatigue and soreness and increase performance.

L.L. Ji, C. Leeuwenburgh and a group of researchers at the University of Illinois carried out a series of studies on muscle injury influenced by free-radical formation. Their objective was to measure the usefulness of GSH in cellular damage control. It is not easy to test the body's adaptive response to exercise. Two metabolic processes in particular are somewhat unpredictable. One is the variability of GSH levels at any particular site. The other relates to the transport of GSH between tissues. Nevertheless, GSH levels were seen to vary in proportion to the level of exertion, the individual's fitness, and his/her nutritional status.

Measuring GSH levels before, immediately afterward, hours after, and days after subjects completed a long-distance run, B. Dufaux's experiments revealed a significant drain of glutathione. Recovery of GSH levels was quite variable, taking from hours to days. Subjects remained susceptible to subsequent illness or injury. Similar studies were conducted on cyclists and other athletes. In all cases, GSH levels in muscle tissue were found to fall with exercise.

Researchers have shown that glutathione levels are more efficiently restored in the elite athlete than in the less well-trained. General bodily fitness encourages the manufacture of GSH and its more efficient release from tissues. Some scientists have gone one step further, suggesting that exercise slows the aging process by increasing one's ability to produce and distribute GSH on demand.

It is known that diabetics in particular can benefit from exercise. This is believed to result in part from the enhanced GSH metabolism of a fit body. It helps diabetics deal with the intense oxidative stress from which they characteristically suffer (see chapter 10). Training in good measure stimulates greater GSH reserves and enhances one's ability to detoxify foreign substances. Tests have show that well-exercised animals suffer less from acetaminophen toxicity than non-active ones. Some theorists even believe that the enhanced glutathione metabolism following exercise explains why the physically fit suffer less from cancer.

Given all this, it seems useful to take antioxidant or GSH-enhancing supplements prior to intensive exercise. J. Sastre and his group from the University of Valencia in Spain tested this idea using vitamin C, NAC (see chapter 4) and GSH on animal subjects. The result was to successfully reduce oxidative damage and maintain reduced glutathione in blood reserves. Another group at the University of California (Berkeley) headed by C.K. Sen proved the corollary—that if greater levels improved antioxidant response, lower levels would worsen it. They forced GSH levels down with the drug BSO and the ability of their subjects to endure exhaustive exercise fell by 50%.

Physiologists investigating the role of GSH in the immune response to exhaustive exercise have shown raised GSH levels to increase the number and activity of white blood cells. Other studies show that taking NAC before a workout diminishes oxidative stress within these white blood cells. Further studies conducted at Baylor College of Medicine in Texas, first on rodents and later on humans, showed that intravenous NAC—which raises GSH levels— enables subjects to perform longer and harder in exhaustive muscle tests.

A dramatic example of increased muscle strength comes from Dr. Larry Lands of McGill University, Montreal. Thinking that oxidative stress contributes to muscular fatigue, his team gave young adults the whey-based GSH precursor Immunocal for three months. During this time they measured peak power and work capacity as indicators of strength and endurance. They found that performance values could be enhanced by a remarkable ten to fifteen percent.

A team at the Peak Wellness Lab in Connecticut examined the effect of whey isolate protein on athletes. They showed that dietary supplementation of this protein could maintain white blood cell levels (CD4 T-lymphocytes and neutrophils) that otherwise fall during extremely intense workouts. Whey proteins have an extraordinarily high 'protein biological value' and are extremely effective in meeting the higher protein demands of athletes, who may require as much as two or three times as much as the average person. For this reason, whey protein is used widely in weight training to increase body mass.

Another study was carried out on AIDS and cancer patients in an attempt to counter the muscle loss (catabolism) they often suffer. This resembles the muscle decline resulting from heavy exercise protein breakdown. A German group led by R. Kinscherf found that NAC could slow this process. Compared to a placebo group, the NAC-supplemented group undergoing anaero-

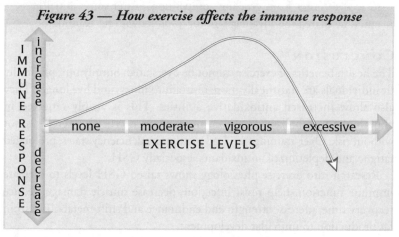

Figure 43 — How exercise affects the immune response

IMMUNE RESPONSE

increase

decrease

none | moderate | vigorous | excessive

EXERCISE LEVELS

bic exertion lost less body cell mass, and interestingly, carried less total body fat. The shift of body fat to body muscle is a strong focus in weight training.

CASE STUDIES

Susan, a 35 year-old fashion merchandiser and mother of two, was a great fitness advocate. Free weights, aerobics, step and spinning classes—over fifteen years she had done them all. She was persistently dissatisfied about "the ten pounds of fat" that prevented her from achieving the muscular definition she wanted. Nutritionally conscious, she also knew that merely restricting her calories would probably just leave her feeling washed out. She started taking 40 grams/day of whey protein isolate in combination with minimal adjustments in fat and carbohydrate intake. In three weeks she noticed better endurance during her cardiovascular workouts and was able to lift heavier weights with greater intensity. Recuperation between workouts improved, enabling her to continue without the usual soreness. Her weight remained unchanged. Despite not having made any great changes to her routine, six weeks after the dietary supplement, people at the gym commented on how "well cut" she was.

John, a national champion cyclist, understood the phenomenon of over-training and its consequences on the immune system. He and his training partners were quite aware of their tendency to get sick before big events if they pushed too hard. Having two children in day-care certainly exposed him to viral illnesses. Hearing that the product Immunocal had potential immune-boosting effects, he incorporated it into his daily diet. The frequency of viral illnesses decreased and when he did get sick, it was for only a day or two, rather than three or four. To his surprise, his performance times were improved as well as his ability to recover faster from grueling competitions. After some initial hesitancy, he shared the advantages of this product with his teammates.

CONCLUSION

The health benefits of exercise cannot be overstated. Simply put, physically fit individuals are statistically more resistant to illness and live longer. They also show increased antioxidative abilities. This is visibly reflected in glutathione metabolism. However, moderation is crucial. Exercise is not without risk. Over-training may lead to immune deficiency states, prolonged fatigue and depletion of antioxidants, especially GSH.

Research into exercise physiology shows raised GSH levels to increase immune function, help resist infection, decrease muscle damage, reduce recovery time, increase strength and endurance and shift metabolism from fat production to muscular development.

EXERCISE & ATHLETIC PERFORMANCE

ALESSIO HM. Exercise-induced oxidative stress. *Med. Sci. Sports Exerc.* 25:218-224, 1993

ALESSIO HM, BLASSI ER. Physical activity as a natural antioxidant booster and its effect on a healthy life span. *Res. Q. Exerc. Sport* 68:292-302, 1997

ATALAY M, MARNILA P, LILIUS EM, ET AL. Glutathione-dependent modulation of exhausting exercise-induced changes in neutrophil function of rats. *Eur. J. Appl. Physiol.* 74:342-347, 1996

CLARKSON PM. Antioxidants and physical performance. *Crit. Rev. Food Sci. Nutr.* 35:131-141, 1995

DEKKERS JC, VAN DOORNEN LJ, KEMPER HC. The role of antioxidant vitamins and enzymes in the prevention of exercise-induced muscle damage. *Sports Med.* 21:213-238, 1996

DUFAUX B, HEINE O, KOTHE A, ET AL. Blood glutathione status following distance running. *Int. J. Sports Med.* 18:89-93, 1997

ERIKSSEN G, LIESTOL K, BJORNHOLT J, ET AL. Changes in physical fitness and changes in mortality. *Lancet* 352: 759-762, 1998

FIELDING RA, MEYDANI M. Exercise, free radical generation, and aging. *Aging* 9:12-18, 1997

FITZGERALD L. Overtraining increases the susceptibility to infection. *Int. J. Sports Med.* 12 (Suppl 1): S5-S8, 1991

GABRIEL H, KINDERMANN W. The acute immune response to exercise: what does it mean? *Int. J. Sports Med.* 18 (Suppl 1): S28-S45, 1997

GOHIL K, VIGUIE C, STANLEY WC, ET AL. Blood glutathione oxidation during human exercise. *J. Appl. Physiol.* 64: 115-119, 1988

HELLSTEN Y, APPLE FS, SJODIN B. Effect of sprint cycle training on activities of antioxidant enzymes in human skeletal muscle. *J. Appl. Physiol.* 81: 1484-1487, 1996

HUUPPONEN MR, MAKINEN LH, HYVONEN PM, ET AL. The effect of N-acetylcysteine on exercise-induced priming of human neutrophils. A chemoluminescence study. *Int. J. Sports Med.* 16: 399-403, 1995

JENKINS RR. Exercise, oxidative stress, and antioxidants: a review. *Int. J. Sports Nutr.* 3: 356-375, 1993

JENKINS RR, GOLDFARB A. Introduction: oxidant stress, aging, and exercise. *Med. Sci. Sports Exerc.* 25: 210-212,1993

JI LL. Oxidative stress during exercise: implication of antioxidant nutrients. *Free Radic. Biol. Med.* 18: 1079-1086, 1995

JI LL. Antioxidant enzyme response to exercise and aging. *Med. Sci. Sports Exerc.* 25: 225-231,1993

JI LL, FU R. Responses of glutathione system and antioxidant enzymes to exhaustive exercise and hydroperoxide. *J. Appl. Physiol.* 72: 549-554, 1992

JI LL, FU R, MITCHELL EW. Glutathione and antioxidant enzymes in skeletal muscle: effects of fiber type and exercise intensity. *J. Appl. Physiol.* 73: 1854-1859, 1992

KARPER WB, HOPEWELL R. Exercise, immunity, acute respiratory infections, and homebound older adults. *Home Care Provider* 3: 41-46, 1998

KINSCHERF R, HACK V, FISCHBACH T, ET AL. Low plasma glutamine in combination with high glutamate levels indicate risk for loss of body cell mass in healthy individuals: the effect of N-acetyl-cysteine. *J. Mol. Med.* 74:393-400. 1996

KRETZSCHMAR M, MULLER D. Aging, training and exercise. A review of effects on plasma glutathione and lipid peroxides. *Sports Med. 15: 196-209, 1993*

LAAKSONEN DE, ATALAY M, NISKANEN L, ET AL. Increased resting and exercise-induced oxidative stress in young IDDM men. *Diabetes Care 19: 569-574, 1996*

LANDS LC, GREY VL, SMOUNTAS AA. Effect of supplementation with a cysteine donor on muscular performance. *J. Appl. Physiol. 87:1381-135, 1999*

LANDS LC, GREY VL, SMOUNTAS AA. The effect of supplementation with a cysteine donor on muscular performance. *American J. Resp. Crit. Care Med 159:A719, 1999*

LEE IM. Exercise and physical health: cancer and immune function. *Res. Q. Exerc. Sport. 66: 286-291, 1995*

LEEUWENBURGH C, JI LL. Glutathione depletion in rested and exercised mice: biochemical consequence and adaptation. *Arch. Biochem. Biophys. 316: 941-949, 1995*

LEMAITRE RN, SISCOVICK DS, RAGHUNATHAN TE, ET AL. Leisure-time physical activity and the risk of primary cardiac arrest. *Arch. Intern. Med. 159: 686-690, 1999*

LEMON PW. Is increased dietary protein necessary or beneficial for individuals with a physically active lifestyle? *Nutr. Rev. 54 (Pt 2): S169-S175, 1996*

LEMON PW. Do athletes need more dietary protein and amino acids? *Int. J. Sports Nutr. 5 (Suppl): S39-S61, 1995*

LEW H, PIKE S, QUINTANILHA A. Changes in the glutathione status of plasma, liver, and muscle following exhaustive exercise in rats. *FEBS Lett. 185: 262-266, 1985*

LEW H, QUINTANILHA A. Effects of endurance training and exercise on tissue antioxidative capacity and acetaminophen detoxification. *Eur. J. Drug Metab. Pharmacokinet. 16: 59-61, 1991*

LIFE EXTENSION EDITORS. The wonders of whey - Restoring youthful anabolic metabolism at the cellular level. *Life Ext. 5:35-38, 1999*

MACKINNON LT. Immunity in athletes. *Int. J. Sports Med. 18 (Suppl): S62-S69, 1997*

MARIN E, KRETZSCHMAR M, AROKOSKI J, ET AL. Enzymes of glutathione synthesis in dog skeletal muscles and their response to training. *Acta. Physiol. Scand. 147: 369-373, 1993*

NASH MS. Exercise and immunology. *Med. Sci. Sports Exerc. 26: 125-127, 1994*

NEHLSEN-CANNARELLA SL, NIEMAN DC, BALK-LAMBERTON AJ, ET AL. The effects of moderate exercise training on immune response. *Med. Sci Sports Exerc. 23: 64-70, 1991*

NIEMAN DC. Exercise and resistance to infection. *Canadian J. Physiol. Pharmacol. 76: 573-580, 1998*

NIEMAN DC. Immune response to heavy exertion. *J. Appl. Physiol. 82: 1385-1394, 1997*

NIEMAN DC. Exercise and immunology: practical applications. *Int. J. Sports Med. 18 (suppl 1): S91-S100, 1997*

NIEMAN DC. Upper respiratory tract infections and exercise. *Thorax 50: 1229-1231, 1995*

NIEMAN DC. Exercise, upper respiratory tract infection, and the immune system. *Med. Sci. Sports Exerc. 26: 128-139, 1994*

NIEMAN DC, HENSON DA, GUSEWITCH G, ET AL. Physical activity and immune function in elderly women. *Med. Sci. Sports Exerc. 25: 823-831, 1993*

NIEMAN DC, PEDERSEN BK. Exercise and immune function. Recent developments. *Sports Med. 27: 73-80, 1999*

OHKUWA T, SATO Y, NAOI M. Glutathione status and reactive oxygen generation in tissues of young and old exercised rats. *Acta. Physiol. Scand. 159: 237-244, 1997*

PACKER L. Oxidants, antioxidants and the athlete. *J. Sports Sci. 15: 353-363, 1997*

PEDERSEN BK. Influence of physical activity on the cellular immune system: mechanisms of action. *Int. J. Sports Med. 12 (Suppl 1): S23-S29, 1991*

PEDERSEN BK, BRUUNSGAARD H. How physical exercise influences the establishment of infections. *Sports Med. 19: 393-400, 1995*

PEDERSEN BK, ROHDE T, ZACHO M. Immunity in athletes. *J. Sports Med. Phys. Fitness 36: 236-245, 1996*

PETERS EM. Exercise, immunology and upper respiratory tract infections. *Int. J. Sports Med. 18 (suppl 1): S69-S77, 1997*

PYKE S, LEW H, QUINTANILHA A. Severe depletion in liver glutathione during physical exercise. *Biochem. Biophys. Res. Commun. 139: 926-931, 1986*

REID MB, STOKIC DS, KOCH SM, ET AL. N-acetylcysteine inhibits muscle fatigue in humans. *J. Clin. Invest. 94: 2468-2474, 1994*

REZNICK AZ, WITT EH, SILBERMANN M, PACKER L. The threshold of age in exercise and antioxidants action. *EXS 62: 423-427, 1992*

ROWBOTTOM DG, KEAST D, GARCIA-WEBB P, MORTON AR. Training adaptation and biological changes among well-trained male athletes. *Med. Sci. Sports Exerc. 29: 1233-1239, 1997*

SASTRE J, ASENSI M, GASCO E, ET AL. Exhaustive physical exercise causes oxidation of glutathione status in blood: prevention by antioxidant administration. *American J. Physiol. 263 (5 Pt 2): R992-R995, 1992*

SEN CK. Oxidants and antioxidants in exercise. *J. Appl. Physiol. 79: 675-686, 1995*

SEN CK, ATALAY M, HANNINEN O. Exercise-induced oxidative stress: glutathione supplementation and deficiency. *J. Appl. Physiol. 77: 2177-2187, 1994*

SEN CK, MARIN E, KRETZCHMAR M, HANNINEN O. Skeletal muscle and liver glutathione homeostasis in response to training, exercise, and immobilization. *J. Appl. Physiol. 73: 1265-1272, 1992*

SEN CK, RANKINEN T, VAISANEN S, RAURAMAA R. Oxidative stress after human exercise: effect of N-acetylcysteine supplementation. *J. Appl. Physiol. 76: 2570-2577, 1994*

SHEPARD RJ, SHEK PN. Impact of physical activity and sport on the immune system. *Rev. Environ. Health 11: 133-147, 1996*

SHEPARD RJ, SHEK PN. Exercise, aging and immune function. *Int. J. Sports Med. 16: 1-6, 1995*

THOMPSON HJ. Effect of treadmill exercise intensity on hepatic glutathione content and its relevance to mammary tumorigenesis. *J. Sports Med. Fitness 32: 59-63, 1992*

WOODS JA, DAVIS JM, SMITH JA, NIEMAN DC. Exercise and cellular innate immune function. *Med. Sci. Sports Exerc. 31: 57-66, 1999*

CHAPTER 25
STRESS, GLUTATHIONE
AND GOOD HEALTH

A person may ask, "I'm healthy. Why worry about GSH?" The answer is simple: "Disease prevention, quality of life, longevity, a sense of well-being." Or, to put it more bluntly, to stay alive as long as possible and to enjoy good health to the end.

One of a doctor's most challenging jobs is to convince a patient with high blood pressure but no symptoms to take his medication every day to prevent heart attack or stroke. The problem is, such people often feel healthy and experience no symptoms. It's even harder to convince a diabetic teenager to avoid junk food, even though the long term consequences can include kidney failure and blindness. Financial advisors presumably have the same difficulty convincing younger clients to tie up their hard-earned income in a retirement savings plan. The truth is, poor health and pain act as powerful motivators. In the absence of any immediate threat, logical arguments rarely provoke a visceral response. Preventive health maintenance requires a lifestyle commitment and special attention to our personal needs. It's no surprise that such strategies are so difficult for many.

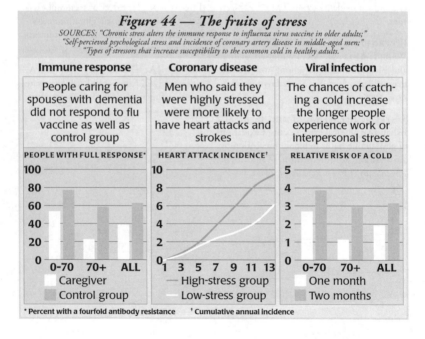

Figure 44 — The fruits of stress

SOURCES: *"Chronic stress alters the immune response to influenza virus vaccine in older adults;"*
"Self-percieved psychological stress and incidence of coronary artery disease in middle-aged men;"
"Types of stressors that increase susceptibility to the common cold in healthy adults."

Immune response	Coronary disease	Viral infection
People caring for spouses with dementia did not respond to flu vaccine as well as control group	Men who said they were highly stressed were more likely to have heart attacks and strokes	The chances of catching a cold increase the longer people experience work or interpersonal stress

* Percent with a fourfold antibody resistance   † Cumulative annual incidence

Preventive medicine has long taken a back seat to treatment-oriented medicine. Much of the slack has been taken up by other health workers, such as nutritionists, naturopaths and those working in complementary fields. More attention is now paid to preventive medicine than ever before and a new school of thought is rapidly evolving. Established medicine as used traditionally by both doctors and patients implied that health was merely the absence of disease. Quality of life was not addressed or was an after-thought. More focus is nowadays being put into "wellness medicine." We owe it to ourselves and to society at large to not only stay healthy but to also maintain a sense of well-being and even a lust for life.

GENERAL RISK OF LOW GLUTATHIONE LEVELS

Is your health really at risk if your GSH levels fall? If we were to impair the GSH effectiveness of young people, would this raise their incidence of disease? A group of Russian researchers found themselves ideally positioned to answer this question. They realized that a large portion of the population was missing the gene for a minor GSH enzyme, glutathione-S-transferase S1 (GSTM1). They measured the population at large for this gene and then a large group suffering from lung and other cancers, alcoholic cirrhosis, cystic fibrosis, chronic bronchitis, endometriosis and other diseases. It was found that a significantly higher portion of the unwell population was missing this gene.

The researchers concluded that impaired GSH effectiveness increased the risk of developing such multifactorial illnesses. They suggest using this as a way to screen those at higher risk for diseases caused by combined environmental and genetic factors, particularly those triggered by accumulated toxins. The table below shows that although less than two-fifths of the population in general is missing this gene, the various disease groups are missing it in at least half of all cases, and sometimes in more than four-fifths. These numbers are very convincing.

Figure 45 — Percentage missing GSTM1 gene	
General population	38.8
Lung cancer patients	81.0
Other cancer patients	65.0
Endometriosis patients	81.0
Alcoholic cirrhosis patients	77.0
Cystic fibrosis patients (*with pulmonary manifestations*)	51.0
Chronic bronchitis patients (*with radiological changes*)	74.0

Aging well

There is little doubt among scientists and medical professionals that good glutathione levels correspond to good health. Look at the number of articles on glutathione and aging appearing recently in major medical journals:

Figure 46 — Number of articles about glutathione			
(LISTING FROM MEDLINE INTERNET SITE, AUGUST 1999)			
Last 1 year	3,165	Last 5 years	14, 560
Last 2 years	6,134	Last 10 years	24, 262

The references at the end of each chapter list the hundreds of scientific papers consulted in the preparation of this book and constitutes overwhelming evidence that adequately maintained GSH levels are necessary for general health. This is particularly true of the aging population. A recent study demonstrates this with glaring simplicity. It was reported in the prestigious British medical journal The Lancet, and was entitled "Glutathione: in sickness and in health." GSH was measured in four groups of people: 1) young healthy volunteers (average 24 years), 2) a healthy elderly population with no hospital admissions, no medications and no major illnesses in the previous five years, 3) elderly patients treated at an out-patient clinic for a variety of chronic illnesses including heart disease, arthritis, diabetes and hypertension, and 4) hospitalized elderly patients. The exact results are shown in figure 47. Those in the poorest health (the hospitalized elderly) have the lowest GSH levels while young volunteers—the healthiest group—have high levels. Raising GSH levels will help keep us well as we age.

Morbidity and mortality

No matter how long we live and how much attention we pay to health maintenance we must eventually face our own mortality. The link between glutathione and all the major causes of death is profound, and the list of research papers supporting this evidence is still growing. The link between GSH and many of the major causes of illness is equally unambiguous, as you can see from figure 48.

Heart disease, stroke and cancer are the leading causes of death in North America. It is truly unfortunate that although these diseases are all to a large degree preventable, their incidence is expected to rise over the next decade. The number of cancer cases alone is expected to increase by 30%. Many of the illnesses from which we commonly suffer are avoidable. These include diabetes, bronchitis, elevated cholesterol levels and infectious diseases. Traditional advice to the health-conscious is aimed at avoiding these problems. We are told to quit smoking, drink moderately, eat well and exercise regu-

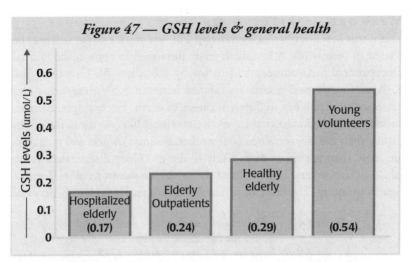

Figure 47 — GSH levels & general health

GSH levels (umol/L)

- Hospitalized elderly (0.17)
- Elderly Outpatients (0.24)
- Healthy elderly (0.29)
- Young volunteers (0.54)

larly. More recently we have learned the advantages of avoiding undue stress, practicing safe sex and using vitamins and other supplements. Now we know that maintenance of glutathione levels belongs near the top of this list. The growing body of scientific evidence is pushing it up there. As general physicians become aware of the health potential of this remarkable protein they will begin to share it with their patients.

Thinking of the years of life lost to these diseases is a chilling reminder of what happens if we ignore our health.

Figure 48 — GSH links	
Major causes of morbidity and mortality	
Heart Disease and Stroke	Chapter 9
Cancer	Chapter 5
Lung disease	Chapter 14
Main causes of chronic illness/hospital admissions *(other than above)*	
Diabetes	Chapter 10
Arthritis	Chapter 6
Dementia, neurodegenerative diseases	Chapters 7, 8, 20
AIDS	Chapter 12
Main causes of acute hospitalization *(other than above)*	
Infectious disease	Chapters 3, 11, 14
Trauma	Chapter 19
Gastrointestinal problems	Chapter 15

MY WORK IS KILLING ME

This is true literally, not just figuratively. The way you die or get sick may be related to your work. A landmark study published in 1999 in the journal Occupational Environmental Medicine by Canadians M. Carpenter and K. Aronson, showed a correspondence between job descriptions and increased susceptibility to different causes of death. For example, barbers, hairdressers, and manicurists are seven times more likely to die of infectious disease than the average blue-collar worker. Business owners and managers are more than ten times more likely to die of kidney disease than other white-collar workers. The results of the survey are shown in more detail in figures 49 and 50. The first rule of health maintenance is to identify personal

Figure 49 — Potential years of life lost (PYLL)
based on life expectancy
(SOURCE: Canadian Cancer Statistics 1999)

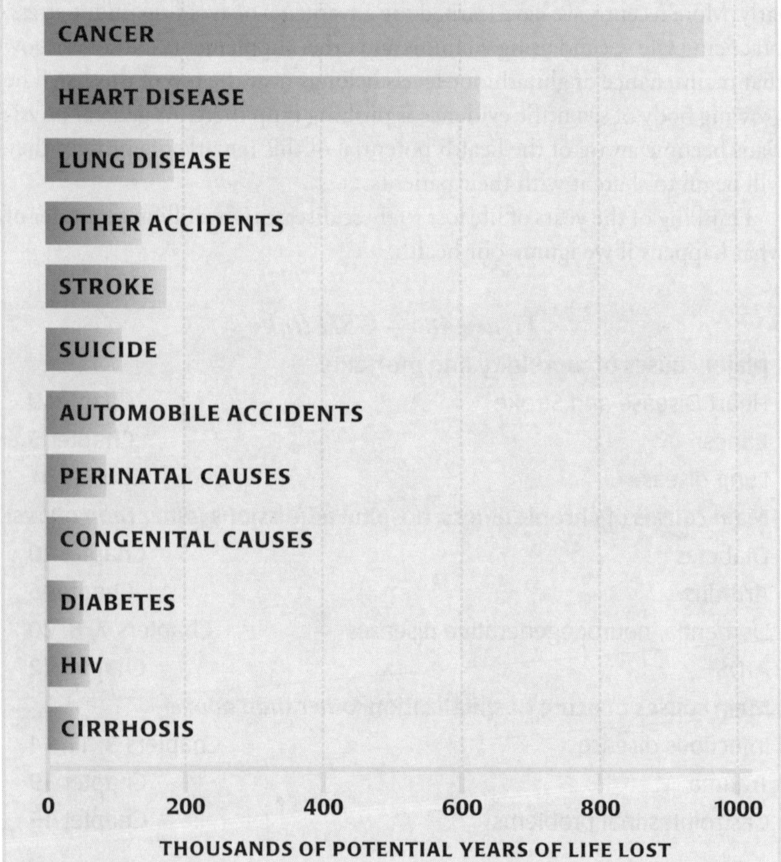

CANCER

HEART DISEASE

LUNG DISEASE

OTHER ACCIDENTS

STROKE

SUICIDE

AUTOMOBILE ACCIDENTS

PERINATAL CAUSES

CONGENITAL CAUSES

DIABETES

HIV

CIRRHOSIS

| 0 | 200 | 400 | 600 | 800 | 1000 |

THOUSANDS OF POTENTIAL YEARS OF LIFE LOST

and environmental risk factors. These figures can help us with part of that process. Whether you need to deal with occupational toxins or just strengthen your immune system, GSH can help.

STRESSED OUT

It has taken the medical community a while, but it has finally acknowledged that stress is not just in the mind. It is in the body too, and can be measured. We all know the effects of stress on sleeping and eating habits. Now strong evidence links it to heart disease, memory problems, obesity and impaired immune defense.

Ronald Glaser of Ohio State University measured the ability of geriatric patients to respond to a flu shot. The purpose of the shot is to stimulate antibody production so that the body is prepared to confront possible infection. Individuals who were each nursing a spouse with dementia, had a significantly lessened response to the vaccine compared to people without this demanding responsibility. Psychologist Sheldon Cohen demonstrated that individuals undergoing either work-related stress or interpersonal stress were more likely to catch a cold when exposed to the virus. Others have documented that men who reported high stress levels were much more likely to suffer from a heart attack than men with low levels. As we have said before, it is not only the consequences of stress that make a demand on glutathione—stress itself depletes GSH levels.

Figure 50 — Occupational hazards for blue-collar workers
ADAPTED FROM ARONSON KJ, HOWE GR, CARPENTER M, FAIR ME OCCUPATIONAL ENVIRONMENTAL MEDICINE (UK), 1999

People working as...	are this many times more likely...	to die of...
Painters*	3.79	brain cancer
Laborers†	5.87	lip cancer
Clerical workers	9.28	influenza
Barbers, hairdressers, manicurists	7.31	Infectious diseases
Maids, service workers	7.79	laryngial cancers
Stenographers	6.91	
Waiters	1.74	lung cancers
Mechanics & repairmen	2.97	chronic myeloid leukemia
Telephone operators	4.22	other leukemia
Construction workers	5.66	

0 2 4 6 8 10

■ Male
□ Female

* Except construction & maintenance workers;
† Except agricultural, fishing, mining & logging workers

THE TWENTY-FIRST CENTURY PLAGUE

"The Killer Germ" shouts Time Magazine (August 1998). "War Against the Microbes" declares Business Week (April 1998). The media and even TV documentaries are all doing their part to sensationalize the problem. We are facing a recurrence of infectious diseases unseen for decades, perhaps centuries.

A very short while ago we thought we were about to annihilate once and for all such scourges as polio, scarlet fever, cholera and smallpox. But the same pharmaceutical technology that almost made these microbes extinct seems also to be partly responsible for the emergence of newer and more resistant ones. Overuse of antibiotics both in the human population and in livestock have given the organisms an opportunity to develop antibiotic resistance. This leaves us without an effective weapon and makes their elimi-

Figure 51 — Occupational hazards for white-collar workers
ADAPTED FROM ARONSON KJ, HOWE GR, CARPENTER M, FAIR ME OCCUPATIONAL ENVIRONMENTAL MEDICINE (UK), 1999

People working as...	are this many times more likely...	to die of...
Inspectors & foremen	3.94	ischemic heart disease
Civil engineers	3.94	prostate cancer
Funeral directors and embalmers	6.00	other cancer
Foremen, textile occupations	5.79	all cancer
Owners & managers	10.45	nephritis
Foremen	5.10	chronic myeloid leukemia
Purchasing agents & buyers	5.90	lung cancers

Male Female 0 2 4 6 8 10

nation difficult, perhaps impossible. Outbreaks of antibiotic-resistant infections are on the rise. Whole wings of hospitals have been shut down to contain the problem. Examples are the 1996 outbreak of toxic E. Coli that sickened and killed Americans in Colorado, rampaging Strep A in Texas in 1997 and the deadly bird flu that struck Japan in 1998. Flesh-eating disease, mad cow disease and super-bugs conjure up nightmarish scenes that have fed the imagination of Hollywood script-writers.

Even the traditionally sober medical establishment is releasing frightening predictions. The World Health Organization (WHO) forecasts more than a billion new cases of tuberculosis over the next generation. In the Clinton-era, U.S. Surgeon General David Satcher warned congress of the global resurgence of infectious diseases, responsible for more than one third of all world deaths. In the United States alone, the death rate from infection jumped almost 60% between 1980 and 1990, partly due to over thirty newly-discovered infections. Ebola, malaria and dengue fever may sound like exotic and very remote diseases, but they are just a plane-ride away from New York, London and Montreal.

Why do some people fall prey to infection while others resist? How is it that two people with the same bug recuperate at a very different rate? These are complex questions with equally complex answers, but it always comes down to the state of the immune system. Rather than spending all our money and time on the development of newer and more powerful antibiotics and antiviral agents, we should apply some of it to enhancing the defensive capabilities of the immune system.

Viral and bacterial mutation and eventual resistance to drugs is inevitable, as we've discovered to our cost. To develop offensive weapons without paying attention to our defense system is an unsound strategy. By enhancing the immune system of the population at large, microbes would have a difficult time getting a foothold. And even when we're infected, we would fight the bug more efficiently. Raising glutathione levels is a powerful way to enhance the immune system. Healthcare professionals, teachers, retail salespersons, restaurant workers and others who work with the public, those who spend time in crowded places such as movie theatres, restaurants, gyms and airports and those prone to illness for any reason can increase their resistance by raising their glutathione levels.

COMPLEMENTARY OR ALTERNATIVE MEDICINE

Alternative medicine is not an alternative to medicine. And traditional medicine does not address the issues of wellness, balance, nutrition or spiritual health in adequate depth. The fusion of these two fields is long overdue. In fact, after years of fruitless conflict, the two approaches are being integrated into what is called "complementary medicine" or "integrative medicine." Instead of choosing between them, we are learning to see how they can and should be used together.

However, the causes of conflict are not imaginary, and any integration of alternative and conventional medicine into a coherent system requires compromise. Alternative therapies will not gain credibility and acceptance unless they are scientifically scrutinized and validated. Traditional doctors must reevaluate the mind-body connection, and especially understand the importance to healing of the doctor-patient relationship.

As is often the case in our society, such changes are ultimately market driven. A nationwide telephone poll in Canada revealed an 81% increase in the use of alternative medicine between 1992 and 1997. Half of these people earned over $60,000/year. As for the class of people using alternative medicine, the answer surprises most traditional practitioners. The highest percentage of users usually are urban-dwelling, high-income earners, and the frequency of use corresponds to higher educational levels. This demand has stimulated the growth of compliementary practices. One U.S. study forecasts a 124% increase between 1994 and 2010. By 1997, more than thirty medical schools in the USA had added courses on alternative medicine, and this number is still growing. U.S. health insurers are beginning to offer coverage for alternative treatments. Independent manufacturers of vitamins, supplements and herbal products are being bought up by brand-name drug companies. At the turn of the millennium, the market for health-food additives and "pharmafoods" or "nutriceuticals" stands at $2.5 billion/year and growing. This is not just a flow of money but a stream of ideas and scientific discovery that is changing how long we live and how well we live.

CONCLUSION

Doctors and patients alike must develop an open-minded but cautious approach to all possible diagnostic and therapeutic tools, whether conventional or compliementary. That is the approach we have taken in this book. We have looked at both conventional and complementary ways of elevating glutathione levels. All information is based on hard scientific research and the reader is encouraged to pursue the references listed at the end of each chapter. The volume, variety and reliability of research data is staggering, and places the importance of glutathione at the forefront of this natural approach to health.

Whether your want to simply treat an existing disease or are attempting to avoid future health problems, raised glutathione levels address the vast majority of the most common and most serious afflictions of modern man. The role of GSH as our body's most important antioxidant, its ability to rid the body of toxins, pollutants and carcinogens, and its critical role in the immune function will establish this molecule as a primary focus of disease prevention and anti-aging.

STRESS, GLUTATHIONE & GOOD HEALTH

ANGELL M, KASSIRER JP. Alternative medicine – the risks of untested and unregulated remedies. *New England J. Med. 17: 339: 839-841, 1998*

ARONSON KJ, HOWE GR, CARPENTER M, FAIR ME. Surveillance of potential associations between occupations and causes of death in Canada, 1965-91. *Occup. Environ. Med. 56:265-269, 1999*

ASTIN JA. Why patients use alternative medicine: results of a national study. *JAMA 279: 1548-1553, 1998*

BARANOV VS, IVASCHENKO T, BAKAY B, ET AL. Proportion of the GSTM1 o/o genotype in some Slavic populations and its correlation with cystic fibrosis and some multifactorial diseases. *Human Genetics 97: 516-520, 1996*

BARNETT PA, SPENCE JD, MANUCK SB, ET AL. Psychological stress and the progression of carotid artery disease. *J. Hypertens. 15: 49-55, 1997*

BERMAN BM, SINGH BK, LAO L, ET AL. Physicians' attitudes toward complementary or alternative medicine: A regional survey. *J. Am. Board Fam. Pract. 8:361-365, 1995*

BLUMBERG DL, GRANT WD, HENDRICKS SR, ET AL. The physician and unconventional medicine. *Altern. Therapies 1: 31-35, 1995*

CACIOPPO JT, BERNTSON GG, MALARKEY WB, ET AL. Autonomic, neuroendocrine, and immune responses to psychological stress: the reactivity hypothesis. *Ann. N. Y. Acad. Sci. 840: 664-673, 1998*

COHEN S, FRANK E, DOYLE WJ, ET AL. Types of stressors that increase susceptibility to the common cold in healthy adults. *Health Psychol. 17: 214-223*

COOPER RA, STOFLET SJ. Trends in the education and practice of alternative medicine clinicians. *Health Aff. 15: 226-238, 1996*

COTTRELL K. Herbal products begin to attract the attention of brand-name drug companies. *Can. Med. Assoc. J. 155: 216-219, 1996*

CTV/ANGUS REID GROUP. Use of alternative medicines and practices. *Angus Reid Group (Winnipeg), 1997*

DROGE W, HACK V, BREITKREUTZ R, ET AL. Role of cysteine and glutathione in signal transduction, immunopathology and cachexia. *Biofactors 8: 97-102, 1998*

EISENBERG DM, KESSLER RC, FOSTER C, ET AL. Unconventional medicine in the United States: Prevalence, cost, and patterns of use. *New England J. Med. 328: 246-252, 1994*

ERNST E, RESCH KL, WHITE AR. Complementary medicine: What physicians think of it: a meta-analysis. *Arch. Inter. Med. 155: 2405-2408, 1995*

EVERSON SA, LYNCH JW, CHESNEY MA, ET AL. Interaction of workplace demands and cardiovascular reactivity in progression of carotid atherosclerosis: population based study. *BMJ 314: 553-558, 1997*

GLASER R, KIECOLT-GLASER JK. Stress-associated immune modulation: relevance to viral infections and chronic fatigue syndrome. *Am. J. Med. 105: 35S-42S, 1998*

GLASER R, KIECOLT-GLASER JK, MALARKEY WB, ET AL. The influence of psychological stress on the immune response to vaccines. *Ann. N. Y. Acad. Sci. 840: 649-655, 1998*

GLASER R, RABIN B, CHESNEY M, ET AL. Stress-induced immune modulation: implications for infectious diseases? *JAMA 281: 2268-2270, 1999*

KHACHATOURIANS GG. Agricultural use of antibiotics and the evolution and transfer of antibiotic-resistant bacteria. *CMAJ 159: 1129-1136, 1998*

KIECOLT-GLASER JK, GLASER R. Psycho-neuroimmunology and immunotoxicology: implications for carcinogenesis. *Psychosom. 61: 271-272, 1999*

KOLESNICHENKO LS, KULINSKII VI, IAS'KO MV, ET AL. The effect of emotional-painful stress, hypoxia, and adaptation to it on the activity of enzymes for metabolizing glutathione and concentration of glutathione in rat organs. *Vopr. Med. Khim. 40: 10-12, 1994*

KOLESNICHENKO LS, MANTOROVA NS, SHAPIRO LA, ET AL. Effect of emotional stress on the activity of enzymes of glutathione me-tabolism. *Vopr. Med. Khim. 33: 85-88, 1987*

KRAL BG, BECKER LC, BLUMENTHAL RS, ET AL. Exaggerated reactivity to mental stress is associated with exercise-induced myocardial ischemia in an asymptomatic high-risk popu-lation. *Circulation 96: 4246-4253, 1997*

LYNCH JW, EVERSON SA, KAPLAN GA, ET AL. Does low socioeconomic status potentiate the ef-fects of heightened cardiovascular responses to stress on the progression of carotid atherosclero-sis? *Am. J. Public Health 8: 389-394*

MARWICK C. Growing use of medicinal bo-tanicals forces assessment by drug regulators. *JAMA 273: 607-609, 1995*

MCEWEN BS, SAPOLSKY RM. Stress and cognitive function. Curr. Opin. *Neurobiol. 5: 205-216, 1995*

McIntosh LJ, Hong KE, Sapolsky RM. Glu-cocorticoids may alter antioxidant enzyme capacity in the brain: baseline studies. *Brain Res. 791: 209-214, 1998*

McINTOSH LJ, SAPOLSKY RM. Glucocor-ticoids may enhance oxygen radical-mediated neurotoxicity. *Neurotoxicology 17: 873-882, 1996*

NATIONAL INSTITUTE OF HEALTH. Alter-native medicine – Expanding medical horizons: A report to the NIH on alternative medical systems and practices in the United States. *NIH publication 94-066. Washington DC. Government Printing Office, 1994*

NUTTAL SL, MARTIN U, SINCLAIR AJ, KENDALL MJ. Glutathione: in sickness and in health. *Lancet 35: 645-646, 1998*

OPARIL S, OBERMAN A. Nontraditional cardiovascular risk factors. *Am. J. Med. Sci. 317: 193-207, 1999*

PEEKE PM, CHROUSOS GP. Hypercortisolism and obesity. *Ann. N. Y. Acad. Sci. 771: 665-676, 1995*

ROZANSKI A, BLUMENTHAL JA, KAPLAN J. Impact of psychological factors on the pathogenesis of cardiovascular disease and implications for therapy. *Circulation 99: 2192-2217, 1999*

SAPOLSKY RM. Why stress is bad for your brain. *Science 273: 749-750, 1996*

SAPOLSKY RM. Stress, Glucocorticoids, and Damage to the Nervous System: The Current State of Confusion. *Stress 1: 1-19, 1996*

SHARPLEY CF. Psychosocial stress-induced heart rate reactivity and atherogenesis: cause or correlation? *J. Behav. Med. 21: 411-432, 1998*

SPENCE JD. Neurocardiology. Stress and ath-erosclerosis. *Baillieres Clin. Neurol. 6: 275-282, 1997*

TOLEIKIS PM, GODIN DV. Alteration of antioxidant status in diabetic rats by chronic exposure to psychological stressors. *Pharmacol. Biochem. Behav. 52: 355-366, 1995*

WU H, WANG J, CACIOPPO JT, ET AL. Chronic stress associated with spousal care giving of patients with Alzheimer's dementia is associated with down-regulation of B-lym-phocyte GH mRNA. *J. Gerontol. A. Biol. Sci. Med. Sci. 54: M212-215, 1999*

GLOSSARY

— A —

Absorb — (nutrition) to draw nutrients from the gastrointestinal tract into the bloodstream

Acetylcholine — ACH; a type of neurotransmitter found in the brain and at all nerve-muscle junctions

Acne — a chronic skin disorder caused by inflammation of hair follicles and sebaceous glands

Acquired immune deficiency syndrome (AIDS) — a deficiency in the immune system due to infection by the human immunodeficiency virus (HIV)

Acute — short-term

Acute gastritis — short-lived inflammation or infection of the stomach

Acute myelogenous leukemia — a type of leukemia causing the excess production of immature non-lymphocyte white blood cells within the marrow

Adaptive immune response — immune system's ability to recognize previously encountered pathogens and to mount a specific response

Adrenal glands — a pair of small, triangular endocrine glands that secrete corticosteroid hormones and aldosterone

Adrenal hormones — corticosteroid hormone and aldosterone; released by adrenal glands

Aflatoxin — a carcinogenic byproduct of fungi found in nuts, seeds, corn and other dried foods

Albumin — a major protein found in blood serum

Alcoholic cirrhosis — a disease of the liver caused by destruction of liver cells through abuse of alcohol, leading to scarring and impaired liver function

Aldosterone — a hormone that helps maintain blood volume and pressure

Allergens — substances that trigger an allergic reaction

Allergy — an inappropriate immune response to a non-pathogen

Alopecia areata — loss of hair in patches

Alopecia universalis — rare condition of total body hair loss

Alpha-lipoic acid — a disulfide compound that acts as an effective antioxidant, a neutralizer of various toxins including some heavy metals, and an important co-enzyme for recycling other antioxidants, including vitamins C and E, and glutathione

Alveoli — microscopic sacs in the lungs where blood is oxygenated

Alzheimer's disease — a degenerative disorder characterized by brain shrinkage

Amenorrhea — cessation of menstruation

Amino acids — organic chemical compounds from which all proteins are made

Anabolic — describes a metabolic action that manufactures complex substances from simple building blocks

Anabolic steroids — synthetic hormones producing a protein-building effect, mimicking testosterone and other male hormones

Anagen — active growing phase of normal hair

Androgen — masculine sex hormone responsible for secondary male characteristics, such as facial hair growth, deepened voice and increased body mass

Androgenic alopecia — male-pattern baldness; the most common cause of hair loss

Andrology — the study of male hormones

Anemia — low hemoglobin (red blood cell) count

Aneurysm — ballooning of blood vessels due to weakened walls

Angina — a strangling or constrictive pain; usually an abbreviation for angina pectoris (chest pain) caused by inadequate oxygen and blood flow to the heart muscle

Antacid — over-the-counter indigestion medication

Anti-androgens — medication that inhibit the production and/or release and/or absorption of androgens; used in treatment of prostate cancer

Antibiotic-resistant infection — newly-developing strains of bacteria that are not destroyed by conventional antibiotic medications

Antibiotics — drugs used to destroy invading bacteria

Anticoagulants — drugs used to prevent or retard the clotting of blood

Anticonvulsants — drugs used to prevent seizures

Antigen — substance foreign to the body that triggers an immune response

Antigen response — immune system's response to an antigen

Antihistamine — anti-allergy medication

Anti-inflammatory — drug that reduces the symptoms of inflammation

Antioxidant — a substance that neutralizes destructive free radicals or prevents oxidation; some are manufactured by the body, others are derived from foods

Antipsychotic drugs — drugs used to treat psychosis

Aorta — the principal artery through which oxygenated blood leaves the heart

APOE — apo-lipo-protein E; a blood protein often altered in Alzheimer's Disease

Apoptosis — cell death

ARDS — adult respiratory distress syndrome; acute, life-threatening respiratory failure following lung injury

Arteriosclerosis — atherosclerosis; hardening of the arteries; a group of disorders that cause artery walls to thicken and narrow

Arthritis — inflammation of joints characterized by pain, swelling and stiffness, sometimes leading to deformation of the joint

Arylamines — a group of volatile chemicals present in cigarette smoke and other toxic sources

Asthma — recurrent bouts of breathlessness of varying severity due to constriction of the small airways

Asymptomatic — presenting no symptoms

Atherogenesis — plaque formation in atherosclerosis

Atherosclerosis — arteriosclerosis; hardening of the arteries

Atopic dermatitis — a type of eczema usually of an allergic or sensitive nature

Autoimmune disease — dysfunctional immune response to healthy processes; disorder caused by inappropriate immune response to one's own tissue

Autopsy — investigation into cause of death by surgical analysis of the corpse

— B —

B cell lymphocyte — immune cell that produces antibodies to attack specific viruses or bacteria

Bacteremia — bacterial infection of the bloodstream

Bacterial mutation — change in cellular DNA of bacteria occasionally leading to antibiotic drug resistance or increased resistance to the immune response

Bacterial pneumonia — pneumonia caused by bacterial infection, as opposed to viral pneumonia

Basal ganglia — area of brain critical for coordination of movement

Baseline levels — original (usually normal) concentration of a body chemical or function

B-cell lymphocyte — lymphocytes that manufacture antibodies

Biliary urea nitrogen — BUN; a breakdown product of proteins; when high, often a marker of diminishing kidney function

Bioactivity — the initiation of specific metabolic activity by a nutrient or other compound

Bioavailability — the amount of a biological substance available for a bodily process

Biochemical — chemical compounds produced by or interacting with the body

Bone outgrowths — osteophytes; bony spurs characteristic of arthritis

Bronchi — airways connecting windpipe to lungs

Bronchitis — inflammation or infection of bronchi

Bronchodilators — drugs that open the airways to the lungs and ease breathing

BUN — biliary urea nitrogen; a breakdown product of proteins; when high, often a marker of diminishing kidney function

Burn-out — a symptom of excessive exposure, for example exercise or stress

— C —

Cancer — a group of diseases characterized by unrestricted growth of cells in general tissue or a specific organ

Candida — thrush or moniliasis; a fungal infection of the vagina or other areas of mucus membrane or moist skin

Carcinogen — cancer-causing agent

Cardiac muscle aging — aging and weakening of the heart's muscularity

Cardiovascular system — the lungs, heart and blood vessels

Cardiovascular workout — systematic raising of the heart rate through physical activity

Carotenoid — yellow or red pigments such as carotenes found widely in plants and animals

Carotid arteries — the principal suppliers of blood to the brain

Carotid atherosclerosis — blockage of the carotid arteries; a major cause of stroke

Cartilage — a type of connective tissue made of collagen; a non-bony component of the skeleton, especially joints

Casein — milk protein; one of the products in milk

Castration — removal of testicles or ovaries; see Chemical castration

Catabolic activity — a metabolic action that breaks down complex proteins into simpler ones

Catabolism — breakdown of complex living tissues into simpler substances or waste matter

Catagen — brief phase of slow hair growth

Cataract — loss of transparency of the lens of the eye due to changes in the delicate protein fibers within the lens

Catecholamine — a type of neuro-chemical normally produced by the body; a substance that functions as a hormone, a neurotransmitter or both, e.g., epinephrine, norepinephrine, and dopamine

Caucasian — originating in the Caucasus; of or relating to the white race classified according to physical features; of European, North African, or southwest Asian ancestry

CD4 helper cells — a type of T-cell lymphocyte

Cell — basic structural element of the body; billions in number and highly differentiated in function

Cell membranes — a double layer of fatty material and proteins constituting the outer barrier of individual cells

Cell receptor — a sort of docking bay on the surface of a cell that attracts specific biochemical substances, enabling the cell's activity to be influenced from the outside

Cerebro-spinal fluid — a clear, watery liquid that surrounds and infuses the brain and the central canal of the spinal cord

Cervical mucus — a secretion of a woman's cervix that changes during the course of the menstrual cycle

Chelation — the attachment of toxins present in the body to organic com-pounds, allowing their excretion and resulting in diminished toxicity

Chelators — organic compounds that attract and stick to metal molecules

Chemical castration — drug-induced reduction of male hormones; a treatment to slow the growth of prostate cancer

Chemical signature — unique feature of a biochemical's activity in the body

Chemotherapeutic agents — toxic drugs used to destroy malignant cells

Chemotherapy — destruction of cells by drugs targeted at cancerous cells

Chemo-toxins — toxic drugs used in chemotherapy

Cholera — an acute bacterial infection of the small intestine resulting in severe diarrhea and dehydration

Cholestasis — impaired drainage of bile from the liver

Cholesterol — an important fatty constituent of body cells; a player in the formation of hormones and the transport of fats to various parts of the body; HDL (good) cholesterol protects against arterial disease; LDL (bad) cholesterol promotes arterial disease

Chronic — of long duration; with diminished likelihood of cure

Chronic gastritis — a stomach disorder with fewer symptoms and longer duration than simple gastritis but which more readily progresses to anemia, stomach ulcers and stomach cancer

Chronic inflammatory change — persistent inflammation and its biochemical changes

Chronic inflammatory disease — persistent diseases characterized by inflammation, such as rheumatoid arthritis

Chronic obstructive pulmonary disease — COPD; a disorder of the lungs in which the airways become blocked or narrowed, such as emphysema, asthma, and chronic bronchitis

Circulating cholesterol — levels of cholesterol in the blood

Circulatory — having to do with blood circulation

Cirrhosis — damage, scarring and subsequent hardening of the liver

Cochlea — a spiral-shaped organ in the inner ear that transforms sound vibrations into nerve impulses

Codeine — a narcotic; a morphine-derived pain medication

Colitis — general inflammation of the bowel

Collagen — tough, fibrous protein important to the structure of bones, tendons, connective tissue and skin

Collagen-vascular diseases — autoimmune disorders of the connective tissues

Colon — the major part of the large intestine

Complementary medicine — the combined application of conventional and alternative health practices

Conductive hearing loss — hearing loss caused by mechanical problems in the middle ear

Congenital problems — birth defects; problems present at birth

Congestive heart failure — compromised ability of the heart to pump blood

Conjugate — to bind to

Connective tissue — material holding together the various structures of the body

Constipation — infrequent and difficult passing of hard feces

Contact dermatitis — skin rash resulting from contact with an external substance

Contraindications — factors in a patient's condition that make it unwise to pursue a particular therapy

COPD — chronic obstructive pulmonary disease; a disorder of the lungs in which the airways become blocked or narrower, impeding air-flow; examples are emphysema, asthma, and chronic bronchitis

Coronary artery disease — a disorder of the arteries supplying blood to the heart muscle, causing oxygen starvation, pain and tissue damage

Correlate — to identify parallel developments between two or more processes

Corticosteroid hormones — hormones that control the body's use of nutrients and the excretion of salts and water in the urine and other critical endocrinological functions

Corticosteroid medications — drugs that simulate the activity of natural corticosteroid hormones produced by the adrenal glands

Creatinine — a waste product of protein metabolism

Crohn's disease — CD; a chronic inflammation in the digestive tract; similar to but more severe than ulcerative colitis

Cushing's disease — abnormally high levels of corticosteroid hormones in the blood

Cyclophosphamide — a chemotherapeutic drug used in the treatment of cancer and a number of kidney diseases

Cysteine — a sulfur-containing amino acid; scarcest of the three constituents of GSH

Cystic fibrosis — mucoviscidosis; an inherited, congenital disease characterized by chronic lung infection and poor absorption of nutrients

Cystoscopy — the introduction of an optical instrument through the urethra to examine the inside of the bladder

Cytarabine chemotherapy — a drug therapy that kills or damages cells, particularly those undergoing rapid multiplication, such as cancer cells; used especially to treat acute myelogenous leukemia in adults

— **D** —

Decidua — the mucous membrane of the uterus cast off in the ordinary process of menstruation

Degenerative disease — physical and/or chemical changes in cells, tissues or organs leading to progressive impairment of both structure and function

Delusion — false and irrational thought taken as true

Dementia — a general decline of mental functioning

Denaturation — change in the physical nature or chemical quality of a substance

Dengue fever — breakbone fever; an acute tropical disease caused by a virus transmitted by certain mosquitoes

Depression — feelings of sadness, hopelessness, pessimism, loss of interest in life and diminished emotional well-being

Dermatitis — inflammation or infection of the skin

Dermatitis herpetiformis — chronic dermatitis characterized by eruption of itching papules, vesicles, and lesions resembling clustered hives

Dermatology — the study of the skin and skin diseases

Dermatomytosis — a rare, sometimes fatal inflammation of muscles and skin

Detoxifier — any substance that neutralizes toxins, pollutants and carcinogens

Diabetes mellitus — diabetes; an insulin disorder of the body that diminishes its ability to metabolize sugar

Dialysate fluid — fluid used in kidney dialysis

Diarrhea — increased fluidity and frequency of bowel movements; a symptom of underlying disease

Distress — stress beyond the body's ability to respond favorably

Diuretic — substance that increases the throughput of urine and causes the body to lose water and salt; used for the symptomatic relief of swelling (edema) due to heart, liver or kidney disorders

Diuretic drugs — preparations that remove excess water from the body by increasing urination

DNA — deoxyribonucleic acid; the genetic material contained in chromosomes

DNA encoding — the information structure of a DNA strand

Dopamine — a neurotransmitter found in the brain

Dopaminergic toxicity — toxicity from dopamine imbalance

Down syndrome — a chromosomal defect resulting in mental handicap and a characteristic physical appearance; formerly known in the western world as mongoloidism

Drug cocktails — a combination of drugs designed to work in unison

Dysfunction — abnormal activity; inability to function

Dyspnea — shortness of breath

— E —

E. Coli — a bacteria normally inhabiting the intestine or colon

Ebola — a virus of African origin that causes an often fatal fever and internal bleeding

Eclampsia — a rare, very serious condition of late pregnancy causing seizures and coma

Eczema — inflammation of the skin

Edema — accumulation of water in the tissues leading to swelling, particularly of the hands, feet and face

Electron transport flux — a chain reaction of atoms grabbing each other's electrons and potentially destabilizing cellular structure

Embryotoxicity — toxic to embryos

Emphysema — pulmonary emphysema; a chronic lung disease in which the air sacs (alveoli) of the lungs degenerate until the elastic fibers in them are destroyed.

Endocrine glands — glands that secrete hormones directly into the bloodstream

Endogenous antioxidants — antioxidants produced within the body

Endometrial cancer — cancer of the lining of the uterus

Endometrial hyperplasia — overgrowth of cells of the uterine lining

Endometriosis — displacement and growth of uterine lining tissue to the pelvic region and elsewhere

Endometrium — lining of the uterus

Endorphins — the body's own natural pain killers

Endothelial — of, relating to, or produced from the endothelium

Endothelium — fine tissue lining lymphatic and blood vessels, the heart, and various other body cavities

Endotoxins — poisons produced by certain bacteria, released when the bacteria die

Enzyme — any protein that promotes or regulates a specific chemical reaction in the body

Epidermis — outer layer of the skin

Epididymis — an oblong structure at the side of the testicle, consisting of a tightly coiled tube 18 to 20 feet long

Erythropoietin — drug intended to stimulate the production of new red blood cells; these cells exhibit elevated GSH levels that are more resistant to lipid peroxidation and breakdown of cell-walls

Essential amino acids — amino acids that must be obtained from dietary sources and cannot be manufactured by the body; arginine, histionine, isoleucine, leucine, lysine, methionine, phenylalanine, threonine, treptophane and valine

Estrogen — the primary female sex hormone

Ethacrynic acid — a diuretic; water or fluid pill

Eustachian tube — passage connecting the middle ear to the rear of the nose

Exacerbate — to make worse

Exercise tolerance — the body's ability to benefit from exercise; limit following which continued exercise become harmful

Exogenous antioxidants — oxyradical scavengers derived from food sources, such as vitamins C and E

— F —

Fat — nutrient providing the body with its most concentrated form of energy; a solid or liquid oil of vegetable or animal origin

Febrile — feverish; related to fever

Fetal tissue implants — implantation into patients of tissue from human fetuses

Fibrinogens — blood-clotting agents

Fibroblast — a cell that manufactures the connective tissue of the brain

Fibrocystic pancreatic disease — a variation of cystic fibrosis affecting the pancreas

Fibroids — a benign tumor made up of muscle and connective tissue, often found in the uterus

Fibrosing alveolitis — pulmonary fibrosis; interstitial fibrosis; scar tissue in the lungs

Fibrous foods — foods containing indigestible plant material that holds water and adds bulk to the feces, aiding normal bowel function

Flavonoids — a variety of crystalline compounds found in plants; some are powerful antioxidants

Follicle — a small cavity; see also Ovarian follicle

Forced menopause — menopause precipitated by a hysterectomy or oophorectomy

Free radical — oxyradical; a highly reactive molecule with one or more unpaired electrons; free radical destruction is implicated in a wide variety of diseases

Fulminant hepatic failure — rapidly-progressing liver failure

— **G** —

GABA — gamma-aminobutyric acid; a neurotransmitter

Gallstones — lumps of solid matter in the gall bladder, sometimes in the bile ducts

Gamma globulin — a plasma protein, a component of blood serum containing antibodies which may be extracted from a person with acquired immunity to a certain infection and used to provide temporary immunity to infectious hepatitis, rubeola (measles), poliomyelitis, tetanus, yellow fever, or smallpox

Gangrene — tissue death due to oxygen starvation following the destruction of blood vessels or infection

Gastric mucosa — stomach lining

Gastritis — inflammation or infection of the stomach lining

Gastrointestinal tract — the pathway of food, including the mouth, esophagus, stomach and intestine

Genotype — genetic make-up

Gingivitis — inflammation or infection of the gums accompanied by any combination of pain, swelling, and bleeding

Glandular — affecting glands, a group of specialized cells that manufacture and release such chemicals as hormones and enzymes

Glaucoma — optic nerve fiber destruction and gradual loss of vision caused by increased fluid pressure within the eye

Glucocorticoids — hormones produced in the outer layer of the adrenal glands that play a part in carbohydrate metabolism and other functions

Glutamine — a crystalline amino acid found in plant and animal protein

Glutathione — GSH; multifunctional tripeptide composed of glutamate, cysteine and glycine

Glutathione peroxidase — a critically important antioxidant enzyme; the only known metabolically active form of selenium in the body

Glycine — an amino acid and neurotransmitter

GNRH agonists — gonadotrophin-releasing hormone agonists; synthetic hormones resembling those released by the hypothalamus gland in the brain

Gonadotrophin — hormones that stimulate activity in the gonads

Gonads — reproductive organs; ovaries and testes

Grafted tissue — transplanted tissue, including organs

Granulocyte — a type of white blood cell

GSH — glutathione; multifunctional tripeptide composed of glutamate, cysteine and glycine

GSH-diester — a form of GSH with two ester side-chains

GSH peroxidase — an enzyme of glutathione critical as an antioxidant, especially against lipid peroxidation

GSH-monoester — a form of GSH with an ester side-chain

Gut — stomach and intestines

— **H** —

Hair follicles — small pits in the epidermis that grow individual hairs

Half-life — period required by the body to eliminate or metabolize a substance to 50% levels

HDL cholesterol — high density lipoprotein; a component of blood that carries cholesterol but protects against arteriosclerosis; also known as "good cholesterol"

Helicobacter pylori — H. pylori; one of a large family of related bacteria that routinely live in the stomachs of most vertebrates

HELLP syndrome — Hemolysis Elevated Liver enzymes and Low

Platelet count; a complication of pre-eclampsia

Helper T-cell — lymphocyte (immune cell) that produce substances to enhance the activity of B-cell lymphocytes and killer T-cell lymphocytes

Hematocrit — a measurement determining the relative amounts of plasma and corpuscles in blood

Hemodialysis — a procedure in which blood is drawn from the body into a mechanical filtering device, cleansed, chemically balanced, and returned to the body

Hemoglobin — a complex protein within red blood cells responsible for carrying oxygen to all other cells

Hemolysis — breakdown of red blood cells

Hemorrhagic shock — death or complications of blood loss

Heparin — an anticoagulant used to prevent blood clotting

Hepatic — pertaining to the liver

Hepatologist — physician specializing in the liver

Hepatotoxic — toxic to the liver

High blood pressure — hypertension; abnormally high blood pressure

Hippocampus — area of the brain involved in short-term memory

Histidine — an amino acid

Hodgkin's disease — HD; lymphoma; cancer of the lymph nodes

Homocysteine — a peptide that either promotes arteriosclerosis or is found in conjunction with arteriosclerosis; a potential risk factor for hardening of the arteries

Homocysteinuria — an enzyme disorder that leads among other things to bone abnormalities

Hormone — a chemical released by an endocrine gland into the bloodstream that affects remote tissues and other hormones in specific ways

Hormone replacement therapy — HRT; replacement of deficient or missing hormones by synthetic methods; commonly synonymous with post-menopausal female hormone therapy

Human growth hormone — hormone produced by the pituitary gland and affecting the development and growth of most body organs and hormonal secretions

Human immunodeficiency virus — HIV; the virus that leads to AIDS

Huntington's disease — Huntington's chorea, hereditary chorea, or chronic progressive chorea; an inherited neurodegenerative movement disorder leading to progressive physical and intellectual deterioration

Hydroxyl radical — the 'OH' radical; the most toxic free radical known

Hyper — a prefix meaning excessive

Hypercalcemia — abnormally high calcium levels

Hypercysteinemia — toxic condition marked by excessive cysteine

Hyperglycemia — high blood sugar levels

Hyperlipidemia — high fat levels in the blood

Hyper-osmolar coma — coma induced by excessively low ratio of water to chemical concentration in the blood

Hyperparathyroidism — over-activity of the parathyroid glands; excess parathyroid hormone in the blood

Hyperplasia — overgrowth of cells

Hypertension — high blood pressure; abnormally high blood pressure even when at rest

Hyperthyroidism — over-activity of the thyroid gland

Hypertrophy — overgrowth and proliferation of cells

Hypo — a prefix meaning insufficient

Hypoalbuminemic — a state of low albumin

Hypoglycemia — low blood sugar levels

Hypoparathyroidism — under-activity of the parathyroid glands

Hypoxemia — inadequate amounts of oxygen in blood

Hypoxia — inadequate oxygen supply to tissues

Hysterectomy — surgical removal of the uterus, sometimes also the ovaries (oophorectomy) and fallopian tubes

— I —

Ideopathic — of unknown cause

Ileum — the end of the small intestine where it joins the large intestine

Immune response — activation of the immune system; ability of the body to protect against microbes, toxins, free radicals and other threats

Immune system — a system of cells and proteins that protect the body from potential harm

Immune system enhancer — a substance or therapy that systematically boosts the immune response

Immune-deficiency — a weakened state in which the patient's defenses against infection and disease are compromised

Immuno-compromised — suffering from weakened immune response

Immunoglobulin — antibody; a protein found in the blood and in tissue fluid

Immunosuppression — diminished immune response caused by disease or drug therapy; sometimes deliberately induced, for example to prevent rejection of transplanted organs

Impact-loading exercise — exercise movements that stimulate bone growth by physical pressure

Impotence — the inability to achieve or maintain a penile erection

In vitro tests — tests conducted on animal or human tissue samples in laboratory experiments; literally, "in glass"

Incidence — frequency; a statistical measure

Inert — inactive; unable to effect a metabolic response

Infection — the establishment and proliferation of a colony of bacteria, viruses, fungi or other disease-causing micro-organisms in the body, usually provoking an immune response

Infectious disease — A transmittable illness caused by a specific micro-organism

Inflammation — redness, swelling, heat and pain in a tissue due to injury or infection

Inflammatory bowel disease — chronic intestinal inflammation, including ulcerative colitis and Crohn's disease

Inflammatory response — biochemical response to tissue damage and/or infection

Insomnia — inability to sleep

Insulin — hormone produced by the pancreas involved in metabolism of sugar

Insult — damage or threat of damage

Integrity — the tendency of a system or organ to maintain its structure and function

Intercellular — between cells

Interferon — a group of proteins produced naturally by the body that inhibits viral spread

Intermittent — of expected occurrence but unpredictable frequency

Interstitial fibrosis — pulmonary fibrosis; fibrosing alveolitis; scar tissue in the lungs

Intestines — the principal part of the gastrointestinal tract, reaching from the exit of the stomach to the anus

Intravenous — within the blood circulation

Ischemia — blood starvation; oxygen deprivation resulting from inhibited blood flow

Ischemic renal failure — kidney failure caused by blood starvation

Isolate — an extract of high concentration (usually over 90%)

— J —

Jaundice — yellow discoloration of the skin usually caused by liver dysfunction

— K —

Karposi's sarcoma — a type of connective tissue cancer characteristic of AIDS

Ketoacidosis — a life-threatening condition caused by acidification of the blood

Kidney stone — stone formed in the kidney from minerals and other substances precipitated from urine

Killer T-cell — lymphocyte (immune cell) that attaches itself to foreign organisms and attempts to destroy them

— L —

Lactalbumin — a specific type of whey protein

Lactic acid — a breakdown product from the overuse of muscle

Lactose — milk sugar

Lactose-intolerance — inability to digest lactose accompanied by nausea, cramps and diarrhea

Laparoscope — a tube with a fiberoptic cable through which the surgeon can see into and work within a body cavity

LDL cholesterol — low density lipoprotein (bad) cholesterol associated with increased risk of arteriosclerosis

Lesion — pathological area of tissue

Leucine — an amino acid

Leukemia — cancer of white blood cells

Leukocyte — any type of white blood cell; component of the immune system

Levothyroxine — a thyroid hormone

LHRH agonists — Luteinizing Hormone Releasing Hormone agonists; pharmaceutical preparation used to treat prostate cancer and other hormonally-related diseases

Libido — sex drive

Liothyronine — a thyroid hormone

Liotrix — a thyroid hormone

Lipid peroxidation — the oxidation of fats from the formation of free radicals and also forming more free radicals

Lipids — fatty substances

Lipofuscinosis — Batten's disease; a neurodegenerative disorder

Lipoprotein-A — LP[A]; a molecule that promotes arteriosclerosis

Lithium — drug used to treat mania and manic-depression

Lou Gehrig's disease — ALS; amyotrophic lateral sclerosis; a rare, fatal progressive degenerative disease of the nervous system that usually begins in middle age; characterized by increasing muscular weakness

Low platelet count — measure of impaired blood clotting ability

Lupus — a chronic autoimmune disease causing inflammation of connective tissue

Lycopene — a carotenoid antioxidant found in brightly-colored vegetables and fruits

Lymph — a milky fluid containing lymphocytes, proteins and fats that originates from the bloodstream and bathes all bodily tissues

Lymph node — a small organ found in the pathways of lymph vessels that filters out harmful organisms from lymph as it reenters the blood circulation

Lymph vessels — channels that drain lymph from the intercellular spaces of body tissues back into the bloodstream

Lymphocyte — a type of white blood cell crucial to the adaptive part of the immune system and made in the lymph nodes, bone marrow, and thymus gland; lymphocytes identify and 'remember' invading disease organisms

Lymphoma — cancer of the lymph nodes

— M —

Macrophage — large, non-adaptive leukocytes that attempt to engulf intruders

Malabsorption — difficulty absorbing nutrients

Malaria — a serious feverish disease caused by a microbe transmitted by the Anopheles mosquito

Male pattern baldness — hereditary onset of baldness in men and not associated with any disease process

Marker — measurable biochemical evidence of a particular metabolic activity

Marrow — the soft, fatty tissue found in bone cavities and responsible for blood production

Marrow plasma cells — a type of white blood cell normally responsible for the production of immunoglobulins

Mediation — facilitation; balance control

Megadosing — the use of vitamins and other concentrated nutrients in quantities greatly exceeding conventional recommendations

Melanoma — a type of skin cancer

Melatonin — hormone secreted by the pineal gland and thought to control daily body rhythms

Melena — black or maroon-colored stools caused by oxidized blood leaking into the digestive tract

Membrane — a layer of usually very thin tissue that covers a bodily surface or forms some sort of barrier

Memory cell lymphocyte — immune cell that 'remembers' specific invading organisms and initiates an accelerated response to subsequent infections

Menopause — the cessation of menstruation often associated with symptoms of hormonal withdrawal

Metabolic disorder — a group of disorders characterized by disturbance of the body's internal chemistry

Metabolism — all chemical processes taking place in the body; catabolic metabolism breaks down complex substances into simpler ones; anabolic metabolism manufactures complex

substances from simple building blocks

Metabolize — to convert foods and other biochemicals into living bodily processes

Metastasis — the spread of cancerous cells throughout the body, usually via the lymphatic and blood circulatory systems

Methionine — a thiol amino acid

MGTC — magnesium thiazolidine carboxylic acid; a glutathione-enhancing drug

Microbes — microscopic living organisms

Migraine — an intermittent disorder of uncertain origin provoking vision disturbances, nausea and severe, long-lasting headaches

Milk-alkali syndrome — high calcium blood levels due to excessive intake of calcium-containing drugs and milk

Mitochondria — energy-generating component of cells

Modality — treatment method

Modulate — to adjust in a controlled manner

Modulation — changing the amount of a substance; regulation of levels

Monitor — to track the progress of a disease or therapy

Monocyte — a type of white blood cell produced mostly in the spleen and the bone marrow

Morbidity — disease rate statistic

Mortality — death rate statistic

Mucolytic — phlegm thinning substance

Mucosal cells — cells lining interior surfaces of the body that secrete mucus

Mucoviscidosis — cystic fibrosis

Multifactorial — having several causes

or effects

Multiple myeloma — the malignant and uncontrolled proliferation of plasma cells in bone marrow

Multiple sclerosis — a progressive, unpredictable disease of the nervous system of uncertain cause

Multi-system organ failure — simultaneous functional deterioration of several bodily systems

Muscle contraction — the action of shortening a muscle so as to draw together the bones to which it is attached

Mutation — abnormal change in a cell's DNA

Mycoplasma — types of microorganism without cell walls that are intermediate between viruses and bacteria and are mostly parasitic

Mycosis fungoides — a type of lymphoma that appears on the skin in chronic scaly patches and progresses over a period of years to form elevated plaques and tumors

Myelin — fatty insulating sheath enclosing nerve fibers

Myocardial infarction — sudden death of part of the heart muscle due to interrupted blood supply; a heart attack

Myopia — short-sightedness

— N —

Nasal application — method of introducing drugs through the nose

Natural killer cell — killer T cell lymphocyte; immune cell that attaches to foreign organisms and attempts to destroy them

Natural product — a substance found in nature as opposed to a pharmaceutical product; also applied to substances found in nature but rendered to

unnatural levels of concentration or purity

Naturopath — one who practices alternative medicine using a non-pharmaceutical approach

Negative feedback inhibition — balancing factor in which increased levels of a biochemical substance cause its continued secretion to slow down or stop

Nephrotic syndrome — disease arising from damage to the filtering units of the kidneys and causing severe proteinuria

Nerve impulses — messages passed between the brain and various parts of the body through the nerves

Neural plaque formation — build-up of protein deposits in brain tissue and spinal cord

Neurobiologist — scientist specializing in the study of the brain and nervous system

Neurochemical — neurotransmitters and other substances active in the brain and nervous system

Neuro-chemical imbalance — a breakdown in the activity of the nervous system due to improper levels or balance of neurotransmitters

Neurodegenerative disorder — any progressive disease of the nervous system caused by physical and/or chemical changes of the brain and its chemical balance

Neurofibrillary tangles — disordered nerve fibers that impair the flow of information

Neurological — having to do with the brain and/or nervous system

Neuron — cell of the brain and nervous system

Neuropathy — disease, damage or

inflammation of peripheral nerves

Neurotransmitter — a chemical released from nerve endings that transmits information among neurons

Neutralize — to render ineffective; antioxidant donation of an electron to stabilize electrical charge

Neutrophil — a type of white blood cell produced in the bone marrow; the principal phagocytic white blood cell

Non-essential amino acid — amino acid that can be manufactured by the body from the essential amino acids found in foods

Noninfectious disease — any illness not caused by a specific micro-organism

Nutriceuticals — new term that describes therapies based on or including foods and food supplements

Nutritionist — health practitioner specializing in nutrition, alimentation and absorption

— O —

Obesity — excessive weight

Oophorectomy — removal of the ovaries

Opacification — rendering less transparent

Opportunistic infections — infection by organisms that do not normally cause disease; prevalent in AIDS patients, chemotherapy patients and others suffering from compromised immune response

Oral antioxidant supplements — concentrated food-like substances that help the body neutralize free radicals

Organic compounds — all compounds containing carbon, except carbon oxides, carbon sulfides and metal carbonates

Organogenesis — organ development

Organomercury content — proportion of mercury found in naturally-occurring organic compounds

Ortho-quinones — a group of powerful oxidants

Osteoarthritis — degeneration of joints due to breakdown of cartilage and/or formation of osteophytes, leading to pain, stiffness and eventual loss of function

Osteophyte — bone outgrowth; accretions of calcium around joints; a common manifestation of osteoarthritis

Osteoporosis — loss of protein matrix tissue from bone causing it to become brittle and to lose structural integrity

Otitis — acute or chronic inflammation or infection of the middle ear characterized by earache, fever, hearing loss, and sometimes rupture of the ear drum

Ova — human egg released from ovarian follicle prior to fertilization

Ovarian follicle — cavities in the ovaries where eggs develop

Ovaries — a pair of almond-shaped glands on either side of the uterus containing numerous follicles

Overgrowth — hyperplasia; over-proliferation of cells

Over-training syndrome — negative effects on the body of excessive amounts or intensity of exercise

Oxidation — the normal process by which matter is metabolized to energy using oxygen

Oxidative stress — cellular and tissue damage resulting from oxidation and leading to bodily disorders

Oxidative stressor — substance that promotes sufficient tissue oxidation to cause bodily disorders

Oxidized glutathione — GSSG; paired glutathione molecules that have neutralized free radicals by absorbing two negatively charged ions

Oxothiazolidine carboxylate — OTC; a potent GSH-enhancing drug

Oxyradical — free radical; a molecule that through the natural process of oxidation is deprived of an electron and rendered toxic

— P —

Pancreas — an elongated gland behind the stomach that produces several biochemicals, including the hormone insulin

Pancreatitis — acute or chronic inflammation of the pancreas

Panic attack — a period of acute anxiety, sometimes focused on the fear of death or loss of reason

Paranoia — a delusion that certain persons or events are especially connected to oneself

Parkinson's disease — shaking palsy; a neurological disorder characterized by muscular tremors, stiffness and weakness and resulting in slow movement and a shuffling gait

Pathogen — any disease-producing micro-organism; an infectious agent; virus, bacteria or parasite

Peer review — the rational and/or empirical scrutiny of published scientific reports by the scientific community at large

Pemphigoid — an uncommon chronic skin disease featuring large blisters that become intensely itchy

Peptide — a molecule made up of amino acids resembling but much smaller than a protein

Peridontium — the tissues surrounding and supporting the teeth

Perinatal period — the period just before, during and just after birth

Periodontal disease — any of several disorders of the peridontium

Periodontitis — Periodontal disease caused by untreated dental cavities or untreated gingivitis

Peritoneal dialysis — cleansing of blood through the peritoneal membrane without its removal from the body

Peritoneal membrane — inner lining of the abdomen

Phagocyte — large white blood cell of the immune system that engulfs and digests microbes, toxic particles and cellular debris

Pharmaceutical drug — drug designed and manufactured in pharmaceutical laboratories; popularly but erroneously considered to be fundamentally different from natural products

Pharmacologists — one who formulates and/or and distributes pharmaceutical products

Philanthropological — for the sake of the greater human good

Physiology — study of the physical and chemical processes of the cells, tissues, organs and systems of the body; the foundation of all medical science

Pituitary gland — the 'master gland' situated in the brain that regulates and controls the activity of other endocrine glands and many body processes

Placebo — an inert substance used in controlled experiments against which the efficacy of a drug or dietary supplement is compared

Placebo group — a group of subjects in a controlled experiment who instead of receiving the therapy under test are given an inert substitute

Placenta — the organ by which a fetus is attached to the inner wall of the uterus and nourished

Plaque — a complex deposit of lipids, platelets, calcium and scar tissue

Plasma — the fluid part of blood that remains when blood cells are removed

Platelet — blood clotting cells

Platelet aggregation — clumping or clotting of blood leading to blockage of blood vessels

Platelet function — the way in which platelets respond to certain conditions

PMS — pre-menstrual syndrome; physical and emotional changes experienced by women in the week or two before menstruation

Pneumonia — inflammation of the lungs due to bacterial or viral infection

Poliomyelitis — polio; a virus that usually provokes only mild illness but sometimes damages the brain and spinal cord and can lead to bodily deformation, paralysis and death

Polyarteritis nodosa — an uncommon inflammation of the walls of medium-sized arteries occasionally leading to the formation of aneurysms

Polycystic kidney disease — the growth of cysts within the kidneys, eventually impairing their function

Polymorphonuclear cells — pus-forming white blood cells that fight bacteria by engulfing and digesting them

Polymyositis — inflammation of several muscles at once

Porous — containing gaps

Post-mortem — after death; during autopsy; analysis of cause of death

Precursor — building block; usually simple proteins combined by the body into more complex molecules

Predispose — to make particularly susceptible to or inclined towards a specific response

Preeclampsia — a serious condition of advanced pregnancy characterized by hypertension, proteinurea and edema

Pre-menstrual syndrome — PMS; various physical and emotional changes experienced by women in the week or two before menstruation

Preventive medicine — prevention of disease states by avoiding causes or conditions under which they develop

Prognosis — probable outcome of a disease process, taking into account the effectiveness of possible therapies

Programmed cell death — apoptosis; the self-destruction of cells initiated by outside causes

Prolactin — a hormone produced by the pituitary gland that stimulates growth of the mammary glands and production of milk

Proliferation — lively growth

Proline — an amino acid

Pro-oxidant stress — exposure or activity contributing to oxidative damage

Prostate cancer — a malignant growth in the outer part of the prostate gland; the most common cancer of men

Prostatic carcinogenesis — initial development of cancerous cells in the prostate gland

Prostatic hyperplasia — an overgrowth of prostate tissue

Prostatitis — inflammation or infection of the prostate gland

Prostheses — artificial replacement for a missing or diseased part of the body

Prosthetic device — artificial, mechanical replacement of a body part

Protein — fundamental component of the body; large molecule consisting of dozens to thousands of amino acids

Proteinuria — loss of protein in the urine

Psoriasis — a chronic skin condition characterized by inflammation and scaling

Psychoneurobiology — an integrated medical science that accounts for brain disorders by combining psychiatry, neurology and human biology

Psychosis — a severe disturbance of normal thought, perception, speech and behavior; mental disorder involving loss of contact with reality

Puberty — the period initiating adolescence during which secondary sexual characteristics develop

Pulmonary — having to do with the lungs and the function of breathing

Pulmonary edema — fluid accumulation in the lungs

Pulmonary fibrosis — fibrosing alveolitis; interstitial fibrosis; scar tissue in the lungs

Pulmonologist — physician specializing in the lungs and breathing

— R —

Radiotherapy — destruction of cells by radiation targeted at cancerous cells

Reactive metabolites — toxic products of normal metabolic oxidation

Reactive oxygen molecules — reactive oxygen species; compounds containing free oxygen radicals

Receptor — a biochemical docking bay on the surface of a cell that attracts certain molecules for specific purposes and enables the cell's activity to be influenced from the outside

Relapse — re-emergence or continued advance of disease after remission

Remission — the withdrawal or temporary halt of disease and its symptoms

Renal dialysis — a technique which replicates the function of the kidneys by removing waste products from the blood

Renal failure — kidney failure; inability to filter waste products from the blood

Renal system — kidneys and associated organs

Renal tubular acidosis — kidney dysfunction leading to high acid levels in the blood

Reperfusion — re-established blood flow, sometimes leading to reperfusion injury

Reperfusion injury — abnormal cellular function following reperfusion

Replication — the multiplication of cells in normal or abnormal growth

Resilience — ability to withstand wear and tear

Respiratory distress syndrome — ARDS; acute, life-threatening respiratory failure following injury to the lungs

Respiratory tract lining fluid — RTLF; a complex mixture of biochemicals and cells of the immune system found in the trachea and lungs

Restorative therapies — medical interventions to correct destruction or dysfunction of any body process

Retina — the light-sensitive area at the back of the eyeball

Retinal detachment — separation of the retina from the outer layers of the back of the eye

Retrolental fibroplasia — retinopathy of prematurity; the build-up of fibrous scar tissue in the retina of premature infants, usually following exposure to high levels of oxygen

Rheumatoid arthritis — systemic arthritis caused by an auto-immune disorder

Rhinorrhea — runny nose

Risk factor — any historical or measurable cause or condition contributing to the onset and development of a disease process

RNA — ribonucleic acid; a nucleic acid that carries out DNA instructions for protein production

Roughage — the indigestible portion of fibrous food

— S —

Salivary gland — the gland in the mouth responsible for the production of saliva and therefore part of the gastrointestinal tract

Sarcoidosis — a condition of unknown etiology leading to inflammation and scarring of tissues throughout the body

Scarlet fever — scarlatina; an acute contagious febrile disease caused by the bacteria streptococcus and characterized by inflammation of the nose, throat, and mouth

Schizophrenia — a chronic, severe, and disabling brain disease often causing patients to suffer symptoms such as hearing internal voices not heard by others, or believing that other people are reading their minds, controlling their thoughts, or plotting to harm them

Scientific study — investigation or research based on scientific principles of accounting and objectivity, open to peer review

Scleroderma — a rare autoimmune disease that can affect many organs and tissues

Scurvy — a disease resulting from vitamin C deficiency

Sebaceous gland — gland in or near hair follicles responsible for secretion of sebum

Seborrheic dermatitis — a skin disorder caused by over-activity of the sebaceous glands and resulting in dandruff, scaling and redness of the eyelids and slight oiliness of the face

Sebum — moisturizing agent in skin secreted by sebaeous glands

Sedentary lifestyle — a life of little physical activity or exercise

Selegiline — a drug used to treat Parkinson's disease

Selenium — a trace element found in meat, fish, whole grains and dairy products

Senescence — the aging process

Senile dementia — a general decline in mental ability related to aging

Sensorineural hearing loss — a problem of the inner ear or auditory nerve

Sepsis — blood-borne infection

Serine — an amino acid

Severe hypotension — critically low blood pressure

Shaking palsy — Parkinson's disease; a neurological disorder characterized by muscular tremors, stiffness and weakness and resulting in slow movement and a shuffling gait

Shock — a condition in which inadequate blood flow in the body's tissue results in physical failure or collapse, together with an extreme drop in blood pressure, sometimes leading to unconsciousness or death

Silymarin — Silybum marianum; the

active component of milk thistle, a traditional herbal cure for liver disorders and poisoning

Sinus cavities — air-filled cavities in the bones near the front of the head, behind the forehead, nose region and cheeks

Sinusitis — inflammation or infection of the membranes lining the sinus cavities

SLE — systemic lupus erythematosus (lupus); chronic inflammation of the connective tissue that holds body structures together

Smallpox — a highly infectious, deadly viral disease now considered to have been eradicated by worldwide vaccination

Specific — tailor-made

Sprue — an intestinal disorder that inhibits absorption of nutrients

SPS — sleep promoting substance; a neurochemical

Steroids — pharmaceutical corticosteroid and anabolic steroid drugs used against disease

Stinging nettle — urtica dioici; a weed common to northern climates able to inject a mild local irritant on contact; occasionally used as medicinal herb

Stomach ulcer — also called peptic ulcers; spots where the lining of stomach has been eroded, leaving an open wound

Stomatitis — inflammation or ulceration of the mouth

Strep A — a streptococcal bacteria that often infects the throat

Stress — physical, emotional, environmental or biochemical pressure

Stroke — death of or damage to brain tissue resulting from blood deprivation

Subcutaneous — under the skin

Substantia nigra — specific area in the basal ganglia

Substrate — source of building material

Sun lamp — electrical device that simulates sunlight, including ultraviolet radiation

Superinfection — one infection on top of another

Super-oxide dismutase — SOD; a naturally-occurring antioxidant

Suppressor T-cell — lymphocyte (immune cell) that slows down or stops the activities of B cell lymphocytes and T cell lymphocytes following the successful destruction of an invader

Surgical excision — cutting out

Synergistic — the mutual enhancement of separate substances by which they enhance each other's efficacy

Systemic lupus erythematosus — SLE; lupus; chronic inflammation of the connective tissue that holds body structures together

— T —

T-4 helper cell — type of T-cell lymphocyte that alerts the immune system and stimulates the growth and differentiation of an appropriate response

Tardive dyskinesia — an involuntary puckering of the lips and writhing of the arms and legs; side-effect of antipsychotic drugs possibly caused by neuronal damage

T-cell — lymphocyte (immune cell) that remembers specific viruses and how to destroy them; damaged T-cells are the dominant feature of AIDS

Telogen — dormant phase of hair growth

Teratogens — substances causing birth defects

Testes — testicles; source of sperm and testosterone

Testosterone — the most important of the androgen (male) hormones

Thermolabile — easily destroyed or altered by heat

Thermoregulatory — helping to maintain constant bodily temperature

Thiol — an amino acid containing sulfur

Thrombophlebitis — blood clots in the veins, usually in the lower extremities

Thrush — infection of the mouth or gullet by the fungus candida albicans

Thyroid gland — one of the main endocrine glands that helps regulate energy levels

Tissue — a collection of cells specialized to perform a specific function

Toxic alopecia — temporary hair loss caused by serious illness, fever, pregnancy, chemotherapeutic drugs, overdoses of vitamin A or other toxins

Toxicity — poisoning leading to impaired bodily function and/or cell damage

TPN — total parenteral nutrition; intravenous nutrition

Transcendental meditation — TM; a meditation technique taught by the Maharishi Mahesh Yogi, a twentieth-century Hindu teacher

Transdermal patch — dressing that releases a drug through the skin into the bloodstream

Trauma — the medical term for injury, usually referring to physical injury but also used to describe psychological injury

Triglyceride — a type of lipid formed from a combination of fatty acids and glycerol; most animal and vegetable fats are triglycerides, but those of animal origin are saturated and have been implicated in various disorders

Tripeptide — a protein consisting of three amino acids.

Tube feeding — nutrition supplied directly to the stomach or intestines

Tumor — a clump of cells resulting from abnormal growth that may be pre-cancerous, cancerous or benign

Tumor load — total tumor mass

Tyrosine — an amino acid

— **U** —

Ulcerative colitis — UC; a chronic inflammatory disease of the mucous membranes of the colon leading to ulcers

Up-regulate — increase

Urethral passage — the path followed by urine from the bladder to the outside of the body

Urinary calcium — calcium excreted from the body in urine

Urologist — physician specializing in disorders of the urinary tract

Uterine fibroids — benign tumors in the uterus

UV-A rays — a type of ultra-violet radiation from sunlight that can burn the skin and may cause several types of cancer; UV-A rays pass further into the skin but are considered to contribute somewhat less to skin cancer than UV-B rays

UV-B rays — a type of ultra-violet radiation from sunlight that is more likely than UV-A rays to cause sunburn

— V —

Valine — an amino acid

Vascular — pertaining to blood vessels

Vasculitis — inflammation of blood vessels

Vertebrae — individual bones of the spine

Viral antibodies — cells of the immune system that identify a virus that has previously infected the body and remember how to combat it

Viral pneumonia — pneumonia caused by viral infection, as opposed to bacterial pneumonia

Vitamins — a group of complex nutrients not providing energy but essential in small amounts to the functioning of the body

— W —

Water-soluble — able to dissolve in water at normal temperature and pressure

Whey isolate protein — protein derived in highly pure concentrations from the liquid portion of cow's milk

White blood cells — leukocytes (neutrophils, lymphocytes and monocytes); cells that help protect the body against disease and infection; the main components of the immune system

WHO — World Health Organization

Workout — exercise regimen

— X —

Xenobiotic — substance foreign to the body and/or biological processes, including infections and toxins

INDEX

ulcers in smokers 148
UV sensitivity 206
Nerve injury 186
Neurodegenerative disorders
   Alzheimer's disease 95
   multiple sclerosis 125
   Parkinson's disease 90
neurodegenerative disorders
   Lou Gehrig's disease 125
Neurology 191, 192
Nickel 26
Nitrogen 52
Nitrosamines 73
Noise exposure 169
Nose 164
Nuclear waste 70

O

Opacification 164
Opthalmology 164
OTC 49
Otitis 171
OTZ 49
Over-training 220
Oxidation 15
Oxygen starvation 136
Ozone depletion 70

P

Pancreatitis 149
Pantoloc 148
Parkinson's disease 90
Pasteurization 56
Pauling, Linus 59, 60
Pemphigoid 203
Periodontal disease 171
Peritoneal dialysis 158
Pesticides 70
Pharmaceutical drugs 48
Phenobarbital 198
Phenytoin 198
Physical trauma 185
Plaque (arteriosclerosis) 99
Platelets (arteriosclerosis) 99
Pneumonia 130
Polio 234
Polyarteritis nodosa 137
Polycystic kidney disease 158

Polymyositis 42, 203
Pre-eclampsia 175
Precursors of glutathione 56
Pregnancy 175
   fetal malformation 177
   hypertension 175
   pre-eclampsia 176
Preventive dentistry 171
Preventive medicine 23
Prostate cancer 211
Prostate problems 210
Prostatic hypertrophy 210
Protein intake and renal failure 161
Proteinurea 175
Proton-pump inhibitor 148
Psoriasis 203
Psychiatry 191
Psychoneurobiology 191
Pulmonary disease 171
Pulmonary edema 136
Pulmonary fibrosis 130, 137
Pulmonary hypertension 134
Pyridoxine 59, 198

R

Radiation therapy 74
   treating side effects 76
Rebamipide 148
Rectal cancer 73
Rectal exam 211
References
   adult respiratory distress syndrome
     (ARDS) 140
   aging 88
   AIDS 124
   Alzheimer's disease 98
   asthma 140
   athletic performance 225
   balding 216
   bronchitis 140
   burns 189
   cancer 79
   childbirth 182
   cholesterol 106
   COPD 140
   cystic fibrosis 140
   diabetes 112
   dialysis 162